The Emergence of Cinematic Time

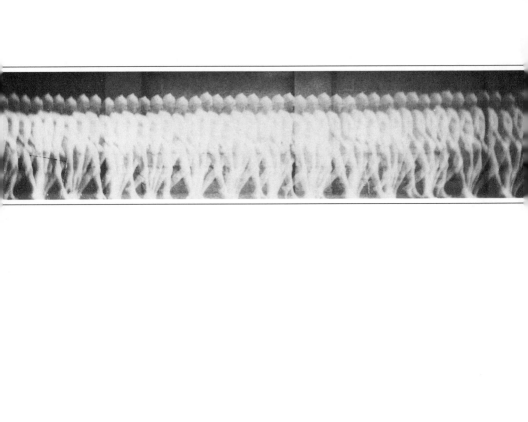

The Emergence of Cinematic Time

MODERNITY, CONTINGENCY,
THE ARCHIVE

Mary Ann Doane

HARVARD UNIVERSITY PRESS

Cambridge, Massachusetts, and London, England · 2002

Library of Congress Cataloging-in-Publication Data
Doane, Mary Ann.
    The emergence of cinematic time : modernity, contingency, the archive /
Mary Ann Doane.
        p. cm.
    Includes bibliographical references and index.
    ISBN 0-674-00729-8 (alk. paper) — ISBN 0-674-00784-0 (pbk. : alk. paper)
    1. Time in motion pictures.   I. Title.
PN1995.9.T55 D63 2002
791.43′684—dc21
2002068727

For Phil and Hannah

Acknowledgments

This book has changed form several times since its inception quite a few years ago. I have many people to thank for their support, guidance, and encouragement at various stages as well as for their sheer patience. I am grateful to the John Simon Guggenheim Foundation for a fellowship that allowed me time to think through the ramifications of a project proposal that is barely visible in the finished product. Brown University provided research support and time as well as a stimulating intellectual milieu in which to test my ideas. My students, with their enthusiasm for ideas and their unrestrained imaginations, have been an energizing and inspirational presence. I thank the English Department of the University of Chicago, especially Miriam Hansen, for inviting me to share my work in progress as a Frederic Ives Carpenter Visiting Professor. I am grateful for the animated conversations I had there and for helpful advice and encouragement from Bill Brown, James Lastra, Tom Mitchell, and Mark Sandberg.

Tom Gunning and an anonymous reader gave the manuscript a rigorous, detailed, and insightful reading; I am deeply indebted to them for their precise criticisms and wise suggestions. The members of a feminist reading group here at Brown—Susan Bernstein, Christina Crosby, Caroline Dean, Coppélia Kahn, Karen Newman, and Ellen Rooney—read several chapters and offered challenging and provocative criticism as well as support. I am very grateful to my hardworking research assistants, Nicole Israel and Rebecca Colesworthy, whose diligence and critical skills match those of the most seasoned of scholars and whose aid was invaluable.

An earlier version of Chapter 2 was published in *Critical Inquiry* 22, no. 2 (Winter 1996) © 1996 by The University of Chicago; and in *Endless Night: Cinema and Psychoanalysis, Parallel Histories,* edited by Janet Bergstrom

(University of California Press, 1999). An earlier and highly condensed version of Chapter 5 appeared in *Language Machines: Technologies of Literary and Cultural Production,* edited by Jeffrey Masten, Peter Stallybrass, and Nancy J. Vickers (London: Routledge, 1997). Sections of Chapter 3 began as part of a very different essay, "Technology's Body: Cinematic Vision in Modernity," *differences* 5, no. 2 (Summer 1993). I am grateful to the editors for permission to reprint this material here.

I would also like to thank my editor at Harvard University Press, Lindsay Waters, for his patience, intelligence, and commitment to the project as well as his academic street wisdom. I am grateful as well to Ann Hawthorne for her diligent and sensitive copyediting. Richard Manning shared his extensive knowledge of films and their availability and assisted in the reproduction of stills. A number of people have offered material support, trenchant advice, acumen, criticism, and wisdom—Katherine Hayles, Marta Braun, Joel Snyder, Dudley Andrew, Meir Wigoder, Anne Friedberg, Lisa Cartwright, Edward O'Neill, Charles Musser, Kristen Whissel, Mark Cooper, Jonathan Buchsbaum, Elizabeth Weed, Susan McNeil, and Liza Hebert.

This book is dedicated to Phil Rosen, who is always there and has an uncanny knowledge of exactly when to withhold advice as well as when to give it, and to Hannah Doane Rosen, whose relation to time I envy.

Contents

1   The Representability of Time   1

2   Temporality, Storage, Legibility: Freud, Marey,
    and the Cinema   33

3   The Afterimage, the Index, and the Accessibility
    of the Present   69

4   Temporal Irreversibility and the Logic of Statistics   108

5   Dead Time, or the Concept of the Event   140

6   Zeno's Paradox: The Emergence of Cinematic Time   172

7   The Instant and the Archive   206

    Notes   235

    Bibliography   267

    Index   279

The Emergence of Cinematic Time

1

The Representability of Time

They laugh and at the same time they shudder. For through the ornamentation of the costume from which the grandmother has disappeared, they think they glimpse a moment of time past, a time that passes without return. Although time is not part of the photograph like the smile or the chignon, the photograph itself, so it seems to them, is a representation of time. Were it the photograph alone that endowed these details with duration, they would not at all outlast mere time; rather, time would create images for itself out of them.

SIEGFRIED KRACAUER, "Photography"

In December 1895, the same month as that of the first public screening of films of the Lumière Cinématographe, a story titled "The Kinetoscope of Time" appeared in *Scribner's Magazine.*[1] The story conveys something of the uncanniness of the new technology's apparent ability to transcend time as corruption by paradoxically fixing life and movement, providing their immutable record. It condenses many of the fears, desires, anxieties, and pleasures attached to the idea of the mechanical representability of time. At the beginning of "The Kinetoscope of Time" the unnamed protagonist finds himself in an unrecognizable and seemingly placeless place, barely furnished and surrounded by walls heavily draped in velvet. The only furnishings are four narrow stands with "eye-pieces" at the top, which, though unnamed, are clearly kinetoscopes, the individual viewing machines invented by Thomas Edison and preceding the cinema. A message projected on the curtains invites the protagonist to look through the eyepieces in order to view "a succession of strange dances." He does so and proceeds to describe a series of scenes that unfold (including the story of Salomé, a scene from *The Scarlet Letter*, and a scene from *Uncle Tom's Cabin* in which Topsy dances). When these cease, the captivated spectator is invited to move to another kinetoscope to view scenes of combat as "memorable" as those of the dances. Here he witnesses scenes from the *Iliad, Don Quixote, Faust,* and the Custer massacre.[2] When the protagonist raises his eyes after this series he becomes aware that he is no longer alone; a mysterious but distinguished-looking middle-aged man is suddenly present. This man appears to claim great age by suggesting that he himself was present at, among others, the filmed scenes of Salomé and the *Iliad.* But when the protagonist asks if he is "Time himself," the figure laughs and denies it. The mysterious man proceeds to offer him two more viewings—one of the protagonist's own past, the other of his future, including "the manner of your end," but this time at a price: "The vision of life must be paid for in life itself. For every ten years of the future which I may unroll before you here, you must assign me a year of your life—twelve months—to do with as I will." The protagonist refuses this Faustian contract and is haughtily dismissed by the kinetoscope's proprietor. After making his way with difficulty through a dark and winding tunnel, the young man finds himself in the "open air:" "I was in a broad street, and over my head an electric light suddenly flared out and whitewashed the pavement at my feet. At the corner a train of the elevated railroad rushed by with a clattering roar and a trailing plume of white steam. Then a cable-car clanged past with incessant bangs upon its gong. Thus it was that I came back to the world of actuality." But within this "world of actuality," the protagonist discovers in a shop window an engraving of the man he has just met. His costume clearly indicates to the protagonist that he lived in the last century, and a legend below the engraving identifies him as Monsieur le Comte de Cagliostro.[3]

The protagonist's viewing of these filmed records of other times and other places occurs in a placeless and timeless space that resembles in many ways (its darkness and otherness to the world outside, its nonidentifiability) the cinema theaters of a much later period. And in the world that the young spectator returns to, normalcy is signified by the technologies of modernity—electric lighting, elevated trains, cable cars—and the series of shocks associated with them. The story conjoins many of the motifs associated with the emerging cinema and its technological promise to capture time: immortality, the denial of the radical finitude of the human body, access to other temporalities, and the issue of the archivability of time. The stories, unlike the space of their projection, are all familiar, and they reinscribe the recognizable tropes of orientalism, racism, and imperialism essential to the nineteenth-century colonialist imperative to conquer other times, other spaces. In the story of Salomé, the narrator-protagonist claims that "the decorations were Eastern in their glowing gorgeousness," and that "in the East women ripen young." In the scene from *Uncle Tom's Cabin,* Topsy was "one of the blackest of her race," and "her black eyes glittered with a kind of wicked drollery." In Custer's last stand, the "red Indians were raging, with exultant hate in their eyes," while the white soldiers were "valiant and defiant" in meeting their fate. These are the recorded times, the other temporalities, that allow the protagonist to disavow, for a while, his own temporality of clattering trains and clanging cable cars. The "kinetoscope of time" constitutes, in Michel Foucault's terms, both a heterotopia and a heterochrony, offering its spectator an immersion in *other* spaces and times, with the assurance of a safe return to his or her own. What the new technologies of vision allow one to see is a record of time.

The story suggests that the mysterious proprietor of the kinetoscope is contaminated by the attributes of his own machine—specifically its ability to access other times (the protagonist's past, his future) and the denial of mortality (the proprietor does not know death). Its rhetoric echoes that which accompanied the reception of the early cinema, with its hyperbolic recourse to the figures of life, death, immortality, and infinity. The cinema would be capable of recording permanently a fleeting moment, the duration of an ephemeral smile or glance. It would preserve the lifelike movements of loved ones after their death and constitute itself as a grand archive of time. As André Bazin would later point out, photographic technology "embalms time, rescuing it simply from its proper corruption."[4] But because time's corruption is "proper" to it, its fixed representation also poses a threat, produces aesthetic and epistemological anxiety. "The Kinetoscope of Time" registers this threat as the complicity of the machine with the demonic; hence the protagonist's refusal to look.

This book is about the representability of time in the late nineteenth and early twentieth centuries. Photographic and cinematic technologies played a central role here precisely because they were so crucial to thinking that representability.[5] Although popular accounts tended to endow the cinema with determinant agency—that is, cinematic technology made possible a new access to time or its "perfect" representation—in fact the emerging cinema participated in a more general cultural imperative, the structuring of time and contingency in capitalist modernity. Although the rupture here is not technologically determined, new technologies of representation, such as photography, phonography, and the cinema, are crucial to modernity's reconceptualization of time and its representability. A sea change in thinking about contingency, indexicality, temporality, and chance deeply marked the epistemologies of time at the turn of the last century. The reverberations of this break are still perceptible today in the continual conjunction of electronic technologies and questions of instantaneity and the archivability of time. As Andreas Huyssen points out, "the issue of media . . . is central to the way we live structures of temporality in our culture."[6] Film, television, and video are frequently specified by the term *time-based media.*

When Walter Benjamin wrote, with respect to Baudelaire's poetry and its relation to early modernity, "In the *spleen,* time becomes palpable: the minutes cover a man like snowflakes," he was not isolating an attitude unique to Baudelaire.[7] One could argue more generally that at the turn of the century time became palpable in a quite different way—one specific to modernity and intimately allied with its new technologies of representation (photography, film, phonography). Time was indeed *felt*—as a weight, as a source of anxiety, and as an acutely pressing problem of representation. Modernity was perceived as a temporal demand. Toward the end of the nineteenth century there was a rapid diffusion of pocket watches in the general population. The German historian Karl Lamprecht noted the importation of 12 million watches for a German population of about 52 million in the 1890s.[8] In 1903 Georg Simmel linked the precision of the money economy to the precision "effected by the universal diffusion of pocket watches." Simmel associated this new obsession with temporal exactitude to the heightened tempo and the "intensification of nervous stimulation" of urban life: "Thus, the technique of metropolitan life is unimaginable without the most punctual integration of all activities and natural relations into a stable and impersonal time schedule."[9] Modernity was characterized by the impulse to *wear* time, to append it to the body so that the watch became a kind of prosthetic device extending the capacity of the body to measure time. The acceleration of events specific to city life was inseparable from the effects of new technologies and a machine culture made possible by developments in modern science. In the realm of physics and beyond, the refinement of the Second Law of Thermodynamics (the law of entropy) engendered a conceptualization of time as the tightness of a direction, an inexorable and irreversible linearity. In the late nineteenth and early twentieth centuries, time became increasingly reified, standardized, stabilized, and rationalized.

This rationalization of time found its fullest realization in a world standardization that took its impetus from the development of railway travel and telegraphy. The standardization of time was originally effected by the railroad companies themselves, which found it extraordinarily difficult to maintain comprehensible schedules in the face of scores of differing local times.[10] In England, London time was four minutes ahead of time in Reading, seven minutes and thirty seconds ahead of Cirencester time, and fourteen minutes ahead of Bridgewater time. Railroad time became general standard time in England in 1880, in Germany in 1893. In 1884 an international conference on time standards held in Washington, D.C., divided the world into twenty-four time zones, established Greenwich as the zero meridian, and set the exact length of a day. In 1913 the first regulating time signal transmitted around the world was sent from the Eiffel Tower. As Stephen Kern points out, "The independence of local times began to collapse once the framework of a global electronic network was established."[11] The sheer speed of transportation and communication worked to annihilate the uniqueness and isolation of the local.

Much of the standardization and rationalization of time can be linked to changes in industrial organization and perceptions of an affinity between the body of the worker and the machine. In 1893 an article in *Scientific American* featured a machine that stamped employees' cards with the time they reported to work and the time they left—a punch-card. The machine had been in use since 1890.[12] This and other techniques emphasized the obsession with efficiency, strict management of time, and the elimination of waste. The most notorious of these techniques is undoubtedly Taylorization, or, as Taylor himself described it, "scientific management."[13] The research of Frederick W. Taylor isolated the crucial gestures of a worker, calculated how they could be most efficiently performed, and timed them with a stopwatch. Various incentives then encouraged workers in a given factory to adopt the most efficient gestures, which then became routinized, reducing the time of a particular operation to a bare minimum. The overall impression is of a form of mechanization of the human body that would further support the alienation of the worker. Taylorism prefigured and was fully consistent with the development of the assembly line. The goal was to eliminate unproductive time from the system.

The lesser-known work of Taylor's disciple, Frank B. Gilbreth, demonstrates that the desire to analyze and to rationalize time was frequently embodied as a desire to make time visualizable. Gilbreth attached a small electric light to the limb of a worker and used a time exposure to photograph the movement as a continuous line in space—he called the result a "cyclograph" (or a chronocyclograph if a motion picture camera was used).[14] For instance, one photograph, titled "Cyclograph of an Expert Surgeon Tying a Knot" (1914), represents the operation as several intersecting curved lines of light against the background of the stable figures of doctor and nurse. In "Girl Folding a Handkerchief," however, the girl has completely disappeared, and only the movement's progress itself is registered as curves of light. Gilbreth's comment on the picture of the surgeon reveals the extent to which he perceived his work as having a certain aesthetic value: "The path of the motion is shown, but not the speed or the direction. The record does show the beautiful smooth repetitive pattern of the expert."[15] This trend toward abstraction in the representation of movement through time is intensified by Gilbreth's translation of the photographed movements (that is, streaks of light) into wire models. One such wire model, titled "Perfect Movement" (1912), is simply an elaborate white curve against a black background. The particularities of the worker's identity or the type of labor involved have completely disappeared in the abstraction of perfection. In his monumental book, *Mechanization Takes Command,* Siegfried Giedion juxtaposes Gilbreth's cyclographs with paintings by Paul Klee and Joan Miró.

The wide diffusion of the pocket watch, the worldwide standardization of time to facilitate railroad schedules and communication by telegraph, as well as Taylorism's precise measurement of the time of labor and its extension in Gilbreth's cyclographs all testify to the intensity of the rationalization of time in the late nineteenth and early twentieth centuries. Time becomes uniform, homogeneous, irreversible, and divisible into verifiable units. A pocket watch allows its carrier to be constantly in sight of time; similarly, railroad schedules give time a visible and rationalizable form. Gilbreth's researches most adamantly illustrate that the scientific analysis of time involves an unrelenting search for its representation in visual terms—visual terms that exceed the capacity of the naked eye.

This rationalized time is a time in complicity with notions of the inevitability of a technologically induced historical progress. It is Benjamin's "homogeneous, empty time." It is also time's abstraction—its transformation into discrete units, its consolidation as a value, its crucial link to processes of pure differentiation and measurability. No longer a medium in which the human subject is situated (it is no longer *lived* or experienced in quite the same way), time is externalized and must be consulted (the phenomenon of the pocket watch). Karl Marx, more thoroughly than anyone, delineated the precise way in which time, in capitalism, has become the measure of value. A commodity has value because it is the objectification of abstract human labor, a labor that has been departicularized, has lost all specificity, and become comparable with any other form of labor. Qualityless, the labor can be measured only by its duration. When Marx asks how the value of the commodity is measured, the answer is "By means of the quantity of the 'value-forming substance,' the labour, contained in the article. The quantity is measured by its duration, and the labour-time is itself measured on the particular scale of hours, days, etc." Labor-time is therefore the measure of the magnitude of value. But the commodity hides its secret—value seems to accrue to the article itself: "The determination of the magnitude of value by labour-time is therefore a secret hidden under the apparent movements in the relative values of commodities." Money, as the commodity chosen as the measure of value of all commodities, becomes the form of appearance of the measure of value residing in commodities, labor-time. The slippage whereby time, as a measure of value, becomes a value in itself is an easy one. Time, in its transubstantiated form in capitalism, becomes money. Simmel compares the "calculative nature of money" and the "new precision" and "certainty in the definition of identities and differences, an unambiguousness in agreements and arrangements" associated with it to the precision aligned with the extensive diffusion of pocket watches.[16]

E. P. Thompson has pointed out that this general diffusion of watches and clocks occurred at "the exact moment when the industrial revolution demanded a greater synchronization of labor." The clock time used to measure labor, according to Thompson, is opposed to the time-sense associated with the task orientation of an agrarian society or one synchronized with "natural" rhythms, such as a fishing or seafaring community. A task-oriented sense of time differs in three ways from industrialized time. First, it is "more humanly comprehensible than timed labour." Thompson links this to the response to a perceived necessity located in the farmer's or fisherman's sensitivity to seasons, weather, tides, the biological rhythms of animals (milking, lambing, and so on). The second difference would be in the relative lack of distinction between "work" and "life" in task-oriented communities. Work and the social are intermingled effortlessly, and there is no great conflict between labor and one's "own" time. Third, this form of work appears to be wasteful and lacking in urgency to those whose labor is timed by the clock. Although it is crucial to avoid a nostalgia for what appears to be a more "natural" relation to time, it is important to recognize the differences between the two modalities. One would be the insistence of a rhetoric of economy associated with industrialized time: "Those who are employed experience a distinction between their employer's time and their 'own' time. And the employer must *use* the time of his labour, and see it is not wasted: not the task but the value of time when reduced to money is dominant. Time is now currency: it is not passed but spent."[17] Both time and money can be used, wasted, spent, and hoarded. More crucially, both exemplify a process of dematerialization and abstraction that fuels a capitalist economy.

As time becomes a value it begins to share the logic of the monetary system—a logic of pure differentiation, quantifiability, and articulation into discrete units. The capitalist buys a certain quantity of the laborer's time in order to produce surplus value. That time must be measurable and therefore divisible. Similarly, the worldwide standardization of time requires the generalized acceptance of minimal units of time for calibration. If the trains are to run on time, there must be only one time—the homogeneous, empty time of Benjamin's "progress." But the rationalization and abstraction of time generally recognized as imperative to capitalism pose certain problems that make their tolerability less assured. The notion of time as abstract differentiation of a homogeneous substance, as eminently divisible for purposes of calculation, clashes with the longstanding philosophical and phenomenological assumption that time is, as Charles Sanders Peirce has put it, "the continuum *par excellence,* through the spectacles of which we envisage every other continuum." Its divisibility is difficult to think. As in "The Kinetoscope of Time," time becomes uncanny, alienated, strange—no longer experienced but read, calculated. For Benjamin, the shock factor characteristic of modernity guarantees that impressions do not "enter experience

(*Erfahrung*)," but instead "remain in the sphere of a certain hour in one's life (*Erlebnis*)." Time is, in a sense, externalized, a surface phenomenon, which the modern subject must ceaselessly attempt to repossess through its multifarious representations. The rationalization of time ruptures the continuum par excellence and generates epistemological and philosophical anxieties exemplified by the work of Henri Bergson, in his adamant reassertion of temporal continuity in the concept of *durée*.[18]

This dilemma of discontinuity and continuity becomes the epistemological conundrum that structures the debates about the representability of time at the turn of the century. It is present in Etienne-Jules Marey's oscillation between graphic inscription (which provides a continuous record of time) and chronophotography (which, though more detailed and precise, is haunted by gaps and discontinuities). The dilemma is manifested in the philosophy of Charles Sanders Peirce as a structuring contradiction produced by his ambivalence about whether instants of time can be truly independent of one another—or indeed, whether there is such a thing as an instant of time. Marey was concerned with the representability of that unknowable instant. Sigmund Freud confronted the dilemma by situating time and memory in two different systems (the conscious and the unconscious), making time, in its articulation as pure process, pure divisibility itself, unrepresentable, alien to the retention of inscriptions characterizing unconscious memory.

The pressure of time's rationalization in the public sphere, and the corresponding atomization that ruptures the sense of time as exemplary continuum, produce a discursive tension that strikes many observers as being embodied or materialized in film form itself. For film is divided into isolated and static frames—"instants" of time, in effect—which when projected produce the illusion of continuous time and movement. Hence there is a renewed attention to Zeno's paradoxes as attempts to demonstrate, philosophically, the impossibility of movement and change given the reducibility of all movement to an accumulation of static states. The cinema is perceived variously as corroborating, undermining, or repeating Zeno's claims. In the realm of physiology, the theory of the afterimage (which supports the concept of the persistence of vision, acting for decades as the explanation for the perception of motion in cinema) grapples with the past's invasion of the present moment, with the persistence of a visual image in time, and with the consequent inseparability of a pure present from the "visible wake" of the past.[19] The intense debates around continuity and discontinuity at the turn of the century, which support and inform discussions of the representability of time, are a symptom of the ideological stress accompanying rationalization and abstraction.

The smooth narrative of a successful and progressive rationalization is also disturbed by an insistent fascination with contingency, indexicality, and chance that manifests itself at many different levels—in aesthetics, debates about photography, physics, biology, and the growth of social statistics and statistical epistemologies in general. Rationalization must entail a reduction or denial of contingency. In Taylorism, each of the laborer's movements must be meaningful; ideally, there is no loss or excess in the system. The body's movements are efficient and purposeful, and time becomes the measure of that efficiency. But modernity is also strongly associated with epistemologies that valorize the contingent, the ephemeral, chance—that which is beyond or resistant to meaning. While in classical thought meaning precedes and determines embodiment, in modernity meaning is associated with immanence and embodiment; it is predetermined not in ideal forms but in a process of emergence and surprise.[20] Impressionism, for instance, has been described as the concerted attempt to fix a moment, to grasp it as, precisely, fugitive.[21] And new technologies of representation—photography in particular—are consistently allied with contingency and the ability to seize the ephemeral. For Peter Galassi, photography is the culmination of a tendency in the history of art that rejects the general, the ideal, and the schematic and focuses upon the particular, the singular, the unique, the contingent.[22] Photography is allied with a "thisness," a certainty in the absolute representability of things and moments. The promise of indexicality is, in effect, the promise of the rematerialization of time—the restoration of a continuum of space in photography, of time in the cinema. Here, time appears to be free in its indeterminacy, reducible to no system or hierarchy (any moment can be the subject of a photograph; any event can be filmed). The technological assurance of indexicality is the guarantee of a privileged relation to chance and the contingent, whose lure would be the escape from the grasp of rationalization and its system.

Are these two tendencies within modernity—abstraction/rationalization and an emphasis upon the contingent, chance, and the ephemeral—irreconcilable? Do they simply represent two different modalities or attitudes operating independently during the same time period, each undisturbed by the other?[23] It is the wager of this book that it is possible to demonstrate their profound connection, their interdependence and alliance in the structuring of temporality in modernity. What is at stake is the representability of time for a subject whose identity is more and more tightly sutured to abstract structures of temporality. The theory of rationalization does not allow for the vicissitudes of the affective, for the subjective play of desire, anxiety, pleasure, trauma, apprehension. Pure rationalization excludes the subject, whose collusion is crucial to the sustenance of a capitalist system. In the face of the abstraction of time, its transformation into the discrete, the measurable, the locus of value, chance and the contingent are assigned an important ideological role—they become the highly cathected sites of both pleasure and anxiety. Contingency appears to offer a vast reservoir of freedom and free play, irreducible to the systematic structuring of "leisure time." What is critical is the production of contingency and ephemerality as graspable, representable, but nevertheless antisystematic. It is the argument of this book that the rationalization of time characterizing industrialization and the expansion of capitalism was accompanied by a structuring of contingency and temporality through emerging technologies of representation—a structuring that attempted to ensure their residence outside structure, to make tolerable an incessant rationalization. Such a strategy is not designed simply to deal with the leakage or by-products of rationalization; it is structurally necessary to the ideologies of capitalist modernization.

Contingency, however, emerges as a form of resistance to rationalization which is saturated with ambivalence. Its lure is that of resistance itself—resistance to system, to structure, to meaning. Contingency proffers to the subject the appearance of absolute freedom, immediacy, directness. Time becomes heterogeneous and unpredictable and harbors the possibility of perpetual newness, difference, the marks of modernity itself. Accident and chance become productive. Nevertheless, these same attributes are also potentially threatening. Their danger resides in their alliance with meaninglessness, even nonsense. The vast continuum of a nonhierarchizable contingency can overwhelm. Baudelaire, in his conflicted confrontation with modernity, feared that in the absence of categories such as the eternal and the immutable, freedom would become anarchy, and a "riot of details" would prevail.[24] For Georg Lukács, in his influential study of naturalism and realism, "Narrate or Describe?," chance and contingency are simultaneously necessary and insufficient:

> The key question is: what is meant by "chance" in fiction? Without chance all narration is dead and abstract. No writer can portray life if he eliminates the fortuitous. On the other hand, in his representation of life he must go beyond crass accident and elevate chance to the inevitable.

Contingency introduces the element of life and the concrete, but *too much* contingency threatens the crucial representational concept of totality, wholeness. Description is a capitulation to the vast and uncontrollable, and ultimately meaningless, realm of the contingent. It is allied with the visual (a "picture") and with the contemporaneous ("one describes what one sees, and the spatial 'present' confers a temporal 'present' on men and objects").[25] Narration, on the other hand, has an intimate relation with the past (it "recounts") and is therefore able to testify to necessity and inevitability. The present moment, contingency, and temporality as indeterminate are hazardous to sense.

Siegfried Kracauer shares this antipathy toward a contingency whose dominance becomes most evident in photography. In eschewing significance, the fullness of a life lived in its proper history, in favor of a slavish adherence to a spatial or temporal continuum, photography attains "a mere surface coherence." Its telos becomes that of historicism—sheer accumulation, coverage, the saturation of detail devoid of the coherent meaning associated with history itself. Photography simply captures a moment, a specific configuration in time and space which lacks necessity. Any moment will do, and time and the archivization of the photograph tend to reveal, to unmask, that lack of necessity as the elements within the configuration disintegrate. Yet Kracauer, unlike Lukács, sees the photographic inscription of contingency as the "go-for-broke game" of history. Photography provokes a confrontation with the meaninglessness of contemporary society; it is a "secretion of the capitalist mode of production." Just as capitalism is haunted by the logic of its own self-destruction, photography is capable of flaunting the logic of a world deprived of meaning and thereby instigating a new organization of knowledge.[26]

It is within the context of a modernity defined by rapid industrialization and the diffusion of new technologies as well as the rapid changes of urban life that contingency emerges as a site of awe and fear, constituted as both lure and threat. Its lure is that of the passing moment, the fascination of the ephemeral, but Walter Benjamin delineates the dark underside of such a relation to contingency as shock or trauma. The concept of shock has received a great deal of attention in contemporary theory, which has linked it to the various blows and assaults upon the subject associated with urban life and modern technologies—traffic, railway travel, electric lighting, newspaper advertising. This is substantiated by Benjamin's own explanation of the "complex kind of training" to which technology has "subjected the human sensorium."[27] But in Benjamin's lengthy appeal to Freud to delineate the psychical mechanism of the distinction between the shock experience associated with mechanical reproduction and the auratic experience associated with traditional art forms, it becomes clear that shock is also, and perhaps most importantly, a way of conceptualizing contingency in modernity.

Freud, in *Beyond the Pleasure Principle*, claims that "consciousness arises instead of a memory-trace" and therefore that the two systems are incompatible. Instead, memory fragments are "often most powerful and most enduring when the incident which left them behind was one that never entered consciousness." In Proustian terms, this means that the involuntary memory is composed of contents that were never experienced consciously; they somehow managed to bypass the level of consciousness. Consciousness, for Freud, does not remember. Its most important function is rather to protect the organism against excessive stimuli, to act as a stimulus shield in operation against external energies. According to Benjamin, "The threat from these energies is one of shocks. The more readily consciousness registers these shocks, the less likely are they to have a traumatic effect."[28]

This stimulus shield would, of course, be tougher, more impenetrable, in a highly developed technological society. In Benjamin's argument, such a society requires a heightened consciousness to parry the shock effects of urban existence. The human organism increasingly becomes surface. For Benjamin, what are lost in this process are memory traces and the full experience of the event exemplified by storytelling, as opposed to the communication of information or mere sensation. This is why it is no longer possible to write like Proust. Shock is, therefore, as opposed to the auratic, a kind of surface phenomenon; experiences do not "take," they simply slip away:

The greater the share of the shock factor in particular impressions, the more constantly consciousness has to be alert as a screen against stimuli; the more efficiently it does so, the less do these impressions enter experience *(Erfahrung)*, tending to remain in the sphere of a certain hour in one's life *(Erlebnis)*. Perhaps the special achievement of shock defense may be seen in its function of assigning to an incident a precise point in time in consciousness at the cost of the integrity of its contents.[29]

Three points need to be made about Benjamin's activation of Freud (and Proust) in his conceptualization of shock. First, shock is specified as that which is unassimilable in experience, a residue of unreadability. In being parried by consciousness it never reaches the subjective depths (of the unconscious, of experience) that could confer upon it a stable meaning. This is the sense in which shock is aligned with the contingent. Second, shock is defined in terms that associate it with a pathology. The subject must defend himself/herself against it at the risk of losing psychical integrity or equilibrium. Consciousness is above all "protective." Third, the defense against shock embodies a privileged relation to time. The rationalization of time (its division into discrete entities—seconds, minutes, hours, and its regulation by the clock) is a symptom of the foreclosure of meaning in the defense against shock (an incident is "assigned a precise point in time in consciousness at the cost of the integrity of its contents"). Rationalization supplants, displaces, or, in a sense, *mimics* meaning.

Nevertheless, shock is not to be avoided or rejected in a historically regressive nostalgia for the auratic. Instead, it must be *worked through*. Benjamin refers to Baudelaire—who in his estimation is the literary figure most sensitive to the phenomenological and epistemological crises of modernity—as a "traumatophile type," actively searching out the shocks of an urban milieu. Similarly, photography and film have a special relation to shock and, in the case of film, a potentially redemptive one. The snapping of the camera shares with other modern technologies the drive to condense time, the aspiration for instantaneity. But photography's impact upon the perception of the "moment" is historically decisive:

Of the countless movements of switching, inserting, pressing and the like, the "snapping" of the photographer has had the greatest conse-

quences. A touch of the finger now sufficed to fix an event for an unlimited period of time. The camera gave the moment a posthumous
shock, as it were.

Here, shock is aligned with photography's ability to arrest the ephemeral, to
represent the contingent. But Benjamin reserves his strongest enthusiasm
for film, in which "perception in the form of shocks was established as a formal principle."[30] Benjamin tends to align shock in film—and hence its "formal principle"—with montage. The very rapidity of the changing images in
film is potentially traumatic for the spectator and allows the cinema to *embody* something of the restructuration of modern perception. For Benjamin,
the shock experience of film makes it adequate to its age, unlike other aesthetic forms, with their adherence to the aura.

Despite Benjamin's explicit equation of filmic shock and montage, it is
clear from his theoretical activation of Freud and Proust and his delineation
of shock as a surface phenomenon unassimilable to meaning, that the cinema's shock effect is ineluctably associated with its indexicality, its ability to
register or represent contingency. Montage functions for Benjamin not so
much to confer order or meaning but to rapidly accumulate and juxtapose
contingencies. In this, the film form mimics and displays for the spectator
the excesses of a technologically saturated modern life. And, comparing this
shock-producing montage to work on the assembly line (where gestures are
isolated and disconnected) and to the unretentive and mechanical gestures
of gambling (the *coup*), Benjamin is necessarily ambivalent about the ideological effects of the cinema (a form that both refuses the depth of experiential meaning—*Erfahrung*—and, at the same time, is a sensitive indicator of
and participant in a vast reorganization of subjectivity in modernity). His
ambivalence here mirrors that associated with the image of contingency as
both lure and threat.

Baudelaire, Lukács, Kracauer, and Benjamin all grapple with the historical
and epistemological implications of the heightened power of contingency
and chance in modernity. Their efforts are located primarily within the domain of aesthetics and the theory of representation. However, the obsession
with contingency and its reconceptualization are pervasive in the nineteenth
and early twentieth centuries, infiltrating the domains of philosophy, physics, history, physiology, evolutionary theory, and psychoanalysis. Charles
Sanders Peirce—who was himself a philosopher, a geographer, a logician,

and a semiotician—seemed to encapsulate this tendency in his claim that "chance itself pours in at every avenue of sense: it is of all things the most obtrusive. That it is absolute is the most manifest of all intellectual perceptions."[31] For Peirce, this dominance of chance dictated the demise of determinism (or necessitarianism in his terms) and the urgency of a recourse to statistics, which alone could deal with the intractability of the unique, the unpredictability of the individual. And this theorization of chance transformed it from a by-product or aberration into a positive historical agent, the ultimate instigator of law. Chance, for Peirce, was the insistence of the singular, the unique, and it was guaranteed by the sheer variety of phenomena and the diversity of events. His conceptualization of chance and the singular is particularly striking in the ways that it echoes his description of indexicality as a semiotic category (and indexicality is the linguistic/semiotic category most frequently activated to define the specificity of photographic media). The indexical sign is the imprint of a once-present and unique moment, the signature of temporality. As pure indication, pure assurance of existence, it is allied with contingency. The new photographic media, whose most prominent attribute is that of indexicality, were available as the potential record of anything and everything that happens, as the guarantee of the representability of the manifold contingencies that seem to specify modernity. These media pay homage to the idea that chance, as Peirce would have it, is "most obtrusive."

Evolutionary theory, and in particular Darwin's concept of natural selection, was instrumental to the diffusion across a range of disciplines of the epistemological centrality of chance. For evolutionary change hinges upon an aberration, a contingent difference that is then retained and consolidated as a characteristic of the species. The evolutionary process is motored by chance rather than by design. Peirce refers to this rubric in the course of his argument that chance, rather than law, is productive and determinant. But the technique which seems to acknowledge most definitively the dominance of contingency while simultaneously attempting to master it is that of statistics. Ian Hacking refers to the "avalanche of numbers"[32] that inaugurated the recourse to statistics, and Theodore Porter claims that

> the great explosion of numbers that made the term statistics indispensable occurred during the 1820s and 1830s. The demands it placed on

people to classify things so that they could be counted and placed in an appropriate box on some official table, and more generally its impact on the character of the information people need to possess before they feel they understand something, are of the greatest interest and importance.[33]

But of course the numbers did not simply appear abruptly as an "explosion" or "avalanche"—a natural catastrophe that society must somehow manage. Rather, the counting, the gathering of numbers, was itself part of a massive project of constructing homogeneities and differences that contributed to a reorganization of knowledge. And it was in the domain of the social sciences—albeit social sciences that aspired to the rigor of the natural sciences—that statistics took hold most vigorously as a technique. The "discovery" that phenomena as seemingly individual and idiosyncratic as crime and suicide and marriage, birth, and death rates evinced certain stable regularities across different societies seemed to promise an epistemological haven from the threat of an overwhelming contingency. In 1844 Adolphe Quetelet announced that the Gaussian curve, originally developed within astronomy to plot the range of errors in measurement, was applicable to a knowledge of the varying characteristics of human beings—height, weight, chest measurements, et cetera—and that it could be used to delineate the features of the "average man." The potential range of this "social physics," to use Quetelet's term, was enormous, and it was capable of organizing and making legible a multitude of variations otherwise inaccessible to understanding. Quetelet's work was influential and was disseminated even more widely by a historian, Henry Thomas Buckle, interested in increasing the rigor of history as a discipline by annexing to it the logic of statistics. Statistics would allow the historian to deal with a plethora of apparently isolated and anomalous events, subordinating their contingency to a lawlike regularity.

While Quetelet, Buckle, and others attempted to use statistics to confer upon sociology and history the authority of the natural sciences, in an ironic twist, physicists were influenced by Quetelet's work to relinquish traditional notions of cause and effect in favor of an emphasis upon probability and statistics. The Second Law of Thermodynamics dictated the inevitable increase of entropy (or the movement toward a stable equilibrium and its attendant dissipation of energy). This law, based on observations of motors and engines and the flow of heat, proclaims that time is irreversible, and is frequently cited as the condition of the possibility of historical thinking. The linear movement in time guarantees an increase in the random, the dissolution of organization. But this "law" was found by physicists, such as James Clerk Maxwell and Ludwig Boltzmann, to be irreconcilable with, or at least inexplicable in terms of, the classical notions of cause and effect associated with Newtonian physics. Thermodynamics emerged as an irreducibly statistical field. There was no "natural law" dictating that entropy would increase, but the overwhelming probability was that it would do so. In terms of the measurement of heat distribution, Maxwell claimed that the same formula as that of Quetelet's error law governed the distribution of molecular velocities in a gas.

Statistics thus emerged as a powerful new epistemological framework during the nineteenth century. Not only did it acknowledge the intractability of the contingent, the unknowability of the individual; it was based on and depended upon these affirmations. The uniqueness and aberration of individual events, their domination by chance, was assured by the displacement of knowledge to the level of the mass. This was both an acknowledgment of and an attempt to control the anxiety of contingency. As Porter points out,

> Statistical writers persuaded their contemporaries that systems consisting of numerous autonomous individuals can be studied at a higher level than that of the diverse atomic constituents. They taught them that such systems could be presumed to generate large-scale order and regularity which would be virtually unaffected by the caprice that seemed to prevail in the actions of individuals. Since significant changes in the state of the system would appear only as a consequence of proportionally large causes, a science could be formulated using relative frequencies as its elemental data.[34]

While this admission and acceptance of "individual caprice" and variation might seem to ensure a new openness and flexibility, its aim was in fact the domination of contingency and chance itself. Chance was granted its own power, but that power was ultimately superseded by general laws of order and regularity. The influence of statistics in a variety of different fields indicated the expansion of the scientific domain itself, the desire to control a

range of phenomena that might otherwise seem unamenable to quantification. In this sense, statistics constitutes an aggressively imperialist epistemology that is fully consonant with the more familiar imperialism of territory.
Historically, statistics has been allied with eugenics in the work of Francis
Galton, and it has been systematically used to outline the specific differences
allegedly associated with such categories as race, gender, class, and ethnicity.
In statistics, knowledge, the management of chance, and dominance are in
collusion.

Nevertheless, it is crucial to insist upon the delicate balance of control and
the privileging of uncertainty in statistics. This involves the conjunction of
rigorous regulation and the simultaneous acknowledgment of inevitable excess and diversity, of that which is beyond the grasp of epistemology. This
gives to statistics a malleability which diminishes none of its force. It is a
technique that might be said to "work indeterminacy." Statistics is, in a
sense, the social praxis, in capitalism, of epistemologies of indeterminism.
It is one response—but an extraordinarily widespread and influential response—to the lure and threat of contingency in modernity. As the organization of the random which nevertheless acknowledges the intractability
and aberrations of the individual, it is the making legible of the contingent.

It is the contention of this book that the epistemology of contingency
which took shape in the nineteenth century was crucial to the emergence
and development of the cinema as a central representational form of the
twentieth century. This is why I deal extensively with disciplines and discourses whose relation to the cinema is not immediately self-evident—thermodynamics, physiology, statistics, psychoanalysis, and philosophy. These
are not isolated and elitist fields of "high culture" or intellectual history
which have no relation to the social regime within which the cinema operates. Thermodynamics emerges from the *praxis* of industrialization and its
obsession with the machine, and it returns to popular culture images of entropy and exhaustion, of the heat-death of the universe. Psychoanalysis is inseparable from the encounter with the urban in modernity, and although
Freud may have seen his work as an analysis of an autonomous psyche, its
intimate links with industrialization, modernization, and, indeed, thermodynamics (with respect to the notion of psychical "economy" and the conservation of energy) have been well documented.[35] Statistics, in its turn,
maintains an intimate relation with the formation of a mass culture.

Yet cinema is not merely an effect or a symptom of epistemological developments in other disciplines. It is a crucial participant in an ongoing re-thinking of temporality in modernity. The relations between cinema and the other disciplines discussed here—psychoanalysis, physiology, physics, statistics, philosophy—are not simple formal analogies or evidence of some general *Zeitgeist*. The pressure to rethink temporality in the nineteenth century is a function of the development of capitalist modernity and its emphases upon distribution, circulation, energy, displacement, quantification, and rationalization. These developments require new conceptualizations of space and time and the *situatedness* of the subject. How does the subject inhabit this new space and time? What are the pressures of contingency and the pleasures of its representability? The ideologies of instantaneity, of temporal compression, of the lure of the present moment that emerge in this period have not disappeared; they confront us now in the form of digital technologies.

The new standards of accuracy, memory, and recordkeeping in modernity traversed the disciplines and in fact encouraged their interaction. Within the terms of their own internal evolution, and acknowledging their relative autonomy, these disciplines were approaching a version of the same problem—the representability of time. Marey in physiology and Freud in psychoanalysis wrestled with the apparent conflict between the accurate recording of time and its legibility. The ability to represent time as irreversible in physics opened up the possibility of an entirely different way of conceptualizing history, as Michel Serres has compellingly demonstrated; and a new paradigm of historical thought had an effect upon the conceptualization of cinema as historical record. The mutual resonances and transformations between these different epistemological frameworks indicate a powerful—and contagious—response to historical trauma, a trauma that involves a refiguring, indeed rupturing, of what had previously been understood as an indivisible temporal continuum, the support and guarantee of a coherent subjectivity. Change becomes synonymous with "newness," which, in its turn, is equated with difference and rupture—a cycle consistent with an intensifying commodification.

The method adopted here certainly has similarities with that of Michel Foucault, particularly with respect to his early use of the term *episteme* to circumscribe the conditions of the possibility of knowledge within a given historical period. While traditional intellectual history might point to the "influences" at work in the period (Helmholtz's "influence" upon Freud or Quetelet's upon thermodynamics, for instance), this is not what is at issue here. Rather, what is at stake is the question of how time took shape as a particular object of knowledge within diverse disciplines and practices. What were the parameters within which time was understood? The epistemological structure allowing for the knowledge or representation of time mobilized a series of binary oppositions—continuity versus discontinuity, rationalization versus contingency, structure versus event, determinism versus chance, storage versus legibility. This structure also embraced representational practices such as photography, optical toys, and cinema. With the shift in his later work to the term *discursive practice,* Foucault maintained that "discursive practices are not purely and simply ways of producing discourse. They are embodied in technical processes, in institutions, in patterns for general behavior, in forms for transmission and diffusion, and in pedagogical forms which, at once, impose and maintain them."[36] The indexical representation of photography, the use of intermittent images to produce the illusion of movement in cinema, and the choice of a standard speed in projection are practices with epistemological underpinnings. They have a knowledge effect. Similarly, the understanding of perception in terms of the concept of the afterimage, or persistence of vision, is a discursive event that cannot be assigned a lower status than the pronouncements of philosophy (Bergson's concept of *durée,* for example). The overlaps or similarities in different disciplinary constructs delineated throughout this book are not coincidental but are effects of a historical pressure to rethink time in relation to its representability.

But here the affinities with Foucault's project end. For the later Foucault, a generalized and immanent notion of power is posited as ultimate determinant. This power resides within and orients a system of institutions, discourses, and practices. It has a positive role rather than a purely negative or interdictory status and cannot be reduced to the functions of law or the concept of the master.[37] Power, however, is disengaged from any explanatory framework, such as Marxism or psychoanalysis, and becomes self-motivating, absolute, unspecifiable as an entity. My contention here, on the other hand, is that the overdetermined possibility of restructuring and rethinking time in modernity is subtended and supported by the historically specific changes within an industrial and commodity capitalism in which labor time as the measure of value is reconceptualized and processes of abstraction and rationalization become crucial to that project.[38] The effects of this restructuring are certainly subject to mediation and displacement, but its recurrent tropes—the machine, energy, the contingent, indexicality, and chance—are highly mobile and challenge the impermeability or rigidity of disciplinary boundaries. Within physics, biology, statistics, psychoanalysis, and physiology, there is an epistemological shift toward the weighting of a legible contingency.

The significance of the cinema, in this context, lies in its apparent capacity to perfectly *represent* the contingent, to provide the pure record of time. And this effort is particularly legible in the most dominant genre of the early cinema—the actuality, which appeared to capture a moment, to register and repeat "that which happens." The hundreds of films in the Lumières' catalogues cover a vast array of activities whose only common denominator (despite the attempt to subject them to a taxonomy) is that they are filmable: a baby eating, a train arriving at a station, workers leaving a factory, photographers arriving at a conference, a snowball fight, the demolition of a wall. The actuality dominated the first decade of film production and produced continual evidence of the drive to fix and make repeatable the ephemeral. Much of the rhetoric accompanying the reception of the earliest films is a sheer celebration of the cinema's ability to represent movement. While photography could fix a moment, the cinema made archivable duration itself. In that sense, it was perceived as a prophylactic against death, ensuring the ability to "see one's loved ones" gesture and smile long after their deaths.[39] What was registered on film was life itself in all its multiplicity, diversity, and contingency.

This archival desire is intimately linked to the technological assurance of indexicality. The fidelity of the image to its referent was no longer dependent upon the skill or honesty of a particular artist. The imprint of the real was automatically guaranteed by the known capability of the machine. For the first time, an aesthetic representation—previously chained to the idea of human control—could be made by accident. This strengthened the medium's alliance with contingency. Film was perceived as the imprint of time itself (as in "The Kinetoscope of Time"), a time unharnessed from rationalization, a nonteleological time in which each moment can produce the unexpected, the unpredictable, and temporality ratifies indeterminacy. Film, in its mechanical and unrelenting forward movement, appears as the incarnation of the thermodynamic law of irreversibility, and as such gives witness to time as the erosion of organization and the free field of chance. Film seems to respond to the dilemma of the representability of time with an easy affirmation. The indexicality of the cinematic sign appears as the guarantee of its status as a record of a temporality outside itself—a pure time or duration which would not be that of its own functioning. This is what imbues cinematic time with historicity. Because it seems to function first and foremost as a *record* of whatever happens in front of the camera, the cinema emerges from and contributes to the archival impulse of the nineteenth century. In it, images are *stored,* time itself is stored. But what is it that is being archived? Once the present as contingency has been seized and stored, it ineluctably becomes the past. Yet this archival artifact becomes strangely immaterial; existing nowhere but in its screening for a spectator in the present, it becomes the experience of presence (this is the sense in which film is usually associated with the present tense rather than the past). What is archived, then, would be the experience of presence. But it is the disjunctiveness of a presence relived, of a presence haunted by historicity. In his essay on photography, Kracauer claims, "A shudder runs through the viewer of old photographs. For they make visible not the knowledge of the original but the spatial configuration of a moment."[40] Similarly, film makes visible not a knowledge of the original but a certain passing temporal configuration. The grandchildren in Kracauer's essay shudder when confronted with the photograph of the grandmother because they see not the grandmother but an image of time, and a time that is not necessary but contingent. This is the pathos of archival desire.

In a sense, the goal of pure inscription or recording was, from the first, self-defeating. The act of filming transforms the contingent into an event characterized by its very filmability, reducing its contingency. The event was there to be filmed. Our current interest in the daily and mundane phenomenon of workers leaving the Lumière factory in 1895 lies in the fact that it constitutes the subject matter of one of the earliest films. Although it proffers to the spectator a wealth of detail and contingency—the different types of clothing of various workers, the use of bicycles, the direction of gazes, et cetera—its significance is ultimately constrained by its association with the "birth" of the cinema. And even in their own time, these early films functioned as both record and performance. The cinema's decisive difference from photography was its ability to inscribe movement through time, and, as Tom Gunning has pointed out, much of the fascination of the earliest Lumière screenings was generated by beginning with a projected still photograph (a form of representation thoroughly familiar to the spectator) and subsequently propelling it into movement so that the temporal work of the apparatus could be displayed as a spectacle in its own right.[41] The representation of time in cinema (its "recording") is also and simultaneously the production of temporalities for the spectator, a structuring of the spectator's time. The cinema is perceived as both record and performance. Recent work on early cinema has tended to focus on its performative dimension. Gunning and André Gaudreault, in their conceptualization of the "cinema of attractions," argue that early films were above all a form of direct display to the spectator, of showing or showmanship.[42] Unabashedly exhibitionistic, they differ from the classical cinema in their direct address, their frequent recourse to a gaze aimed at the camera. The "cinema of attractions," in its emphasis on theatrical display, is opposed to the diegetic absorption of the later classical cinema. It is a confrontational cinema, emphasizing shock and surprise.

Yet it is important to emphasize that notions of film as record and film as performance/display are not necessarily contradictory or incompatible. While the earliest screenings of film clearly functioned as demonstrations of the capabilities of the machine itself (so much so that advertisements frequently mentioned the name of the machine/apparatus—the Biograph or Vitascope—rather than the titles of films), one of the most prominent capabilities exhibited was that of indexicality, the ability to represent motion and temporal duration. Contingency was itself a display. Gunning and Gaudreault buttress their argument about the cinema of attractions by situating the cinema in the context of other popular forms of entertainment, including fairs, vaudeville, and the magic theater. My intention here is both to emphasize the specific difference of photographic media and to extend the range of relevant extracinematic determinants to include a variety of discourses on contingency. The cinema's central role as entertainment does not preclude its intimate relation with new epistemologies, its inextricability from the reorganization of knowledge taking place in modernity. For photographic media offered new standards of accuracy, memory, knowability. The cinema, unlike fairs, vaudeville, and magic theater, requires a permanent in-scription, an archival record. While all of these forms celebrate the ephem-eral, it is the cinema which directly confronts the problematic question of the *representability* of the ephemeral, of the archivability of presence.

Thus, it is necessary to re-engage the issue of indexicality. The notion of indexicality has almost always been anathema to film theory (with the major exception of André Bazin). From Rudolf Arnheim, for whom the deviation from the real assured the status of film as art, to *Screen* film theory of the 1970s and its critique of realism as ideological, the cinema's alleged adher-ence to the referent was something to be denied, rejected, transcended. But indexicality can and must be dissociated from its sole connection to the concept of realism, the reflection of a coherent, familiar, and recognizable world. Indexicality is a function that is essentially without content—in lan-guage, it is allied with the pure denotation of "this" or "here it is." Essentially contentless, it is free to convey anything and everything. In the cinema, it is the guarantee that anything and everything is filmable, the implicit thesis of the Lumière catalogues and the plethora of actualities produced in the earliest years. And while the notion that film as a record of time is suf-ficient rationale for its existence and dissemination disappeared fairly rap-idly, the concept of the filmability of the contingent without limit persists and subtends/supports mainstream classical narrative. It explains the over-whelming multiplicity and diversity of detail which contributes to the sense that a film must be experienced rather than described, that it is fundamen-tally alien to interpretation or translation. It allies the cinema with the logic of statistics and the imperative to domesticate contingency.

Chapters 2, 3, and 4 trace the circulation of debates about the storage and legibility of time, accessibility or representability of the present, continuity versus discontinuity, irreversibility, and contingency in various discourses within physiology, psychoanalysis, aesthetics, logic, thermodynamics, evolu-tionary theory, and statistics. These are the domains within which time becomes an insistent question and where the reconceptualization of tempo-rality and its effects is coincident with a major epistemological shift. In Chapters 5 and 6, I delineate in a more specific fashion the representational dilemmas associated with the emergence of time in cinema. This involves a discussion of the issues of "real time" and the cinematic structuring of time effected by editing. The concluding chapter (Chapter 7) attempts to shed light on the links between the reconceptualization of time that took place at the turn of the twentieth century and the representational developments associated with more recent technologies such as television and digital media. The fate of cinephilia—a love of cinema hinging on its indexicality and link to contingency—is examined to aid in clarifying this relationship.

In Chapter 2, an initial analysis of theoretical questions about the representability of time focuses on the disparate approaches of Sigmund Freud and Etienne-Jules Marey. While Marey's intellectual domain was that of physiology and Freud's the quite differently oriented new science of his own creation, psychoanalysis, they share the project of defamiliarizing time and a conceptual framework for its analysis. For each, the understanding of time was informed by the tension between storage (or representation) and legibility. For Marey, time was an objective plenitude that always seemed to escape the grasp of his differential photographic technique. It could be adequately "represented" only at the risk of illegibility. For Freud, time was pure difference, the effect of the operation of a system designed to store timeless memories and simultaneously protect the subject from the excess stimulation of the external world. Time was associated with consciousness, which is opaque and illegible; it is the unconscious which is readable. The cinema's relation to legibility was also an impossible one for Freud and Marey. Its failure was an inability to abstract, a predilection for overpresence, for excessive coverage without limitation. What Marey and Freud share, in this respect, is the desire to move beyond the visible, to locate, on the one hand, the unit of time/movement that cannot be seen and, on the other, unconscious desire. All three—the cinema, Freud, and Marey—invested in a conceptual framework that foregrounded the tension between the representation of time and legibility, and did so in relation to the opposition between continuity and discontinuity.

Chapter 3 continues the investigation of temporality and storage through an analysis of two concepts of the temporal trace that emerged in the nineteenth century: the afterimage in physiology and the index in Charles Sanders Peirce's theory of signs. The afterimage was instrumental to the notion of the persistence of vision, which for decades constituted the major explanation for the illusion of motion in the cinema. Similarly, the index has functioned as the semiotic concept delineating the specificity of photographic and cinematographic representation. Both the afterimage and the index assume a certain inextricability of past and present, and both rely on the idea of imprinting. They are concepts that illustrate the role of the present as an object of fascination and as an impossible limit within modernity. I delineate the way in which the theory of the afterimage has had a direct impact on aesthetics, particularly in relation to the problem of the representation of motion, in Paul Souriau's theory and in Futurism. I go on to discuss the relation of Peirce's concept of the index, in a sense the semiotic equivalent of the afterimage, to his theory of chance and contingency. Chance, for Peirce, is absolute, and indexicality, contingency, and chance, as well as the notion of the present instant as a point of discontinuity, are wedded in his theory. The dominance of chance leads him to embrace a statistical logic. The final section of this chapter elucidates the cinema's relation to presence and the present tense in view of modernity's fascination with the present moment and its archive, as well as in relation to the growing influence of a statistical logic.

Peirce was not the only theorist to insist upon the importance of statistics in this period, and in Chapter 4 I analyze the emergence of a statistical epistemology in a different field, physics, in relation to the concept of temporal irreversibility. Thermodynamics arose as a response to the centrality of the engine in modernity and the need to deal with the crucial but highly malleable concept of energy. Its second law recognizes that usable energy ultimately and irreversibly exhausts itself in the process of transformation and dissipates, leading inevitably to the degeneration and death of a closed system. This is the law of entropy and mandates temporal irreversibility. In the first section of this chapter, I examine the concept of temporal irreversibility in physics and the way in which the cinematic apparatus, given its indexically based representation of movement and time, is often perceived as *the* exemplar of temporal irreversibility. Although experimentation with reversing filmic temporality is not uncommon in the early days of cinema and is often produced as a novelty or curiosity, mainstream film has worked historically to familiarize temporal irreversibility, in its unrelenting forward movement. The temporal irreversibility associated with entropy breaks down organization and leads to the domination of chance and the contingent. It is not explicable through the classical laws of cause and effect in dynamics and requires a recourse to a statistical methodology. While acknowledging or paying homage to singularity, particularity, contingency, and chance, a statistical epistemology ultimately constrains them within an overriding system. It is a method of dealing simultaneously with both the particular and the general, the contingent and the lawful. The final section of Chapter 4 analyzes how contingency and chance within cinematic exhibition was gradually reduced as the temporality of the diegesis began to dominate, and even attempted to annihilate, the temporality of the viewing situation. In contrast, the films of Lumière and Méliès, in foregrounding contingency and chance in quite different ways, constituted a form of resistance to the systematicity of a statistical logic and were symptomatic of the nineteenth-century epistemological crisis that undermined ideas of law, necessity, and determinism.

Chapters 5 and 6 deal with the way in which the interdisciplinary epistemology of contingency discussed in the previous three chapters leaves its traces in the representational struggles of an emerging cinema and how that cinema contributes to the articulation of contingency and system in modernity. In Chapter 5, I focus on the inscription of the contingent and of temporality in two early actualities, *Electrocuting an Elephant* (Edison, 1903) and *Execution of Czolgosz, with Panorama of Auburn Prison* (Porter/Edison, 1901). My major concern in this chapter is with the cinematic representation of time, focusing on the cinematic construction of the event as the most condensed and semantically wealthy unit of time. The event which these execution films seek to represent could be defined as one of the most intractable of contingencies—death. Although each of these films clings to a referential event, a historically specific moment, what they demonstrate above all is the indeterminacy, the instability and imprecision of cinematic time. The final section of Chapter 5 entails a discussion of the way in which structuralism, later in the century, consolidates an opposition between structure and event that is much less stable at the turn of the century. These instabilities are played out in the work of two theorists—Sigmund Freud and Charles Baudelaire—whose writing is contemporary with the epistemological shift outlined here.

Chapter 6 directly confronts the question of the role of continuity and discontinuity in the cinema, filtering this discussion through the debates about Zeno's paradoxes and their relation to the phenomenon of intermittent motion in the cinema. Given the fact that movement in the cinema is based on an illusion generated by a series of still frames, a number of theorists (for example, Henri Bergson and Jean Epstein) have situated the cinema as either the corroboration or the refutation of Zeno's claim that movement and change do not really exist and are only apparent. The dialectic of discontinuity and continuity, so crucial to theorists like Bergson or Peirce, operates in the cinema at two levels: in the gap between frames, which is effaced in the production of the illusion of movement, and in the cut, which is also often concealed through techniques of continuity editing. In this chapter, I examine three early logics of editing and their assumptions about the potential form of a cinematic time. These logics also reveal the intimate relation between the formation of a cinematic syntax and the reafirmation of heterosexuality. Chapter 6 ends with an analysis of Thom Andersen's 1974 documentary, *Eadward Muybridge, Zoopraxographer,* which praises Muybridge for transforming photography into cinema and, in the process, "bridging the darkness" that constitutes the abyss between individual frames. In this way, according to Andersen, Muybridge demonstrated how cinema decisively refuted Zeno's paradoxes. Cinematic narrative's denial of the darkness that subtends it gains credibility by weaving together a series of apparently obvious "truths"—the truths of movement, instantaneity, heterosexuality, and visibility.

My concluding chapter delineates the relations between the nineteenth-/ early twentieth-century epistemology of contingency and contemporary processes of digital and televisual imaging, which inscribe/produce temporality in forms echoing, in many respects, those of earlier technologies of representation. I argue that there is no radical rupture and that what is still very much at stake is the attempt to structure contingency. The work of both modern and "postmodern" technologies of representation is characterized by the tension between a desire for instantaneity and an archival aspiration. This chapter returns to Marey as a nodal figure in the nineteenth-century debates about continuity, discontinuity, and the representability of time. Marey's chronophotography demonstrates the crucial role of the photographic instant and instantaneity in the representation of movement and time (the aspiration to instantaneity is a feature of television and digital media as well). His conceptualization of the image/instant as point (revealed by the continuing lure, for him, of the graphic method of representing time) laid the groundwork for the synthesis of movement that was to become cinema. The *point* is a particularly potent trope here, given its theorization as simultaneously the ultimate abstraction and the ultimate indicator of the concrete, the particular, the present instant in its absolute singularity. It condenses in a single figure the aspirations of the epistemology of contingency—to acknowledge and pay homage to the power of contingency and at the same time to subject it to a system.

The other governing figure of this epistemological shift is that of the archive, which is often in tension with the fascination with instantaneity. Ultimately, the focus of archival desire in the cinema is an impossible one—the reproduction of presence, a presence perceived to be the victim of rationalization and estrangement. Yet the archive's historicizing impulse, together with its inextricability from the concept of value, resonates uneasily with the desire to represent presence and instantaneity, with cinema's alliance with contingency and ephemerality, and with its apparent ability to represent anything whatsoever. The final section of Chapter 7, a reconsideration of cinephilia, is an attempt to demonstrate how value becomes attached not to the content of the contingent detail itself, but to the power of the very form of cinematic contingency and its relation to historical possibility.

The cinema engages multiple temporalities, and it is helpful, at least temporarily, to disentangle them. There is the temporality of the apparatus itself—linear, irreversible, "mechanical." And there is the temporality of the diegesis, the way in which time is represented by the image, the varying invocations of present, past, future, historicity. Flashbacks would be the most prominent example of how the temporal content of the narrative can seemingly contest or counter the irreversibility of the apparatus itself. And finally, there is the temporality of reception, theoretically distinct but nevertheless a temporality which the developing classical cinema attempted to fuse as tightly as possible to that of the apparatus, conferring upon it the same linear predictability and irreversibility. Historically, experimentation with this form of temporality has been relegated to an avant-garde at the margins of mainstream cinema. Everything about the theatrical setting—the placement of the screen in relation to the audience, the darkness of the auditorium and its enclosed space—encourages the spectator to honor the relentless temporality of the apparatus. It is possible to look away or to exit momentarily, but in the process something is lost and is felt as such. Similarly, the historical trajectory of the cinema has seemed to effect a reduction in the function of film as pure record of a time and a movement outside itself. Even in the early days of the cinema, the use of camera stoppage and editing allowed the film to construct its own temporality, independently of the external event or situation. The specific technology of the cinema—its apparent ability to represent the contingent without limit—posed the threat of an overwhelming detail, a denial of representation itself. The frame, of course, constitutes a spatial limit, but it is intriguing to note that histories and theories of early cinema continually pinpoint the temporal limit of the *cut,* the interruption in the linear forward movement of the film strip, as the crucial moment in the elaboration of film language. The cinema moves from the status of a machine that amazes and astonishes through its capacity as a record of time and movement to a machine for the production of temporalities that mimic "real time." Nevertheless, the production of temporalities in the classical cinema is ultimately not separable from the idea of the image as a record of time outside itself. At the macroscopic level, in its maintenance of continuity and the illusion of "real time," the film mimics and reiterates the microscopic level of the shot itself. In this way, it borrows and activates the fascination of the shot's privileged relation to contingency and a temporality emancipated from rationalization. Contingency becomes a form of graspable effectivity.

The fully developed classical cinema, like statistics, acknowledges contingency and indeterminacy while at the same time offering the law of their regularity. In 1848 Quetelet, in an attempt to banish chance, wrote: "What we call an anomaly deviates in our eyes from the general law only because we are incapable of embracing enough things in a single glance."[43] The cinema emerges as the materialization of the drive to "embrace enough things in a single glance." An advertisement for the American Biograph Company in 1900 proclaimed: "Our Films Are Seven Times the Size of Others, We Show Twice as Many Pictures Per Second, and Our Pictures on the Canvas are LARGER, BRIGHTER, STEADIER and More INTERESTING Than Others . . . We Have a Stock of Over Three Thousand Subjects and They are Coming all the Time from Europe, Asia, Africa and America."[44] Indexicality has acted historically not solely as the assurance of realism but as the guarantee that anything and everything—any moment whatever—is representable, cinematographic. Contingency is brought under the rein of semiosis. But the earliest films display more vividly the fact that chance and contingency are the highly cathected sites not only of pleasure but of anxiety. The threat is that of an excess of designation, an excess of sensation that excludes meaning and control. The developing classical conventions structure time and contingency in ways consonant with the broader rationalization and abstraction of time in an industrialized modernity. Efficiency becomes a crucial value, and time is filled with meaning. Nevertheless, contingency is by no means banished. The structuring of time also involves its (structure's) denegation. Cinema comprises simultaneously the rationalization of time and an homage to contingency. Classical cinematic form involves the strict regulation of a mode that never ceases to strike the spectator as open, fluid, malleable—the site of newness and difference itself.

2

Temporality, Storage, Legibility: Freud, Marey, and the Cinema

The advent of mechanical reproduction inaugurated a discursive thematics of excess and oversaturation that is still with us. The sheer quantity of images and sounds is perceived as the threat of overwhelming or suffocating the subject. In his 1927 essay on photography, Siegfried Kracauer appeals to figures of natural disaster to capture the anxiety attendant upon the accelerated diffusion of photographic images; he refers to "the blizzard of photographs" and the "flood of photos" that "sweep away the dams of memory."[1] Excess is embodied in the form of the photograph itself to the extent that it represents a spatial continuum, without the gaps or lacks conducive to the production of historical significance. This continuum of the photograph becomes, in Kracauer's argument, the continuum of a practice of photography that supports an overwhelming and ultimately meaningless historicism. Hence we have the crucial and yet puzzling problem of the development and maintenance of a photographic archive, as so provocatively delineated by Allan Sekula.[2] What taxonomic principle can govern the breakdown and ordering of a "flood" or a "blizzard"?

The excess and unrelenting continuum of mechanical reproduction are not, however, limited to the consideration of space (and Kracauer himself is insistent upon historicism's dependence upon the fullness of a temporal continuum). The emergence of mechanical reproduction is accompanied by modernity's increasing understanding of temporality as assault, acceleration, speed. There is too much, too fast. From Georg Simmel to Walter Benjamin, modernity is conceptualized as an increase in the speed and intensity of stimuli. Time emerges as a problem intimately linked to the theorization of modernity as trauma or shock. Time is no longer the benign phenomenon most easily grasped by the notion of flow but a troublesome and anxiety-producing entity that must be thought in relation to management, regulation, storage, and representation. One of the most important apparatuses for regulating and storing time was the cinema. As Friedrich Kittler has pointed out, the cinema and phonography held out the promise of storing time even as they posed a potential threat to an entire symbolic system.

> What was new about the storage capability of the phonograph and cinematograph—and both names refer, not accidentally, to writing—was their ability to store time: as a mixture of audio frequencies in the acoustic realm, as a movement of single picture sequences in the optic realm. Time, however, is what determines the limits of all art. The quotidian data flow must be arrested before it can become image or sign . . . whatever runs as time on a physical or . . . real level, blindly and unpredictably, could by no means be encoded. Therefore all data flows, if they were real streams of data, had to pass through the defile of the signifier.[3]

Before the invention of phonography and cinema, written texts and musical scores were the only means of preserving time. Each was clearly dependent upon writing as a symbolic system and eschewed the apparent fullness, presence, and unrelenting continuum of the forms of imagistic mechanical reproduction.

Time hence became very insistently a problem of representation. Accompanying the cinema as a new technology of temporality was a sustained discourse on time in the philosophical, psychoanalytic, and scientific realms. This chapter explores two very disparate, if not diametrically opposed, attempts to analyze time that nevertheless converge in their specification of the framework of terms in which time can be understood—a framework crucial to the representational/historical trajectory of the cinema. In Freud's work, time is an undertheorized concept that seems to operate as a symptom whose effects are intensified by the excessive trauma of modernity, so that modernity becomes, in part, a pathology of temporality. The impasse of his spatial model of memory forces him to produce a theory of temporality as the discontinuous mode of operation of the psyche itself. Time is not "out there," to be measured, but is instead the effect of a protective configuration of the psyche. Freud chose for his exemplary machine and model not the cinema, photography, or phonography, but the comparatively old-fashioned Mystic Writing-Pad. In contrast, Etienne-Jules Marey marshaled the latest technologies of sequential photography (and, in most historical accounts, anticipated the cinema) in order to capture and measure an objective temporality that nevertheless always seemed to elude representation. Together, Freud and Marey figure the limits of the representational problematic within which the cinema developed as a specific mode of organizing and regulating time. Both theorists conceptualized time as a problem of storage or representation and its failure.

Freud and Marey do not simply overlap chronologically but share a certain conceptual rubric within which the question of temporality is raised. Freud, particularly in his early work, which is still infused with terminology drawn from physiology (for instance, *The Project for a Scientific Psychology*, 1895), is obsessed with the issues of traces and recording, of a space of psychical representation and the problem of its limits. For a subject who is in some sense molded by time, what keeps the space of memory from becoming oversaturated, disallowing fresh impressions? Physiology provides Freud with some of the terms crucial to thinking the work of memory, whose traces are intimately linked with the phenomenon of resistance. Marey, whose field is physiology, is more directly concerned with the representation of time as it is incarnated in physical movement. But his fascination with the technologies required for that inscription forces him to confront issues of material resistance and the limits of space as well. For both theorists, these difficulties are figured in relation to the opposition between continuity and discontinuity, a critical opposition of the period with which Henri Bergson and Charles Sanders Peirce also grapple and whose insistence is indicated by the resuscitation of the questions posed by Zeno's paradoxes. Marey's work is undergirded by an investment in time as continuum, a fact attested to by his continuing nostalgia for the graphic method despite his later embrace of the intermittent method of chronophotography. Freud, on the other hand, in the process of constructing a theory of subjectivity based on loss and lack, produces an understanding of time as the very work of discontinuity. Both approaches hinge on the question of whether time is located inside or outside the apparatus—whether time is an effect of the operation of the apparatus or the neutral object of its representation. This is also a pivotal question for the emerging cinema.

At first glance it would seem that psychoanalysis is infused with questions of temporality, that temporality would be one of its most indispensable concepts. For the psychoanalytic subject is delineated as the site of historical inscriptions and the psychoanalytic encounter specified as a process of remembering, repeating, and working through. Whether or not Freud is accountable for espousing a notion of stages or phases of development, it is clear that for him the specificity of sexuality in the human being is linked to its diphasic nature—the fact that sexuality is expressed freely and abundantly in the infantile period, undergoes repression, and is finally resuscitated in puberty in a different form. The French rereading of Freud has isolated the concept of *Nachträglichkeit,* or deferred action *(après coup),* as crucial to the thinking of psychical determination, so that the traumatic effect of an event is understood as the reverberation between two events separated across time. Freud also exerts an extraordinary amount of effort searching for an apparatus capable of representing memory. And Jacques Derrida can claim, particularly insofar as it supports his own theory of writing and the logic of the trace, that "memory . . . is not a psychical property among others; it is the very essence of the psyche: resistance, and precisely, thereby, an opening to the effraction of the trace." Michel Serres, on the basis of Freud's adherence to the thermodynamic principles of conservation of energy (the economic point of view) and the tendency toward death (the death drive), claims that "Freudian time is irreversible" and therefore in line with contemporary movements in physics and the other sciences of the late nineteenth century, as well as with technological innovations ("As soon as one can build them and theorize about them—steam or combustion engines, chemical, electrical, and turbine engines, and so forth—the notion of time changes").[4]

On the other hand, and despite the marks of its apparent importance, the concept of temporality is also, in a way, radically absent from Freud's work. In his 1915 metapsychological paper "The Unconscious," Freud made it quite clear that the unconscious lacks a concept of time: "The processes of the system *Ucs.* are *timeless; i.e.* they are not ordered temporally, are not altered by the passage of time; they have no reference to time at all. Reference to time is bound up, once again, with the work of the system *Cs* [Consciousness]." The same negative characteristics are reiterated in *Beyond the Pleasure Principle.*[5] The unconscious is described in *The Interpretation of Dreams* as a storehouse of contents and processes that are immune to the corrosive effects of temporality. In fact, according to Freud, the idea that wear and tear *are* fundamental effects of time is a commonly held but mistaken one:

> Indeed it is a prominent feature of unconscious processes that they are indestructible. In the unconscious nothing can be brought to an end, nothing is past or forgotten . . . For the fading of memories and the emotional weakness of impressions which are no longer recent, which we are inclined to regard as self-evident and to explain as a primary effect of time upon mental memory-traces, are in reality secondary modifications which are only brought about by laborious work.[6]

Freud elaborates here the counterintuitive idea that the passage of time does not diminish "memories" and "impressions" in the unconscious, which remain at some level as vivid for the adult as for the child. The unconscious stores all, relinquishes nothing, and is, most insistently, outside of time. Given the fact that the major impulse of psychoanalysis is the depriviledging of consciousness and that time is resolutely linked to the phenomenon of consciousness, it is perhaps not surprising that Freud nowhere expounds a full-fledged theory of temporality.

Freud's very few direct references to time as a concept have always struck me as enigmatic, if not opaque. "A Note upon the 'Mystic Writing-Pad'" (1925) is devoted to a problem concerning memory that Freud had isolated as early as the 1895 *Project for a Scientific Psychology.* In order to understand memory and its operation it is crucial to conceptualize a surface that can both retain a limitless number of traces or inscriptions and yet be continually open to the reception of fresh impressions. Freud resolves the difficulty by appealing to an apparatus—a toy, in effect—the Mystic Writing-Pad, in order to represent memory. It is appropriate as an analogy because it is a multilevel system, its three layers constituted by a wax slab, a thin sheet of translucent waxed paper, and a transparent piece of celluloid. When written on, the wax slab permanently retains the traces of that writing, but when the two upper sheets are raised, the writing is erased from them, and they are free to receive new impressions. In Freud's analogy, the two upper sheets correspond to the system perception-consciousness, while the wax slab is comparable to the unconscious—a storehouse of traces. The "appearance and disappearance of the writing" is analogous to the "flickering-up and passing-away of consciousness in the process of perception." Freud is particularly interested in the working of the system. Because the layers continually break contact, discontinuity and periodicity are the basis of the pad's operation. He ends the short essay with a speculation: "I further had a suspicion that this discontinuous method of functioning of the system *Pcpt.-Cs.* [Perception-Consciousness] lies at the bottom of the origin of the concept of time."[7] This tantalizing theoretical proposition is simply left dangling, and it is nowhere followed through or elaborated. Time appears here as the afterthought of an attempt to deal with memory.

"A Note upon the 'Mystic Writing-Pad,'" which, after all, is extremely brief and speculative, is not the only place where Freud confronts the concept of time yet manages to make it marginal within his own discourse as well as theoretically a by-product or aftereffect of some other process. In his investigation of the hypothetical life processes of the simplest living organism in *Beyond the Pleasure Principle,* Freud takes a discursive detour to consider the question of time: "our abstract idea of time seems to be wholly derived from the method of working of the system *Pcpt.-Cs.* and to correspond to a perception on its own part of that method of working. This mode of functioning may perhaps constitute another way of providing a shield against stimuli. I know that these remarks must sound very obscure, but I must limit myself to these hints."[8] It is not clear why Freud has to limit himself to "these hints" in a work as highly speculative, wide-ranging, and ambitious as *Beyond the Pleasure Principle.* But certainly time's alliance with consciousness determines its displacement as a category. For within psychoanalysis it is the familiar, everyday concept of consciousness that becomes strange (Freud refers to the "inexplicable phenomenon of consciousness").[9]

Given the obscurity or even opaqueness of Freud's direct references to temporality, it might be useful to take a detour through his theorization of memory before returning to the concept of time. A close examination of Freud's treatment of memory and temporality reveals the continual recurrence of three themes: (1) the insistence upon inscription as a metaphor for the processes of memory; (2) the retention of a notion of storage and the corresponding problem of localization; (3) the close association established between time and protection of the organism from external stimuli. All these motifs—inscription or trace as representation, storage, and protection from an overload of stimuli—have been activated in an attempt to theorize the nascent cinema. My discussion of the psychoanalytic texts is preparatory to an analysis of the conceptual encounters and intersections between the two institutions in their formulation of a relation to time in modernity.

Although time is a concept that is marginalized in Freud's work, it is clear that he was obsessed throughout his career, at both the clinical and the metapsychological levels, with the problem of memory. He invoked a plethora of apparatuses (the camera, the telescope, the microscope), metaphors, analogies, and mythologies in an attempt to find its proper theoretical representation. But the metaphorical complex that insistently returns, from the 1895 *Project* to "A Note upon the 'Mystic Writing-Pad,'" where Freud believes he has finally found what he is looking for, is that of inscription, mark or trace, pathway. This vocabulary is most persistent in the construction of the elaborate neurological fable begun and quickly abandoned by Freud in the unpublished "Project." Searching for a scientific basis for the study of the psyche, he here appropriates the terminology and theoretical paradigms of late nineteenth-century neurophysiology and even utilizes its concept of the neurone as the material particle or minimal unit in question. He makes a distinction, roughly equivalent to that between consciousness and the unconscious, between permeable and impermeable neurones. The impermeable neurones are the "vehicles of memory and so probably of psychical processes in general" precisely because they offer difficulty or resistance to the passage of quantity. Retention of traces is a direct result of resistance, and the permeable neurones retain nothing. The impermeable neurones, the vehicles of memory, are "permanently altered by the passage of an excitation."[10]

"Facilitation" is the *Standard Edition*'s translation of *Bahnung*, which is derived from "road" and means "pathbreaking." The translator of Derrida's "Freud and the Scene of Writing" uses the term *breaching* (for Derrida's "frayage") and claims that "it is crucial to maintain the sense of the *force* that breaks open a pathway, and the *space* opened by the force." A metaphorics of pathbreaking is certainly appropriate, for Freud understands the process of

facilitation as one that makes the neurones more capable of conduction—
less impermeable. Facilitation opens up a space, engraves a course, eases a
movement. But the initial resistance is absolutely crucial. As Derrida points
out, "If there were only perception, pure permeability to breaching, there
would be no breaches. We would be written, but nothing would be recorded;
no writing would be produced, retained, repeated as legibility."[11] Recording
and legibility are precisely the stakes.

Although Freud abandons quite quickly the neurophysiological framework of the *Project*, its terms and descriptions persistently infect his discourse and leave their mark on his attempts to find a new way of representing psychical processes. As late as *Beyond the Pleasure Principle*, in the course
of constructing the fantasy of a simple organism and its relations with the
external world, Freud invokes the same terminology and the same scenario
as in the *Project*: "It may be supposed that, in passing from one element to
another, an excitation has to overcome a resistance, and that the diminution
of resistance thus effected is what lays down a permanent trace of the excitation, that is, a facilitation. In the system *Cs.*, then, resistance of this kind to
passage from one element to another would no longer exist."[12] He continues
to theorize memory in terms of resistance and engraving. In "A Note upon
the 'Mystic Writing-Pad,'" a stylus will do, rather than a pen, since only an
instrument whose pressure will leave its mark is required. The wax slab is
cut into, its material permanently altered or displaced. Derrida predictably
celebrates Freud's choice of a writing apparatus as the culminating analogy
in his theory of memory, but it is crucial to remember that the Mystic Writing-Pad will accept any type of mark or engraving. The traces on the pad are
not necessarily phonetic writing. It is enough that they are retained without
disallowing further receptivity to fresh impressions. Indeed, given the fact
that the Mystic Writing-Pad is, after all, a child's toy (and as Derrida himself
points out, more sophisticated technologies of recording were readily available at this time), it might be more likely to receive iconic representations or
nonsense.[13]

What is noteworthy about Freud's vocabulary and complex metaphorics
in his search for an adequate means of representing memory is not their relation to any concept of writing but their resolute materialism. Memory is
the effect of a blockage, the resistance of some unthinkable material, and its
ultimate failure. A barrier is *breached* and a certain violence is suggested in

the notion of "breaking a path." Memory traces are conceptualized as an actual etching into a material. Long after Freud relinquishes the neurophysiological model, he retains its dream of a material ground that would support a true "scientific" endeavor.

Such a resolute materialism in the description of memory demands a corresponding notion of storage, location, place. It is difficult to conceive of an etching or a trace that is not located *somewhere*. One of the aspects of neurophysiology first and most adamantly rejected by Freud, however, was precisely the idea of physiological localization. In "The Unconscious," he states,

> Research has given irrefutable proof that mental activity is bound up with the function of the brain as it is with no other organ. We are taken a step further—we do not know how much—by the discovery of the unequal importance of the different parts of the brain and their special relations to particular parts of the body and to particular mental activities. But every attempt to go on from there to discover a localization of mental processes, every endeavor to think of ideas as stored up in nerve cells and of excitations as travelling along nerve-fibres, has miscarried completely.

Nevertheless, Freud retains the idea of a "psychical topography" and "regions in the mental apparatus."[14] Figures of space and place are pervasive in much of his writing, and the topographic point of view continues to compete successfully with the dynamic and economic points of view. The very terms in which Freud describes his quandary in the attempt to represent memory are indicative of the critical need for a concept of space. The difficulty in thinking about memory has to do with two seemingly incompatible needs: unlimited receptive capacity (a "clean" or "open" space) and the retention of permanent traces (a space of storage). A notepad is an impossible metaphor because it will soon "fill up"; it constitutes a finite space. Similarly, a chalkboard is infinitely receptive but can retain no traces. The dilemma posed by a spatial conceptualization leads Freud to the notion of layering and depths as well as that of a periodic contact between the layers. But the terms are clearly posed as those of space, room for inscription, emptiness, and fullness. And, ultimately, Freud's desire is to think of both the receptive layer and the retentive layer as infinite spaces. For the unconscious, the site of memory, is in a sense a truly ideal space of unlimited storage, a perfect library in which nothing is ever lost. Perhaps this is why, in the context of elaborating an earlier analogy—that of the compound microscope or photographic apparatus—Freud emphasizes the ideality of place (location): "psychical locality will correspond to a point inside the apparatus at which one of the preliminary stages of an image comes into being. In the microscope and telescope, as we know, these occur in part at ideal points, regions in which no tangible component of the apparatus is situated."[15] What Freud requires is a virtual space—a space that is thinkable but not localizable.

It may be true that Freud, given his pre-Saussurean relation to linguistic phenomena, was unable to think what much of his own theory suggests quite palpably—that the unconscious is structured like a language. But he *was* able to think of the unconscious as a space, a storehouse, a place outside of time, infinitely accommodating, where nothing is ever lost or destroyed. It is also a place where processes occur, where thing-representations are cathected to a greater or lesser degree. But there is no contradiction between its elements, which are all simply *there*. The link between the unconscious and the idea of storage or a reservoir is elaborated by Jean Laplanche in an essay on psychoanalysis, time, and translation: "It is the inexhaustible stores of material that each human being in the course of his existence strives as a last resort to translate into his acts, his speech, and the manner in which he represents himself to himself—it is this untranslatable that I term the unconscious."[16] It is only at the cost of a serious distortion of Freud's work that one could see the unconscious as *only* or even primarily a place of storage. But it is also problematic to ignore completely this vein of his thought.

The first two thematic motifs—the insistence upon a metaphorics of inscription or engraving, and the resultant requirement for some kind of notion of locality or storage—are elaborated in the course of developing a theory of memory. The third motif—the close connection Freud established between the concept of time and the need for protection from external stimuli—brings memory back into relation with temporality.

Freud claims, in *Beyond the Pleasure Principle*, that "*Protection against stimuli is an almost more important function for the living organism than reception of stimuli.*"[17] His understanding of the "external world" does not change much from the 1895 *Project* to the 1920 speculative tract. It is consistently envisioned as a surplus of stimulations, an overwhelming mass of energies perpetually assaulting the subject and liable to break through its defenses. In the *Project* he states: "there is no question but that the external world is the origin of all major quantities of energy, since, according to the discoveries of physics, it consists of powerful masses which are in violent motion and which transmit their motion." This same thermodynamic conception reemerges in *Beyond the Pleasure Principle* in the speculative hypothesis of the "simplest organism:" "This little fragment of living substance is suspended in the middle of an external world charged with the most powerful energies; and it would be killed by the stimulation emanating from these if it were not provided with a protective shield against stimuli."[18] The intensity of the concern in this text for external energies and the phenomena of shock and trauma has been linked directly to the extensive shellshock resulting from a highly technologized World War I, but it is also an expression of generalized anxieties about modernity and its assault on the senses. It is not surprising that Walter Benjamin fastens on *Beyond the Pleasure Principle* in his attempt to theorize the relation of Proust and Baudelaire to the concepts of shock, memory, and modernity.[19]

The top layer of the Mystic Writing-Pad—the transparent celluloid sheet—is conceived of entirely in terms of protection—it functions "to keep off injurious effects from without" and is "a protective shield against stimuli."[20] The celluloid and the waxed paper together are analogous to the system perception-consciousness and its protective shield, and the intermittent and discontinuous operation of these two layers together is directly linked to Freud's enigmatic reference to time. The reference is immediately preceded by a discussion of a notion that Freud says he has "long had" but "hitherto kept to" himself—a notion about the perceptual apparatus's method of operation. The unconscious sends out cathectic innervations in "rapid periodic impulses" into the system perception-consciousness. When this system is cathected, it can receive perceptions that are then transmitted as impressions to the unconscious system of memory; when the cathexis is rapidly and periodically withdrawn, consciousness is "extinguished" (remember the previous reference to the "flickering-up and passing-away" of consciousness),[21] and the system cannot function. The description of this process is strikingly similar to that of intermittent motion in the cinema (Freud refers to the "periodic non-excitability of the perceptual system"). Freud claims:

"It is as though the unconscious stretches out feelers, through the medium of the system *Pcpt.-Cs.,* towards the external world and hastily withdraws them as soon as they have sampled the excitations coming from it." This entire discussion ushers in the tantalizingly brief reference to time—"I further had a suspicion that this discontinuous method of functioning of the system *Pcpt.-Cs.* lies at the bottom of the origin of the concept of time."[22] Time as discontinuity emerges as a secondary effect of the organism's need to protect itself from the stimuli of the outer world. And since modernity is perceived as an astonishing increase in the stimuli bombarding the subject, it follows that time would become a particularly acute problem in modernity.

In "A Note upon the 'Mystic Writing-Pad,'" perception-consciousness is a transparent protective sheet and a layer of waxed paper; in *Beyond the Pleasure Principle,* it is a hardened shell, resistant to the massive energies of the external world. But nowhere is it a surface that is capable of retaining traces. Indeed, consciousness in Freud's view is absolutely antithetical to the notion of storage or retention—"excitatory processes do not leave behind any permanent change in its elements but expire, as it were, in the phenomenon of becoming conscious."[23] The dilemma of memory and its relation to storage assigns to consciousness the function of pure receptivity. Consciousness is the site of all that is transitory, in flux, impermanent. The retention or representation of memory traces is reserved for the unconscious.

In some respects, this theoretical construction might appear excessive or radically impractical in relation to Freud's own psychoanalytic practice. For it might seem at first glance that his therapeutic approach demands the recall or retrieval by consciousness of ancient unconscious memories, hence requiring some form of compatibility between consciousness and memory. However, Freud struggled with the question of therapy's relation to memory throughout his career. Essays like "Constructions in Analysis" and "Remembering Repeating and Working-Through" trace the difficulties Freud encountered with the idea of a simple "recall" of childhood memories and elaborate how he favored, instead, a belief that a laborious process of construction was required in the course of the analysis.[24] Memories are quite "real" and reside in the unconscious, continually producing effects. But they are not simply and transparently accessible to consciousness.[25] In this respect, Freud's therapeutic practice is consistent with the more apparent radicalness of his highly speculative and often literally incredible metapsychological texts. For instance, in *Beyond the Pleasure Principle* Freud claims that "becoming conscious and leaving behind a memory-trace are processes incompatible with each other within one and the same system," and *"consciousness arises instead of a memory-trace."*[26] What can "instead of" mean here? "In place of"? "In order to block (memory)"? "At the expense of"? What remains clear is the incompatibility of memory and consciousness. And because consciousness is so fully bound up with the concept of time—through the periodicity or discontinuity of its functioning—it would seem inevitable that in Freud's system, time and memory are absolutely incompatible as well. Time is that which leaves no record—it emerges from the failure of representation. This scenario produces the unconscious as the dream of a memory uncorrupted by time. Time is not an inert process, external to the subject, weighing down on memories, contributing to their weakening and diminishment. Instead, it is an effect, a kind of mirroring of the operation of the psychical system. Within psychoanalysis, the commonly held view that memory is the residue of time is an impossible one.

Time is therefore conceptualized within the problematic of determining what is storable, what is representable. Memory is representation itself; time, its inconceivability. Time is antithetical to the notions of storage and retention of traces. This is a rare point of contact between Freud and Bergson, who condemns the pervasive attempt to spatialize time (particularly in a positivist science) and argues the indivisibility of movement and the impossibility of real instants. However, for Bergson, time is unrepresentable because it is flux, absolute unity, indivisibility.[27] For Freud, time is intimately linked with the very phenomena of discontinuity and difference. Furthermore, for Bergson time is a crucial and central concept in the delineation of subjectivity, whereas for Freud it is a by-product of more significant psychical processes. It could almost be said that for Freud time is a *symptom* of the subject's agonistic relationship with its environment.

The psychoanalysis of time, which produces through negation an image of its operation in its association with an inexplicable consciousness, needs to be seen in the context of another endeavor at the turn of the century to analyze time. Whereas time was for Freud what is, above all, unrepresentable, there was a widespread and concerted, if not obsessive, attempt in a number of fields, including physiology, to isolate and analyze the instant, to make an invisible time optically legible—in other words, to represent adequately the phenomenon that Freud opposes to the trace. What determines the direction of much of this research is the overwhelming desire to know what happens within the duration of a fraction of a second, that is, to know that aspect of time which is not accessible to ordinary vision. In an essay on photography, Benjamin reiterates this impulse to dissect time: "While it is possible to give an account of how people walk, if only in the most inexact way, all the same we know nothing definite of the positions involved in the fraction of a second when the step is taken."[28] The best-known proponent of this endeavor, and the figure who is most frequently isolated as a primary scientific precursor of the cinema, is Etienne-Jules Marey, who spent his life generating careful and detailed depictions of bodies in movement, first through graphic inscriptors and, later, through photographic apparatuses. Marey's photographic technique was labeled "chronophotography," literally, the photography of time.

Marey participated in a general movement in physiology in the latter half of the nineteenth century that involved the production of a concept of life adequate to modernity—a concept of life as movement, process, change. As Lisa Cartwright has eloquently argued, instruments and techniques were developed as the support of a "vivifying physiological gaze."[29] Autopsy and vivisection interfered with or annihilated life processes and were therefore antithetical to the aims of physiology. Physiologists could have no interest in the "dead instant." Marey proclaimed that "motion is the most apparent characteristic of life; it manifests itself in all the functions; it is even the essence of several of them."[30]

Thus, Marey's ostensible object was movement, that is, the correlation of space and time as a body successively changes its position. It is therefore arguable that his interest in time was merely secondary, a by-product of the obsessive concern—more proper to a physiologist—with the analysis of bodies in motion. Nevertheless, the trajectory of Marey's own career, his incessant struggle with the development of newer, more readable modes of representation of his object, and his explicit awareness of the tension between spatial and temporal categories in his work all suggest the ultimate privileging of temporality and its scientific representation and measurement. Marey's dream, whether acknowledged or not, was that of cutting into time, slicing it in such a way that it could become representable. Movement remained the clearest and most accessible expression of duration. Initially and apparently adhering to a body, movement was progressively disengaged from that body first through the techniques of geometric chronophotography and later through Marey's growing interest in the more apparently abstract and bodiless realms of fluid dynamics and the flow of air currents.

Marey's obsessive concern with the measurement and graphing of movement across time emerged from the problems involved in understanding physiological time, a project he inherited from Hermann von Helmholtz, one of the figures most closely connected with the "discovery" of the laws of thermodynamics. Initially at stake was internal physiological time, a time inaccessible to the naked eye. Helmholtz was the first to investigate the speed of the transference of a shock along the extension of a nerve to the point of muscular contraction. Marey was particularly interested in the concept of "lost time" invoked by Helmholtz to label the time during which nothing seems to happen—the time between the reception of the nervous shock or impulse by the muscle and the muscle's contraction: "Now, it results from the experiments of Helmholtz, that all the time which elapses between the excitement and the motion is not occupied by the transference of the nervous agent; but that the muscle, when it has received the order carried by the nerve, remains an instant before acting." Marey disputes the reigning hypothesis that the speed of the "nervous agent" varies under certain influences, and instead proposes that the variable duration is attributable to "those still unknown phenomena which are produced in the muscle during the *lost time* of Helmholtz."[31] According to Anson Rabinbach, in his study of energy and fatigue, "This lost time, which consists of the relationship between duration and energy expenditure, is for Marey a basic component of the economy of the body."[32] Already, at this early stage, the urge to make a "lost time" visible and knowable is in evidence.

In his early work, Marey constructed a series of instruments (the sphymograph, the myograph) designed to expand or replace the deficient human senses in the measurement of internal processes. He later applied this refined and altered instrumentation to the production of graphic inscriptions capable of representing the movement of horses cantering, trotting, or galloping, the movement of insect wings, and the flight of birds. From the start, indexicality was the major stake of Marey's representational practices. It was crucial that the body whose movement was being measured be the direct source for the tracing. This process required a complex apparatus of wires,

India-rubber tubing, and other connectors between body and recording instrument. Marey repeatedly refers to this type of tracing as "automatic." The phenomenon is the author of its own record: "In experiments . . . which deal with time measurements, it is of immense importance that the graphic record should be automatically registered, in fact, that the phenomenon should give on paper its own record of duration, and of the moment of production. This method, in the cases in which it is applicable, is almost perfect."[33] Marey was not unaware of the resistant properties of the conducting material itself and diligently searched for the most "immaterial," the most self-effacing, link between the body and the recording instrument, tending ultimately to favor air pressure. Photography was, in this respect, ideal, since its means of connecting object and representation—light waves—were literally intangible and greatly reduced the potentially corruptive effects of mediation. It is telling that François Dagognet subtitled his study of Marey "A Passion for the Trace" and that this work is an extended celebration of indexicality. "Marey's brilliance lay in the discovery of how to make recordings without recourse to the hidden hand or eye. Nature had to testify to itself, to translate itself through the inflection of curves and subtle trajectories that were truly representative . . . The 'trace' . . . was to be considered nature's own expression, without screen, echo or interference: it was faithful, clear and, above all, universal."[34] Attempting to disengage entirely the notion of human authorship from Marey's graphic method, Dagognet repeatedly refers to it as "direct writing" or "direct inscription."

Inextricably linked, for Marey, with the obsession with indexicality was the attribute of the clarity or lucidity of the representation—its *legibility*. The curve of a graph tracing the path of a moving object was eminently readable, assimilable in little more than a glance. Marey consistently contrasted the graphic method favorably to phonetic language and statistics, heavily mediated forms of representation that were potentially obscure and unappealing (as well as slow—instantaneity was an aspiration): "Language is as slow and obscure a method of expressing the duration and sequence of events as the graphic method is lucid and easy to understand. As a matter of fact, it is the only natural mode of expressing such events; and, further, the information which this kind of record conveys is that which appeals to the eyes, usually the most reliable form in which it can be expressed."[35] All the positive attributes Marey associates with the graphic method—indexicality, instantaneity, readability—illuminate his later predilection for photography as a privileged mode of scientific representation.

And, indeed, after Marey's contact with the work of Eadward Muybridge, published in a French journal in 1878, he replaced some of his graphic inscriptors with photographic ones and developed the technique that finally lodged his name in histories of the cinema—chronophotography. The photographic method did not necessarily increase the precision or the accuracy of the graphic method of inscription. But it did allow for greater detail and ease in specifying the successive spatial positions of the subject. Unlike Muybridge, Marey used a single camera and photographic plate to register these successive positions. As a result, and in contrast to Muybridge's separately framed images (Figure 2.1), the chronophotograph included all the recorded successive positions of a single subject in the same frame (Figure 2.2). As Marta Braun points out, this technique compromised an entire tradition of Western representation:

Their [the chronophotographs'] novelty would certainly have been disconcerting to the untutored viewer, because the traditional Western pictorial delineation of time and space would make them hard to read. Since the advent of linear perspective in the Renaissance, the frame of an image has, with rare exceptions, been understood to enclose a temporal and spatial unity. We read what occurs within the frame as happening at a single instant in time and in a single space. Marey's photographs shattered that unity; viewers now had to unravel the successive parts of the work in order to understand that they were looking not at several men moving in single file, but at a single figure successively occupying a series of positions in space.[36]

Given Marey's desire to decrease the intervals between the successive positions of the subject in order to clarify the movement's temporal progression, these positions were inevitably superimposed and blurred, figures overlapped, and outlines became indistinct (Figures 2.3, 2.4). There was an overcrowding of detail in the photographic method.

In *Movement,* Marey illustrates this confusion with the image of an "Arab horse at a gallop" in which he claims that "the large surface covered by each image cause[s] almost complete superposition." He concludes that "the ap-

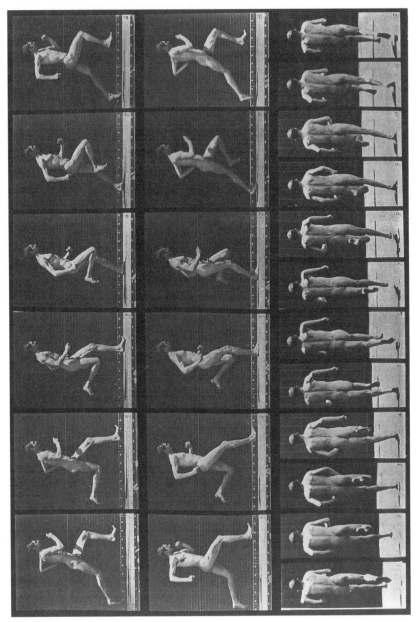

2.1 *Man Running* (c. 1887). Eadweard Muybridge. Courtesy George Eastman House.

2.2　*Schenkel, Long Jump* (July 1886). Etienne-Jules Marey. Cinémathèque Française.

2.3 *Demeny Walking* (1883). Etienne-Jules Marey. Collège de France.

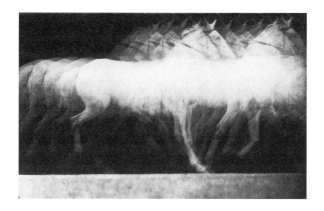

2.4 *Movements of a White Horse* (1885–1886). Etienne-Jules Marey. Collège de France.

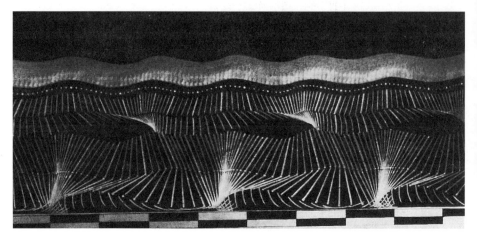

2.5 *Joinville Soldier Walking* (1883). Etienne-Jules Marey. Collège de France.

plications of chronophotography are, as we have seen, limited by interference from superposition and consequent confusion." This is a spatial difficulty—a finite space (on a fixed plate) must accommodate a minimum number of images. As a consequence of the resulting superimposition, the legibility of time is seriously impaired, since it requires the distinct separation of legible units and Marey has already stipulated that a pronounced advantage of photography is that it "would permit the exact measurement of time intervals."[37] Problems of legibility linked to the overlapping, blurring, and superimposition of figures were due, in a sense, to the fact that there was *too much* detail in the photographic method.

Marey attempted to solve that problem by gradually excising details that might be distracting and using blacker backgrounds. This tendency in his work ultimately resulted in some amazingly abstract representations. Marey clothed his subjects completely in black, attaching luminous dots to their joints and connecting them with luminous striping, and then he photographed them against a black background (Figures 2.5, 2.6, and 2.7). The outcome was a series of chronophotographs consisting only of lines and curves in space ("geometric chronophotography"). Marey's trajectory here is quite astonishing. He moves from the graphic method to the photographic method only to defamiliarize, derealize, even de-iconize the photographic image. Why, then, did Marey use photography at all? Pragmatically speaking, photography, and not the graphic method, worked when it was difficult or

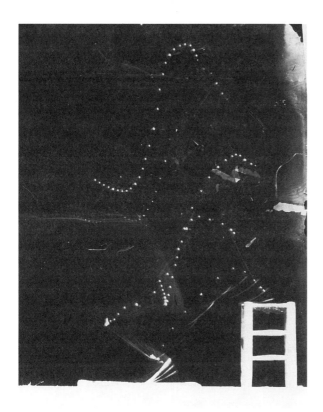

2.6 *Jump from a Height with Knees Bent* (1884). Etienne-Jules
   Marey. Collège de France.

impossible to maintain a physical connection between the moving object
and the recording instrument. The flight of birds would be an exemplary instance of this problem, and Marey's first attempts, in the realm of photographic methods, involved the development of a "photographic gun" inspired by a similar instrument employed by the astronomer Jules Janssen.
But Marey was also drawn to the wealth of detail automatically made available by photography and was excited about the possibilities the new medium harbored of making visible the previously hidden secrets of movement: "When it is a matter of registering all the details of a man's
movements, both as regards change of position and attitude of the body and
limbs, mechanical registration is out of the question. It is at this point that
chronophotography comes to the rescue."[38]

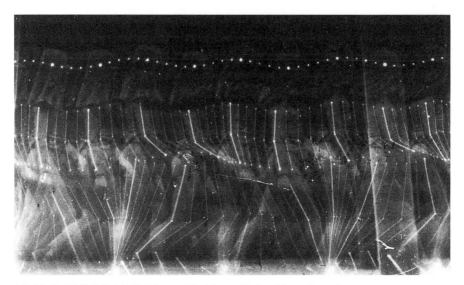

2.7 *Morin, Walk* (July 1886). Etienne-Jules Marey. Cinémathèque Française.

Chronophotography is much more suited to the representation of space than is the graphic method. And Marey in fact viewed the antagonistic relationship between space and time as a potential obstruction to his project, which, because it was explicitly concerned with movement, required references to both spatial and temporal coordinates. He referred to the difficulty of "harmoniz[ing] two such incompatible notions."[39] In fixed-plate chronophotography, a moving object that covers only a small surface area will allow the registration of a large number of images, enhancing the representation of time while restricting that of space. A large animal or human being, on the other hand, uses up so much space in its movements that it is difficult to get the necessary quantity of images without superimposition and confusion. With a very small number of different positions, the legibility of time is diminished. Marey himself was intensely aware of the tension between the two categories:

In this method of photographic analysis the two elements of movement, time and space, cannot both be estimated in a perfect manner. Knowledge of the positions the body occupies in space presumes that complete and distinct images are possessed; yet to have such images, a relatively long temporal interval must be had between two successive photographs. But *if it is the notion of time one desires to bring to perfection* [my emphasis], the only way of doing so is to greatly augment the frequency of images, and this forces each of them to be reduced to lines.[40]

The legibility of the image is directly affected by the desire to perfect a representation of time. In fixed-plate chronophotography, this is true even if the figures are reduced to lines, for the finite surface area of the plate will eventually limit the number of lines that can be recorded without superimposition and consequent illegibility.

Geometric chronophotography and increasing the number of openings (windows) in the disk shutter were two strategies Marey adopted for dealing with the dilemma. Marey, however, never embraced wholeheartedly the most obvious resolution of the problem—the substitution of moving film for the fixed plates, which would theoretically increase almost limitlessly the surface area of the recording medium. Although his experiments with moving film are crucial to arguments that Marey was deeply involved in the "invention of cinematography,"[41] he had serious difficulties with the problem of stabilizing a fast-moving strip of film for an adequate (unblurred) registration of the image. Furthermore, Marey had little interest in the synthesis of movement, which was the goal of cinematography, and, in an extraordinary move, he would attempt to rearrange the images taken with moving film so that they embodied the characteristics of fixed-plate chronophotography. In other words, he would laboriously cut out the individual images from a strip of film, place them next to one another so that they slightly overlapped, and rephotograph them. Or he would project the images and trace their outlines onto another image that would then resemble those of his geometric chronophotography (Figures 2.8 and 2.9). This drive toward horizontality worked to suppress the separation between individual film frames (the site of loss, discontinuity in film). It is as though Marey were obsessed by a graphic aspiration so that he devised ever more ingenious methods, through geometric chronophotography and his manipulation of the images of moving film, to transform photographic modes of representation into graphic ones.

For the graphic method had one distinct advantage over the photo-

2.8 *Flexioned March, Subject Commandant de Raoul* (1895). Etienne-Jules Marey. Cinémathèque Française.

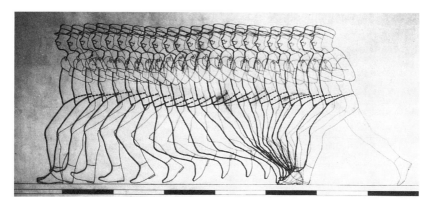

2.9 *Flexioned March* (1895). Etienne-Jules Marey. Rephotographed tracings made from projected and overlapped filmed images. Collège de France.

graphic: its record of a movement left no temporal gaps, and its inscription therefore allowed complete continuity. Chronophotography, on the other hand, was based on intermittency, and, despite Marey's strategy of increasing the number of windows in the disk shutter, it would always entail a necessary temporal elision. Marey was haunted by this lost time. With respect to the chronophotography of a tortoise's cardiac cycle, Marey maintains:

> these [temporal] measurements do not pretend to rival in exactness those derived from the graphic method, which are almost infinitely accurate. When the commencement and termination of a phenomenon is measured by means of a discontinuous series of images, there may be an error as regards both stages. The commencement and termination may occur between two exposures of the photographic plate, and it is impossible to say exactly when they occur.

By the nature of the technique, something is invariably lost. Marey consistently compares this unavoidable temporal loss with the fullness, the "almost infinite accuracy," the "perfection" of the graphic method. Chronophotography "only gives an approximate idea of the sequence of the various phases of movement, because its record is one of intermittent indications, instead of the continuous record of a curve." The points, lines, and curves of geometric chronophotography not only reduce the overwhelming and excessive detail of the photographic image but also allow chronophotography to mimic the graphic method. Indeed, the points traced by the movement of a joint on the body can be readily connected to form a graph. Marey claims with delight, "In geometrical photographs, thanks to the great number of the images, the discontinuity of the phases almost entirely disappears, and the actual path followed by each point of the body can be seen represented almost as a continuous curve."[42] In a roundabout way, Marey returns to the goal of producing a pure graph of time.

The technical problems that continually confronted Marey and drove him to refine and laboriously perfect his equipment all emerge from the conflict between legibility and illegibility in sequential photography. Because the various positions of Muybridge's figures were separated in distinct frames, he did not experience this difficulty. But this aspect of his work was also a cause of Marey's criticism of it. Not only did Muybridge have no way of measuring the time of the movements he recorded; the positions of the figures were too far apart—it was often impossible to determine how the figure moved from one position to the next. Too much time was lost. Since Marey had always been primarily interested in "a technical apparatus that could make visible minute changes over time—'les infiniment petits du temps'"[43]—his search led him to desire smaller and smaller units of a continuum that he himself conceptualized as "infinitely divisible." If, in his photographic work, Marey respected the integrity of time and attempted to register its smallest displacements, he produced an unreadable record (as a result of excessive overlapping and superimposition). If he strove for legibility in his documents, he betrayed his object (time) and compromised his attempt to represent it adequately. Marey's oscillation between the graphic and the photographic is symptomatic of the extent to which he constantly grappled with the problems of legibility and recording. It is significant that the limit or failure of Marey's scientific endeavor—the blurred image—was subsequently taken up by modernism (especially Italian Futurism) as evidence that the perfect representation of time (particularly its more "modern" aspects of speed and dynamism) was precisely illegibility (nondifferentiation).[44]

The quandary emerges, of course, from the very technology of the photographic apparatus—the need for a hiatus between exposures of the photographic plate or plates to ensure an unblurred image. As deficient as Muybridge's technique was, his series produced a representation of that hiatus in the form of the frames separating images. Most of Marey's chronophotography did not. Such an absence, together with the subjection of photography to the graphic aspiration as outlined above, points to a desire to represent *all* time—to a dream of representation without loss.

In his theory of the psychical apparatus, Freud acknowledged the necessity of intervals of nonreceptivity in the registration/inscription of mnemic traces. Recording (of memory) is not continuous; there must be gaps, lacks, losses in order to protect against overwhelming energies.[45] And it is the discontinuous functioning of the system perception-consciousness that produces those gaps and in this way produces the notion of time. For Marey, on the other hand, time is "out there"—a continuum that, though infinitely divisible, is divisible nevertheless. He is faced with the dilemma, however, that pure and direct recording of time would result only in noise. Freud's theory of the unconscious exhibits an aspiration for perfect storage that is antithetical to the concept of time (the unconscious is "timeless"); Marey's chronophotography evinces a desire for a pure representation of time that would ultimately, if it were attainable, be antithetical to the notion of the legible trace (which was the support and goal of his endeavor). Although both of these discourses are imbued with contradictions, they put into play in decisively important ways concepts of temporality and storage that are crucial to much thinking about the cinema as the medium, par excellence, of time.

It is well known that both Freud and Marey resisted the cinema. In addition to his refusal to contemplate or authorize a film about psychoanalysis, Freud also systematically avoided using cinema and photography as analogies for the psyche in favor of other, optical but nonphotographic technologies (such as the microscope and telescope). As we have seen, in 1925 Freud insisted upon using the Mystic Writing-Pad, a fairly antiquated technology, as an analogy for memory.[46] Marey, in his turn, condemned the cinema's collaboration with defective senses: "Cinema produces only what the eye can see in any case. It adds nothing to the power of our sight, nor does it remove its illusions, and the real character of a scientific method is to supplant the insufficiency of our senses and correct their errors. To get to this point, chronophotography should renounce the representation of phenomena as they are seen by the eye."[47] Cinema presents the illusion—and the commercially successful illusion—of what Marey could only dream about, the possibility of a continuous and nonselective recording of real time. In concealing the division between frames, it refuses to acknowledge the loss of time on which it is based. From Marey's point of view there is a double deception at work here: the lie that truth resides in visibility, in what the eye can see, and the pretense that the cinema replicates time perfectly, without loss.

Nevertheless, the cinema has been conceptualized in ways that reinscribe the terms of Freud's and Marey's attempts to correlate storage and time. The early cinema was quickly embraced as the site of an ideal storage, a medium capable of recording images that would then be impervious to the passage of time. Hence the recurrent motif of the cinema as a machine that conquers death. Noël Burch cites, in this context, two journalistic reviews of the Lumières' first screening, both of which contain references to the conquest of death—*Le Radical:* "Speech has already been collected and reproduced, now life is collected and reproduced. For example, it will be possible to see one's loved ones active long after they have passed away"; and *La Poste:* "When these cameras are made available to the public, when everyone can photograph their dear ones, no longer in a motionless form but in their movements, their activity, their familiar gestures, with words on their lips, death will have ceased to be absolute."[48] Even Marey's assistant, Georges Demeny, whose conflicts with Marey were partially fueled by his avid interest in cinematography, invoked the rhetoric of a conquest over death when referring to the potential of moving and speaking images:

> How many people would be happy if they could for a moment see again the living features of someone who had passed away! The future will replace the still photograph, locked in its frame, with the moving portrait, which can be given life at the turn of a wheel! The expression of the physiognomy will be preserved as the voice is by the phonograph. The latter could even be added to the phonoscope to complete the illusion . . . We shall do more than analyze [the face]; we shall bring it to life again.[49]

Death, the most corrosive effect of time, is vanquished by an apparatus understood to contain the potential for flawless storage.

On the other hand, both the cinema's novelty and its decisive difference from photography were linked to its ability not to resist time but to store or represent it. The first films could easily risk banality in their subject matter,

since their fascination was indissociably linked with their sheer representation of movement through time. The more familiar, everyday, and recognizable the activity, the more appreciable the pure act of its re-presentation.
The Lumières filmed such subjects as the demolition of a wall, a snowball
fight, workers leaving the factory, the arrival of a train, children clamdigging
and jumping off a pier into the sea. Perhaps this fascination with the technologically supported ability to inscribe time helps to explain the dominance
of the actuality, the presentation of an unstaged incident, during the first ten
or so years of the cinema. But these tendencies to exploit the familiar and
the recognizable would seem to remove the cinema decisively from the
problematic confronting both Freud and Marey—that of the difficult relations among time, representability, and legibility. The early cinema would
seem to be, above all, eminently readable.

Yet one characteristic of the cinema set it apart from earlier processes of
representing time, such as writing and music, and associated it with the
ever-present and consistently disturbing potential of meaninglessness, of
providing the spectator with *nothing to read.* And that is the camera's capacity to record indiscriminately.[50] Beyond the inevitable selectivity of framing and angle, the camera always seems to evade the issues of subjectivity,
agency, and intentionality in the process of an unthought and mechanical
recording. In reception, this lack can readily be transformed into the questions What does it mean? and What is it for? In his attempt to differentiate
the "discourse network of 1900" from the "discourse network of 1800,"
Friedrich Kittler specifies the former, at least partly, as the generating, recording, and collecting of nonsense, an endeavor in which the new technological media were particularly determinant. Whereas the discourse network
of 1800 stressed the mother's voice as the anchor of meaning and understanding, the discourse network of 1900 dissociated memory and meaning
and stressed the materialism of signs—to the extent of excluding subjectivity. For Kittler, the master science of this discourse network is psychophysics,
whose experiments transformed memory into pure registration or inscription at the physiological level. In 1879–80 and 1883–84 Hermann Ebbinghaus, its founder, conducted experiments in which he measured the amount
of repetitions necessary to memorize strings of varying lengths of nonsense syllables. Because the individual syllabic combinations were deliberately chosen for their meaninglessness, their inability to be associated with

any significant context, the purity of memory as a physiological function was allegedly guaranteed. For Kittler, this is evidence that around 1900 "memory is taken from people and delegated to a material organization of discourse."[51]

Kittler, in an astonishing gesture, goes so far as to make psychoanalysis subordinate to (and in league with) the positivist science of psychophysics: "This is the reason for psychoanalysis. Material discarded by psychophysics can be resorted and then decoded. Freud's discourse was a response not to individual miseries but to a discourse network that exhaustively records nonsense, its purpose being to inscribe people with the network's logic of the signifier." This would explain Freud's peculiar attentiveness to slips of the tongue, errors, and symptoms, which he organized into the material phenomena of psychical life. Kittler analyzes the extent to which the case histories deal with submeaningful elements, such as letters ("S.P." or "Espe" in the Wolf-Man case): "All of Freud's case histories demonstrate that the romanticism of the soul has yielded to a materialism of written signs."[52]

Similarly, film deals with the idiosyncratic, the detail, the element that cannot automatically be integrated into an immediately meaningful context: "Technology makes it possible for the first time to record single and accidental messages . . . The entire discourse network of 1900 is fed by the return of an opaque thisness." Such a "thisness" is indisputable—it is simply there, while the sheer act of recording it transforms it into an archival moment that cannot be ignored. Kittler makes film, as well as psychoanalysis, subordinate to the master discourse of psychophysics—"In the discourse network of 1900, discourse is produced by RANDOM GENERATORS. Psychophysics constructed such sources of noise; the new technological media stored their output."[53] Kittler takes the term *noise* from information theory; and computer technology, in fact, infuses his analysis of both discourse networks. He activates the term *noise* as the polar opposite of information in order to stress the resistance to meaning that characterizes the contemporary discourse network. Nevertheless, the idea that the new technological media "store noise" is a paradoxical one at best. For noise is defined as "an unwanted signal or a disturbance" or "a disturbance interfering with the operation of a mechanical device or system." In information theory, it refers to "irrelevant or meaningless bits or words occurring along with desired information (as in a computer output)."[54] In the language of technicians, the term *noise* often refers to an interference generated by the apparatus itself, and from that point of view the idea of "storing noise" suggests that the sharpness of the distinction between what is "out there" to be recorded and what is traced by the machine is lost.

In any event, the concept of an archive of noise is a difficult one. But it does speak to the enormity of the changes introduced by mechanical reproduction. Certainly the capacity to record the singular and the opacity of the "thisness" captured and presented by the machine that Kittler describes are linked to the promise of an ability to represent the unforeseen, the unintended. Dai Vaughan's homage to the Lumières is based on the notion that both the principal promise and the principal effect of the early cinema were of spontaneity, of unwilled communication. He points to the unexpected and disturbing wave (a wave that appears suddenly and seems to interrupt the smooth progress of the boat being rowed) in *A Boat Leaving Harbour* (*Barque sortant du port*, 1897) as evidence of the force of contingency in the new medium:

> such an invasion of the spontaneous into the human arts, being unprecedented, must have assumed the character of a threat not only to the "performers" but to the whole idea of controlled, willed, obedient communication. And conversely, since the idea of communication had in the past been inseparable from the assumption of willed control, this invasion must have seemed a veritable doubling-back of the world into its own imagery, a denial of the order of a coded system: an escape of the represented from the representational act . . . [*A Boat Leaving Harbour*] survives as a reminder of that moment when the question of spontaneity was posed and not yet found to be insoluble: when the cinema seemed free, not only of its proper connotations, but of the threat of its absorption into meanings beyond it.[55]

Vaughan perceives this spontaneity, the capacity to represent the unforeseen, as an exhilarating potential of the cinema that was subsequently annihilated in the management and control exerted over filmic significations. But the ability to represent everything—both the planned and the unplanned—also constituted, as Vaughan suggests, a threat. The anxiety generated would be that of sheer undivided extension, of a "real time" without significant moments, of a confusion about where or why to look. If everything is recordable, nothing matters except the act of recording itself.

Something of the overwhelming effect of this recording process is visible in the very bulk of the archives left by Muybridge and Marey—thousands of stills of the sequential gestures of animals, men, women, and children performing everyday movements. Although he never mentioned Marey by name, Bergson was quite critical of the leveling of temporal moments that was an inevitable effect of sequential photography.[56] And he did not acknowledge the distinction Marey himself saw between his own enterprise and that of cinematography, because both were based on dividing time into a series of static images. When Bergson claims that "the mechanism of our ordinary knowledge is of a cinematographical kind," it is in defiance of the concept of "ordinary knowledge" and its ability to apprehend time. Both the ancients and the moderns, according to Bergson, were guilty of spatializing time and hence of a "cinematographical mechanism," but at least the ancients were capable of isolating moments and lending them an aesthetic significance:

> Of the gallop of a horse our eye perceives chiefly a characteristic, essential or rather schematic attitude that sculpture has fixed on the frieze of the Parthenon. But instantaneous photography isolates any moment; it puts them all in the same rank, and thus the gallop of a horse spreads out for it into as many successive attitudes as it wishes, instead of massing itself into a single attitude, which is supposed to flash out in a privileged moment and to illuminate a whole period.[57]

Time, in effect, becomes banal and meaningless. Any moment is as "exemplary" as any other and hence none provides that privileged "flash" or spark of knowledge.

The problem of the early cinema's relation to time hence becomes one of generating difference. The actuality's embodiment of "real time" very quickly becomes only an aspiration (actualities contain cuts), and the cinema avoids the representational difficulties posed by the notion of a "globe on the scale of the earth."[58] According to Bergson, the Greeks could isolate the exemplary moment and compel it to signify, whereas Marey and the cinema level all moments until each is the same as the other—producing an overwhelming sameness and banality. The problem the cinema must address early in the century is precisely its ability to record singularity. The cinema confronts the difficult task of endowing the singular with significance, of manufacturing an event in a medium designed to record, without predilection, all moments. It is not surprising, from this point of view, that the cinema embraces narrative as its primary means of making time legible. Despite the dominance of the actuality in the first decade of the cinema, despite the extensive fascination with the camera's relation to "real time" and movement, narrative very quickly becomes its dominant method of structuring time. Born of the aspiration to represent or store time, the cinema must content itself with producing time as an effect.

Freud, Marey, and the cinema all grapple, in quite different ways, with the relations among the concepts of time, storage, representation, and legibility. For Marey, the desire to represent a time that he conceives of as objective and measurable inevitably produces dilemmas of legibility. In Freud, the very concept of time emerges from the failure of storage or representation, the discontinuous functioning of a psychical apparatus designed to protect the subject from overwhelming energies. For Marey, time is infinitely divisible; for Freud, time is division itself. What both theorists disallow, however, is a notion of time as degradation, degeneration, wearing down. For Marey, time is the support of movement and hence of life—it enables them. For Freud, the unconscious is a site of perfect storage characterized by its time-lessness. Time, instead of gnawing away at memories, is the effect of a system that protects them. The unconscious is a haven, the pure space of representation, and the subject becomes the site of a perfect reading, without loss. Such a scenario guarantees legibility for the psychoanalyst, since no memory, no detail, no minute clue to the working of the psyche can be irrevocably lost. But it also helps to explain Freud's resistance to technology. If the unconscious provides us with a perfect record, the cinema as a prosthetic memory is simply unnecessary.

In the work of Freud and Marey, time seems to be continually at odds with legibility. For Freud, temporality is indissociably linked with a consciousness that is opaque or "obscure"—it is the unconscious which is readable. For Marey, time is an entity that resists his instruments, his scientific technology for the production of readability. Time as homogeneous and continuous is antithetical to the differential mapping of photographic technology. For both, time disallows its own record. What temporality eschews is representation. Freud and Marey, in different ways, stake out the terms of the impossibility of cinema insofar as it strives to be a legible record of time.

Freud and Marey resisted the cinema because it adhered to the senses and was not amenable to the abstraction required either to illustrate the basic concepts of psychoanalysis or to produce scientific knowledge. In its hyperindexicality it could not dissociate itself from the realm of the contingent or the material. It is clear, as Vaughan suggests, that cinema posed a threat to an entire system of representation. But for Freud and Marey the danger lay not so much in the loss of control and agency in willed communication as in the implicit refusal of limit or limitation. The threat was one of overpresence, of excessive coverage, of a refusal of the distinction or differentiation that would ensure legibility. To the extent that cinema strove for the status of total record, strove to confirm the senses and their potential apprehension of anything and everything, it constituted itself as a failure of representation. Such a logic anticipates Kracauer's anxieties about photography's and film's inscriptions of a spatial and temporal continuum without gap, of a "blizzard" or "flood" of images. The historical transition in the early cinema from a focus on actualities to an insistence upon narrative would be one way of ameliorating such fears. From this point of view, I do not think it is too far-fetched to suggest that in the cinema, as in psychoanalysis, time is produced as an effect, at least in part to protect the subject from the anxieties of total representation generated by the new technological media.

Yet Freud's and Marey's conscious rejection of the cinema was accompanied by an unconscious complicity with its very aspirations—the desire to store or represent time, the rejection of mortality (especially in the case of Freud, who continually attempted to demonstrate that death was accidental, contingent rather than inevitable). Freud, Marey, and the early cinema collaborate in a tendency to perceive time as a persistent and troubling problem that holds in tension two different understandings of representation: representation as the record, trace, or inscription of that which is outside itself (for instance, time, as elusive as it may be); and representation as the production of temporalities with no referent other than that of the representational system itself (the psyche, the cinema). The latter understanding of representation persists and is strengthened in modernity, but only at the cost of harboring within itself the dream of the first.

3

The Afterimage, the Index, and the Accessibility of the Present

The nineteenth century witnessed the emergence of two theories of the temporal trace that have had an enormous impact on attempts to explain the effects of the cinema. In the realm of optics and physiology, investigations of vision focused on illusions, or "tricks" of the eye, central among these the afterimage. Goethe, Joseph Plateau, David Brewster, Charles Wheatstone, and Helmholtz all studied the phenomena associated with the posited retention of an image on the retina for varied durations after the removal of a stimulus (usually a bright light or color). The theory was based on the assumption that the image *persists* in time, that it has a substantive duration, and hence that vision is not instantaneous. Later in the century Charles Sanders Peirce, an American scientist and philosopher, elaborated an extraordinarily complex theory of signs that rested on the tripartite division of icon, index, and symbol. Of these, it is the indexical sign that acts as a temporal trace and has an existential relation to its object; it "takes hold of our eyes, as it were, and forcibly directs them to a particular object."[1] A pointing finger is the "type of the class," but Peirce gives a number of other examples: a footprint, a weathercock, demonstrative pronouns such as *this, here, now,* and, most relevant here, the photographic image (which the viewer knows has a direct, physical connection to its object). Both the afterimage and the index posit vision as subject to compulsion, to an irresistible force—one by stressing the inescapable temporal effects of imaging processes, the other by the imperative to "Look here, see this." Furthermore, the theory of the afterimage in one sense inscribes the indexical image within it by assuming the analogy between the eye and a camera, in which the retina acts as a kind of photographic plate, registering and retaining, if only momentarily, an image.[2]

Nevertheless, the two concepts stake out markedly different relations to referentiality. As Jonathan Crary has compellingly shown, the afterimage is a crucial component of a more extensive discourse stressing the dissociation of the human senses from the external world in a scientific movement away from referentiality and toward the subjectivization of vision. In this context, the afterimage proves the possibility of vision in the absence of an object/referent. After looking at a bright object and then looking away, one will see an afterimage whether the original bright object continues to exist or not. An electrical stimulus can generate afterimages in the absence of any object. The concept of the index, on the other hand, seems to acknowledge the invasion of semiotic systems by the real. The footprint, the weathercock, the photographic image—all testify to the fact that the referent was present and left its legible trace directly in representation. One of Peirce's favorite examples, the demonstrative pronoun *this,* displays the persistent adherence of the present to signs. Both the afterimage and the index are yoked to the problematic of time in representation. The afterimage, precisely, comes *after*—it is the deferred effect of a stimulus/object. The indexical sign comes after as well (except in those instances in which it is simultaneous with its referent—for example, smoke signaling fire); however, in all cases, in embodying within its form the existential traces of its referent, it posits as its limit the present moment. Both the theory of the afterimage and the theory of the index (embedded, as it is, in Peirce's larger epistemological universe) circulate around the question of the accessibility of the present in representation. An investigation of the historical work of these two concepts can shed light on the cinema's role in discourses about the present in modernity—the present as an object of fascination, the present as impossible limit.

The concept of the afterimage is the basis of the theory of persistence of vision, which from the late nineteenth century until very recently functioned as *the* psychoscientific explanation for the perception of motion in the cinema.[3] The theory of persistence of vision assumes that the retinal impression provoked by one frame of film persists and blends with the next frame so that the slightly different images merge to produce the illusion of motion. One classic invocation of the theory appears in C. W. Ceram's *Archaeology of the Cinema:* "Cinematography is technically based on the phenomenon of persistence of vision—the capacity of the retina of the eye to retain the impression of an object for the fraction of a second after its disappearance." The observations of Peter Mark Roget and Michael Faraday about optical illusions in viewing spokes of a turning wheel through vertical apertures are often cited as the origin of the theory in the early nineteenth century (even though it can be traced back to some observations made by Newton). But the figure who is most frequently given credit for the establishment of the theory is Joseph Plateau, who not only elaborated the principles of the effect but invented an optical toy—the Phenakistiscope—to demonstrate it. In 1830 he wrote: "If several objects, progressively different in form and position, are presented to the eye for very short intervals and sufficiently close together, the impressions they make upon the retina will join together without being confused, and one will believe one is seeing a single object gradually changing form and position."[4] The Phenakistiscope was a disc with a series of changing designs on one side and a series of evenly placed slots around the circumference. When rotated in front of a mirror, the designs viewed through the slits appeared to merge into one moving figure. At about the same time, the Austrian mathematician Simon Stampfer invented a similar device and called it the stroboscopic disc. An earlier toy, the Thaumatrope (invented by Dr. J. A. Paris in 1825), was based on the theory of persistence of vision but produced an illusion of superimposition rather than movement. It was a circular card with a design on the front and one on the back (a bird and a cage, a bald man and a wig, and so on). When twirled by means of two attached strings, the images were superimposed so that, for instance, the bird appeared to be in the cage. Throughout the nineteenth century there was an extensive fascination with a host of optical toys that seemed to corroborate the theory of persistence of vision.

The toys "worked," but the theory has been largely discredited in the realm of cognitive psychology and replaced by theories of the phi phenomenon, masking, and critical flicker fusion.[5] The assumptions underlying the theory of persistence of vision—retinal retention, the physiological duration of images—have been rejected in favor of the notion of critical thresholds beyond which the human eye is incapable of perceiving difference.[6] As early as 1916, Hugo Münsterberg, in one of the first extended theories of film, questioned the validity of persistence of vision and, influenced by the 1912 studies of Max Wertheimer, proposed that the viewer fills in the gap between two still images and that motion is "superadded by the action of the mind."[7] The theory of persistence of vision may be "wrong," but the question remains—why was it so firmly ensconced, and why did it endure for so long?

The answer is not that persistence of vision was handy, available, or the only explanation for the illusion of motion at the time, but that it was so fully imbricated with insistent concerns in the nineteenth and early twentieth centuries about representation, inscription, temporality, and the archive.

Accompanying the theory of persistence of vision is an insistent vocabulary of deception and failure. The etymological meaning of *phenakistiscope* is "deceptive view." In his 1912 explanation of the movies, *Moving Pictures: How They Are Made and Worked,* Frederick A. Talbot elaborated upon the way in which the cinematographer exploits a "deficiency" of the human eye: "This wonderful organ of ours has a defect which is known as 'visual persistence.'" The concept of persistence of vision presupposes that a delayed image (an afterimage) blurs empirical distinctions between imperceptible stages of movement in time. Hence the afterimage is the symptom of a failure in human vision that is reinscribed in the very technology of the cinema. The afterimage points to a flawed temporality. Michael Chanan, in his discussion of the (to him inaccurate and misguided) theory of persistence of vision, claims that it "is invoked in order to explain what appears to be a failing in our perception: our failure to notice the gaps between successive images. The image is said to *persist* during these gaps." In an 1880 article on optical illusions of motion, Silvanus Phillips Thompson states: "Of all the senses none is more frequently the seat of such deceptive judgments than that of sight."[8] The thaumatrope, the phenakistiscope, the zoetrope, and finally the cinema are all said to "work" because of a defect, a deficiency of the human body.

The theory of persistence of vision, when invoked to explain the illusion of motion, is propped upon the concept of the afterimage, which has a distinguished scientific lineage. In his *Theory of Colours,* Goethe referred to afterimages as "physiological colours" (they have also been referred to by others as accidental colors, phantasms, and ocular spectra). Goethe's phenomenological researches led to a fascination with the phenomenon in which the act of looking at a brilliant color and then turning away induces the afterimage of the complementary color:

> I had entered an inn towards evening, and, as a well-formed girl, with a
> brilliantly fair complexion, black hair, and a scarlet bodice, came into
> the room, I looked attentively at her as she stood before me at some

distance in half shadow. As she presently afterwards turned away, I saw on the white wall, which was now before me, a black face surrounded with a bright light, while the dress of the perfectly distinct figure appeared of a beautiful sea-green.

The eroticism of vision here underlines the fact that the afterimage is accessible only through an experience of intensity, of dazzlement (and, here, of the anxiety attached to the possibility of racial instability that accompanies visual instability). For ordinarily, "In glancing from one object to another; the succession of images appears to us distinct; we are not aware that some portion of the impression derived from the object first contemplated passes to that which is next looked at." A dazzling object, on the other hand, "makes a strong lasting impression," and its afterimage is accompanied by a series of shifts in coloration—from red to blue to black. Goethe explains that in this process "the retina recovers itself by a succession of vibrations after the powerful external impression it received."[9] He is particularly interested in tracing the various durations of afterimages—the image of the sun constituting the absolute limit. The idea that temporality invades vision hinges upon the conceptualization of a force producing an impression upon the retina—an impression that only gradually fades away.

Sir David Brewster, whose research in optics led to the invention of the kaleidoscope and a version of the stereoscope, was also intensely interested in the theory of afterimages. In an 1830 encyclopedia entry he offered a definition of what he referred to as "accidental colours:"

> When we look steadily, and for a considerable time, at a small square of red paper placed upon a white ground, we perceive a light green border surrounding the red square: by removing the eye from the red square and directing it to another part of the white ground, we perceive very distinctly a square of light-green approaching a little to blue, and of the same size as the real red square. This imaginary *green* is the *accidental colour of red,* and continues to be visible till the impression made upon the retina by the red square has been effaced by other images.[10]

Brewster goes on to specify the accidental color proper to each color, in the process demonstrating that "accidental" colors are actually quite regularized and predictable. Much of the research on optical illusions was, in fact, phenomenologically based, the result of observations of the scientist's own perceptions. Brewster, Plateau, and Gustav Fechner all damaged their eyesight by staring into the sun in the investigation of the afterimage (Plateau became permanently blind). Yet the purpose was not at all to trace the idiosyncratic or subjective differences of vision, but to demonstrate the regularization of its effects. Jan Purkinje, a Czech psychologist, in his doctoral dissertation (1819) and subsequent studies (1825), recorded a series of his own personally experienced afterimages, induced by a variety of stimuli—alternating light and darkness (stroboscopic patterns), pressure on the eyeball, and electrical stimulation around the eye. He also noted the figures seen when the eye was closed or in darkness and the ephemeral small bright dots perceived when the eyes are fixed on a large illuminated surface.[11] Purkinje published drawings representing the afterimages he saw (Figure 3.1), and these drawings seem to have an affinity with avant-garde art rather than representation based on classical verisimilitude (with the exception of Figures 21–24 in Purkinje's numbering system, which are supposed to represent the blood vessels of the eye itself and the "free blood-globules in the aqueous humour"—the eye literally viewing itself). Purkinje was interested in tracing the transformations in the afterimage through time—hence, for example, Figures 1–4 in Purkinje's numbering system record the changes in an afterimage induced by rapid alternations of light and shade. Although Purkinje pointed out that these were his subjective impressions, he requested that others perform the same experiments, and the results were similar. Sir Charles Wheatstone (who translated Purkinje into English) inferred that "we may therefore, perhaps, be justified in concluding that the above phenomena do not depend on a morbid or individual condition, but physiologically result from the very organization of the human eye."[12]

The afterimage demonstrated that the "very organization of the human eye" was imbued with a temporal dimension, that vision was subject to delay. In addition, the retina was conceptualized as a slate or screen that retains, if only briefly, imprints or impressions. According to A. R. Luria, "The psychology of the nineteenth century regarded perception as a passive imprint made by external stimuli on the retina, and later in the visual cortex." A strong enough stimulus or force will *impress itself* upon the retina, causing actual physical changes often described in terms reminiscent of engraving,

3.1 Plate II from "Contributions of the Physiology of Vision No. I," *Journal of the Royal Institution*, 1830. Engraving by Jan Purkinje (1787–1869). The Royal Institution, London / Bridgeman Art Library.

printing, or other processes of mechanical reproduction. Helmholtz, for whom the eye was analogous to a *camera obscura*, claimed that "On the surface of this membrane [the retina] a real optical image is projected of the external objects in view, which is inverted and very much reduced in size."[13] He buttressed this explanation by citing the fact that when an eye is removed from a corpse and pointed toward the light, a small inverted image can be seen sharply defined on the retina. It is, of course, only at the moment of death that the image is stabilized for any length of time—in general, we are dealing with impressions of short duration. Nevertheless, the problem that emerges in this account is a problem of space, storage, and legibility, and is similar to the quandary outlined by Jacques Derrida in his discussion of Freud's mystic writing-pad and attempts to theorize memory (see Chapter 2)—how is the retention of impressions compatible with the need to receive fresh impressions on a blank surface? The temporal operation of an apparatus (the mystic writing-pad, the layered psyche) was Freud's solution, and it was invoked in optical theories of the afterimage as well. In a discussion of afterimages produced by viewing the sun (and the transfer of the retinal image from one eye to the other), Brewster claimed that he could "refresh" the afterimage by closing the eye, since "the images of external objects efface the impression upon the retina."[14] In other words, an external object annihilates the retinal imprint in order to make room for its own impression. The retina *retains* impressions, but only briefly, long enough to merge with succeeding impressions and make a pure present inaccessible.

This inaccessibility of the present becomes a theme within philosophy as well. Henri Bergson's theory of perception and memory echoes in its formulations physiological theories of vision. The theory of the afterimage presupposes a temporal aberration, an incessant invasion of the present moment by the past, the inability of the eye to relinquish an impression once it is made and the consequent superimposition of two images. Paralleling the psychoscientific dominance of the afterimage in the period preceding and coinciding with the emergence of the cinema is a philosophical obsession with a nonlinear temporality as the mark of human subjectivity par excellence. Bergson's work is perhaps most striking in this respect.

Bergson asserts, in *Matter and Memory*, the importance of duration, of waiting—of the gap between stimulus (sensation) and response. Perception is not in its essence subjective but resides in things; it is external rather than internal; it is lodged within the real. However, this perception exists only in theory, because it is continually invaded by memory:

> this perception, which coincides with its object, exists rather in theory than in fact: it could only happen if we were shut up within the present moment. In concrete perception, memory intervenes, and the subjectivity of sensible qualities is due precisely to the fact that our consciousness, which begins by being only memory, prolongs a plurality of moments into each other, contracting them into a single intuition.

Perception, from this point of view, is only an "occasion for remembering," and "there is for us nothing that is instantaneous. In all that goes by that name there is already some work of our memory."[15]

The human experience of perception hence pivots upon a temporal lag, a superimposition of images, an inextricability of past and present. To that extent it is a perverse temporality, a nonlinear temporality that cannot be defined as a succession of instants. According to Gilles Deleuze, "Bergsonian duration is defined less by succession than by coexistence."[16] And it is this peculiar temporality that for Bergson is the mark of the human.

The physiology and optical theory that situate the human body as the site of the inextricability of past and present recognize the finitude, the frailty of this body, which is subject to fatigue.[17] And fatigue is, ultimately, the explanation for "accidental colours" or complementary afterimages such as Goethe's lasting impression of the "well-favoured girl" at the inn. Afterimages are the result of very strong, powerful forces—bright lights rather than dim ones, impressions that assault the senses and are often described in terms reminiscent of the phenomenon of "shock" in discourses on modernity. After describing the series of colors characterizing an afterimage, Goethe notes: "Here again we see how the retina recovers itself by a succession of vibrations after the powerful external impression it received." This recovery *takes time*, which is why the afterimage endures. Brewster explains the phenomena of accidental colours in terms of excitability, tension, and release. When the eye is fixed for a long time on a red square, the portion of the retina that receives the image of the red square is highly excited by the continuous action of the red rays. The continuity of the red rays gradually makes the retina less sensitive to red ("in the same way as the palate, when accustomed to a particular taste, ceases to feel its impression"), so that when the eye is shifted to a white or gray surface, the "debilitated portion" of the retina will not be susceptible to the red rays, which are part of the composition of white light. As Brewster explains it, the resulting color will be a combination of all the other colors except red, in this case, green or bluish green. Helmholtz also refers to a "local fatigue of the retina" in his discussion of afterimages and notes that a portion of the retina becomes "red-blind" for a time, hence ensuring that the afterimage will be the complementary color of red.[18] From this point of view, Plateau, Brewster, and Fechner, staring at the sun, would subject the retina to a surfeit of impressions, reach the limit of fatigue, and become blind (temporarily or permanently), incapable of receiving any impressions.

When persistence of vision is used to explain the illusion of movement in the cinema, the concept of the afterimage carries in its wake the connotations of flaw, deficiency, failure, and fatigue. The afterimage weds human finitude to the machine—it becomes the biotechnical support of the illusion of motion. The nineteenth century's scientific discourse on the afterimage situates it as a form of proof against the instantaneity of vision. In vision, there is always an inscription (the evidence of which is there on the dead retina, presumably recorded forever) and hence a delay in clearing the "slate" for new impressions. This is a delay linked to metaphors of imprinting, recording, and the duration involved in that process. What is at stake here is the possibility of a stable representation of the present. Within the theory of the afterimage, what appears to us as instantaneous, as without duration— as, precisely, the present—is riven by delay. For the human subject, the images of past and present are inextricable, at a grounding, physiological level. On the one hand, this theory will lead to an acknowledgment that the present is infused with the past (Proust, Bergson's theory of memory) and on the other hand, and simultaneously to an obsession with instantaneity, with isolating and analyzing the instant, with the accessibility of the present (Marey, Muybridge, the Futurists).

Jonathan Crary's analysis of the afterimage stresses the fact that its theorization made human vision subject to temporality and physical embodiment. The afterimage demonstrated, above all, that vision was dissociable from any concept of a referent: "the privileging of the afterimage allowed one to conceive of sensory perception as cut from any necessary link with an external referent. The afterimage—the presence of sensation in the absence of a stimulus—and its subsequent modulations posed a theoretical and empirical demonstration of autonomous vision, of an optical experience that was produced by and within the subject." Furthermore, the afterimage's insistence upon the temporalization of vision indicated that the act of seeing was inseparable from "the shifting processes of one's own subjectivity experienced in time."[19] This alliance of subjectivity and vision is in contradistinction to the decorporealization of the observer in the camera obscura model of vision, which reigned from the late 1500s to the end of the 1700s. Crary describes how, in the early years of the nineteenth century, investigations of vision shifted from a focus upon optics and the physics of the transmission of light to the physiological properties of seeing.

In Crary's argument, the rupture that separated thinking about vision as a function of a perfectly operating camera obscura from thinking about vision as a physiological phenomenon linked to the body and temporality is the historical rupture that pinpoints the emergence of modernity. He claims that the increasing embodiment and subjectivization of vision lead to its increasing abstraction. As an attribute of the subject, vision becomes divorced from the realm of the referential and open to specific social manipulations. This, for Crary, is the project of modernity—to make the subject adequate to the construction of a new reality of fleeting images, exchangeability, flow. Modernity is here defined by the mobility of signs and commodities, the circulation of "vast new amounts of visual imagery and information."[20] Ultimately, for Crary, both modernity and modernism (as an aesthetic movement) are antireferential.

Crary's stress upon the disciplining and "normalizing" of subjectivity in order to make it adequate to modernity leads him to neglect or dismiss the motifs of failure, deception, deficiency, and flaw that accompany the discussion of the afterimage. For the idea of deception depends upon a comparison between a sensory image and external reality as the ground of truth. But according to Crary, this form of truth was proper to the era of the camera obscura and was displaced by the nineteenth century's positioning of human subjectivity itself as object. It is certainly the case that in the discourse of many scientists working at the time, the opposition between truth and deception was rejected in favor of an analysis of the forms of sensory know-ing. Ernst Mach, physicist-philosopher-psychologist, made this point clearly in *The Analysis of Sensations:*

> The expression "sense-illusion" proves that we are not yet fully con-scious, or at least have not yet deemed it necessary to incorporate the fact into our ordinary language, *that the senses represent things neither wrongly nor correctly.* All that can be truly said of the sense organs is, that, *under different circumstances they produced different sensations and perceptions.* As these "circumstances," now, are extremely manifold in character, being partly external (inherent in the objects), partly internal (inherent in the sensory organs), and partly interior (having their seat in the central organs), it would naturally seem, especially when atten-tion is paid only to external circumstances, as if the organs acted differ-ently under the same conditions. And it is customary to call the un-usual effects, deceptions or illusions.[21]

Johannes Müller, whose theory of the specific sensory energies was ex-tremely influential, believed that the senses gave us knowledge not of exter-nal reality but of the "nerves of sense themselves." Hence, he claimed that without the organ of hearing, sound would not exist, and without the eyes, "there would be no light, colour nor darkness, but merely a corresponding presence or absence of the oscillation of the imponderable matter of light."[22] These arguments tend to support Crary's contention that the subjectiviza-tion of vision opened the way to the manipulation, discipline, and normal-ization of subjects in a capitalist economy of exchange and flow. But in invoking a Foucauldian methodology that emphasizes manipulation and discipline of the subject, Crary is unable to consider the psychical dimension of the subjectivization of vision, its inevitable production of anxiety linked with the revelation of a body that cannot even trust its own senses, when vi-sion is uprooted from the world and destabilized. For certainly, as outlined earlier, the vocabulary of failure, deficiency, and flaw is an insistent one, par-ticularly in the scientific explanations provided for the illusion of movement produced in such technologies as the phenakistiscope, the zoetrope, and the cinema (which are defined as exploiting a defect in human vision). At the same time, photography and the cinema become forms of prosthetic devices that compensate for a flawed body, for the finitude of human vision. In the scientific subjection of the body to the status of object, it becomes disempowered, feminized in effect.[23] The body is no longer a transparent entity taken for granted but is subject to temporality and error.

While much of this discourse of deficiency and failure is linked to direct discussion of optical toys and new technologies such as the cinema, the anxiety accompanying the subjectivization of vision is also present in less technically oriented scientific works. Helmholtz, for instance, while acknowledging the significance of Müller's theories, continues to mourn the loss of the external world and to elaborate complex, though not necessarily mimetic, theories of the relation between sensory images and the real. These theories locate the qualities of the sensation of sight as *signs* of the qualities of light of the objects it illuminates.[24] He notes that despite "all this imperfection" of vision and "so inconstant a system of signs," despite the fatigue of the retina, "we are able to determine the proper colour of any object, the one constant phenomenon which corresponds to a constant quality of its surface; and this we can do, not after long consideration, but by an instantaneous and involuntary decision." In the face of the afterimage, the desire for instantaneity emerges as a guarantee of a grounded referentiality. It is perhaps not surprising in this context that time is situated as one of three types of relations (time, space, equality) that are common to the outer and inner world— "and here we may indeed look for a complete correspondence between our conceptions and the objects which excite them."[25] Müller himself makes certain temporal processes ("progressive and tremulous motion" and chemical change)—as well as "extension"—properties that "may belong wholly to external nature."[26] Temporality is lodged firmly in the external world.

Crary's insistence on the antireferentiality of nineteenth-century optical research also leads him to neglect the consistent recourse to the tropes of "imprint" and "impression" so crucial to the elaboration of the theory of the afterimage. Indeed, it is the assault on the retina by strong external forces which leave "impressions" on the retina that leads to fatigue. Fatigue in its turn determines a certain lack of susceptibility to new impressions. Fatigue here is the mark of the body's finitude, the limits of its endurance and its capability of storage/retention and is a recurrent theme in much nineteenth-century thinking (including nascent time-and-motion studies later deployed in Taylorism).[27] The tropes of imprint, impression, and recording and their alliance with a theory of fatigue point to insistent anxieties concerning representation, storage, and time as they coalesce in the problem of the archive. The nineteenth century witnessed an upsurge of interest in archival processes—museums and zoos that could document the loot of colonial expansion as well as a series of new archival technologies—photography, the typewriter, the phonograph, cinema. It is not accidental that in this context vision would be conceptualized in terms of retinal impressions that *endure* (if only for a brief time). The archive would expand and supplement human vision. As Jacques Derrida has pointed out, there would be no archive desire without radical finitude.[28] Although he links this finitude to a forgetfulness not limited to repression (as well as to the destructive death drive), in the case of the afterimage the radical finitude is a failure/inability to access the present due to retention of an image—not forgetfulness. The images accumulate and interfere with one another. The archive is a form of protection against time, but in the nineteenth century it becomes, in addition, a quandary, since what is at stake is the problem of archiving time (photography, studies of movement in time—Marey, Muybridge—the cinema). The obsession with instantaneity and the instant, with the present, leads to the contradictory desire of archiving presence. For what is archivable loses its presence, becomes immediately the past. Hence, what is archived is not so much a material object as an experience—an experience of the present. And since the present is the mark of contingency in time, the problem of the archive in the nineteenth century participates in the epistemological struggles over contingency. If the afterimage disallows visual access to the present, and this failure is one of the marks of human finitude, the problem is to produce and sustain an archival technology that will compensate for, or perhaps even deny, this form of finitude by successfully representing the present. The cinema participates in this compulsion.

Physiological theories of the afterimage had a strong impact on aesthetic theory and particularly on debates over the possibility of the representation of movement in a static art form—painting. At stake here were issues of realism and legibility: if movement were represented as the eye "really" sees it, it would be characterized by a certain illegibility, constituting itself as blur. This understanding was based on current optical theories, in particular the theory of the afterimage as the retention across time of an image. The aesthetician Paul Souriau, who read the work of Helmholtz and other physiologists on vision, described retinal images in his 1889 *Aesthetics of Movement* as "the reflections of an anterior reality" and wrote of fatigue and the retina's constant efforts "to repair and reconstitute itself after a light has impinged on it." Souriau extended the implications of afterimage theory to encompass all of vision so that any moving object would leave a "visible wake" behind it:

> Any luminous point displacing itself in the visual field leaves behind it a visible wake, the existence of which we can easily ascertain if we make sure to keep our eye really motionless.
>
> The result is that an animated object moving rapidly will become completely invisible. For, when the object displaces itself, each of its points leaves behind it a wake into which enters the next point, so that all of them tend to melt into a continuous line.

Unlike Bergson, Souriau does not appeal to the afterimage in order to demonstrate the invasion of the present by the past, but instead indicates the *absorption* of the past into the present, the "presencing" of the past moment through an expansion of the length of the present. The inscription upon the retina of an "actual image" is opposed to memory: "Owing to the duration of the luminous perceptions, the object literally describes its trajectory and permits us to appreciate its nature extremely well by leaving with us not just a memory but an actual image, a persistent tracing of its successive positions."[29] Here, the perception of movement in time is of an indexical nature and forces the past to become a form of present experience.

Souriau provides an extensive discussion of the consequences of the afterimage for aesthetic representation. Because the afterimage prevents the sharp perception of objects—indeed, for Souriau, the moving object is accessible only through its traces—a literal representation of movement in painting would be a blur, a "diaphanous" image. The integrity of objects would be threatened by such a representation. Before the advent of photography, persistence of vision led to mistakes in painting the various positions of horses or other animals in motion. Souriau advocates a limited recourse to instantaneous photography by artists but not a literal recapitulation of its results. There are two reasons for this. First, a position of a body in motion may be photographically accurate, but "implausible" and ungraceful. Artists should not be bound by such a literal truth—they have the license to "cheat" a little. Second, and perhaps more important, photographic images are, in a sense, physiologically false; they fail to represent movement as we really see it, since what is lacking is the "real token" of movement—its luminous tracing or visible wake. But our actual perception of motion is no less implausible than photographic poses: "For the watching eye, the flying bird does not have two wings, it has at least four; the trotting horse does not have four legs, it has at least eight." The artistic mode that for Souriau is most conducive to the representation of movement is the sketch. It is as if the speed, momentum, and necessary imprecision of the sketch embodied all the attributes of our perception of motion. An artist sketching a dancing woman "imagines this feminine body coming and going, an unseizable ghost," but in the final painting or drawing, "the image attaches itself gradually to the paper" and is finally "completely stiffened into it." Ultimately, Souriau's solution to the dilemma is to advocate a sketchy execution for the parts of an artwork that represent mobility and "in order that these blurred parts should not make a hole in the painting, give them a secondary place. In this way, we will not be tempted to look too hard at something we are supposed not to see well."[30] What seems to be at stake for Souriau is the constraint of illegibility (this was also a problem for Marey). The truth of motion is imprecision of form and indecipherability, but that truth is too stark for, and indeed in contradiction with, the goals of representation.

The Italian Futurists, on the other hand, only two decades later, would fully embrace illegibility as a necessary effect and as the pure signifier of speed and mobility. Anton Giulio Bragaglia, in his 1911 manifesto, "Futurist Photodynamism," claimed that it was both "desirable and correct to record the images in a distorted state, since images themselves are inevitably transformed in movement."[31] Just as Souriau claimed that the object disappeared when in movement, the Futurist painters (Umberto Boccioni, Carlo Carrà, Luigi Russolo, Giacomo Balla, and Gino Severini) wrote that "movement and light destroy the materiality of bodies," and Bragaglia referred to the "dematerialization consequent upon motion."[32] The Futurists in general were enamored with the idea of modernity as speed, acceleration, simultaneity, and with the accompanying technologies of mobility (the automobile, the train). A discourse of simultaneity is persistent in their aesthetic theory—"simultaneity is a lyrical exaltation, a plastic manifestation of a new

3.2 *Dynamism of a Dog on a Leash* (1912). Giacomo Balla. Oil on canvas, 35⅜ × 43¼".
Collection Albright-Knox Art Gallery, Buffalo, New York. Bequest of A. Conger
Goodyear and Gift of George F. Goodyear, 1964. © 2002 Artists Rights Society (ARS),
New York / SIAE, Rome.

absolute, speed; a new and marvelous spectacle, modern life; a new fever,
scientific discovery."[33] Absolute speed equals simultaneity, and communication becomes instantaneous.

A number of the Futurist painters were influenced by the work of Marey
and by the scientific theory of persistence of vision. Giacomo Balla's work in
particular is often cited in this context. In *Dynamism of a Dog on a Leash*
(1912) (Figure 3.2), the legs of the dog and its human companion are multiple and blurred, while in *The Hand of the Violinist* or *Rhythm of the Violinist*
(1912) there are at least five hands with imprecise outlines, suggesting mobility. In their "Technical Manifesto" of 1910, the Futurist painters echoed
Souriau's description of the horse with multiple legs in a more positive light:
"On account of the persisting of an image upon the retina, moving objects

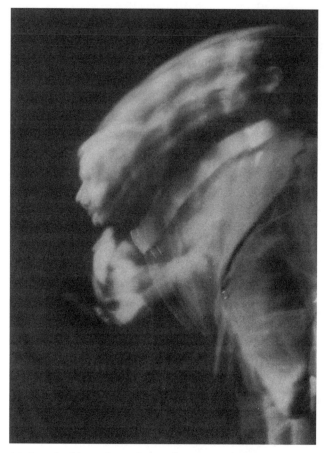

3.3 *Portrait of Arturo Bragaglia* (1911). Anton Giulio Bragaglia.
  Gelatin silver print, 16.5 × 11.9 cm. Gilman Paper Company
  Collection, New York.

constantly multiply themselves; their form changes like rapid vibrations in
their mad career. Thus a running horse has not four legs, but twenty, and
their movements are triangular."[34] Unlike Souriau, however, the Futurists
embraced the "implausible" and attempted to give it its proper representation. This effort took place primarily within the realm of painting, but
Bragaglia pursued his concern with the trajectories of moving objects
through photography. The technique of photodynamism (Bragaglia's term,
paralleling the painters' "plastic dynamism") involved a rejection of instan-

3.4 *Change of Position* (1911). Anton Giulio Bragaglia. Gelatin silver print, 12.8 × 17.9 cm. Gilman Paper Company Collection, New York.

taneity in photography. Instead, the shutter was left open to record Souriau's "visible wake" of the moving object (Figures 3.3, 3.4). Bragaglia claimed that cinematography and Marey's chronophotography are incapable of achieving the intensity or precision of photodynamism's analysis of movement, and, more important, they cannot represent/produce the *sensation* of movement—the "inner, sensorial, cerebral and psychic emotions that we feel when an action leaves its superb, unbroken trace." Cinematography "shatters" movement in the frames of the film strip with cold and mechanical arbitrariness. The different poses of Marey's subjects, more widely separated in time, could be said to belong to different subjects:

> To put it crudely, chronophotography could be compared with a clock on the face of which only the quarter-hours are marked, cinematography to one on which the minutes too are indicated, and Photodynamism to a third on which are marked not only the seconds, but also the *intermovemental* fractions existing in the passages between seconds. This becomes an almost infinitesimal calculation of movement.

Although Bragaglia characterizes the instantaneous exposure as a "laughable absurdity," here he seems to be very much in pursuit of the instant as the unattainable object of desire.[35] Despite the fact that the passage above stresses finer and finer divisions and discriminations, the trajectory traced by Bragaglia's photographs effectively lengthens the duration of the present—the instant—to make it accessible to representation, even if it is a representation characterized by a certain illegibility. It sacrifices the object.

The Futurists' embrace of the implausible over and against a slavish, photographic adherence to reality ultimately led them to reject Bragaglia's work in photography. As Marta Braun has pointed out, it is ironic that the Futurists, who displayed great enthusiasm for the machine and modern technology in general, favored the traditional and hierarchically dominant arts—painting, sculpture, architecture.[36] Nevertheless, and in line with the numerous contradictions riddling their manifestos, the Futurists rejected the culturally acknowledged archives for these traditional arts; the tenth tenet of F. T. Marinetti's original 1909 manifesto claims: "We will destroy the museums, libraries, academies of every kind." He goes on to proclaim, "Museums: cemeteries! . . . Identical, surely in the sinister promiscuity of so many bodies unknown to one another."[37] Museums harbored the dead weight of the past, the dead bodies of so many histories that could only suffocate the young Futurist artist who embraced the present. Exaltation of simultaneity, the instant, the present moment led to the desire for annihilation of the past and of the architectures of cultural memory. But in the censuring of Bragaglia and his photographic work this antiarchival impulse was extended to the new archival technologies of photography and cinema.[38] The Futurists, ironically, favored a premodern form (painting) to represent the strange volatility of the instant.

Souriau and the Futurists have in common the theory of vision as the imprint/tracing of a trajectory or visible wake. In their work, the physiological afterimage of Goethe, Plateau, and Brewster becomes a sign—a sign of mobility, speed, simultaneity, in effect—modernity (this sign has become highly conventionalized in our own time; witness the time-exposure photographs of car headlights in a cityscape at night). If the sign that the afterimage comes to constitute could be characterized more specifically, it would be in terms of Peirce's description of the index. The extensive use of the terms *impression, imprint,* and *trace* in these discussions confirms the relevance of this category. The "visible wake" of Souriau is the existential tracing of an object's movement in time. For Helmholtz, vision could be understood as a sign system characterized by signifiers of varying stability. The theory of retinal impressions that supports the concept of the afterimage provides a physiological parallel for the semiotic phenomenon of indexicality. And indexicality becomes an issue of intense concern in the nineteenth century, expressed primarily in the debates over photography. Although these debates circulate around the question of photography's absolute mimesis—its excess of *similarity* to the real—what is at stake is photography's indexicality, not its iconicity (painting had always allowed for iconicity). In instantaneous photography, it is the automatic rendering of an instant, the forceful "taking" of a picture that becomes problematic.[39] It is the overadherence to the real guaranteed by its indexicality which promotes resistance to photography, particularly in the aesthetic realm. The arguments about time and movement and the possibility of their representation (which become so much more intense in the second half of the nineteenth century and the beginning of the twentieth) circulate around the question of what is photographable and indicate that the issue here is one of representing what we *cannot* see—time. The index belongs very much to the temporality of the moment and its accessibility. It is not accidental that it becomes an important component of Peirce's semiotics and, indeed, of his general epistemological system.

Peirce, employed as a measurer, observer, and designer of instruments by the U.S. Government Coast Survey for thirty years, managed to write prolifically on a wide range of issues in logic, mathematics, philosophy, ethics, and semiotics. In the course of his essays on time and logic as well as indexicality it becomes clear that Peirce did not believe in instantaneous photography, because he denied any philosophical validity to the concept of the instant. In an essay on the semiotic implications of judgment and inference, Peirce writes, "Even what is called an 'instantaneous photograph,' taken with a camera, is a composite of the effects of intervals of exposure more numerous by far than the sands of the sea."[40] For Peirce, a belief in the reality of the instant, as the basic and indivisible unit of time, disallows the possibility of logical thought, which requires that two thoughts be held in the mind during the same interval of time in order to be compared. An idea exists only when it is present to the mind and has no qualities other than those attributed to it by the mind at the moment when it thinks the idea. According to Peirce, it follows from this that "if the succession of time were by separate steps, no idea could resemble another; for these ideas if they are distinct, are present to the mind at different times."[41] The conceptualization of the present as composed of fleeting instants, of ultimately separable, absolute steps, negates the possibility of logical reasoning (which Peirce assumes). In the face of the threat, time must be thought of as a continuum, which in turn disallows thinking of the instant as anything other than an ideal limit:

> A continuum such as we suppose time and space to be, is defined as something any part of which itself has parts of the same kind. So that the point of time or the point of space is nothing but the ideal limit towards which we approach, but which we can never reach in dividing time or space; and consequently nothing is true of a point which is not true of a space or a time . . . We are accustomed to say that nothing is present but a fleeting instant, a point of time. But this is a wrong view of the matter because a point differs in no respect from a space of time, except that it is the ideal limit which, in the division of time, we can never reach. It can not therefore be that it differs from an interval of time in this respect that what is present is only in a fleeting instant, and does not occupy a whole interval of time, unless what is present be an ideal something which can never be reached, and not something real.

Hence there is no immediacy, and Peirce substitutes for the term *more immediately present,* "less mediately present." Any unit of time, no matter how small, will always be an *interval,* composed of smaller units of time. Thoughts, therefore, always take place within an interval in which they are enabled by the presence of other thoughts. In a logic resembling that of the afterimage (and Peirce's only example in this essay is, appropriately, the idea of the color red), he claims that what is present during one instant (defined as an interval) will have an effect on what is present during the "lapse of time which follows that instant." Since that effect is "memory in its most elementary form," and time is theorized as a continuum whose units are not separate and discrete, for Peirce as for Bergson, memory inevitably prevents a pure access to the present.[42]

One of the founding assumptions of this logic, for Peirce, is that thought takes time—nothing is present to the mind for an instant. There is, therefore, for Peirce, no thought that could be defined as intuition, that is, as in the immediate present. Intuition is also, traditionally, considered to take place outside any sign system, and Peirce denies the possibility of thought not in signs. Only thought in signs can be "evidenced by external facts." Every thought, as a sign, must address itself to some other, and this activity takes time: "To say, therefore, that thought cannot happen in an instant, but requires a time, is but another way of saying that every thought must be interpreted in another, or that all thought is in signs."[43] Thought and signs, welded together, resist instantaneity or any notion of an immediate present. It would seem, therefore, that there can be no sign that fully or accurately represents or embodies instantaneity. The instant—as an ideal limit—can yield no adequate sign of itself.

Nevertheless, within Peirce's own extremely elaborate taxonomy of signs, the index is in fact the form of sign that comes closest to this ideal limit. Just as the present is the effect of the "pure denotative power of the mind" (that is, attention), the power of the index is a denotative one, forcing the attention to a particular object, here and now.[44] Peirce's theory of signs is relentlessly triadic—he eventually developed ten different triads and sixty-six different types of sign.[45] His definition of the sign itself invokes a triad: a sign is "anything which determines something else (its *interpretant*) to refer to an object to which itself refers (its *object*) in the same way, the interpretant becoming in turn a sign, and so on *ad infinitum*." The interpretant is not a psychologizing notion in the sense that would have it describe a human individual. Instead, it is a meaning or idea that takes the form of a sign itself and is therefore capable of continuing the life of the sign indefinitely. Looking up a word in the dictionary and being directed only to other words in the dictionary would be emblematic of Peirce's "*ad infinitum*." Nevertheless, there is certainly a subjective dimension associated with the concept of an interpretant. Peirce immediately adds, after his definition, "No doubt, intelligent consciousness must enter into the series. If the series of successive interpretants comes to an end, the sign is thereby rendered imperfect, at least." In an earlier piece he claims that there are three classes of signs because "there is a triple connection of *sign, thing signified, cognition produced in the mind*." And in an essay titled "On the Nature of Signs" (1873), he is most explicit on the subjectivity of semiosis: "it is necessary for a sign to be a sign that it should be regarded as a sign for it is only a sign to that mind which so considers and if it is not a sign to any mind it is not a sign at all."[46] The triad of signs most central to Peirce's exposition of his semiotics is consistently that of icon, index, and symbol. In an icon (for example, a picture or a graph) there is a relation of similarity or reason between the sign and the object signified. The index signifies by virtue of an existential bond between the sign and its object (for example, a footprint), and the symbol is sustained by a conventional, or habitual, or lawlike relation between itself and its object (for example, language).

According to Peirce, most signs are mixed in character; it is difficult, for instance, to find examples of a "pure index." However, signs do have a dominant dimension, and he proceeds to elaborate these dimensions in great detail. Indices are characterized by a certain singularity and uniqueness; they always refer to individuals, single units, single collections of units, or single continua. They are dependent upon certain unique contingencies: the wind blowing at the moment in a certain direction, a foot having landed in the mud at precisely this place, the camera's shutter opening at a given time. Unlike icons, indices have no resemblance to their objects, which, nevertheless, directly cause them. This phenomenon reflects the fact that the index is evacuated of content; it is a hollowed-out sign. It (for instance, a pointing finger) designates something without describing it ("The index asserts nothing; it only says 'There!'").[47] An index is a particularly forceful and compelling form of sign—it directs the attention to an object by "blind compulsion:" "A rap on the door is an index. Anything which focuses the attention is an index. Anything which startles us is an index, in so far as it marks the junction between two portions of experience. Thus a tremendous thunderbolt indicates that *something* considerable happened, though we may not know precisely what the event was. But it may be expected to connect itself with some other experience."[48] Unlike icons and symbols, which rely upon association by resemblance or intellectual operations, the work of the index depends upon association by contiguity (the foot touches the ground and leaves a trace, the wind pushes the weathercock, the pointing finger indicates an adjoining site, the light rays reflected from the object "touch" the film). The object is made "present" to the addressee. The specificity and singularity associated with the index are evidenced most clearly in Peirce's designation of the demonstrative pronouns (for example, *this, that*) as "nearly pure indices" (although, existing within language, they must be symbols as well).[49] As Oswald Ducrot and Tzvetan Todorov point out in their *Encyclopedic Dictionary of the Sciences of Language,* "In language everything that relates to *deixis* is an index: words such as *I, you, here, now.*"[50] Roman Jakobson calls deictics *shifters* because their reference is entirely dependent upon the situation of speaking itself and shifts from one implementation to the next.[51] *This* is evacuated of all content and simply designates a specific and singular object or situation, comprehensible only within the given discourse. In Peirce's philosophy, "thisness" is equivalent to "firstness." *Deixis* is the moment when language seems to touch ground, to adhere as closely as it can to the present reality of speech. Peirce was acutely aware of this and hence contested the traditional wisdom, which dictates that a pronoun (such as *this, that, I*) is a substitute for a noun. These pronouns have a directness and immediacy that all nouns lack; they are capable of indicating things in the most straightforward way. Therefore, Peirce claims that "a noun is an imperfect substitute for a pronoun."[52]

Photography and film would seem to be excellent examples of sign systems that merge icon, index, and, to some extent, symbol. Though indexical because the photographic image has an existential bond with its object, they are also iconic in relying upon a similarity with that object. To the extent that photography and film have recourse to language (or are labeled themselves) they invoke the symbolic realm. Peter Wollen has cited Peirce's semiotics as a more flexible and precise method of describing cinema than Christian Metz's linguistically based schema because it allows the possibility of thinking film as a heterogeneous sign system.[53] Although this analysis is undoubtedly accurate, it is interesting that Peirce himself seemed to situate photography as primarily indexical, subordinating the iconic dimension to secondary status; photography's iconicity was a by-product of its indexicality:

Photographs, especially instantaneous photographs, are very instructive, because we know that they are in certain respects exactly like the objects they represent. But this resemblance is due to the photographs having been produced under such circumstances that they were physically forced to correspond point by point to nature. In that aspect, then, they belong to the second class of signs, those by physical connection.[54]

For Peirce, the iconicity of the photographic image is reduced by the sign's overadherence to its object (elsewhere he claims that an icon, in order to resemble its object, must also be noticeably different).

The index, more insistently than any other type of sign, is haunted by its object. The index is "actually modified" by its object.[55] It puts its addressee into a "real connection" with its object, and at one point Peirce defines the index as "being really and in its individual existence connected with the individual object." Indices "furnish positive assurance of the reality and the nearness of their Objects." But they are limited to the assurance of an existence; they provide no insight into the nature of their objects; they have no cognitive value but simply indicate that something is "there." The indices that are traces of the forces of the natural world (tracks, a weathercock) can even deny the dimension of subjectivity altogether:

> An *index* is a sign which would, at once, lose the character which makes it a sign if its object were removed, but would not lose that character if there were no interpretant. Such, for instance, is a piece of mould with a bullet-hole in it as a sign of a shot; for without the shot there would have been no hole; but there is a hole there, whether anybody has the sense to attribute it to a shot or not.[56]

Yet the structure of the sign itself is fundamentally triadic, and if either the object or the interpretant is eliminated, the sign will no longer exist. With this move, Peirce seems to be situating the index on the very threshold of semiosis; for to deprive the index of its interpretant while leaving its status as sign unaffected is to open up the possibility of the index isolating itself from semiosis, the chain of signification sustained by the presence of a continuing line of interpretants. The index is reduced to its own singularity; it appears as a brute and opaque fact, wedded to contingency. In this way, Peirce theorizes the index as potentially outside the domain of human subjectivity and meaning. It is pure indication, pure assurance of existence. The photographic image would, in this sense, appear to be its perfect representative. In photography, for the first time, an aesthetic or spatial representation could be made by chance, by accident, without human control.[57] And it would still be a sign of something, perched precariously on the threshold of semiosis. As the sign most clearly connected to the present and presence, perhaps it is the ideal limit of the instant that is approached by the index.

This curious capacity of the index to be simultaneously inside and outside of semiosis is illuminated by Peirce's more extended treatment of the epistemological issues associated with singularity, contingency, and irregularity in his theory of chance. Chance, for Peirce, was not a negative concept—it was not simply the absence of law or our ignorance of actual operational causes. Rather, it was a positive force and far from being reduced to the leakage or occasional exception to law:

> For a long time, I myself strove to make chance that diversity in the universe which laws leave room for, instead of a violation of law, or lawlessness. That was truly believing in chance that was not absolute chance . . . Chance itself pours in at every avenue of sense: it is of all things the most obtrusive. That it is absolute is the most manifest of all intellectual perceptions. That it is a being, living and conscious, is what all the dullness that belongs to ratiocination's self can scarce muster hardihood to deny.[58]

Peirce argued vociferously against the doctrine of necessity, which he defined as "the common belief that every single fact in the universe is precisely determined by law." In the face of the necessitarian position that certain continuous qualities have exact values, Peirce pointed to the impossibility of exact measurement, to the notorious and insurmountable differences in producing mathematically exact measurement of masses, lengths, and angles. Furthermore, irregularities abound: "Try to verify any law of nature, and you will find that the more precise your observations, the more certain they will be to show irregular departures from the law . . . Trace their causes back far enough and you will be forced to admit they are always due to arbitrary determination, or chance." The sheer variety of phenomena and the diversity and "specificalness" of events were, for Peirce, proof of the operation of chance, for law produces only uniformity, regularity, and, consequently, banality. Indeed, in Peirce's view, the most important law formulated in the nineteenth century—the Second Law of Thermodynamics, which prescribed a continual increase in entropy and the eventual heat-death of the universe—was not simply confronted with occasional exceptions but everywhere violated by growth and increasing complexity. For Peirce, "Death and corruption are mere accidents or secondary phenomena."[59] The very force and significance of the Second Law of Thermodynamics made its violation even more remarkable and corroborated the power of chance:

> You have all heard of the dissipation of energy. It is found that in all transformations of energy a part is converted into heat and heat is always tending to equalize its temperature. The consequence is that the energy of the universe is tending by virtue of its necessary laws toward a death of the universe in which there shall be no force but heat and the temperature everywhere the same. This is a truly astounding result, and the most materialistic the most anti-teleological conceivable.
>
> We may say that we know enough of the forces at work in the universe to know that there is none that can counteract this tendency away from every definite end but death.
>
> But although no force can counteract this tendency, chance may and will have the opposite influence. Force is in the long run dissipative; chance is in the long run concentrative. The dissipation of energy by the regular laws of nature is by those very laws accompanied by circumstances more and more favorable to its reconcentration by chance. There must therefore be a point at which the two tendencies are balanced and that is no doubt the actual condition of the whole universe at the present time.[60]

Chance, in Peirce's view, is on the side of life and spontaneity.

Peirce, like many other philosophers of his era, was profoundly influenced by Darwin's theory of evolution, in which a strong element of chance is inescapable. In natural selection, the only positive agent of change, in the transition from monkey to man for instance, is fortuitous variation, or, in effect, chance. Variations in the species are accidents, aberrations that are then corroborated or not by their function in survival. Chance hence propels biological transformation and the evolution of the species. It is in this sense that Peirce claims that the theory of natural selection in evolution promotes the idea that chance begets order. This idea is also one of the "cornerstones of modern physics" and is prevalent in chemistry, history, and sociology as well. Peirce associates it with the names of Quetelet, Herschel, Buckle, Clausius, and Maxwell. Peirce was a great admirer of the probability curve invoked by Quetelet in the realm of biological and social phenomena. For Peirce, chance, "as an objective phenomenon, is a property of a distribution."[61] In a fortuitous distribution, the elements are mixed together with a "perfect" irregularity.

Hence, Peirce's epistemology was invested in the growing popularity of the statistical method. Knowledge was a matter of defining probabilities and tendencies and was therefore always provisional. It depended upon the possibility of an indefinite extension of experience, to cover all possible events, with the assumption that "our approximations will become indefinitely close in the long run; that is to say, close to the experience *to come*."[62] Knowledge is asymptotic, and it is chance that makes our epistemological claims provisional and experiential. If one had an infinite amount of time and experience, statistics and probability would give us certainty. But the fact that humans are mortal introduces uncertainty:

> All human affairs rest upon probabilities, and the same thing is true everywhere. If man were immortal he could be perfectly sure of seeing the day when everything in which he had trusted should betray his trust, and, in short, of coming eventually to hopeless misery. He would break down, at last, as every great fortune, as every dynasty, as every civilization does. In place of this we have death.
>
> But what, without death, would happen to every man, with death must happen to some man. At the same time, death makes the number of our risks, of our inferences, finite, and so makes their mean result uncertain. The very idea of probability and of reasoning rests on the assumption that this number is indefinitely great.

The only solution to this conundrum, according to Peirce, is to acknowledge that logicality requires that our interests *not* be limited. We must not be concerned solely with our own fate (which is, in a sense, epistemologically impoverished) but must be concerned with the community (which, in its turn, cannot be limited by such factors as race, geography, time): "Logic is rooted in the social principle."[63]

Necessitarianism, in Peirce's view, is defeated by the ubiquity of chance, but chance, curiously, becomes the very foundation of regularity, habit, and, ultimately, law. In this way, Peirce participates in the "taming of chance," which Ian Hacking situates in the nineteenth century as a prelude to the erosion of determinism in twentieth-century physics. Probability was, after all, a new type of law—a more flexible and in a way more powerful law. In Hacking's words, "Society became statistical,"[64] and Peirce's philosophy is complicit with this form of normalization. Although Peirce, in his battle with the necessitarians, gave as one of his reasons for believing in absolute chance that law, like everything else, must be explained and can be explained only by non-law or by chance, in the process he established a significant relation between chance and law resembling that of cause and effect. In "The Doctrine of Necessity" Peirce claims: "I make use of chance chiefly to make room for a principle of generalization, or tendency to form habits, which I hold has produced all regularities"; and in "Design and Chance" he states": "Chance is indeterminacy, is freedom. But the action of freedom issues in the strictest rule of law." Peirce based this move on the precedents of Darwin's theory of natural selection (wherein chance indeed becomes law) and molecular physics, wherein the inconceivable number of molecules and the frequency of their encounters call out for probability and its laws. A mark may be accidental, made by chance, but "no further progress beyond this can be made, until a mark will *stay* for a little while; that is, until some beginning of a *habit* has been established by virtue of which the accident acquires some incipient staying quality, some tendency toward consistency."[65] Habit is the tendency toward repetition; it is associated with uniformity and predictability while chance is associated with diversity and the specific.

Peirce, who believed in a continuity between matter and mind, maintained that matter was mind whose habits had become so fixed that it could not lose them or form new ones. Mind, on the other hand, was the very seat of complexity and instability with an enormous capacity for taking on and laying aside habits, entailing frequent divergences from law. Thus Peirce went so far as to claim that the laws of mind "simulate divergences from law." Although Pierce held that the law of mind was the law of habit, it was a curious law since it required its own violation to allow for the possibility of acquiring new habits—he referred to it as "that mental law the violation of which is so included in its essence that unless it were violated it would cease to exist." Ultimately, this violability of the law of mind becomes a fundamental feature of all law for Peirce when he claims that all law is the result of evolution and therefore imperfect.[66] Law must be perceived as evolutionary in character, since the inevitable chance variations from it that increase the diversity of the world result in transformations of the law. For Peirce, this is what is meant by the "action of chance." Chance is no longer an aberration, a by-product, a leakage, but a positive historical agent.

But how can chance have lasting effects? Peirce's attempt to solve this problem brings him back to his theory of time and continuity, and in fact leads him inexorably to embrace a contradiction in his own thinking. He claims that the "natural answer" to the question of why chance produces permanent effects has to do with the independence of different instants of time. Once a chance variation takes place there is no particular reason why it should ever be undone. Thus, the effects of the discontinuity can persist. But, given Peirce's investment in continuity and in time as the continuity par excellence which cannot be reduced to a series of points, he himself is taken aback by his own answer: "But we have no sooner let slip the remark about the independence of the instants of time than we are shocked by it. What can be less independent than the parts of the continuum *par excellence,* through the spectacles of which we envisage every other continuum?" Peirce had already claimed that the instant, time as isolated point, had no reality other than as an ideal limit that we could never reach. A continuous line or a continuum such as time has no points. And yet, though scandalous, the scandal is true—"Yet it undoubtedly is true that the permanence of chance effects is due to the independence of the instants of time. How are we to resolve this puzzle? The solution of it lies in this, that time has a point of discontinuity at the present." This is true only of that instant we call the present; the actual instant (the present) differs form all other instants absolutely: the others differ from each other only in degree. Time is a true continuum except at the moment of the actual present. The absolute break between past and future is a symptom in our consciousness of this discontinuity. The present as instant suddenly becomes accessible in order to buttress Peirce's theory of chance—indeed, it is the condition of possibility of chance: "Perhaps all fortuitous distribution originates from a fortuitous distribution of events in time." But just as chance produces law, the errors that are fortuitous variations of our actions in time are responsible for intellectual growth: "It is a truth well worthy of rumination that all the intellectual development of man rests upon the circumstance that all our action is subject to error."[67] Failure and error, chance and accident, become enabling forces, *in* time.

The scandal, the contradiction at the heart of Peirce's system, is necessitated by his simultaneous investment in chance and in continuity (in his terms, Tychism and Synechism). What the scandal allows is what is so dear to modernity—the possibility of the new, novelty, the continual difference and variation that constitutes the sensory basis of the modern. For although Peirce embraces habit as a crucial philosophical concept, that habit must always be animated, nourished by chance. Only chance can explain the new; only chance can account for the overwhelming diversity and variety in the universe. And only the fact that time has a point of discontinuity at the present can explain the lasting imprint or impression left by chance, its contribution to the formulation of the new. Peirce states: "time is the form under which logic presents itself to objective intuition; and the signification of the discontinuity at the actual instant is that here new premises, not logically derived by Firsts, are introduced."[68] The instant is the condition of the possibility of newness, novelty, modernity. The power of chance and its effects is bound to a belief in the absolute discontinuity of the instant. Peirce succumbs to that lure of the present instant, of chance, of contingency that is so characteristic of much nineteenth-century thinking. And in the process, the present instant becomes philosophically representable, within his grasp. It is figurable as a "point" and as "discontinuity."

In his theory of chance, Peirce is searching for an explanation for contingency, not for regularity. And far from an ideal limit never reached, the present as point of discontinuity becomes the mark of the real and the condition of possibility of chance. Manifesting itself in the singular, chance is in a sense the insistence of the real. The real, for Peirce, is not something sensed or vaguely felt. It exists as an insistence, a compulsion, an absolute demand. In "Notes on Metaphysics," he claims:

> to say that a singular is known by sense is a confusion of thought. It is not known by the feeling-element of sense, but by the compulsion, the insistency, that characterizes experience. For the singular subject is real; and reality is insistency. That is what we mean by "reality." It is the brute irrational insistency that forces us to acknowledge the reality of what we experience, that gives us our conviction of any singular.[69]

These are the same terms that are used to describe the work of the index. The index "takes hold of our eyes, as it were, and forcibly directs them to a particular object." Indices always refer to singulars—single units, individuals, unique events. They direct the attention to an object by "blind compulsion."[70] The function of the index is that of sheer indication, denotation, and it serves primarily as an assurance of an existence. It leaves its mark in language in the empty signifier "this," ready to take on any singular entity. "Thisness," indexicality, and chance, as well as the notion of the present instant as a point of discontinuity, are wedded in Peirce's theory. All are attributes of the photographic image. Although Peirce never, to my knowledge, wrote about the cinema, and made only brief references to photography, the photographic image and its representational logic haunted his philosophical moves and informed the tensions and contradictions in his discourse. The index, sign and not-sign, is perched on the threshold of semiosis; chance opposes and yet consolidates law; the present instant—inaccessible because of its submersion in the vast continuum of time—becomes graspable as the pure point of discontinuity that is the condition of the possibility of modernity. Peirce struggled to come to terms with a conceptualization of a contingency suddenly more powerful than it had ever been in classical thought.

The physiology and the philosophy of the nineteenth century work to delineate the theoretical impossibility of instantaneity, the inaccessibility of the present moment. Peirce's and Bergson's investment in time as the ultimate continuum disallows the possibility of a pure experience of the present—past and present are inextricably bound together. For Bergson, instantaneity and a pure apprehension of the present are negated by the incessant work of memory and the continual invasion of the present by the past. For Peirce, the ungraspability of the present is a consequence of the fact that thought (and its necessary embeddedness in signs) *takes time.* These philosophical arguments find a physiological basis in the theory of the afterimage and persistence of vision. If the retinal image persists in time, the instantaneous image will always be contaminated by past images; the object will be inseparable from its visual wake. What appears to us as the present instant is in fact riven by delay. It is the very archivability of the retinal image—its ability to leave an enduring (if brief) impression—that makes the present moment out of reach.

Yet the physiological and philosophical discourses that serve to construct the present as distant and unattainable limit are accompanied, both internally and externally, by an insatiable desire to represent it. The sequential photography of Marey and Muybridge constitutes an attempt to isolate and analyze the instant, to make an invisible time optically legible. The Futurist desire to represent the "*intermovemental* fractions existing in the passages between seconds" indicates a compulsion to figure instantaneity even if it meant risking illegibility.[71] And even in Peirce's work, the inaccessible present ultimately emerges to be figured as a point of discontinuity that enables modernity. In an essay on literary history and literary modernity, Paul de Man has claimed that modernity attempts to annihilate the past in order to support its fascination with the present: "Modernity exists in the form of a desire to wipe out whatever came earlier, in the hope of reaching at last a point that could be called a true present, a point of origin that marks a new departure."[72] The tension is between modernity and history, and de Man cites Nietzsche's exhortation to forget history as well as Baudelaire's celebration of the present in his famous essay on Constantin Guys, "The Painter of Modern Life." The aspiration to represent movement and instantaneity is revealed in Guys's predilection—reminiscent of Souriau's injunction to the painter of movement—for the sketch as favored mode of representation/ technique. The sketch is an attempt to fix the moment, to effectively "outrun time," and Baudelaire's invocation of the phrase "representation of the present" is, as de Man points out, paradoxical—combining repetition and instantaneity without awareness of the contradiction. But it is finally in the new representational technologies of vision—photography, the cinema— that one witnesses the insistency of the impossible desire to represent—to archive—the present. And if a perception of radical finitude is a condition for archival desire, the longing to grasp the present in representation finds its basis in an image of a body whose visual powers are defective, lacking, riven by delay—a body which cannot "see" that present which is so crucial to modernity.

With photography, the instants can be disentangled. The point of discontinuity that is Peirce's present can be caught—"embalmed," as André Bazin would say. The photograph isolates a moment in time and engraves what would otherwise be an ephemeral instant, unarchivable. As Siegfried Kracauer points out in his 1927 essay on photography, the photograph "must be essentially associated with the moment in time at which it came into existence." But Kracauer contrasts this mechanical preservation of the spatial configuration of a moment to authentic memory and history, which isolate and store only significant moments that have a relation to truth. The problem with photography, according to Kracauer, is its lack of meaning, its association with pure contingency, and its disconnectedness: "The photographic archive assembles in effigy the last elements of a nature alienated from meaning." The illustrated magazines accumulate these moments deprived of a meaningful context, and in them "the world has become a photographable present."[73]

Nevertheless, although the photograph has been associated with this feverish desire to "warehouse" the present, it is more frequently linked to a relentless assertion of pastness—a "that-has-been." In instantaneous photography (the snapshot), the instants blurred together in human vision, through the work of the afterimage, can be disentangled, but in the process they become inevitably past. Roland Barthes analyzes the photograph as a curious conjunction of the "here" and "then": "what I see has been here, in this place which extends between infinity and the subject (*operator* or *spectator*); it has been here, and yet immediately separated; it has been absolutely, irrefutably present, and yet already deferred."[74] The insistent referentiality of the photograph is linked, for Barthes, with the spectator's knowledge that the object *had been* there, in front of the camera, and that the image carries its trace. But he also claims that in the cinema, photography's "*having-been-there* gives way before a *being-there* of the thing." The spectator always experiences the film as in the present tense, and this is for Barthes what lends to the cinema the "more projective, more 'magical' fictional consciousness" denied to the photograph, which is chained to the brute facticity of the past.[75] Christian Metz agrees with this assessment of film's amenability to spectatorial projection and extends the argument to claim that the extraordinary affective and perceptual participation of the spectator in a film is linked to its ability to generate belief (the impression of the real) based on its mode of *presence*. And this sense of experiencing the present is due to the representation of movement—"the spectator always sees movement as being present (even if it duplicates a past movement)."[76] The moving images are, for the spectator, "here" and "now." Photography, it would seem, is theorized as the representation of isolated present moments (which must be experienced by the spectator as already past), whereas filmic representation produces the spectatorial experience of presence.

But one must immediately add to this the observation that there is also a certain instability of the present tense in the cinema, as a result of its archivability and the consequent intrusion of historicity. As soon as one is aware that a film can be viewed again—that this experience of presence can be repeated—it becomes a record, more precisely a specifically historical record (of its own performance, of its place in a cultural history, of its production/preservation of an event). Watching a Humphrey Bogart film in the 1990s is undoubtedly a different experience from watching the same film in the 1940s (the 1990s viewing has the added frisson of historicity attached to it). Michael Chanan has argued that film has had a radical effect on our sense of history. Film exposed people to aspects and events of the world that had previously been distant and inaccessible; it made them immediate, but at the same time mediated: "Because a camera happened to record them, the moments film was exposed to thus became historical moments of a new order. In a sense, therefore, film turned the present into a kind of immediate history; it made history out of the present. Film was therefore an entirely new mode of production of human perception; that is, it provided a new way of looking." But to assume that film records neutral moments that subsequently become historical is to assume a certain transparency in the apparatus itself. It would be more accurate to say that photography and the cinema produce the sense of a present moment laden with historicity at the same time that they encourage a belief in our access to pure presence, instantaneity. As Derrida points out, "what is no longer archived in the same way is no longer lived in the same way. Archivable meaning is also and in advance codetermined by the structure that archives."[77]

In an essay titled "Observations on the Long Take," Pier Paolo Pasolini analyzes the intricate relation between present and past tenses in the cinema, focusing on a consideration of the famous Abraham Zapruder film—the 8-millimeter film of Kennedy's assassination—which has become, perhaps, the filmed historical moment par excellence. Pasolini, for whom reality is a language for which we do not yet have an adequate semiology, claims that reality can be perceived only as it happens and from a single point of view. The long take, duplicating this single point of view, presents us with reality as it happens. The long take is, therefore, always in the present tense:

Reality seen and heard as it happens is *always in the present tense.*

The long take, the schematic and primordial element of cinema, is thus in the present tense. Cinema therefore "reproduces the present."

> Live television is a paradigmatic reproduction of something happening in the present.[78]

From this perspective, Kennedy would always die, over and over again with each screening of Zapruder's film, in the present tense.[79] For Pasolini, it is montage which transforms the absolute present of the long take into the past—montage which, in Chanan's terminology, translates the present into "immediate history." Although Pasolini defines the cinema as the "reproduction of the present," "as soon as montage intervenes, when we pass from cinema to film . . . the present becomes past: a past that, for cinematographic and not aesthetic reasons, is always in the present mode *(that is, it is a historic present)*." For Pasolini, what makes a filmic discourse past tense is not its repeatability but something interior to the discourse itself—the cut that coordinates two separate presences and reconfigures them as a historic, that is, meaningful, present. He goes even further, to claim that the cut is equivalent to death, which, on the individual biographic level, converts "our present, which is infinite, unstable, and uncertain, and thus linguistically undescribable, into a clear, stable, certain, and thus linguistically describable past."[80] The present moment, for Pasolini as for Kracauer, is imbued with contingency and, hence, meaninglessness. In the long take, the cinema incarnates the meaninglessness of a lived reality. The cut, like the dead eye of Helmholtz's fresh corpse, stabilizes the image.

But what is a historic present if not a present that can be successfully archived? What is at stake in modernity is not just, as in Crary's argument, a logic of mobility, circulation, and accelerated exchange, but also a logic of the archive and, especially, the archivability of time. Photography renders a present moment as past; cinema transforms the present into immediate history (a historic present); both deal with the problematic and contradictory task of archiving the present. This fascination with the present, with instantaneity, is evident in a large array of discourses of the period—in those of the Futurists, Souriau's and Baudelaire's aesthetics, Marey, Muybridge, and Peirce. The problem becomes how to theorize the instant, how to think the possibility of its representation. How can one maintain the accessibility of the present—as the pure point of departure so crucial to modernity—in the face of its seemingly inevitable contamination by the past? In this respect, there is no radical rupture between modernity and what is called postmodernity. The fascination with an impossible instantaneity is still with us, perhaps even more insistently, corroborated by a continuing chain of new technologies of representation—photography, cinema, television, the computer—that seem to put instantaneity more fully within our grasp. The televisual obsession with the "live" coverage of catastrophe—the ultimate representation of contingency, chance, the instantaneous—is symptomatic of this enduring preoccupation with the present as a kind of limit of representation.

The present, in this context, acts as a zero or placeholder for something outside of what is perceived as a more and more rigorously ordered social system, organized by technological, industrial, economic, and political determinants—the intricate web of commodity capitalism. The present can be figured (as Peirce does) as a point of discontinuity (and hence the condition of the possibility of chance) in an otherwise continuous stream of time. This flow of time, in a capitalist economy, is increasingly regularized, systematized, normalized both in the realm of work and in the domain of leisure. The present as point of discontinuity marks the promise of something other, something outside of systematicity. This otherness is, perhaps more accurately, the lure not only of the nonsystematic but of the antisystematic (which is why catastrophe—as the rupture of system and the mark of unpredictability—is so fascinating and why television is so obsessed with its discursive control).[81] But the present instant also and simultaneously poses a threat, that of meaninglessness, pure and uncontrollable contingency. Hence, it is contained, but at the same time deployed. Its appeal as that which is asystematic, spontaneous, is, in many respects, deceptive; for chance, contingency, the present moment become themselves the building blocks of a system designed to deal with asystematicity. Such a logic is closer to that of statistics and probability than to that of narrative. But the two logics are subtly interwoven and coordinated in the cinema's "reproduction of the present."

For Pasolini, death (incarnated in the cinematic cut) enables a story, a meaningful narrative.[82] It is the single shot, the life as it is lived, which embodies all the contingency, uncertainty, and instability of the real. However, Peirce's analysis of death is quite different. It is immortality which bestows the certainty, the sure knowledge of a person's inevitable ruin and destruction. Death brings uncertainty and the domination of chance; it makes our risks finite, and therefore their "mean result" is uncertain. For probability and statistics to "work," the number of risks must be indefinitely great. For Peirce, this is an argument for expanding our interests beyond those of the individual (the self) in order to create a statistically meaningful pool. What is at stake for Pasolini is a meaning, a knowledge referred to (modeled on) the life of an individual. It is, precisely, a narrative meaning. Peirce's meaning, referred to the "indefinitely great" pool of humanity, is a statistical meaning, following the laws of probability and making chance the motor of its knowledge.

Cinema, born in a period when the battle over contingency, determinism, and meaning was strong, embodies both epistemologies. In its dominant historical development, it has become the narrativization of chance, the historicization of the present. A large part of its pleasure and fascination is no doubt due to the lure of contingency, the promise of its indexicality, and hence its access to the present. But such a lure and such a promise carry with them the threat of meaninglessness. In narrative, the contingency, singularity, and uniqueness associated with the bourgeois notion of the individual can be yoked to a meaning guaranteed by his or her mortality. All the beauty and fascination of the world's diversity and variety—so admired by Peirce—can become the spectacular and erotic backdrop, the field of restrained possibility, for the playing out of this meaning. The lure of contingency, the fascination of a present moment in which anything can happen, is safely deployed. The present—as the mark of contingency in time—is made tolerable, readable, archivable, and, not least, pleasurable.

4

Temporal Irreversibility and the
Logic of Statistics

Part of the fascination of the early cinema was its status as a machine. Advertisements highlighted the projector itself and often named the specific invention (the Vitascope, the Bioscope, and so forth) rather than the individual films as the source of the attraction.[1] As a machine, a motor, the cinema shared the automatic appeal of other nineteenth-century machines—their harnessing of energy in an unrelenting movement seemingly independent of human labor. But in this case, the fascination of the technology did not differ in kind from the fascination of the images projected upon the screen. Unlike previous forms of visual representation, in which comprehension *took time* (writing, sculpture, painting), the cinema, because it was mechanical, subjected its spectator to the time of its own inexorable and unvarying forward movement.[2] Previously, the time of viewing had been in the control of the subject, allowing for contemplation at leisure. The technological basis of the cinema incarnated the regimentation of time in modernity, its irreversibility.

Certain types of phenomena would seem to contest such an interpretation. One was quite basic and consisted simply of a technological reversal: in the early days of the cinema, the film was sometimes run backward, exploiting a curiosity about the limits of the machine, its uses and abuses, together with the titillation of witnessing time apparently flow backward—a man leaping backward from the water into a diving position on a pier, the pieces of a broken glass reassembling themselves into a whole. A Rochester newspaper announcing such an experiment in a local theater in 1897 claimed: "Whatever else it may prove the experiment will at least be a curious novelty and one which everyone who has seen the Cinématographe will be desirous to witness." But the desire imputed to this spectator is a transgressive one, emanating from the knowledge that such a procedure apparently contradicts not only the laws of nature (of movement) but also, and perhaps more importantly, the laws of the cinematic machine itself, which incessantly and unrelentingly inscribes time as a succession of instants whose "true" directionality is ultimately incontestable. The "trick" corroborates the dominance and determinant status of the rule. Similarly, and in contrast to the frequently noted "consumability" of the fully developed classical Hollywood narrative, the tendency of early audiences to re-view films, often in succession, was not merely a function of their shorter length but also an acknowledgment of the temporal hold over meaning existing even in films not yet saturated with narrative linearity. As the Rochester *Post-Express* remarked of Lumière's *Repas de bébé* (1895), "So intent is the spectator usually in watching the proceedings of the happy trio at table that he fails to notice the pretty background of trees and shrubbery, whose waving branches indicate that a stiff breeze is blowing. So it is in each of the pictures shown; they are full of interesting little details that come out one by one when the same views are seen several times."[3]

Because it does not involve such an obvious tampering with the technology but rather the *semiosis* of the cinema's own technological conditions of existence—the transformation of those conditions into legible *signs*—the incorporation of temporal reversibility within the diegesis would seem to pose a greater challenge to the dominance of irreversibility. And in fact it has frequently been remarked that early films exploit more extensively, along with other "special effects," the possibilities of reverse motion. A particularly provocative example is offered by a 1900 Vitagraph/Edison film titled *The Artist's Dilemma.*[4] In his studio, the space of which is constituted by a stage for models, a grandfather clock, and an easel, an artist dozes in a chair next to the clock. A model opens the central panel (Figure 4.1) and emerges from the clock to awaken the artist and assume her pose on the stage. As the artist painstakingly begins to paint her, another figure emerges from the clock—a ghostly figure with supernatural connotations who seems to resemble a clown or a demon (Figure 4.2). The clown/demon, admiring the model, displaces the artist and, after grabbing a special bucket and paintbrush from the clock, proceeds to paint—or, more accurately, *unpaint*—the portrait of the model (Figure 4.3). It is clear that this section of the film is reverse motion: a film strip in which the clown/demon had painted black over an already ex-

4.1 *The Artist's Dilemma* (1900). Vitagraph/Edison.

4.2 *The Artist's Dilemma.*

4.3 *The Artist's Dilemma.*

4.4 *The Artist's Dilemma.*

isting picture of the model is simply run backward so that it appears as if an impressive likeness of the model emerges magically from the broad, careless strokes of the demon's brush. The demon helps his representation to step down from the portrait and become alive (Figure 4.4).[5] The model comes down from the stage, bows to her own likeness, and the two women begin to dance together, ending the short dance by kicking the gaping artist and demon. They arise, and first the model's likeness disappears, and then the demon. The artist attempts to kiss the model, who is suddenly transformed into the demon figure. The demon figure then knocks down the artist, jumps up in front of the clock, and disappears. The artist reassumes his position dozing in front of the clock, which remains at four o'clock from beginning to end of the film, perhaps suggesting, as does the artist's sleeping position, that the diegesis has the status of a dream.

Although it is not clear what the artist's dilemma is (since *dilemma* implies a choice), the film is richly suggestive of some of the problems of representation faced by the new technology. The seemingly flawless mimesis of the model effected by the demon's magical trick (which is supported by the specifically cinematic "trick" of reverse motion) is activated to blur the line between life and image, object and representation. The parallel between the realistic portrait and the film image—both inhabit a frame and emerge out of blackness—demonstrates that the film seeks to reinscribe the uncanny likeness of the cinematic image as magic, and magic as the underside of science. It is no less significant that the entire "dilemma" emerges from the clock, a machine for the representation of time which here dominates the mise-en-scène. What is at stake in the film's own signifying operation is, at least in part, the relation between reversible and irreversible time. Although, according to the clock, time does not advance in the space of this dream, a quasi-narrative unfolds, and it is clear that something advances, something happens in a time that is linear.[6] And reversible time is subordinate to the rationale of the event. For ultimately, in *The Artist's Dilemma,* as in many other magic films of the period, reverse motion is subjected to a textual logic if not yet a fully developed narrative logic. It is not gratuitous.

The fascination with the tension between reversible and irreversible time evidenced in these examples and phenomena from the early cinema is not confined to the realm of film, which seems in many ways to be the mechanical incarnation of representational irreversibility. The last half of the nineteenth century is witness to the intersection of various new conceptualizations of temporality, including those of physics, psychoanalysis, biology/physiology, archaeology, history, and evolution, as well as the emergent technologies of modernity. All pay homage, at some level, to the concept of irreversibility. This chapter explores the emerging conceptualization of time as an "arrow," focusing on the development of the idea of irreversibility in thermodynamics and its broader cultural impact. Irreversibility is significant not only as crucial rethinking of temporality but also—because its validity is statistical rather than causal—as the occasion of an epistemological break with traditional notions of determination. The work of Charles Sanders Peirce, as outlined in the previous chapter, is entirely consistent with this rethinking of causality, necessity, and determinism and with the new emphasis upon statistics. Here, I analyze statistics as rupturing classical ways of thinking the relation between the particular and the general, the individual and the mass, as a logic particularly appropriate for a mass culture. The alliance of thermodynamics with statistics yokes time to the domain of chance rather than destiny, somewhat parodoxically since irreversibility seems to connote rigidity, certainty, and directionality. Yet irreversibility is a probability rather than a certainty, and, in addition, its intimate association in physics with entropy allies it with increasing disorder and disorganization.

Film in its mainstream form seems to embody the very principle of irreversibility. At its most basic level, the film moves forward relentlessly, reproducing the familiar directionality of movements with regularity despite its capability of doing exactly the opposite. And even the relatively infrequent recourse to reversed time/movement in genres such as slapstick comedy is subject to the mechanized and regularized forward movement of the projector. As Jacques Aumont has pointed out, "From the outset filmic time was given as a time to which one submits and simultaneously as an acknowledged, identified time: unable to escape the time of projection, we nevertheless accept this time, recognize it as our own and experience it as such."[7] This irreversible linearity forms the substrate and support for any particular film's temporal experimentation with repetition, memory, projection, or stasis. Such a mechanical irreversibility also, however, forms the basis for film's affiliation with time as chance. The longer a shot is held, the more likely the unraveling of the profilmic as the controlled order of events, the more likely the intrusion of chance and the unexpected. This process is most apparent in the early cinema chronicling events, most famously that of Lumière, but the appeal to chance and time as disorder is also an attribute of Méliès's filmmaking practice. In the final section of this chapter I contest the classical polarization of Lumière and Méliès by rethinking their relation to chance and the contingent in time.

The discourse that enables the thinking of irreversibility has been pinpointed by many theorists and historians as that of thermodynamics. Before the elaboration of the laws of thermodynamics, physics had no formulations that allowed one to specify the directionality of time. The material world and its laws were analyzable without recourse to the dimension of the temporal. Newton's law of gravitation and Kepler's laws of planetary motion deal with processes that are symmetrical in time (this symmetry is a property not only of orbital motion, but of molecular collisions and nuclear reactions as well).[8] But thermodynamics, as the name suggests, deals with the phenomenon of heat dissipation, which, in the absence of an external source of energy—that is, in an isolated system—is a one-way process. Hot objects spontaneously lose heat to cooler objects. And this process is not reversible in a closed system. This is why, in physics, thermodynamics is the basis of the idea of an "arrow of time."

According to Michel Serres, who has consistently emphasized the crucial historical importance of thermodynamics in the nineteenth century, the concept of system and its relation to time is subject to historical change. A system may be logicomathematical, dependent upon the formulation of postulates and the elaboration of deductions from these postulates (the "classical idea of knowledge" for figures such as Descartes, Spinoza, or Leibniz). Such a system is completely independent of temporality as a variable. Or a system may be mechanical, consisting of a set characterized by stability despite the movement or variations of its objects (Laplace's definition of the solar system). Here, there is time, but its directionality is irrelevant. Reversing time will produce no significant physical or material change. But the third type of system, that of thermodynamics, based as it is on the circulation of energy and the production of movement, generates the notion of temporal irreversibility, its second law (of increasing entropy) dictating the ultimate "heat death" of the universe, a state of maximum entropy in which total equilibrium would mean the cessation of all process, work, change. According to Serres (and a number of other writers as well), thermodynamics arises as an attempt to explain, to theorize the work of the steam engine: "As soon as one can build them and theorize about them—steam or combustion engines, chemical, electrical, and turbine engines, and so forth—the notion of time changes . . . From this moment on, time is endowed with a direction. It is irreversible and drifts from order to disorder, or from difference to the dissolution or dissemination of a homogeneous mixture from which no energy, no force, and no motion can arise."[9] The one temporally specific field of physics emerges from the problematic of the machine.

Elaborated in the realm of physics in the 1840s, the two laws of thermodynamics have had an extraordinary impact—both subtle and explicit—on a range of fields including literature, biology, psychoanalysis, and information theory. The first law, commonly known as the conservation of energy, stipulates that energy may change in form, but the total quantity of that energy always remains constant—it cannot disappear altogether. Although this law was anticipated and "discovered" by various figures working at slightly different times in different places (for example, Sadi Carnot, James Prescott Joule, Robert Mayer), the figure most closely associated with it is Hermann von Helmholtz, who provided its mathematical formulation. The second law is also associated with several figures, including Helmholtz, Rudolf Clausius, and Sir William Thomson (Lord Kelvin). This law recognizes that usable energy ultimately and irreversibly exhausts itself in the process of transformation and dissipates, leading inevitably to the degeneration and death of a closed system. This is the law of entropy.

The two laws are at least seemingly inconsistent, and it could be said that their apparent contradiction in fact conditions the terms of understanding of the late nineteenth century. Anson Rabinbach argues that the tension between the two laws, their "paradoxical relation," defines the contours of modernity.[10] On the one hand, the law of conservation fuels the optimistic view of progress, of an ever-increasing efficiency and rational control over nature. On the other, the Second Law of Thermodynamics supports theories of inevitable decline and degeneration, of an ultimate descent into disorder and chaos that seems to be accelerated by developments within modernity. However, the two laws are only apparently contradictory, since the first concerns the quantity of energy while the second deals with its quality (that is, whether it is "usable" or not). The first law describes a system that has no necessary relation to temporality—whether progressive or regressive. It is the second law that makes the temporal dimension inescapable. Hence it would be more accurate to revise Rabinbach's argument to claim that both the idea of progress and the idea of degeneration and decline are intimately linked to each other and to the Second Law of Thermodynamics. As soon as the theory of energy is injected with temporal directionality, the ideas of both historical progress and historical decline become possible.[11]

It is not, however, as though there is a direct cause-and-effect relation between theoretical physics and history. Both thermodynamics and the disciplining of history in relation to issues of progress and degeneration emerge in the context of an ongoing Industrial Revolution, in which the issue of time becomes insistent and compelling, and in which the machine begins to destabilize traditional notions of work and production in line with the imperatives of a strengthening capitalism. While "work" had been a technical concept within classical physics (dynamics),[12] its contours begin to change as the focus is shifted to efficiency and loss in relation to the machine. Thermodynamics is about the inevitability of loss, of dissipation and hence the impossibility of a perfect machine. Yet it is also accompanied by the desire to minimize loss, to manage inevitability, and therefore to manage time.

The crucial position of the steam engine in the technological imaginary spawned by the Industrial Revolution affected the central importance of heat in thermodynamics. The fact that heat and work were perceived as equivalent suggested the basic principle of the transformability of energy. And it is energy that ultimately became *the* privileged concept in both laws of thermodynamics. This centrality of energy conferred upon the theory an astounding generality, allowing it not only to cover the various phenomena of physics—heat, light, electricity, and magnetism—but also to extend into the domains of other sciences dealing with energy, including biology and chemistry. According to P. M. Harman, "The fundamental status of energy derived from its immutability and convertibility, and from its unifying role in linking all physical phenomena within a web of energy transformations."[13] From the mid-nineteenth century on, thermodynamics functioned as a kind of master discourse that destabilized the boundary between the living and the nonliving, making the universe and the human body analogous to the extent that each serves as a system for the conservation, transformation, and deployment of energy (although the universe is a closed system while the human body is not). Energy and work were the passwords and constituted the basic elements of this expansive epistemology. Thermodynamics encouraged an intensive investigation of labor power (a concept first applied to machines and only later extended to the human body) and the allied concepts of work and fatigue. In that context, as Anson Rabinbach has thoroughly demonstrated, the working body became central, and Emil Kraepelin, one of the founders of psychophysics and a psychologist who made fatigue a central aspect of his investigations, could proclaim: "the nature of man is to be a tool . . . his vocation is to be set in his place and set to work."[14] One of the results of that thinking was the extensively and rigorously pursued time-and-motion studies of the turn of the century (to which Marey was a strong contributor), in which the central and determinant category was "homo faber."

Energy is ubiquitous and highly malleable, but the logical relations between the two laws of thermodynamics demand that it be divided into two critical categories—usable and unusable. The first law states that the *quantity* of energy will remain constant in an isolated system; it may change in form or nature but energy can neither be created, nor destroyed. Hence, when the second law claims that energy will inevitably dissipate, the notion of dissipation is not equivalent to destruction. When energy dissipates, it changes form so that it becomes unusable—that is, unable to produce work. This transformation levels differences so that, for instance, the flow of heat to a cooler space will in time cause equilibrium (according to the theory this will eventually lead to the death of the universe, its absolute stasis). Usable energy—that is, energy capable of producing work—is therefore defined in terms of the critical presence of differences. The gravitational energy in water is usable—it will turn the wheel of a mill, for instance—only if there is a difference of levels so that the water falls from one height to another. The gravitational energy in a body of water—a lake or the ocean—is unusable without these differences.

From this point of view, entropy can be defined as the annihilation of difference. As Richard Morris has pointed out, the second law can be stated somewhat differently so that it stipulates that in an isolated system, entropy will always increase (or, more accurately, since it sometimes remains constant, it will never decrease). An increase in entropy will be equivalent to a progressive loss of disequilibrium, and, therefore, "Entropy can be defined as the absence of disequilibrium."[15] This strikes one as a fairly convoluted definition, containing as it does a double negativity. According to this logic, the Second Law of Thermodynamics dictates what is effectively an increase in an absence—as entropy increases, there will be less and less difference. As Morris points out, it is not possible to simplify matters by defining entropy as equilibrium, because equilibrium is a final state, and entropy increases on the way to that state. There is no way of avoiding the fact that in a thermodynamic logic what is increasing is lack, or loss. Entropy is popularly understood in another, slightly different, negative sense as disorder, the second law prescribing (dictating) the continual increase of disorder in the universe. Here, disorder indicates a state in which there are no differences and hence no possibilities of categorization and knowledge—a bland and nondynamic homogeneity. The temporal irreversibility of the second law manifests itself in the diminishing possibility of differentiation, in the movement toward a state in which there would be no motor of change. Such a situation generates an epistemological imperative to multiply and intensify differences in the face of anxiety about the passage of time. Difference is perceived as both a social motor and a physical/mechanical one.

It is striking that many discussions of thermodynamics resort to film or video in an attempt to explicate the second law and to make the concept of entropy more accessible. Such a move indicates that film is in some sense popularly understood as *the* exemplar of temporal irreversibility, as the most effective means of clarifying the idea of an "arrow of time." For instance, in

François Jacob's discussion of thermodynamics and its relation to biological knowledge (including evolution), he states:

> In physics, the second law of thermodynamics imposes a direction on phenomena; no event can go in a direction different from that observed, for that would mean a decrease in entropy. No part of the universe's substance can return to a former condition, as might be imagined in a purely mechanical system such as an imaginary clock. In neither the organic nor the inanimate physical world can the film sequences disclosing evolution be run backwards.[16]

Similarly, in Warren Weaver's attempt to explain the significance of thermodynamics and, in particular, its impact on information theory, he also has recourse to film as an exemplary medium of temporality:

> In the physical sciences, the entropy associated with a situation is a measure of the degree of randomness, or of "shuffledness" if you will, in the situation; and the tendency of physical systems to become less and less organized, to become more and more perfectly shuffled, is so basic that Eddington argues that it is primarily this tendency which gives time its arrow—which would reveal to us, for example, whether a movie of the physical world is being run forward or backward.[17]

But the most elaborate and extensive use of the film/video illustration is in Richard Morris's explication of the concept of entropy in *Time's Arrows*. He opens the discussion by elaborating a fantasy in which an extraterrestrial space vessel moves close enough to the Earth to be reached by a space shuttle. Although there has clearly been some sort of accident and the crew has been dead for a long time, there are some discs resembling videotapes that seem to be recordings. Earth scientists can devise a means to play the discs, but it is not immediately obvious in which direction they should be played. The content of the first few discs—a planet rotating on its axis, a planet revolving around a star, an animated cartoon depicting either the collision of an alpha particle and a thorium-234 nucleus to form uranium-238 or the decay of a uranium-238 nucleus into thorium-234 and an alpha particle, a scene in which a number of unfamiliar-looking vehicles move around on a paved surface—gives the scientists no indication whatsoever which direction is forward and which backward. But they finally come upon a disc depicting a pair of tongs holding a hot, glowing piece of metal that gradually becomes dimmer, losing heat to the tongs and then its own surroundings. This immediately indicates to the scientists that they are playing the tape in the "right," that is, the forward, direction, since the Second Law of Thermodynamics stipulates that heat always flows spontaneously from hot objects to cool ones and never the reverse. The scenario functions for Morris as a means of demonstrating the radical importance of thermodynamics as an indicator of temporal direction in physics.

All these activations of film or video in the effort to explicate thermodynamics entail an assumption of referentiality—that is, knowledge of temporal directionality is linked to what are perceived as the specifically referential properties of film. The first two (the discourses of Jacob and Weaver) take for granted that film is a transparent window on the world, that it simply records physical processes of the material realm. Morris's use of film/video is somewhat more complicated, since two of his examples are animated cartoons, which would seem to diminish the significance of the medium's indexicality. Yet the examples of animation are not the decisive ones in terms of the determination of temporal direction (and in fact they could not be, since animation would raise undesirable questions concerning the fictional or nonfictional status of the representation). The argumentation of all these writers is precisely dependent upon *not* raising the issue of the filmic image's status as a representation. With respect to film's position as an exemplary illustration of the Second Law of Thermodynamics, irreversible temporality and referentiality are in collusion, or, more accurately, inextricable. Film incarnates the certainty and inevitability of temporal direction only at the cost of enslavement to its status as an indexical record. The automatic assumption that film indicates "real" or accurate temporal direction is coincident with the automatic assumption of its direct and unmediated referentiality.[18] From this point of view, the filmic image must be read as the imprint or trace of a specific moment in time.

In a sense, then, film has worked historically to familiarize the concept of temporal irreversibility, so much so that Ilya Prigogine and Isabelle Stengers can claim that the "strangeness" of classical (prethermodynamic) physics is equivalent to the "strangeness" of a film run backward.[19] But in the nineteenth century, in the discursive realms submitted to the codification of "science," irreversibility was radically unfamiliar and, in many respects, threatening.[20] Within classical physics (dynamics), time was fully reversible, making past and future equivalent. All change was reduced to the displacement from one position to another of material bodies along given trajectories. As Prigogine and Stengers have pointed out, the basic characteristics of trajectories are "lawfulness, determinism, and reversibility."[21] As long as the forces at work are known, one can deduce past and future states from any given initial state. Hence, "everything is given," as Prigogine and Stengers echo Bergson. The trajectory in classical dynamics is curiously static. Law and determinism within such a problematic can be formulated only at the expense of time, in a timeless order in which the effects of the movements, accelerations, and collisions of material objects are fully reversible. Alexandre Koyré describes motion in dynamics as "a motion unrelated to time or, more strangely, a motion which proceeds in an intemporal time—a motion as paradoxical as that of a change without change."[22] The notions of law and harmony that governed classical physics were mirrored in the life sciences by pre-Darwinian theories of harmony and necessity in the forms of living species.

Irreversibility, however, became a crucial concept in a number of disciplines in the nineteenth century, in biology (evolution), for example, as well as in thermodynamics. In its incarnation in physics, it is often thought of as the condition of possibility of thinking history. Before thermodynamics, according to Serres, the world was "without age": "The theory of heat, of motors and of reservoirs, assumes difference, mixture and irreversibility. History and entropy are invented in the same stroke. Here we have the new time, the tragic idea of a degradation, and the pathetic hope of a flow of life which would go in the opposite direction."[23] In the wake of the steam engine, thermodynamics responded to the concern with loss of energy and waste. Although the term *entropy* in itself appears neutral—it is derived from the Greek *en* (in) and *tropos* (turning), signaling a capacity for change, transformation—the widely used *dissipation* and *degradation* are not. Energy dissipates, it is degraded, with all the negative connotations associated with these terms. Entropy was the haunting underside of the nineteenth-century faith in progress. As Prigogine and Stengers point out, the model of nature for classical science was the clock; for nineteenth-century science, it was the engine running down, or the reservoir of energy always threatened with exhaustion.[24] Irreversibility here denotes the certainty of doom, the inevitable "heat death" of the universe. In Prigogine and Stenger's analysis, "the specific form in which time was introduced in physics, as a tendency toward homogeneity and death, reminds us more of ancient mythological and religious archetypes than of the progressive complexification and diversification described by biology and the social sciences."[25] They link the resuscitation of this ancient mythology to a deep anxiety in the nineteenth century about the rapidity of technological change and the consequent accelerated pace of everyday life. The leap from engine technology to cosmology would indicate something of the stakes of such anxiety about temporality.

The other major theory of irreversibility in the nineteenth century—the theory of evolution—produced a diametrically opposed understanding of time, to the extent that the work of Carnot and that of Darwin were often thought to be irreconcilable. Whereas irreversibility in thermodynamics leads to dissipation, dedifferentiation, and simplification (or leveling), irreversibility in evolution produces greater and greater diversification and complexity. Within biology, life itself is often seen as a contradiction of the Second Law of Thermodynamics and is situated as an instance of "negentropy."[26] On the other hand, evolution and thermodynamics share a large number of theoretical assumptions, and Ludwig Boltzmann (who was associated with the development of statistical thermodynamics) was a great admirer of Darwin. Temporal irreversibility is perhaps the major attribute shared by both theories. Once natural selection has been effected and a species has undergone a series of changes, that transformation is irreversible. According to Jacob, the species can undergo further changes, but it cannot return to its former state.[27] Furthermore, evolutionary theory deindividualizes; it focuses on large populations at the expense of the individual. Individual deviation or variation has meaning only if it has an impact on the species as a whole. Similarly, thermodynamics was developed as an explanation of macroscopic events. Although the second law is applicable only to isolated, closed systems, the closed system generally invoked is that of the universe (hence the cosmological consequences of increasing entropy). Thermodynamics also activates the law of large numbers in its reliance on statistics and probability. It purports to describe not the movements of individual molecules but the movements of large populations, which, over time, tend toward a state of least organization. Finally, both thermodynamics and evolutionary theory establish an intimate connection between contingency and law, undermining the foundations of determinism in physics and biology. It is the rare occurrence, the contingent fact of variation, which is subject to natural selection and hence "directs" the course of evolution. Nothing in the form of a species is preordained—it could have been different. Thermodynamics, instead of dealing with a cause-and-effect determinism, deals in probabilities; entropy or disorganization is the most probable state. Statistics is not simply an accouterment, a handy mathematical model for thermodynamics. It has a fundamental explanatory power. There is no secret law forbidding heat to flow from a cooler object to a hotter one, but this would be a great deal less probable than the reverse. According to François Jacob, "it never happens in practice, without being absolutely impossible in theory."[28]

There is a sense, then, in which the Second Law of Thermodynamics put the very idea of "law" into question, and this in fact may be its most important effect. According to Prigogine and Stengers, thermodynamics was at the origin of a reconceptualization of physics that shifted the emphasis from deterministic, reversible processes to stochastic, irreversible, and statistically describable ones.[29] The recourse to a statistical explanatory framework was, at least in part, linked to a strong resistance to the concept of irreversibility in the domain of physics. The Second Law of Thermodynamics contradicted the bases of the Newtonian heritage of classical dynamics, and could not be reconciled with its long-accepted laws and its intellectual triumphs. Skepticism about irreversibility was often linked to its association with macroscopic processes and hence with a fallible observer. In 1902 Josiah Gibbs provided a popular example buttressing the idea that irreversibility was inherently subjective.[30] If one puts a drop of black ink into water, the ink will dissolve and the water will soon look gray. Such a process appears to us as irreversible. However, if we could distinguish each molecule at the microscopic level, we would realize that the system remains heterogeneous. The scale of the heterogeneity has simply changed from the macroscopic, visible to the human eye, to the microscopic. Temporal irreversibility was perceived as an illusion (Einstein also strongly held this view) and due primarily to the limitations of our knowledge and perception. This view was strongly allied to the perception that the phenomena associated with the discovery of the Second Law of Thermodynamics—the friction, viscosity, and waste of the steam engine—were rectifiable and only temporarily a problem arising from our technical/technological incompetence. In contrast to the objective and stable laws of Newtonian physics, irreversibility emerged as "subjective."

The difficulty lay in the conceptual status accorded to a "law" that was not compatible with a classical dynamics readily seen as still applicable in many areas. The problem came to a head with the study of gases and heat in relation to the velocity of molecules. A given volume's heat is defined in relation to the *average* velocity of its molecules—fast-moving molecules being associated with heat, slow-moving molecules with coolness. But the collisions and the subsequent velocity of *individual* molecules will be randomly distributed, determined by the rules of classical dynamics. It is only at the level of large populations of molecules that heat will be observed to flow irreversibly toward cooler areas to reach thermal equilibrium (or maximum entropy). Hence, attempts to derive the Second Law of Thermodynamics from classical dynamics failed. The determination of collisions and velocity of individual molecules using Newtonian physics predicted nothing about the behavior of large volumes of gas. In 1871 James Clerk Maxwell tried to resolve the issue by demonstrating that, in the face of the failure of a dynamic explanation, a statistical method of calculation was required. He did so by producing a prosopopoeia (subsequently labeled "Maxwell's demon" by William Thomson).[31] Maxwell's demon was a finite being, like us, but with faculties "so sharpened that he can follow every molecule in its course."[32] Able to see individual molecules, he would be capable of sliding a frictionless door to allow fast-moving molecules to collect in the right-hand compartment of a gas-filled vessel and slow-moving molecules to congregate in the left-hand compartment. In this way, the demon would defeat the Second Law of Thermodynamics by maintaining a heat differential and hence decreasing entropy.[33]

The purpose of such a "thought experiment" was not to demonstrate that such a being does or could exist. While a being such as Maxwell's demon with sharper powers of observation/perception would be necessary to produce an *observable* flow of heat from a cold body to a warmer one, this happens spontaneously at the level of individual molecules, given their random motions. One of the effects of Maxwell's thought experiment was to demonstrate that the Second Law of Thermodynamics did not meet the criteria of strict causality or necessity. It dealt not with certainties, but with probabilities.[34] Maxwell claimed that the second law was an irreducibly statistical law. There was an unbridgeable gap between dynamics and thermodynamics. Because one could conceive of a mechanism (Maxwell's demon) that could violate the second law while remaining entirely consistent with the classical laws of mechanics, thermodynamics could not be described as a dynamic law that would describe the motions of individual molecules. Although it was possible that entropy would decrease in certain observable events/phenomena, it was highly improbable. Ludwig Boltzman also realized that the conceptual status of the second law was ambiguous in comparison with the secure status of the law of energy conservation. After several failed attempts to find a theorem in dynamics that could correspond to the second law, Boltzmann also became convinced by the early 1870s that it was an irreducibly statistical law. He redefined entropy as a measure of probability. Thermal equilibrium, or maximum entropy, was the most probable molecular distribution.

Maxwell's movement away from attributing significance to the motion of individual molecules in favor of calculating the behavior of large populations is often linked to the influence of Adolphe Quetelet, the founder of "social physics" and the inventor of the "average man."[35] Quetelet applied the well-known "bell-shaped curve," or Gaussian distribution, developed in astronomy, to social phenomena. For Quetelet, the bell-shaped curve was "the very expression of randomness."[36] In physics, the specification of thermodynamics as an essentially statistical law challenged the very nature of law. For this was a "law" based on contingency or chance, repudiating necessity and the logic of cause and effect. As Jacob points out, "with statistical mechanics, as with the theory of evolution, the notion of contingency became established in the very heart of nature," and "statistical thermodynamics completely transformed the way of looking at nature, mainly because it brought together and gave the status of related and measurable quantities to order and chance—two concepts which until then had been incompatible."[37] Conventional notions associated with law—continuity, necessity, determinism, reversibility—were displaced by an emphasis upon contingency, irreversibility, discontinuities, and probability.

The status of the individual was subject to a historic reconceptualization as well. Although a statistical epistemology might seem to negate the individual in favor of the mass, there is a sense in which it makes the individual more profoundly *individual,* characterized by irreducible differences, random attributes. For this reason—and because analysis of such an individual yields no usable knowledge—the statistical method renounces knowledge of the concrete individual and concentrates on large populations. For Jacob, this constitutes an affirmation of the individual over and against the type, and heralds a radical change in the very way of looking at objects. This transformation took place in the middle of the nineteenth century, and is seen most clearly in the rise of evolutionary theory and statistical thermodynamics. Jacob claims that there are two ways of conceptualizing a collection of objects of the same kind (such as molecules of a gas or organisms of the same species). Members of the group can be considered as essentially identical, all patterned on the same type. The type, not the individual member, constitutes the reality to be known. Any individual deviations or differences from the type are assumed to be negligible or insignificant. The second approach, according to Jacob, operates by positing the group as a collection of individuals who are unique, irreducibly different, never identical. The type does not exist: "There is no longer a pattern to which all individuals conform, but a composite picture, which merely summarizes the average of each individual's properties. What has to be known, then, is the population and its distribution as a whole. The average type is just an abstraction. Only individuals, with their particularities, differences and variations, have reality." According to Jacob, the passage from the first epistemology to the second "marked the beginning of modern scientific thought."[38] In evolution, no immutable type preordained the course of variation in species. Change was dependent upon contingency. In physics, rigidly deterministic laws were put in crisis. Jacob's reading pits an investment in the reality of the individual against an investment in the reality of the type. But it would be more accurate to speak of an aggregate of individuals who are subject to statistical explanation. Although only individuals, with their irreducible differences, have reality, it is an inconsequential reality—not epistemologically viable. Statistics refuses certainties, precision, and necessity in favor of tendencies, directions, and probabilities. It acknowledges and tolerates individual difference by transcending it.

The ambiguities and difficulties of the individual-versus-type paradigm become highly visible in the work of Quetelet. Quetelet was a Belgian astronomer and therefore highly familiar with the binomial, or Gaussian, curve of errors (the bell-shaped curve). The Gaussian curve was constructed in 1809 to trace and map inevitable errors in astronomical measurement, and to demonstrate that the distribution of random errors clustered around a central mean. Quetelet transferred the epistemological assumptions of the Gaussian curve to the realm of human and social measurement, arguing that it represented a fundamental social law and buttressed his idea of the "average man" *(homme type)*. The "average man" would be at the center of the curve, and all anomalies or extremes would be located at the edges. The movement from astronomical measurement to social measurement entailed, as Ian Hacking has shown, an enormous conceptual leap, one absolutely fundamental to the establishment of social statistics and its immense prestige from the 1800s on.

The Gaussian curve was utilized to obtain the measurement of a real entity (the position of one star or planet, for instance) as precisely as possible. Quetelet maintained that the same curve applied to the situation of measuring a single man's height. But he went further to claim that if one is confronted with a series of measurements of height, and they conform to the Gaussian curve (even if they do not represent the height of one man but the heights of different men within a given population), the "average height" produced by such a strategy will be a real quantity, the accurate measure of a real characteristic of a homogeneous population. As Hacking points out, "Here we pass from a real physical unknown, the height of one person, to a postulated reality, an objective property of a population at a time, its mean height or longevity or whatever." Although there has been a general consensus since Quetelet that there is no such thing as an "average man," the concept has nevertheless come to define the contours of real experience. Hacking claims that Quetelet

transformed the theory of measuring unknown physical quantities, with a definite probable error, into the theory of measuring ideal or abstract properties of a population. Because these could be subjected to the same formal techniques they became real quantities. This is a crucial step in the taming of chance. It began to turn statistical laws that were merely descriptive of large-scale regularities into laws of nature and society that dealt in underlying truths and causes.[39]

Quetelet's "average man" subsumes a host of individualities in a single figure, a quantity/number that exists nowhere but that performs work, resulting in a vast reconceptualization of reality (ultimately as predictable, manageable risk).[40] While Jacob may be right in insisting that within science (physics, biology) a statistical methodology constitutes a massive rejection of the idea of the type in favor of an avowal of irreducible individual difference, the social sciences from Quetelet to the present have been haunted by typology, reemerging surreptitiously through the concept of the "average man."

Statistics within Quetelet's "social physics" is also a way of acknowledging, paying homage to, singularity, contingency, individuality, while nevertheless overriding all of these. They do not constitute usable knowledge. Knowability is a function of probabilities, which, as Hacking shows, construct a new reality. The use of the Gaussian curve means that those characteristics (extreme shortness of height, for instance) that do not fall in the center of the bell curve are classified as "errors," with the center constituting the norm. Hence, in the nineteenth century, the growing recourse to statistics is allied with an obsession with various forms of social pathology—criminality, disease, prostitution, homosexuality. But above all, the "new reality" constructed by statistics, in an age of imperialism and anxieties about the redefinition of sexual identities, is one of particularly strategic groupings—nation, race, gender. It is not simply a question of measuring ideal or abstract properties of a population, but of creating the coherence of an imaginary or abstract population. "Average height" makes sense only if one assumes a well-defined homogeneous group within which values will cluster around a mean. The presumption of the classification and its unity confers intelligibility upon the statistical figuration. Hence, statistics makes it possible to define and control new populations and annexes its method to various forms of nationalism, imperialism, racism, and sexism.

Statistics, in its privileging of the purest, the most abstract of symbolical systems—the numerical, might seem to be very far removed from the indexical image, from photography and cinematography. But the power of the statistical method in the nineteenth century is evidenced by the work of Francis Galton and his attempt to merge a statistical epistemology with photography's predilection for the individual, the contingent. For Galton, photography allowed the visualization, the realization in effect, of Quetelet's *homme type*. In order to determine the ideal type of each race or group (the English, criminals, the consumptive, the Jew), he developed a method of composite portraiture, in which he made multiple exposures of different faces, carefully aligning the major features, on a single photographic plate. The human ability to recognize a single known face in a crowd of thousands is for Galton evidence of the great multiplicity and minuteness of individual differences: "The general expression of a face is the sum of a multitude of small details, which are viewed in such rapid succession that we seem to perceive them all at a single glance." For this reason, ordinary statistical methods will fail to uncover "the true physiognomy of a race." Composite portraiture, on the other hand, is able to isolate the general features of a type, which emerge with clarity, while it cancels out individual anomalies—it leaves "but a ghost of a trace of individual peculiarities." Galton attempted to distill a quality—criminality, insanity, Jewishness—as an essentially visible feature of the face. The tuberculosis patient, predictably enough, could be identified by an "ideal wan face."[41] Galton's primary interest was in the possibilities of eugenics, in cultivating the best exemplars of the English race in the face of a constant tendency toward social decline and degeneration, partially linked to the negative effects of modernity and partially to a general thermodynamic logic of entropy.[42] That Galton embraced the thermodynamic logic is seen in his celebration of energy as the most crucial characteristic to cultivate in any eugenics program: "Energy is an attribute of the higher races, being favoured beyond all other qualities by natural selection."[43]

Galton's achievement, idiosyncratic and historically marginal though it might have been, was to conjoin the work and configuration of the face, usually the very guarantee of individuality, to a statistical epistemology. His desire to embed the bell curve in a photographic form is manifest in his language: "It is the essential notion of a race that there should be some ideal typical form from which the individuals may deviate in all directions, but about which they chiefly cluster, and towards which their descendants will continue to cluster."[44] That "typical form" emerges with clarity and recognizability as long as a sufficient number of faces are superimposed. Any blurriness of the image is relegated to the margins and is effectively inessential (ears tend not to survive the process of composite portraiture). Allan Sekula has argued that Galton's relegation of blurring to the edges of the composite, when in fact it would occur over the entire surface, illuminates his epistemological bias: "Only an imagination that wanted to *see* a visual analogue of the binomial curve would make the mistake, finding the type at the center and the idiosyncratic and individual at the outer periphery."[45] Galton's composite portraiture is simultaneously a denial of the indexical status of the photograph in favor of its symbolic status (its ability to embody a type) and an exploitation of that indexicality (the photographic realism verifies, *authenticates* the reality of the type). Instead of an abstract, bland, and uncompelling binomial curve, one can "see with one's own eyes" the saturation of social reality with races and types, and the consequent necessity for eugenic direction. Sekula points to another figure of roughly the same period—Alphonse Bertillon, a Paris police official—who also attempted a merger of optics and statistics but in a diametrically opposed fashion. Rather than implanting the bell curve within the individual photograph, Bertillon accumulated vast numbers of photographs of criminals and developed a system of filing these photographs along with linguistic descriptions and physiological statistics. The purpose here was the recognition and identification of the criminal recidivist.

A confrontation with the overwhelming contingency of the medium—its ability to accumulate a hoard of uncataloguable details—results in the nineteenth century's urge to make photographic meaning accountable to a statistical epistemology. Statistics in this regard constitutes a form of reconciliation of law and contingency, as well as of the individual with the increasing centrality of a concept of the masses. It derives from an epistemology that forecloses knowledge of the individual while maintaining an absolute belief in his or her viability as irreducible difference. At the birth of mass culture, statistics regulate and manage the threat of overwhelming numbers. In his discussion of mechanical reproduction's destruction of the aura, Walter Benjamin aligns the social bases of such a decay with the growing importance of statistics. In a by now familiar definition, the aura is specified as "the unique phenomenon of a distance, however close it may be." Benjamin also allies the concept of aura with the notions of "presence," "unique existence," "authenticity," and the "authority of the object." The masses are endowed with a form of agency in the destruction of the aura—it is linked to their desire to bring things closer and their "bent toward overcoming the uniqueness of every reality by accepting its reproduction." Mechanical reproduction robs the object of its uniqueness and permanence:

> To pry an object from its shell, to destroy its aura, is the mark of a perception whose "sense of the universal equality of things" has increased to such a degree that it extracts it even from a unique object by means of reproduction. Thus is manifested in the field of perception what in the theoretical sphere is noticeable in the increasing importance of statistics. The adjustment of reality to the masses and of the masses to reality is a process of unlimited scope, as much for thinking as for perception.[46]

For Benjamin, statistics have a leveling effect. Through translation into an abstract numerical system in which all phenomena become comparable and hence "equal" to some degree, uniqueness and individuality are lost. Regardless of the rich multiplicity and contingency of photographic modes of representation, the technical process of reproduction reduces all things to a common denominator. They become *photographable,* and hence can circulate far from the time and space in which they were originally embedded. For Benjamin, the photograph does not have to be rigorously manipulated into a composite portrait, in the manner of Galton, in order to transcend/deny all individual aberrations or idiosyncrasies. Yet even Galton grounds his imagistic statistics in the acknowledgment of a multiplicity of minute individual differences that make recognition possible. Benjamin neglects the extent to which the individual plays a crucial role in the operation of statistics. The individual is there as a placeholder, a latent meaning or even potential determination (as in evolution), but one that does not *figure* as such in the production of knowledge. Similarly, contingency and the idea of uniqueness are critical to the signifying effect of photographic modes of representation and are not annihilated by the undeniable leveling effect of transforming the world into a series of photographs (a photographable reality).[47]

The cinema, by projecting the photograph into a temporal domain, brings into play yet another aspect of contingency—its relation to expectation and predictability. To the extent that statistics deals in probabilities, it engages the future. Thermodynamics, in effect, makes that future quite predictable; it is one of increasing entropy and hence randomness: "Time is linked by thermodynamics to ideas about organization and randomness. The flow of time becomes apparent because there is an inexorable tendency in any system left to its own devices for organization to diminish and randomness to increase."[48] Such irreversibility is not observable in the individual molecule but only at the level of the aggregate, the masses. Film has become the privileged illustration of irreversibility in so many physics textbooks because its history in its mainstream forms so readily allies it with referentiality, realism, and an associated idea of "common sense," or the probable/plausible (avant-garde films such as Paul Sharits' *Ray Gun Virus* or Tony Conrad's *The Flicker* are eminently reversible). The strangeness or disbelief experienced when one is confronted with images of a man walking backward or a diver jumping backward out of the water onto a pier acts as a guarantee of the ultimate reality of irreversibility. The film, driven by a machine, moves inexorably forward, demonstrating the inevitable nature of irreversibility.

The temporal irreversibility at issue here is, indeed, a mechanical one— that of the cinematic apparatus and its representation of movement. It is not narrative irreversibility, although it is arguable that narrative as a temporal form tends, overall, to corroborate the directionality, linearity, and hence irreversibility of time. Yet film narrative can and does depend upon the temporal aberrations of memories and projections, incarnated in flashbacks, flashforwards, and radical ellipses. Each of these, however, depends upon the cut, which allows the disarticulation of filmic time and profilmic time. Within the single shot, the two are glued together, and the primary marker of the passage of time is movement. The ability to represent movement is, of course, what distinguishes film from photography. Within the unit of time covered by the flashback, time is irreversible; the linear "forward" nature of movement is acknowledged and honored. This basic commitment to the irreversibility of movement subtends and supports all the various experimentations with narrative temporality that punctuate the history of cinema.[49] It is this basic commitment which impresses the spectator with the inexorably forward movement of film, with the "truth" of irreversibility.

To some extent, however, this expectation of irreversibility is a projection

backward of our contemporary experience of film spectatorship: in a dark-
ened theater, spectators are isolated and immobilized, in seats facing forward, while the film unwinds with no turning back. But in the earliest years
of the cinema there were several factors mitigating against such resolute irreversibility beyond the novelty "trick" of showing the occasional film backward. For the Vitascope, films were spliced end to end to make a continuous
band or loop. This allowed a brief film (fifteen to twenty seconds) to be
shown over and over again (sometimes while a second projector was being
threaded). Although the Lumière Cinématographe did not use loops, the
exhibitor could repeat a film if the audience demanded, since the scenes
were shown separately and fell into a basket instead of rolling onto a reel.[50]
As Charles Musser points out, "By projecting one-shot films in an endless
band, the vitascope emphasized movement and lifelike images at the expense of narrative." In this respect the cinema originally mimicked the temporal structure of the many optical toys that preceded it—the Zoetrope,
the Praxinoscope, the Thaumatrope, and so on. In the Zoetrope and the
Praxiniscope, the circular shape of the apparatus ensured repetition, while
the Stereopticon encouraged the repetitive gesture of exchanging cards in
the machine. But it was not very long (approximately one year, according to
Musser—the length of the cinema's "novelty period") before the cinema disengaged itself from the structure of temporal repetition. By 1897, according
to Musser, "Though not totally replaced, the endless-band technique of exhibition, typified by the vitascope, gave way to a more linear, singular unfolding of the film through the projector."[51] This was a function not simply
of technological development, but of the tendency toward sequencing of
film shots/scenes in exhibition. The difference between optical toys and the
cinema—that is, the cinema's possibility of expansive duration—came to
the fore in the earliest years.

In contrast, conditions of spectatorship or audience reception varied
widely according to the venue (fairground, storefront nickelodeon, church-
sponsored setting), and their stabilization, which took place slowly, was
overdetermined by a number of economic, aesthetic, and ideological factors.
Even if the form of the films had encouraged spectatorial absorption and
submission to an irreversible time, achieving these would have been difficult, given the often chaotic nature of the viewing situation. As Roy Rosenzweig's research on workers and leisure in Worcester at the turn of the cen-

tury has shown, working-class movie theater conduct was built on a long tradition ranging from behavior in saloons, to July Fourth picnics, to working-class parks.[52] This behavior was boisterous, lively, sociable, and interactive. The films were often a pretext for other types of amusements. Given the brevity of the films, schedules encouraged customers to drop in at various times. In other words, the relentless linearity of the film's forward movement, which became central later, had not yet displaced the temporality of the theater or viewing situation itself, in which "events" in the audience could compete with those on the screen. After 1907–08, gradual changes in movie theater architecture encouraged more sedate and directed spectatorship. Sloping as opposed to flat floors aimed attention at the screen. Classical styles of architecture for new theaters built from 1908 to 1916 inspired a new sense of control, order, and safety.[53] In the attempt to lure the middle and upper-middle classes to the movies, theater owners favored an architecture that supported the more restrained, less sociable behavior associated with those classes. By the time of the vogue in grandiose picture palaces in the 1920s, the organization of theater space, as well as the form of the films, ensured the dominance of the projected film's irreversible temporality.[54]

In physics, irreversibility has the character of a "law" only at the macroscopic level—where events are visible to human perception and can be *seen*.[55] This is why it was so readily labeled "subjective" by those clinging to the stability of classical Newtonian physics. At the microscopic level, where scientific technology and analysis dissect observable phenomena, and the individual and random nature of collisions between molecules becomes apparent, irreversibility is by no means assured. The cinema, much to Marey's dismay, reconfirms the human senses, recapitulates the common sense and common vision of the everyday. Its alliance with irreversibility is wedded to this dependence upon visibility and referentiality. Nevertheless, as Benjamin attempted to stress with his concept of the optical unconscious, cinema was capable of much more. Through slow motion, microscopic photography, and other "special effects," cinema could make visible what was not in ordinary, everyday experience. The section of reversed film in *The Artist's Dilemma* is just such a special effect, making visible what we do not ordinarily see—a reversed temporality. The clown/demon of the Edison film is like Maxwell's demon; just as Maxwell's demon defeats the law of increasing entropy, forcing organization out of randomness, "Edison's demon" makes an image of a woman emerge from a reversed time. With his broad strokes of the paintbrush, the clown/demon undoes the work of time. The fact that it is an image of a woman is by no means unimportant. For the spectacle of the woman has historically acted as an impediment to the linear narrative trajectory in film.[56]

The "special effect" in *The Artist's Dilemma,* however, is ultimately subordinated to a narrative logic that is weaker—or even nonexistent—in the vast majority of films in the genre to which it belongs, the magic film. This genre is associated primarily with the work of Georges Méliès, but it also encompasses a host of imitations, including preeminently Pathé in France and Edison in the United States. The magic film is structured by repetition, based on the alternation of presence and absence rather than a linear forward trajectory.[57] Its primary "special effect" is the substitution splice. A shot of a woman dancing followed by a shot of the same space without the woman will be read as her appearance and sudden disappearance. If the second shot is that of a magician, the shot will be read as the transformation of the woman *into* the magician. The cut will not be seen. Méliès' "invisible editing" preceded that of the classical continuity system by many years. The difference between the two is that in Méliès' films, the frame is static and the space is completely homogeneous across the cut; the manipulation is in the dimension of time.[58] Méliès' 1899 *The Conjurer (Le Magicien),* for example, centers on two characters, a ballerina and a magician, each of whom appears and disappears or is transformed into the other. At one point the woman "becomes" a pile of confetti—all within the same static frame of a space resembling a stage, the characters facing toward the audience/camera. Even in the more rigorously narrative films such as *A Trip to the Moon* (1902) or *The Palace of the Arabian Nights* (1905), special effects or tricks take on a crucial role and often impede the linear movement of the film. The aesthetic is one of implausibility, of impossible things happening in a world in which impossibility is the norm. As Paul Hammond points out,

> Méliès' aesthetic consists of periodical dislocations, of spectacular, metamorphic images supported by subservient ones, of lawless unpredictable pantomime . . .
>
> An object can be transformed either instantaneously or gradually into another object; an object can grow or diminish before our eyes,

while the rest of the image remains a constant size; an object, usually human, can disintegrate into its parts, then these can assume a life of their own; an inanimate object can begin to move and an animate one to defy the laws of gravity; and an object can appear or disappear instantaneously or gradually.[59]

Méliès' work elaborates the instability and unpredictability of the phenomenal world. Objects and human beings have difficulty retaining their identity. There is an active resistance to the plausible or probable. The popularity of the magic show in the late nineteenth century (Robert Houdin, Maskelyne and Cooke) is the underside of fears about an encroaching science, a science attributed with powers that, combined with new technologies, could potentially transform everyday life. Magic is opposed to science in its celebration of mystery, of unknowability, of the impossibility of connecting cause to effect, indeed, of causeless effects. Magic seeks to distance effects from causes and to extol singularity, instability, undecidability.

Lucy Fischer and Linda Williams have each claimed, albeit in very different ways, that the figure of the magician/Méliès exerts control over the female body in the face of its potential threat. While Fischer argues that the magician's control over the appearance and disappearance of the female body is a manifestation of envy of the female procreative function, Williams links the magician's ability to orchestrate the visibility of men and women *and* objects to the psychical mechanism of fetishism, as a defense against castration anxiety.[60] But I think it is crucial to be sensitive to the films' work as a *dramatization* of control and its loss. Although the magician figure has varying levels of control in the films (at times he is surprised by objects or persons which escape his mastery—*The Treasures of Satan* [1902], *Extraordinary Illusions* [1903], *A Trip to the Moon* [1902]), the environment is always one of ceaseless transformation, of the instability of identity. The mise-en-scène is one of chance and contingency, where identity does not imply duration. The magic films are, in fact, coming to grips with a science that increasingly diminishes confidence in necessity and determinism in favor of tendencies and probabilities. In a way, they both resist and confirm that science. Centering upon the figure of the woman, the films play out an epistemological crisis provoked by the seemingly limitless advances of science.[61] But they pit themselves against the statistical transformation of everyday life, against the reign of the probable, preferring to insist upon the representational viability of implausibility. The magic film must be seen in the context not only of the magic theater of the nineteenth century, but also of the carnival attractions and amusements with which early films competed. The freak show, in particular, with its bearded women, dwarves, limbless human beings, and so on, constituted a morbid play with Quetelet's bell curve, dwelling on its edges or excesses, both refusing and confirming its assertion of a norm. Similarly, in a Méliès film, what is most probable is the improbable, the excessive, the stochastic.

Histories of the cinema have traditionally pitted Méliès against Lumière, situating them as the "fathers" of two tendencies followed by later films. In this account, Méliès represents fantasy and the fantastic, the Ur-text of all genres that celebrate the "magic" effects of fictional cinema, while Lumière is said to anticipate the insistence upon realism, particularly in documentary films. Undoubtedly, the filmmaking practices of the two are quite divergent, particularly with respect to their relation to time. Lumière films honor the notion of "real time," the ability of cinema to inscribe ordinary everyday movements with their familiar duration. In Méliès time is above all *extraordinary,* elastic, producing unpredictable effects, insisting upon the uncanny instantaneity of appearance, disappearance, and transformation. Historically, classical cinema has confirmed Lumière's status as the victor. It has reaffirmed the technological irreversibility of the medium with the second-order irreversibility of narrative, and consolidated the filmic centrality of ordinary movement. The "special effect," which for Méliès was the raison d'être of film, was progressively marginalized, localized, and subdued in the classical form.

Nevertheless, it is crucial to disrupt this teleological history by reflecting upon what is usually neglected—that which conjoins Lumière and Méliès and sets their work radically apart from, rather than as progenitors of, the cinema that follows them.[62] Both make contingency central to their representational practice in a medium in which the experience of temporality is crucial. The theory of entropy in thermodynamics has insistently proclaimed the inextricability of time and randomness, time and contingency. Time's relentless movement is synonymous with the dissolving of organization, the dominance of the random and uncontrolled. It is the potential of time to gnaw away at organization, and this potential becomes most evident in the long take and its inscription of "real time." As the camera holds on the departing boat in Lumière's *A Boat Leaving Harbor* (*Barque sortant du port*, 1897), the sheer duration of filmic time allows for the random event, the surprise of the unexpected wave. This representation of time carries with it both the frisson and the threat/anxiety of the unexpected and is culturally tolerable only for a very brief period at the turn of the century. In the classical cinema, the cut aborts the problem of an excess of the random, of chance in time.

Méliès' relation to contingency and the random event is somewhat different. In spite of the extensive control and mastery exhibited in Méliès' films, they dramatize—often quite explicitly—the effect of a loss of control. The inexplicable appearances and disappearances of bodies and objects, the transformation of entities into each other, the independent action of limbs, and unexpected exaggerations of scale all pay homage to contingency despite the fact that they are carefully orchestrated. Given this effect of contingency, so dominant in his filmmaking practice, it is striking that Méliès' own account, in 1906, of the discovery of stop-motion cinematography or the substitution trick makes it hinge on an accident, a contingency.

> One day, when I was photographing as usual at the Place de l'Opéra, the camera I used at the beginning (a primitive one in which the film tore or frequently caught and refused to advance) jammed and produced an unexpected result; a minute was needed to disengage the film and to make the camera work again. During this minute, the passersby, a horse trolley, and the vehicles had, of course, changed positions. In projecting the strip, rejoined at the point of the break, I suddenly saw a Madeleine-Bastille trolley change into a hearse and men changed into women.[63]

Although this account is undoubtedly apocryphal, it has had a certain discursive resilience and appears frequently in surveys of film history, indicating the lure of contingency as an explanation.[64] Méliès constructs a history whose effect is similar to that of his films—a history in which a central component of his signifying practice is allegedly based on an accident, an error. In this account, a chance event is transformed into an innovation and, from there, into a system. The historical strength of this anecdote, whether it is accurate or not, indicates a cultural investment in the link between contingency and system. The camera's function, for Méliès, was, in a sense, like that of Lumière—to register contingency, to transform it into a representational system while maintaining both its threat and its allure.

The celebration of the unexpected chance event—the implausibility of a Méliès film—and the risky duration of a Lumière film, which opens the stage for contingency, are resolutely rejected by the classical narrative system. Narrative binds any access to the contingent and adds a second-order level of irreversibility that seems to confirm its own historical inevitability (so much so that traditional histories of cinema do not question the idea of "progress" toward a narrative form). Lumière and Méliès certainly can be (and have been) read as contributing to a cumulative process of advancing and "perfecting" cinematic form. But they are more compellingly read as aberrations, moments of resistance, symptoms of the nineteenth-century epistemological crisis that undermined ideas of law, necessity, and determinism. Against this, the classical cinema allies itself with the logic of statistics, as a way of measuring and hence mapping chance events, contingency.

Statistics emerges as a way of coping with the acknowledgment of the irreducibility of individual difference and deviation, of a contingency unassimilable to traditional notions of law or cause. It preserves the idea of an unknowable or unrepresentable individual deviation as the guarantee of the necessity of its own method—the mapping or graphing of large numbers, of masses, of aggregates. It is an epistemology well suited to a mass culture. And the forms of representation that constitute this mass culture do not escape its logic. The classical cinema, in line with the logic of statistics, acknowledges the force of contingency and mobilizes chance, but ultimately it overrides both. This process allows for a containment of difference that is astonishingly flexible, since it provides a mechanism for thinking the coherence of varying groups, varying audiences. In the cinema, as in statistics, both chance and order become measurable and hence comparable, compatible. The temporal contingency celebrated by Méliès and Lumière is tamed through its incorporation into a rigidly codified system of producing a temporality that can fully absorb the spectator. Foucault has classified the cinema, along with the beach, the museum, the fairground, the cemetery, and other locations, as a form of *heterotopia*—an other space that is adjacent to, but experientially detached from and "absolutely different from," the space of ordinary everyday life.[65] Heterotopias also, according to Foucault, open onto *heterochronies,* since they can fully function only when their inhabitants experience a radical break with their traditional time. But the time of classical cinema, clearly manufactured for the desires of the spectator seated in the timeless space of the theater, is disconcertingly familiar insofar as it consistently reaffirms the plausibility, the probability, the irreversibility, and the fundamental recognizability of "real time." Classical form in the cinema has functioned to restabilize a time subject to multiple disruptions in the nineteenth century's confrontation with the epistemological implications of the loss of determinism and law. But the traces of these disruptions are still legible in many of the earliest films.

5

Dead Time, or the
Concept of the Event

Because a fascination with contingency raises the specter of pure loss, the possibility of complete obliteration of the passing moment, the degradation of meaning, it also elicits a desire for its opposite—the possibility of structure. Jean-François Lyotard claims that modernity is "a way of shaping a sequence of moments in such a way that it accepts a high rate of contingency."[1] In this definition, contingency coexists happily with the process of "shaping." In the same way, the concept of the *event* is on the cusp between contingency and structure, history and theory. Although the term *event* implies the fortuitous, the accidental, transience, and unpredictability (as in "events overtake us"), it also can be used to connote a high degree of constructedness, as in the notions of a media event or social event. The *Oxford English Dictionary* traces the etymological roots of *event* to the Latin *eventus,* occurrence, issue, and the French *évenir,* to come out, happen, result. The event is a deictic marker of time, a "this is happening, this is taking place." As such, it is pure indication, deprived of meaning. In Freudian psychoanalysis, trauma is the consequence of the nonassimilation of an event that has its psychical impact years later, after the fact. But the event somehow persists, in a semiotic limbo, as a kernel of the real that awaits only a second event whose collision with the first generates readability. In a sense, any event is by its nature that which is unassimilable, that which resists meaning, that which, like the index, serves primarily as an assurance of the real— "something is happening." It allies itself with the factual, with history. Hence the event finds itself on the side of diachrony rather than synchrony. Time itself resists structure.

Insofar as the cinema presented itself as the indexical record of time, it allied itself with the event and the unfolding of events as aleatory, stochastic, contingent. It was capable of trapping events in all their unpredictability and pure factualness. However, the fact of its own finitude—the limits imposed by both the frame and the length of the reel—resulted in the necessity of conceiving the event simultaneously in terms of structure, as a unit of time, as not simply a happening, but a significant happening that nevertheless remained tinged by the contingent, by the unassimilable. This curious merger of contingency and structure lends specificity to the early formations of cinematic temporality.

My aim here is to investigate the temporalities of the early cinema, to try to recover something of their historical and representational novelty, as well as their destabilizing potential. The excesses of the discursive rhetoric that greeted the cinema, its invocation of the grandiose tropes of life, death, waste, and eternity, as well as its elicitation of both fascination and antipathy, indicate the traumatic nature of its cultural/representational intervention. I have already discussed the temporality of the apparatus and its links to the temporality of reception in Chapter 4. Here my main concern is with the cinematic image as a representation *of* time, focusing on the cinematic construction of the event as the most condensed and semantically wealthy unit of time, but also as the site of intense internal contradictions.

In contrast to the security and certainty of the irreversible flow of time incarnated in the projector's relentless forward movement, there is an intolerable instability in the image's representation of temporality (where one might be led to expect, in fact, a grounding referentiality). This instability is linked to the early cinema's predilection for the contingent and the resistance the contingent offers to any notion of structuration. *The Artist's Dilemma* (discussed in Chapter 4), to the extent that it incorporates a form of narrative logic, is already an example of a somewhat "late" development in the emerging cinema. Although magic films were quite popular, many of the earliest films were in fact "occasional" films, dealing in a documentary fashion with an incident, a place, an activity—the stuff of everyday life. The overwhelming hegemony of narrative in the later Hollywood cinema of the classical era led earlier film historians to construct a teleology that organized silent films and hierarchized them according to their ability to anticipate the dominant narrative function and "invent," or "discover," its most salient signifying strategies. More recently, film historians such as Charles Musser and Tom Gunning have pointed out that this teleological approach tends to mask the fact that the dominant genre of the early silent cinema was the actuality, or topical film, which dealt with current events or incidents of general interest (the demolition of buildings, fires, the aftermath of natural disasters such as floods, prizefights, as well as family scenes, work scenes, and travelogues, or scenics). Although there is some debate about the precise timing of the transition, it is clear that sometime between 1902–03 and 1907 the popularity of actualities declined and narrative films began to take precedence in the various studios' productions. This transition indicates a crucial representational shift. But for a brief time the cinema seemed to be preoccupied with the minute examination of the realm of the contingent, persistently displaying the camera's aptitude for recording.

This predilection for the contingent is yoked to the photographic base of the cinema. Historical analyses of photography consistently demonstrate photography's inclination toward the contingent, the particular, the detail. For Peter Galassi, photography is simply the culmination of a movement in the history of art away from the general and schematic, and toward the precise, the partial, the transient, and embodied view. In the two centuries preceding the birth of photography, artistic representation strove "to present a new and fundamentally modern pictorial syntax of immediate, synoptic perceptions and discontinuous, unexpected forms. It is the syntax of an art devoted to the singular and contingent, rather than the universal and stable. It is also the syntax of photography." In Galassi's argument, the technology of photography itself constitutes an instant consolidation and stabilization of a form of perception arduously and painstakingly developed, with numerous lags and setbacks over a protracted period, in art. Photographic technology is the automatic, unthinking guarantee of the predilection for the contingent: "In photography, the camera's inability to compose rendered the old standards nearly obsolete from the outset."[2] Such a quasi-technological determinism solders the photographic to the contingent. But whether or not the camera is in fact incapable of composing (a notion subject to debate, especially given the history of "art photography"), the specificity of photography as a representational form has been, and continues to be, situated as a privileged link to the contingent.

It is a theme that recurs continually in discourses on photography. In "A Small History of Photography" (1931), Benjamin claims: "No matter how artful the photographer, no matter how carefully posed his subject, the beholder feels an irresistible urge to search such a picture for the tiny spark of contingency, of the Here and Now, with which reality has so to speak seared the subject." Writing in 1927, Siegfried Kracauer examines the role of the detail, the accessory, in photography and argues that the photograph "must be essentially associated with the moment in time at which it came into existence."[3] Such an appeal to the indexicality of the photograph grounds Roland Barthes's more recent investigation of photography in *Camera Lucida* and underwrites the very category of the *"punctum"* (the unstructured, unanticipated detail that fascinates the individual spectator).[4]

But the analysis of photography's alliance with contingency is predicated upon the acknowledgment that photography freezes a moment in time (Kracauer's "essential" association with the "moment in time in which it came into existence"). In a sense, as Barthes has argued, the photograph is imbued with an immediate "pastness." In the cinema, the appeal to contingency is from the start saturated with temporality. Filmic duration is the factor that leads Barthes to posit the absoluteness of the gap between photography and film as modes of representation; their temporal references are distinct and opposed. Whereas photography is inevitably in the past tense, evoking the recognition of a *"having-been-there,"* the cinema makes an inexorable appeal to the present tense—a *"being-there* of the thing."[5] Yet Barthes is wrong or, at the very least, incomplete. For there are always at least two temporalities at work in film. Accompanying the spectatorial experience of the present tense of the filmic flow is the recognition that the images were produced at a particular time, that they are inevitably stained with their own historicity. This is what allows film to age—quickly and visibly—in a way similar to that of the photograph. Not only does the technology itself become "dated" (the use of black and white, Cinemascope, film noir lighting), but the contents of the image inevitably bear the traces of the moment at which they were produced (fashion, cars, interior design, architecture). As André Gaudreault points out, unlike literature, a fiction film is "necessarily compelled to give an account of some sort of reality—that is, the one that appeared in front of the camera—even though it has been disguised in a fiction in order to be recorded," and "it is indeed by using portions of historical time that cinema builds up *fictional* time, hence the always-already-given historiographical character of cinematographic time."[6] In this respect the cinema's alliance with contingency, like that of photography, would appear to be irreducible.

The plethora of actualities produced between 1895 and 1904–05 testifies to the strength of such a recognition. Seemingly *anything* could constitute the occasion for a film—most famously, perhaps, the simple activity of workers leaving a factory, the arrival of a train, a snowball fight, children swimming, feeding a baby, a bargain day at a department store, delivering newspapers, bass fishing, and the like. The cinema was assigned the task of producing a record of time that allowed for the spontaneous and unexpected—a look at the camera, a shadowy figure passing in front of the lens. What was intended as "event" could, at least theoretically, be overshadowed. This is not to suggest, however, that actualities were uncomposed or unstructured, that they did in fact constitute simply a transparent record. As Thomas Elsaesser points out, "Actualities obliged the film-maker to create, even as he records an event, a specific sequential or spatial logic, which becomes in some sense the event's (intensified) abstracted representation, as opposed to reproducing its (extensive) duration."[7] However, Elsaesser's claim is haunted by the difficulties and contradictions that always seem to adhere to the concept of the event. The event precedes its record; it possesses its own duration, which can, in a subsequent moment, be intensified or abstracted. The argument enacts a theoretical (and popular) tendency to situate the event as the site of residence of the contingent (a tendency to which I will return). Nevertheless, it would be more accurate to note that the cinema, together with other technologies of modernity, is instrumental in producing and corroborating an investment in events, in dividing temporality to elicit eventful and uneventful time. The confusion of construction and contingency around the concept of the event is crucial in the historical elaboration of a cinematic syntax. At the turn of the century, contingency is both lure and threat, and this double valence is played out in the rapid representational transformations of the cinema. The embarrassment of contingency is that it is everywhere and that it everywhere poses the threat of an evacuation of meaning. The concept of the event provides a limit—not everything is equally filmable—and reinvests the contingent with significance. The contingent is, in effect, harnessed.

In this respect, the short-lived genre of the actuality provides a particularly fertile field of investigation, since it harbors the contradictory dream of re-presenting the contingent. The inscription of the contingent in two early actualities (one at the scene of the event, the other reenacted) has powerful implications for the conceptualization of the cinema's relation to time, its status as a quite precise type of technology of temporality. The films are *Electrocuting an Elephant* (Edison, 1903) and *Execution of Czolgosz, with Panorama of Auburn Prison* (Porter/Edison, 1901). Both films inhabit the particularly popular subgenre of the execution film, which included titles such as *Execution by Hanging* (Mutoscope/Biograph, 1905), *Reading the Death Sentence* (Mutoscope/Biograph, 1905), *Execution of a Spy* (Mutoscope/Biograph, 1902), *Beheading the Chinese Prisoner* (Lubin, 1900), and *The Execution of Mary Queen of Scots* (Edison, 1895).[8] The subgenre manifests an intense fascination with the representation of death, or the conjunction of life and death (contemporary sources describe the paradox of the image of death in a medium that makes represented bodies so "life-like").[9] Death and the contingent have something in common insofar as both are often situated as that which is unassimilable to meaning.[10] Death would seem to mark the insistence and intractability of the real in representation.

Electrocuting an Elephant utilizes authentic footage of the execution of an elephant who had killed three men. The film begins as the elephant is led toward the camera. The camera pans to the right to keep the elephant in frame, and the elephant effectively walks into a close-up. There is then a jump cut (probably caused by a camera stoppage to elide the time necessary to attach the animal to the electrocuting apparatus). In the following shot, the elephant stands facing the camera, tied down, with two of her feet attached to wooden sandals. A sign in the background advertises Luna Park as the "Heart of Coney Island." Suddenly, smoke rises from the elephant's feet and envelops her as she stiffens and collapses forward (Figure 5.1). A shadowy figure passes in front of the camera, which holds on the scene a while longer as the elephant produces a few more jerks and twitches. *Electrocuting an Elephant* was released on January 12, 1903. The *New York World* of January 5 reported the incident: "While fifteen hundred persons looked on in breathless excitement, an electric bolt of 6,000 volts sent Topsy, the man-killing elephant, staggering to the ground yesterday afternoon at Luna Park, Coney Island. With her own life [she] paid for the lives of the three men she had killed . . . It was all over in a moment." The newspaper account provides an additional detail that underlines the fascination of electricity as a lethal weapon: "Joseph Johansen, the electrician in charge of the Edison electric-light station, narrowly escaped death in turning the switches that threw the entire voltage into the wire that was to carry death to Topsy. As he threw the

5.1 *Electrocuting an Elephant* (1903). Edison.
Photograph by Patrick G. Loughney. Courtesy
American Federation of the Arts.

last switch he got the full force of the current through his arm and down
his right side to the calf of his leg."[11] The reference to the fifteen hundred
persons looking on "in breathless excitement" indicates that the elephant's
death constituted a spectacle for the Coney Island audience as well. The crucial difference is that the film managed to reach an audience not physically
present at the scene, as well as to act as an indexical record of Topsy's
death.[12] And although the newspaper account reached its audience faster, the
film allowed spectators not actually present at the event to see with their
own eyes the exhibition of an elephant's death throes. Hence the nickname
given to the early cinema—the "visual newspaper."[13]

The Execution of Czolgosz also exploits an interest in current events. On
September 6, 1901, while President McKinley was visiting the Pan-American

Exposition in Buffalo, New York, he was shot by the Cleveland anarchist Leon Czolgosz and died eight days later. Czolgosz was tried, found guilty, and executed on October 29. An Edison camera crew was present in Buffalo with a special concession to cover the exposition. A number of short films, including one of McKinley's speeches, a panorama of the crowd outside the Temple of Music after the announcement of the shooting, and the travels of McKinley's body from Buffalo to Washington to his hometown in Canton, Ohio, were released by the company. Edison continued to exploit interest in the assassination by producing a reenactment of the assassin's execution, whose complete title was *Execution of Czolgosz, with Panorama of Auburn Prison*. It is clear that Edison would have liked to film the actual execution, or at least Czolgosz entering the death chamber, but in the absence of permission to do so the crew had to settle for a panorama of the prison walls taken the morning of the execution joined with a reenactment of the electrocution, which the company labeled "a realistic imitation of the last scene in the electric chair."[14] The film begins with a pan following a train moving in front of the prison walls (Figure 5.2). There is a jump cut (possibly indicating only missing footage) to the same type of pan moving along a stationary train (Figure 5.3) and ending after the last empty car. The next shot is a pan, also moving to the right, over the massive prison walls (Figure 5.4), ending with the image of bare trees in the prison yard. There is a dissolve to the next shot, in which Czolgosz waits in his cell (Figure 5.5). Prison guards stand motionless on the right side of the frame and begin to move toward the cell several seconds after the initiation of the shot. As they approach, Czolgosz shrinks back. The guards lead him from the cell (Figure 5.6) and exit frame right. In the second interior shot, the electric chair is prominently centered in the frame, and the state electrician, wardens, and doctor are making a final test of the electricity with a bank of electric light bulbs (Figure 5.7). The bulbs are removed, and Czolgosz is escorted into the frame from the right. He stumbles briefly as he is seated in the chair and is strapped in. The warden gives the signal, the electric switch is pulled, and Czolgosz heaves three times and is still (Figure 5.8). The warden and doctor confirm that he is dead (Figure 5.9).

The two films have a great deal in common. Both exhibit a marked fascination with electricity as a conveyor of death. In the 1880s, the electric chair had become the socially acceptable form of execution, and at the turn of the

5.2 *Execution of Czolgosz, with Panorama of Auburn Prison* (1901). Porter/Edison. Photograph by Charles Musser. Courtesy Motion Picture, Broadcasting, and Recorded Sound Division, Library of Congress.

5.3 *Execution of Czolgosz, with Panorama of Auburn Prison.*

5.4 *Execution of Czolgosz, with Panorama of Auburn Prison.*

5.5 *Execution of Czolgosz, with Panorama of Auburn Prison.*

5.6 *Execution of Czolgosz, with Panorama of Auburn Prison.*

5.7 *Execution of Czolgosz, with Panorama of Auburn Prison.*

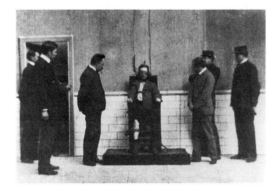

5.8 *Execution of Czolgosz, with Panorama of Auburn Prison.*

5.9 *Execution of Czolgosz, with Panorama of Auburn Prison.*

century, electricity was still an intriguing phenomenon in its own right. David E. Nye outlines some of the aspects of this fascination: "Electricity was the sign of Edison's genius, the wonder of the age, the hallmark of progress. It was a mysterious power Americans had long connected to magnetism, the nervous system, heat, power, lightning, sex, health, and light. One of Nathaniel Hawthorne's characters exclaimed, 'Then there is electricity, the demon, the angel, the mighty physical power, the all-pervading intelligence!' He went on: 'Is it a fact—or have I dreamt it—that, by means of electricity, the world of matter has become a great nerve, vibrating thousands of miles in a breathless point of time?'" As David Levy has pointed out, it may have seemed particularly appropriate to use electricity to execute McKinley's assassin. Part of McKinley's speech praised the advances of modern technology, and the exposition constituted the first use of electricity for display lighting. Niagara Falls provided the power, and part of the exposition included the 405-foot Electric Tower with 35,000 light bulbs.[15] Similarly, the *New York World* underlined the power and danger of electricity in emphasizing the injury sustained by the electrician who threw the switch to electrocute Topsy. In the face of the massive size and sheer physical resistance represented by an elephant, electricity suggests an almost magical lethal force.

Electricity signifies not only a technological form of death, but also a compression of time and process. For electricity seems to effectively annihilate delay, the distance between cause and effect, and to evoke the idea of the instantaneous. Mark Seltzer describes the impact of electricity at the turn of the century:

> The electric switch, ready to hand, promises to reconnect the interrupted links between conception and execution, agency and expression. Such a violent immediacy posits an identity between signal and act and an identity between communication and execution—"execution" in its several senses. It would be possible to trace out, along these lines, the fascination with the sense of immediacy and of the pure present conveyed by the electric technology's "magical" and lightning transgression of the barriers of time and distance.[16]

This "fascination with the sense of immediacy and of the pure present" is associated not only with electric technology but with the cinema itself as a technology of images that seem automatically to connote a certain presence. The image is registered instantly, apparently without intermediary, and conveys in its screening a sense of the immediacy of the real, which is confirmed in the popularity of actualities. The actuality would seem to answer the question "What is the cinema for?" with a conception of the cinema as document of the real, capturing and fixing a moment. For Walter Benjamin, flipping an electric switch is only one of a series of gestures made possible by new technologies that had a major impact upon the shape of modernity: "Of the countless movements of switching, inserting, pressing and the like, the 'snapping' of the photographer has had the greatest consequences. A touch of the finger now sufficed to fix an event for an unlimited period of time. The camera gave the moment a posthumous shock, as it were."[17] Benjamin is referring to still photography here, but later he designates "shock" as a formal principle of film. The concept of "giving the moment a posthumous shock" implies that when photographed or filmed, time is already dead. In executing images, one also executes time.

A second attribute shared by the two films is their status as the orchestration of guilt and punishment around the concept of a criminality understood in relation to otherness. Czolgosz is tinged with the threat of the foreign, the immigrant, the unfamiliar.[18] Topsy's name ineluctably reverberates with the racial politics of *Uncle Tom's Cabin* as well as with the colonialist aspirations distilled in the representational repertoire of the circus. Benjamin claimed that Eugène Atget's work demonstrated the close allegiance between the space of photography and the scene of a crime.[19] The transformation of the contingent into evidence allies it with a legal hermeneutics. When any detail can become the sign of a crime, can make legible guilt or innocence, photographic and cinematographic evidence enables the subordination of the contingent to the rule of law, ultimately imbued with a power over life and death. Electrocution simultaneously provides a "clean" way, an efficient and punctual method, of dealing with such tainted criminality, and a forum for the exhibition of technological prowess.[20]

Although both *Electrocuting an Elephant* and *Execution of Czolgosz* activate curiosity about electricity and the lure of witnessing an electrical death, there is one difference between the two films that to today's spectator of film, photography, and television would seem far to outweigh any similarities. For the relations to time sustained by the two films are quite different, if not opposed. In *Electrocuting an Elephant,* the camera operator is actually present at the scene of the execution, and the death recorded is a "real" death. There are various textual assurances of this fact: the camera operator's presence is marked by the pan that follows the movement of the elephant into close-up; the break in the footage or camera stoppage functions to elide time but is not concealed as a rupture (the implication being that it is a pragmatic break that simply excises "uneventful" time); the image is composed in depth (as opposed to the flatness of staged productions); and its content is not entirely predictable (a shadowy figure passes in front of the camera after the elephant collapses). None of this, of course, guarantees that the image is actually documentary, but certain stylistic traits had already been attached to the on-the-scene actuality, giving it a rudimentary form and recognizability.

The epistemological status of the image is less certain with *Execution of*

Czolgosz, which was a reenactment and advertised as a "realistic imitation." In a reenactment, the time of the image does not coincide with the time of the event signified. The construction of the Czolgosz film is evidence of an awareness of that disjunction and of an attempt to rectify it. As Charles Musser has pointed out, the film is a hybrid, joining the panorama with the dramatic reenactment.[21] The opening pans of Auburn Prison were taken on the day of Czolgosz's execution, thus providing the spectator with images whose temporality did in fact coincide with that of the actual event being represented. Nevertheless, once the film circulates as a product, that temporality becomes illegible, effaced from the image, which is disengaged from its origins. In the absence of outside information about their origin, the temporality of the pans receives specification internally, as a function of their juxtaposition with the reenacted scene of the execution and their own duration on the screen.

It is significant that the shots of Auburn Prison are moving shots, whereas in the reenactment the camera is still. Such a division was typical in the early years of the silent cinema, when the pan was generally reserved for the unstaged, on-the-scene actuality, while staged scenes were static. Films such as *The Burning of Durland's Riding Academy* (Edison, 1902) consisted primarily of lengthy pans of the fire and firefighters, and *Scenes of the Wreckage from the Waterfront* (Lubin, 1900), a topical about the aftermath of the Galveston hurricane (advertised with the phrase "Lubin's Operators the First on the Scene"), is a single panorama that travels almost 360 degrees. The term panorama is derived from the Greek *pan,* or "all," and *orama,* "to see," and the cinematic pan inherits its name from the popular panoramas that predated the cinema by a hundred years. These panoramas took for their subject matter extensive landscapes or cityscapes (when Robert Barker, usually cited as the inventor of the panorama, took out a patent for it he labeled it "La nature à coup d'oeil"), as well as historical scenes.[22] The timing of the image was frequently an obsession here as well, particularly with the historical panoramas. Dolf Sternberger stresses the fact that the written material accompanying Anton von Werner's *The Battle of Sedan* (1883) set the time of the events depicted between 1:30 and 2:00 P.M. on September 1, 1870. Such precise timing reinforced the enormous work of reconstructing a moment in its minutest details and the striving after a realism that surrounded and even enveloped the spectator. As Sternberger points out, the spectator was transformed from a "passerby" into an "eyewitness," and in the panorama "relentless illusionistic unity forbade even the faintest hint of a frame and required negating the pictorial character in any way whatsoever as well as reducing or bridging the viewing distance." Part of the task of negating the pictorial involved the integration of objects—rocks, bushes, implements, wood, even stairs—seemingly allowing access to the painted space. In the diorama, a form of panorama relying heavily on certain lighting effects that often simulated the passage of time (day to night), the space of the spectator was negated; shrouded in darkness it became a nonspace that yielded its rights to the representation. Yet despite the obsessiveness of these efforts to attain realism, Sternberger, who sees the panorama as *the* trope of the nineteenth century, insists that there was no attempt to deceive. The spectator, far from being "taken in" by the illusion, was invited to admire the virtuosity of the creators of the panorama, the painstaking labor required to construct an illusion that did not have to "work" to be appreciated—"in a word, illusionistic virtuosity became an end in itself."[23]

Given the representational history of the panorama, it is not surprising that the pan in the cinema was first activated in the on-the-scene footage of the actuality, which fully exploited the indexicality associated with its photographic base. Here the illusionistic virtuosity is a function not of the skill of the camera operator (whose task has been largely appropriated by the automatism associated with the machine), but of simply being there at the right time. The accumulation of historical detail was one of the assumed properties of the apparatus, and the unpredictability of the random movement of figures within the frame consolidated the impression of the real. The cinematic pan, like the panorama, constituted a denial of the frame as boundary and hence promised access to a seemingly limitless vision.

Since the pan in the early cinema signified a certain presence in relation to the event, the stylistic disjunction of *Execution of Czolgosz, with Panorama of Auburn Prison* is quite striking. The "event," inside the prison, is filmed with a static camera, on a set that has no hint of depth. The camera movements, which ought to guarantee the authenticity of the footage, its license to represent, are allied with shots of a space where nothing happens but which has at least a metonymic link to the site in question. It is almost as though the filmmakers hoped that the panoramas' temporal coincidence with the event would somehow bleed over into the restaged scenes and contaminate them with their veracity or authenticity. The pans of Auburn Prison act as an alibi (in the etymological sense of invoking "another place") or an excuse that entails being elsewhere.

Nevertheless, as with Werner's panorama, there is no attempt to deceive the spectator, who is forewarned that this is a "realistic imitation." In fact *Execution of Czolgosz* fits readily into the well-accepted category of the dramatic reenactment, a subgenre that lost its currency around 1907.[24] These films modeled themselves on important current events and often used newspaper accounts as pre-texts. They were advertised as "faithful duplications," "reproductions," "dramatic representations of current events." Subject matter for this subgenre of topicality included prizefights, war scenes, fires, natural disasters, and the police's apprehension of criminals. As David Levy points out, there was a "weak ontological frontier" between the categories of newsreel, documentary, drama, and reproduction. Kemp Niver, in his categorization of films in the Library of Congress's paper print collection, lists *An Execution by Hanging,* for example, as both a reproduction and a newsreel.[25] Méliès labeled his reenactments "Artificially Arranged Scenes."[26] These films were not necessarily perceived primarily as "fakes," although there was certainly discussion about their origin and legitimacy, particularly in the case of war films, which were often shot in bathtubs and deserted New Jersey fields. Levy cites the advice of a British trade journal on how to tell the difference between a "sham" war film and the real thing: one clue to the existence of a sham is the presence of "gentlemen with tall hats, accompanied by ladies apparently looking on."[27] Raymond Fielding constructs a taxonomy of reconstituted newsreels whose divisions are specified primarily by the intent of the films to deceive. A 1906 Biograph film about the San Francisco earthquake, for example, was shot on a miniature set with cardboard buildings and controlled fires. No description of this technique accompanied the exhibition of the film, which allegedly "fooled" the mayor of San Francisco. Fielding also claims that this early "fake" made it impossible for audiences to accept footage of the quake screened later as authentic.[28] But what is most striking are not the debates about faking or deception, which seem in fact to be quite minimal and marginal in relation to the phenomenon itself. Rather, what is interesting to us today is that such a genre (the dramatic reenactment) was tolerable and even popular among audiences before 1907. As Miriam Hansen points out, "Though occasional complaints were heard early on, the standard of authenticity by which all such films would be rejected as 'fake pictures' evolved with the classical paradigm and became one of the war cries in the campaign against primitive modes."[29] Hansen claims, instead, that any distinctions between documentary and narrative were overshadowed by the sensationalism and unmediated sadism of the films (particularly the execution films). To the extent that the impact of the films mattered more than their origin, realism was not yet yoked to a strident morality. As late as 1911, a writer for *Moving Picture World* could claim: "Cinematography cannot be made to *lie*, it is a machine that merely records what is happening."[30] But it is not clear that such a question (that of the image's relation to honesty) shaped the reception of films before 1907.

The slipperiness associated with the ontological status of the image was not unrelated to the largely unregulated entrepreneurship characterizing the business of cinema in its early years. After an Edison crew arrived too late to photograph the devastating Paterson, New Jersey, fire of 1902, Edison renamed *The Burning of Durland's Riding Academy* and distributed it as *Firemen Fighting the Flames at Paterson*. According to Musser, this was "neither unusual nor 'naive' but consistent with the highly opportunistic business ethics of Edison and other film producers."[31] Plagiarism and duping films were also widespread practices and contributed to the instability of the cinematic image, which seemed, in the early years, to play out all the difficulties revolving around the notions of property, original, and origin delineated by Benjamin's considerations of art in the age of mechanical reproduction. Particularly illuminating are the copyright battles, which, though to a large extent determined by marketing strategies, reveal a great deal about the conceptualization of the early cinema. Initially photography was the only available model for copyrighting films. Since most films were very short actualities, this made sense: two paper prints were sent to the Library of Congress together with the fifty-cent fee required for copyrighting a photograph. In the court case of *Edison v. Lubin*, in which the Edison Company attempted to keep Lubin from duping parts of the actuality *Christening and Launching Kaiser Wilhelm's Yacht "Meteor"* (1902), Lubin made two basic arguments: (1) an actuality was not an original creative and hence copyrightable work because it used a mechanical device (the camera) to record what anyone present could see; (2) a film could not be copyrighted as a single photograph, since it consisted of many different exposures each one of which required the protection of copyright. The second argument was the determinant one for the judge, although his ruling was later overturned in favor of an understanding of a film as a single entity on account of its single point of view ("one camera at one operation"), its constitution by separate pictures whose difference was "not detectable by the human eye," and its value as a single commodity.[32]

This case does not address the issue of editing, and both André Gaudreault and David Levy single out a later case in which Biograph brought legal proceedings against Edison for its remake of the multishot film *Personal* (1904) as *How a French Nobleman Got a Wife through the New York Herald "Personal" Columns* (later remade by Lubin as well). Both film historians agree that Edison's already outdated marketing strategy of offering portions of multiple-shot films separately for sale shaped its legal arguments, claiming that a longer film was simply a discontinuous aggregate of shots taken at different places and at different times (the "whole" film was therefore not copyrightable). Although the judge ultimately decided that the copyrightable unity of a film could be based on its narrative status (using literature as a model rather than simply the photograph),[33] the arguments made during the trial suggest that the dilemma has a great deal to do with the conceptualization of the spectator—whether that spectator is indeed "one," and where he or she is situated. Testifying for Edison, Edwin S. Porter claimed that a film like *Personal* could not be copyrighted as a single photograph because it was composed of different scenes, each constituting a different viewpoint widely separated in time and space. Porter stated that the settings were so distant from one another that they could not have been recorded "even with a camera pivoted so as to take a panorama," and emphasized that the distant views were "seldom taken the same day."[34] Spatial and temporal disjunctions were not reconcilable with the unity suggested by a single copyright. This disjunction was a problem in conceptualizing the spectator as well, who could no longer be thought of as an "onlooker":

Another fact noted . . . in the Lubin case was that the negative simply photographically reproduced "in continuous form the view which would be represented to the eye of an onlooker on the spot occupied by the camera." Complainant's so-called negative reproduces in discontinuous form several views . . . which could not possibly be presented to the eye of an onlooker, unless he travelled with the photographer and his pantomimic troupe from Grant's tomb through and around the surrounding country.[35]

Gaudreault argues persuasively that this discourse traces a movement from the monstrator (film simply *shows* the event) to the narrator (who functions to conceal/override the gap between different events/views). I would add that the legal discourse also designates a certain quandary in thinking the cinematic spectator. As film becomes a syntax whose unity is not a direct reflection of the space and time it records, the spectator is no longer an "onlooker" or "bystander," but occupies an unthinkable space or site. This discourse, together with the development of the narrative cinema, traces the reduction of the embodiment and contingency of the spectator.

The confusion in formulating questions of morality and legality in relation to the cinematic image allowed a period of apparent anarchy in filmmaking, a certain heterogeneity of styles, subjects, and marketing strategies. Out of this relatively chaotic moment emerged the anomalous category of the dramatic reenactment, which seemed to grasp simultaneously at two contradictory temporal modes of the cinematic image. On the one hand, the reenactment exploited the temporal specificity of the image, its ability to record a quite precise temporal event, and hence to be "timely," or topical. Thus the "visual newspaper" rushed to represent the most newsworthy current events, the more quickly the better. On the other hand, the very acceptability of the reconstruction of an event constituted an acknowledgment of the atemporality of the image, the fact that it did not speak its own relation to time. From this perspective, the temporal aspirations of the cinema would seem to be contained in the notion of making the event "present" to the spectator. David Levy argues quite convincingly that the reenactment was a kind of transitional object between the actuality and the narrative film, that techniques developed in relation to the changing conditions in shooting actualities (pans, shooting in depth, non-eye-level angles, and so on) were taken up by narrative films to enhance their realism.[36] It seems equally plausible (and not necessarily in contradiction to such a hypothesis) to argue that narrative functioned as a displacement of unanswerable questions about the ontology of the image. What came to be known eventually as "deception" in the reenactment was made harmless as "illusion" in the narrative film. Clearly, the progressive domination of the industry by narrative was overdetermined (culturally, economically, technologically), but from this point of view, narrative would constitute a certain taming or securing of the instability of the cinematic image. In the same way, narrative became the model for the apprehension of the legal unity of film.

From this perspective, *Electrocuting an Elephant,* which postdates *Execution of Czolgosz* by two years, would appear to be the more "primitive" film. The time and space of the image coincide with the time and space of the referent; the spectator is positioned as an "onlooker" with a stable spatial viewpoint. The camera simply substitutes for the spectator who cannot manage to be at Coney Island at the appropriate moment. Hence the film spectator sees nothing that the Coney Island spectator does not see. But this account is not quite true. For the film spectator sees both less and more. His or her vision is limited by the frame and the access it allows to the execution—when the camera pans, that vision shifts. Yet the film spectator also sees something that the Coney Island spectator cannot see—a break in the film where the camera is stopped and then started again. Because this break constitutes an ellipsis, it is arguable that the film spectator again, or in another way, sees less, but I want to focus on the sight of the break itself, which is by no means concealed. This visibility of the cut is in contrast to a later execution film, *Execution by Hanging* (Mutoscope/Biograph, 1905), in which a camera stoppage is the condition of possibility of the representation of a death. In this reenactment of an execution, a woman is led up to a stage, a black hood is placed over her face, and a noose is placed around her neck. At this point there is a barely perceptible break in which, evidently, the actors freeze in position, the woman is removed, and a dummy is substituted for her so that the execution can continue unimpeded. When the film is screened, the break is all but invisible. Such a strategy is a denial of process and ensures the spectator's experience of continuous time. In *Electrocuting an Elephant,* there is no attempt to conceal the break or to deny its existence. That break functions to elide time that is perceived as "uneventful"—the work of situating the elephant and binding her in the electrical apparatus. The disruption is itself a signifier of a certain closeness to the real. The aspiration to convey the "real time" of the event is only ever that—an aspiration—despite its claim to be grounded in the technological specificity of the medium. Even without cuts or camera stoppages of any sort, the actuality is destined to produce only the *sign* of time.

In an actuality, the time that is excluded or elided is constituted as "dead time"—time which, by definition, is outside of the event, "uneventful." But such an explanation assumes that the event is simply "out there" and dead time a by-product of grasping the event's clear-cut and inherent structure. It would be more accurate, I think, to assume that an understanding of "dead time"—time in which nothing happens, time which is in some sense "wasted," expended without product—is the condition of a conceptualization of the "event." From this point of view the documentary event is not so far from the narrative event. The event may take time, but it is packaged as a moment: time is condensed and becomes eminently meaningful. Such a conceptualization of time as punctual is fully consistent with the fascination with electricity. Part of the lure of electricity is the lure of an escape from process, duration, work. This conjunction of cinematic time and a temporality owing much to an understanding of electricity is suggested by Benjamin's notion of giving the moment a posthumous shock.

In *Electrocuting an Elephant,* time is certainly condensed and abstracted, but it also bears the stamp of an authenticity that is derived from the technological capabilities of the camera. Since the camera could not "be there" at the moment of the execution in *Execution of Czolgosz,* the film borrows the aura of technological authenticity by connecting the temporality of the pan (already a prime signifier of the actuality) and the temporality of the event. But the effectiveness of taking the panorama shots on the day of the execution is lost unless the spectator has external knowledge about their origin, for the image is not self-sufficient in this respect—its own temporal history is not legible. In the earliest years of the cinema, this requirement of external spectatorial knowledge was not atypical but, rather, constituted something of a norm. The spectator was often expected to have knowledge of another text (for example, newspaper accounts of a current event or a familiar story such as the Passion plays or Jack and the Beanstalk, which the films alluded to or illustrated but did not fully develop). Or, in many cases, the lecturer (a person hired to accompany the film with comments, explaining to the audience what was happening) would act as an external source, pointing out aspects of the image whose readability might be a function of external information. Conditions of exhibition were grounded in an acknowledgment that the image was not self-sufficient.

In the actuality, the time of the image is determined to a large extent externally—ideally the time of the image and the time of the referent would coincide. The camera would act purely as a recording device. The dramatic reenactment of current events aspires to that temporal relation. But actualities, which dominated film production up until 1903, gradually lost ground with the ascendancy of narrative. Around 1907 the dramatic reenactment disappeared as a genre despite the persistence of isolated examples.[37] The subordination of documentary to a marginal cinematic mode was simultaneous with the inscription of temporality as an internal attribute. Even within the realm of narrative, temporality attained a new level of significance. Narrative constructed its own coherent and linear temporality, enhancing the autonomy of the film and the self-sufficiency of its own projected spectator. The initial centrifugal momentum of film exhibition—in which the spectator was thrown outward from the viewing situation to other texts, other sources of knowledge, was halted. As André Gaudreault points out, "an insistence on temporality [in narrative film] is a phenomenon which grows in importance during 1907. By the following year, many themes will emphasize story elements tied to temporality."[38] Gaudreault notes in particular the growing emphasis on clocks in the mise-en-scène and on suspense as a structuring agent. Because the time flow was now an imaginary one, situated in the realm of fiction and mimicking a sense of ordinary everyday time, it could not be tested against an external measure, thus contributing to the stabilization of a potentially deceptive or disruptive image.

From this point of view, the pans in *Execution of Czolgosz* constitute a type of hinge phenomenon, since their temporality is readable as a function of both external and internal determinants. Although the spectator would need external knowledge to verify the fact that the pans were taken on the day of the execution, there are other, internal signals of simultaneity drawn from a narrative imaginary: the dissolve, which links the panoramas to the reenacted scenes; the resulting construction of an opposition between inside and outside, which situates the pans as establishing shots; and the succession of shots, which yokes the pans to a precisely timed story. In other words, the film exploits both the technology's relation to time (that of recording) and the technology's ability to construct a time that has the imaginary coherence of "real time," everyday time. It hedges its bets.

It would be inaccurate to suggest that the first relation to time (that of the actuality) is abandoned. Rather, it is rewritten in such a way that contingency and unpredictability are reduced as a part of the process, reemerging as the signified. The pan, resolutely linked to the real in the early days of the cinema, is also, in comparison with the panoramas of the early and mid-nineteenth century, a way of mechanizing and regulating the subject's relation to time. The cinema participates in the rationalization of time characterizing the industrial age. "Economy" is a fundamental value of the developed narrative film, and the efficiency of electricity is paralleled by the efficiency of narrative. Resolute linearity, efficiency, and economy are also crucial goals of scientific management in its attempt to deploy the human body in labor with a maximum reduction of wasted time. "Dead time" is, again, anathema. As Michael Chanan has argued, "It is this fixing of our experience of time which constitutes the dominant ideological form of time in commoditized society . . . You could also say that the two processes—'scientific' management and 'mass culture'—have in common the practice of *time economy* insofar as they both structure the flow of time."[39] This analysis is consistent with Kracauer's understanding of mass culture in the 1920s as, at least in part, the negation of unorganized, unstructured time. In this context, boredom becomes the "only proper occupation" if not a radical resistance to the media's incessant production of images and sounds: "In the evening one saunters through the streets, replete with an unfulfillment from which a fullness could sprout. Illuminated words glide by on the rooftops, and already one is banished from one's own emptiness into the alien *advertisement*." Boredom ensures one's presence, one's refusal to be absorbed into and overcome by the regulated temporality of mass culture; "If one were never bored, one would presumably not really be present at all and would thus be merely one more object of boredom, as was claimed at the outset. One would light up on the rooftops or spool by as a filmstrip."[40] Mass culture seeks to annihilate the possibility of boredom, of dead time, of a monochrome, unpunctuated time. Modernity, in contrast, becomes the persistent production of events.[41]

From this point of view, the inevitably historiographic tendency of cinema, its ability to record "real" time and its duration, at first a source of seemingly endless fascination, poses critical difficulties for the early cinema. Cinema's time is surely referential; it is a record of time with the weight of indexicality. But its time is also always characterized by a certain indeterminacy, an intolerable instability. The image is the imprint of a particular moment whose particularity becomes indeterminable precisely because the image does not speak its own relation to time. Film *is*, therefore, a record of time, but a nonspecific, nonidentifiable time, a disembodied, unanchored time. The cinema hence becomes the production of a generalized experience of time, a duration. The unreadability and uncertainty concerning the image's relation to temporality and to its origin are not problems that are resolved—they are, in fact, insoluble. But they are displaced through the elaborate development of structures that produce the image of a coherent and unified "real time" that is much more "real" than "real time" itself. The resulting cinema delicately negotiates the contradiction between recording and signification.

It is striking that these dilemmas concerning the cinematic representation of time should emerge so starkly in films depicting executions. If cinematic narrative develops, in part, as a structuring of contingency (and hence its reduction as such), the most intractable contingencies would seem to be those having to do with the body and death. Early actualities exploit the cinema's apparent predilection for the contingent, its capacity to record whatever happens to be there at the moment. As highly structured as these actualities were, they left a space open for the unpredictable, the spontaneous—that which would differentiate the cinema from all previous forms of signification precisely because it appears to reject the very idea of meaning. Death is perhaps the ultimate trauma insofar as it is situated as that which is unassimilable to meaning (for Benjamin, "shock" named that which was unassimilable in experience, a residue of unreadability). Freud consistently emphasized that what the subject could never fully accept or grasp was the fact of his or her own death. In "Thoughts for the Times on War and Death," Freud claimed: "It is indeed impossible to imagine our own death; and whenever we attempt to do so we can perceive that we are in fact still present as spectators. Hence the psychoanalytic school could venture on the assertion that at bottom no one believes in his own death, or, to put the same thing in another way, that in the unconscious every one of us is convinced of his own immortality."[42]

Perhaps the execution films circulate around the phenomenon of death, striving to capture the moment of death, in order to celebrate the contingency of the cinematic image, a celebration that is always already too late, since the contingent, in the face of the cinematic apparatus, has already received a "posthumous shock." *Electrocuting an Elephant* does not bring to its spectator the moment of death but its image, its sign, underscored by the film's inscription of lost time. In a dramatic reenactment such as *Execution of Czolgosz*, the inevitable secondariness of such "immediacy" is even more visibly marked. The lure of "seeing death" must have been such that the secondariness of the representation was overshadowed. Nevertheless, the fascination with death was clearly fully consistent with the conceptualization of the cinema's capabilities as an unbiased record of the moment.

In the cinema, the tendency to depict death in this form, in a direct and unmediated way for the gaze of the spectator, lasted for only a brief period of film history,[43] a period that is also bound up with speculations about the new technology itself (what it is for, what it can do). Just as electricity could be activated as a technological control over life and death, the cinema must have seemed to offer the same promise in the field of representation. Topsy and Czolgosz are kept alive through the representations of their deaths. Technology's veiled assurance of compensating for the limitations of the body, that is, its finitude, would be synonymous with a hope of conquering death. But to the extent that the spontaneous and the unpredictable seemed to invade the image of the actuality, to the extent that that image cannot speak its own relation to temporality, narrative proved to be a more effective and surer means of assimilating the unassimilable by conferring on death a meaning. The direct presentation of death to the spectator as pure event, as shock, was displaced in mainstream cinema by its narrativization. Technology and narrative form an alliance in modernity to ameliorate the corrosiveness of the relation between time and subjectivity.

Perhaps death functions as a kind of cinematic Ur-event because it appears as the zero degree of meaning, its evacuation. With death we are suddenly confronted with pure event, pure contingency, what ought to be inaccessible to representation (hence the various social and legal bans against the direct, nonfictional filming of death). Such a problematic is possible only where contingency and meaning, event and structure are radically opposed. The extreme instance of such a formulation is familiar to us in a more recent historical incarnation, that of structuralism. In "Structure, Sign, and Play in the Discourse of the Human Sciences," Jacques Derrida opens a discussion of Claude Lévi-Strauss's structuralism with a reference to the incompatibility of the concepts of structure and event, where the event emerges as a concept that is intolerable within a structuralist epistemology (to the extent that it is precisely that which is supposed to escape structure): "Perhaps something has occurred in the history of the concept of structure that could be called an 'event,' if this loaded word did not entail a meaning which it is precisely the function of structural—or structuralist—thought to reduce or suspect."[44] And Lévi-Strauss himself does, indeed, explicitly and extensively activate the opposition between structure and event, particularly in "The Science of the Concrete." The stability of the opposition becomes more critical to the extent that structuralism claims a scientific status. As Lévi-Strauss puts it, "Science as a whole is based on the distinction between the contingent and the necessary, this being also what distinguishes event and structure. The qualities it claimed at its outset as peculiarly scientific were precisely those which formed no part of living experience and remained outside and, as it were, unrelated to events." The concepts of structure and event are opposed as ends and means in order to distinguish between two equally valid modes of apprehending the world and producing knowledge: science (or "engineering") and bricolage (which is the process of mythmaking). The scientist activates structures in order to produce events ("changing the world"), while the bricoleur gathers events (or the remains and debris of events) in order to create structures.[45]

Art emerges as a somewhat anomalous category in this context; it mediates between structure and event, design and accident, and is even defined as the "union between the structural order and the order of events." However, art does not produce cognition, does not generate knowledge; instead, Lévi-Strauss specifies as its outcome an "aesthetic emotion." And even art must take care not to "come entirely under the sway of extraneous contingencies . . . Even the most professional art succeeds in moving us only if it arrests in time this dissipation of the contingent in favor of the pretext."[46] Unalloyed contingency is constituted as a danger, as the site of semiotic failure. Structuralism as a movement, in order to produce knowledge, evicts the event from its epistemological domain; it disdains the contingent. As Derrida points out, "in the work of Lévi-Strauss it must be recognized that the respect for structurality, for the internal originality of the structure, compels a neutralization of time and history." The event, within structuralism, is unthinkable, or, perhaps more accurately, the event can be thought only as rupture or catastrophe, as a kind of time or nontime between, marking the lack of a causal or developmental explanation for the historical change from one structure to another. As Derrida argues, "In this 'structuralist' moment, the concepts of chance and discontinuity are indispensable."[47] However, chance and discontinuity are relegated to the epistemological margins; they are unanalyzable.

Structuralism should be historically out of place in this discussion of early cinema. But I would argue that it effectively consolidates an opposition between structure and event that at the turn of the century is emergent and in many respects less stable. The pressure of resolving the contradiction between the two seems more intense, and staking out a meaningful place for contingency becomes paramount. This is particularly striking in the work of Freud, who struggled incessantly, throughout his career, with the oppositions between constitution and event, fantasy and the real. But this struggle in and around the concept of the contingent is also visible even earlier, in the efforts of Baudelaire to come to terms with the trauma of modernity. Before returning to the process through which the cinema grapples with this problematic, let us examine briefly the way in which the opposition between structure and event (and its variants the general and the particular, constitution and event, the necessary and the contingent) plays itself out in the work of these two figures.

It could be said that Freud's entire project is a battle against contingency, an attempt violently to yoke it to meaning. In *The Interpretation of Dreams* and *The Psychopathology of Everyday Life,* no detail is immune from significance, and meaning is located where one would most expect opacity, unreadability. But it is the theory of the screen memory which condenses most strikingly Freud's confrontation with the concept of the contingent.[48] For the screen memory is a detail, a contingency, which is nevertheless richly vivid and sensuous in its cognitive opacity. It stands out in a scene and constitutes itself as the marker of specificity itself. Screen memories are characterized by their intensity; they are, in Freud's words, recollected "*too* clearly." What is lost in meaning is gained in affective force. For these memories fasten on the trivial, the indifferent, and ultimately strike us as hollow or empty. In this respect the screen memory is deceptive, for it is above all a displacement—both temporally and semantically. The trivial, the indifferent, the contingent come to act as a veil, covering over significance; "an unsuspected wealth of meaning lies concealed behind their [the screen memories'] apparent innocence."[49] The detail—that which stands out in a scene— becomes a *screen.* Itself emptied of content, the screen memory attains value through a relation, a spatial and temporal connection; it is in the "neighborhood" of meaning. The screen memory becomes legible through this connection and is ultimately subordinated to a more significant psychical scenario.

The Psychopathology of Everyday Life is an extended demonstration of the impossibility of the concepts of chance or meaninglessness in psychical life. Every moment of forgetting, every gesture, every slip of the tongue, is legible. But toward the end of this work, Freud becomes somewhat nervous about the extensiveness of the implied determinism and devotes a chapter to "Determinism, Belief in Chance and Superstition," in which he attempts to defend himself against charges of paranoia and superstition. The paranoiac believes that everything is saturated with meaning and can be interpreted, and, in this sense, he or she attains a glimmer of truth (there is a very thin line here, since Freud clearly admires the systematicity of paranoia and often compares it to psychoanalysis). Yet the paranoiac makes the mistake of projecting that meaning and interpretive process onto other people when it is simply a figuring of his or her own drives and desires. Similarly, the superstitious person differs from the psychoanalyst (that is, Freud) insofar as he or she projects meaning outward, onto "external chance happenings" or "real events." Freud claims: "he [the superstitious person] interprets chance as due to an event, while I trace it back to a thought," and "I believe in external (real) chance, it is true, but not in internal (psychical) accidental events."[50] With this gesture, Freud effectively relegates contingency to the event, defined as external, nonpsychical, "real." Perhaps this is why Freud resisted the cinema; chained to the domain of the visible, to the external surface of events, the cinema must have struck him as a veritable reservoir of meaninglessness. Nevertheless, the distinctions Freud struggled to maintain at the end of *The Psychopathology*—between psychoanalysis and superstition, structure and event, the internal and the external—were always fragile and subject to collapse in the course of his own analyses. And at times he actively attempted to dismantle them. The very concept of phylogenesis, one of the weakest and most speculative in psychoanalysis, is, as Jean Laplanche and Jean-Bertrand Pontalis point out, a vain attempt "to overcome the opposition between event and constitution."[51] Contingency haunted Freud as the mark of interpretive failure, and frequently his texts bear witness to a troubled and uneasy relation to the category of the event.

In Baudelaire, the opposition is cast in somewhat different terms. The

logic of the essay "The Painter of Modern Life," most famous for its production of the figure taken by many to be emblematic of modernity—the
flâneur—is structured by the tension between the general and the particular, the eternal and the contingent, oppositions whose deployment ultimately hinges on the figure of the woman. For Baudelaire, modernity is "the
ephemeral, the fugitive, the contingent, the half of art whose other half is the
eternal and the immutable." His endeavor is to collapse the opposition between the two, to situate the contingent as the only possible means of access
to the eternal, to "distill the eternal from the transitory." Any attempt to relinquish the contingent, to attain pure and unadulterated access to eternal
and immutable beauty, courts danger and can be figured only as a confrontation with a gaping hole, an abyss that is figured in its turn as originary and
timeless female beauty: "This transitory, fugitive element, whose metamor-
phoses are so rapid, must on no account be despised or dispensed with. By
neglecting it, you cannot fail to tumble into the abyss of an abstract and indeterminate beauty, like that of the first woman before the fall of man." The
first woman is naked, exposed, and it is fashion which, for Baudelaire, is the
very site of contingency and acts as a defense against this abyss. It is the
woman's clothing—the "muslins, the gauzes, the vast, iridescent clouds of
stuff in which she envelops herself"—which protects the man against the
blinding abyss of the abstract, the indeterminable, and, ultimately, against
meaninglessness.[52] It is the contingent which, in Baudelaire as in Freud,
comes to bear the weight of meaning.

Yet Baudelaire, like Freud, vacillates. For both the lure and the threat of
the contingent are played out in his attempt to come to terms with the role
of art in modernity. The artist must beware of the potential danger of a "riot
of details" and the consequent "state of anarchy." Here, the presence or absence of the model is crucial: "When a true artist has come to the point of
the final execution of his work, the model would be more of an embarrassment than a help to him," and "the physical presence of the model and its
multiplicity of details disconcerts and as it were paralyses [the artist's] principal faculty."[53] The absence of the model during the process of production of the representation is, of course, impossible in the photography that
Baudelaire disdained and hence effectively excluded from the domain of art.
Photography adhered *too* closely to the contingent, and, like Lévi-Strauss,
Baudelaire was concerned that art not come too completely under the sway

of the contingent. Although Baudelaire was certainly drawn toward the ephemeral, the fleeting, the effervescent, which he associated with modernity, his nostalgia for the eternal is also quite apparent. He strives to maintain a precarious balance between structure and event.

The last half of the nineteenth century witnesses the growth of the perception of contingency as both threat and lure. And both could be said to be linked to its tenuous and unstable relation to meaning. The cinema emerges in this context as a technology that appears to be capable of *representing* the contingent, of providing the ephemeral with a durable record. This capability is the source of both fascination and anxiety. For the idea of representation without meaning involves the forfeiture of limits, and hence of semiotic control. The cinema is forced to confront the episteme wherein structure and event both oppose and tantalize each other. The polarization of structure and event which underwrites structuralism is less tenable at the turn of the century, and Freud, Baudelaire, and the cinema all contest, in some manner, its logic.

The cinematic image's privileged relation to the contingent renders it unstable. As certain as the spectator may be that this image is a record of a real duration, a unique temporality, that temporality is unspecifiable and unverifiable. This temporal instability is dealt with historically in two ways. The first can be traced in the movement from the actuality, with its allegiance to the ephemeral and the contingent, to narrative as a tightly structured web of manufactured temporalities. In both, it is the event which comes to bear the weight of meaning—the event, where time coagulates and where the contingent can be readily imbued with meaning through its very framing *as* event. The elision of time that structures *Electrocuting an Elephant* actively undercuts the dissipation of the contingent, the "riot of details" feared by Baudelaire, to produce simultaneously the event and its significance. In *Execution of Czolgosz,* a transitional form between actuality and narrative, the contingency that seems to be specific to the medium is subjected to a temporal domain, where it is transformed into a second-order signifier of the real. The internal lack of temporal specificity of the opening pan is retrospectively endowed with historical certainty by the highly structured narrative of Czolgosz's death, at the same time that the pan lends to the narrative the authority of the contingent. At what point does the shadowy figure who passes in front of the camera in *Electrocuting an Elephant* cease to be a marker of instability, of potential spontaneity, and become the signifier of a medium's power to access the real?

The second attempt to deal with the temporal instability of the image involves not the taming of the contingent, but its denial. Like the event, spectacle effects a coagulation of time, but, in its effort to evoke an "abstract and indeterminate beauty," it courts the outcome feared by Baudelaire—that of tumbling into the "abyss" of femininity. The event bears a relation to time; spectacle does not. Spectacle is, as Laura Mulvey has pointed out, fundamentally atemporal, associated with stasis and the antilinear.[54] And it is not accidental that Mulvey's influential attempt to delineate the production of sexual difference in the cinema is forged through the crucial categories of narrative (as a chain of *events*) and spectacle. In a film, the event furthers and supports narrative progression, whereas the spectacle halts it in a protracted stare. Spectacle, in its psychoanalytic conceptualization, is not a self-evident category in the early cinema, and it, together with its allied fetishistic and voyeuristic spectator, has been analyzed as a relatively late formation, synonymous with the development of the classical system.[55] Nevertheless, I would argue that it emerges sporadically much earlier as a crucial component of the representational struggle with contingency. Spectacle functions to localize desire, fantasy, and longing in a timeless time, outside contingency. In this respect, spectacle, in contrast to the event, is epistemologically reactionary, decidedly *unmodern* (in the terms outlined by Baudelaire); for the spectacle of female beauty becomes the nostalgia for pure structure—a world without contingency. In this context, the 1900 Edison film *The Artist's Dilemma* is quite telling. For its scenario of the endeavor to represent female beauty unfolds in a timeless time; both the model and the demon who paints her *too* adequately emerge from a clock whose hands do not move.

The cinema's struggles with contingency repeat, in the field of representation, the "taming of chance" that takes place in sociology, philosophy, and the sciences during roughly the same time period.[56] And, as we have seen, the growing acknowledgment and acceptance of chance and indeterminism did not imply chaos or a loss of control. To the contrary, it consolidated the lawlike regularities of statistics and probability, and encouraged the growing numerical quality of knowledge. The idea of the normal produced in such a context implied an even greater control over that situated as deviant, aberrant, other. The cinema's predilection for the contingent was accompanied by the threat of excess and representational indeterminacy. In many respects, this was most evident in its capacity to record/represent a duration, unanchored and potentially without limits. Temporality hence became the site of the critical control and regulation of cinematic meaning. The cinema had a stake in *not* allowing the event to fall outside the domain of structure. In the cinema, as in much theoretical writing of the period, it would be more accurate to say that the event comes to harbor contingency within its very structure.

6

Zeno's Paradox: The Emergence
of Cinematic Time

In the technical language of filmmaking, the term *real time* refers to the duration of a single shot (assuming the shot is neither fast nor slow motion). If the physical film is not cut and its projection speed equals its shooting speed (usually somewhere between sixteen and twenty-four frames per second), the movement on the screen will unfold in a time that is isomorphic with profilmic time, or what is generally thought to be our everyday lived experience of time—hence the term *real*. The time of the apparatus matches, is married to, the time of the action or the scene. This "real time" is marked by an apparent plenitude. No lack or loss of time is visible to the eye or accessible to the spectator. But this temporal continuity is in fact haunted by absence, by the lost time represented by the division between frames. During the projection of a film, the spectator is sitting in an unperceived darkness for almost 40 percent of the running time. Hence, much of the movement or the time allegedly recorded by the camera is simply not there, lost in the interstices between frames. These interstices, crucial to the representation of movement, must themselves remain unacknowledged. The cinema presents us with a simulacrum of time. Nevertheless, knowledge of the indexicality of the cinematic image sustains a belief that something of time, something of movement or its imprint, or, at the very least, its adequate representation, is there.

Because an adequate representation of motion in time appeared to be a powerful result of cinematic technology, the cinema seemed to address, or even resolve, an ancient philosophical argument. Theoretical and philosophical discourses on the cinema have from a very early point paired the cinema's production of continuous movement from discontinuous images with Zeno's paradoxes. In the 1920s Jean Epstein, under the heading "The transmutation of the discontinuous into the continuous, negated by Zeno, but accomplished by the cinematograph," wrote: "the cinematograph seems to be a mysterious mechanism intended to assess the false accuracy of Zeno's famous argument about the arrow, intended for the analysis of the subtle metamorphosis of stasis into mobility, of emptiness into solid, of continuous into discontinuous, a transformation as stupefying as the generation of life from inanimate elements." In 1907 Henri Bergson directly linked a discussion of the cinematographic illusion of motion and Zeno's paradoxes, and accused both of the same error—that of attempting to reconstitute movement from static states or instants. Real movement, he claimed, escapes the grasp of both: "The movement slips through the interval, because every attempt to reconstitute change out of states implies the absurd proposition, that movement is made of immobilities."[1]

Zeno was the perfect nemesis for Bergson because, as a member of the Eleatic School of pre-Socratic philosophers, he was fully invested in the denial of movement, change, and plurality. His paradoxes were designed to demonstrate the absurdity of a commonsense belief in the reality of such concepts. The paradox of the arrow to which Epstein refers is an account that undermines our belief in its movement. At any given moment, the arrow occupies a space equal to its volume and simply is where it is. Therefore, at any moment it is at rest. Therefore, it is always at rest and never moves. At each point of its course, it is motionless; hence it is motionless during the entire time it is allegedly moving. A second paradox attempts to prove that it is impossible for a person to reach the far end of a stadium, since before attaining the goal the person must reach the halfway mark and, before that, the halfway mark of the halfway mark, and so on, in perpetuity. Because space is infinitely divisible, it is impossible to cross it with a finite number of steps. A third paradox concerns the famous race between Achilles and the tortoise. The tortoise is given a head start of ten units, but Achilles runs ten times faster. Zeno argued that Achilles would never pass the tortoise because every time Achilles attains the point where the tortoise was, the tortoise has progressed a tenth of the distance Achilles has run. The tortoise will always be ahead.

Epstein gives Zeno credit for understanding that "the analysis of movement yielded a collection of stops," but faults him for failing to envisage the seemingly impossible—their absurd synthesis in the cinema, which demolishes the opposition between the continuous and the discontinuous ("Hardly anyone has realized that the cinematic image carries a warning of something monstrous, that it bears a subtle venom which could corrupt the entire rational order so painstakingly imagined in the destiny of the universe").[2] Epstein's discourse is an avant-gardist celebration of this monstrous cinema. Bergson, on the other hand, rejects any claim the cinema might make to representing the truth of time or movement. Zeno's fallacy finds its technological embodiment in the cinema—in its spatialization of time, its investment in the reality of instants. According to Bergson, all Zeno's paradoxes are essentially the same, and that one paradox in its different varieties errs in its misrecognition of the essence of movement. The arrow's movement is not confronted as such but instead is reduced to its trajectory, a line in space tracing the path of the moving body. This trajectory is, indeed, divisible and, furthermore, infinitely divisible, as Zeno's paradox of the stadium emphasizes. But the trajectory is only the shadow, the trace of the movement, which is in itself indivisible. Since movement is qualitative rather than quantitative, its divisibility is unthinkable. The arrow is not at rest at any point in its course, for those instants of immobility are only potential, not actual. When the arrow does come to rest, its movement is over, and any new movement departing from that point is a qualitatively different movement. Zeno's mistake lies in assuming that what is true of the trajectory or line is true of the movement, but the trajectory simply subtends the movement—it does not define it. Movement takes place in the interval, in the transition *between* states, not in their accumulation. This explains, for Bergson, the profound unreality of cinematic "real time." Movement cannot be reconstituted from immobilities.

Yet how does Bergson deal with the fact of cinema? It becomes emblematic, for him, of our ordinary, everyday, pragmatic knowledge of time. Such knowledge is, of necessity, discontinuous and has what Bergson refers to as a cinematographic quality. But for Bergson it is crucial to move beyond that cinematographic impulse to grasp the true nature of duration and movement. The cinema attempts to reconstitute movement with a series of still photographs, but none of these photographs has anything to do with movement. Their gestures are static, frozen. Bergson admits that in order to produce the illusion of movement there must be real movement somewhere. He locates it in the apparatus, the projector, which moves the film forward. The movement of the projector is always the same and succeeds in abstracting a kind of general movement from the individual, particular movements recorded by the camera:

> The process then consists in extracting from all the movements peculiar to all the figures an impersonal movement abstract and simple, *movement in general,* so to speak: we put this into the apparatus and we reconstitute the individuality of each particular movement by combining this nameless movement with the personal attitudes. Such is the contrivance of the cinematograph. And such is also that of our knowledge . . . Whether we would think becoming, or express it, or even perceive it, we hardly do anything else than set going a kind of cinematograph inside us.

Yet, as Bergson later claims, "the movement slips through the interval."[3] The cinematograph can produce only the illusion of mobility.

Bergson's adamant rejection of the cinema as an adequate representation of time poses problems for Gilles Deleuze, who, in his massive two-volume treatment of the cinema, movement, and time, appeals to Bergson for the guiding framework of his discussion. One way of circumventing the problem is to claim, as Deleuze does, that the cinema Bergson dismissed in *Creative Evolution* was a primitive cinema and that "things are never defined by their primitive state, but by the tendency concealed in this state." Another approach involves the claim that Bergson actually anticipated the cinema in his groundbreaking discussion of movement and duration in the first chapter of *Matter and Memory* (published in 1896). From this point of view, the cinema emerges as a philosophical machine for the demonstration of duration in its truth—for the presentation of "time in the pure state."[4]

Bergson's misrecognition of the cinema's true capabilities, according to Deleuze, is linked to his insistence upon locating the cinema's access to real movement in the projector, in a homogeneous mechanical time subject to the "abstract idea of a succession" and "copied from space." Bergson therefore believed that cinematic movement was reducible to the formula "immobile sections + abstract time." Deleuze claims, on the other hand, that the movement needs to be thought in relation to the spectator rather than in relation to the apparatus, and that, for the spectator, movement is immediately given in an "intermediate image." The spectator does not see the succession of photograms but, instead, an intermediate image, which is a "mobile section" not an immobility.[5] This mobile section is not the illusion of movement but its reality; it is imbued with qualitative change and duration. In Deleuze's view, the cinema constitutes a massive refutation of Zeno; it does not participate in his error, as Bergson, who ironically produced a philosophy consonant with the cinema, claimed.

Zeno's paradoxes have provoked extensive and long-lived discussion in mathematics and philosophy. In general, the attempt has *not* been to ascertain the truth or falsity of Zeno's contention (that there is no such thing as movement or change), but to determine why he was wrong, what fatal flaw marred his reasoning in the paradoxes. Bergson believed that our intuition that movement and change exist is correct and simply requires philosophical corroboration. His entire philosophy is in fact a celebration of movement, change, duration. It should not be surprising that an obsession with the limits of Zeno's paradoxes should be resuscitated in modernity, or in the wake of the emergence of the cinema. For in modernity time seems to change its contours, to become more insistently present as a problem, to be subject to acceleration and manipulation. Representational systems (art, literature) address themselves to the ephemeral, the contingent, the moment. The credibility of any static universal or eternal is diminished. And, in this context, the cinema seems to offer a direct answer to Zeno in insisting that movement can indeed be born from immobilities. Cinema works by obliterating the photogram, annihilating that which is static. It appears to extract a magical continuity from what is acknowledged to be discontinuous. The moment of fascination in the early cinema is the moment when the still image projected on the screen bursts into movement.[6]

Epstein, writing in the 1920s, was under no illusion that the movement in cinema was "real"; it was experienced only within the spectator as a kind of phantom. In the cinema itself, "there is no movement, no flux, no life in the mosaics of light and shadow which the screen always presents as fixed." Christian Metz, on the other hand, in an early piece inspired by phenomenology on the impression of reality in the cinema, argued that there is no such thing as the reproduction, or representation, or illusion of motion; the appearance of movement *is* movement: "Because movement is never material but is *always* visual, to reproduce its appearance is to duplicate its reality."[7] Movement is the annihilation of the distinction between object and copy and ensures the reality-effect of the cinema. Similarly, Deleuze has a stake in the idea that the cinema gives us real movement, for he allies himself with Bergson's claim that both movement and time constitute irreducible continuities. The investment in plenitude and consequent rejection of any underlying lack or absence are clear. For the moment, I simply want to reemphasize that a belief in the cinema's alliance with real movement rests on a denial of discontinuity, or of the significance of the distance separating photograms and incarnated in the frameline.

In their insistence upon the reality of cinematic movement, these theorists are duplicating the gesture of much of the earliest cinema—the constant reiteration of the cinematic fact of movement, of the capabilities of the machine. Much of this cinema could be characterized as the sheer celebration of movement for its own sake. This is particularly true of the earliest actualities, especially those of the Lumières, the most famous of which, *Workers Leaving the Lumière Factory* (*Sortie d'usine,* 1895), is content to chronicle the steady stream of workers emerging from the factory yard and moving toward and beyond the edges of the frame.[8] The Lumières were adept at framing their subjects in depth so that the movement of the figures, traversing the frame diagonally, would be extended, would consume more time; examples include *Course en sacs* (*Sack Race,* 1896), *Stuttgart: 26ᵉ Dragons. Sauts d'obstacles* (*German Hussars Jumping Fences,* 1896), *Arrivée en gondole* (*Gondola Party,* 1896), *Arrivée d'un train en gare de La Ciotat* (*Arrival of a Train at the Station of La Ciotat,* 1897), *Barque sortant du port* (*Boat Leaving the Harbor,* 1897).[9] Other films extol movement through its insistent repetition, as in *Sauts au cheval en longueur* (*Leaping over a Horse,* 1897), *Baignade de négrillons* (*Negroes Bathing,* 1897). The anecdote detailing Méliès's fascination with the moving leaves in the background of *Repas de Bébé* (1895), rather than with the concerted (and centered) efforts of the parents to feed the child, is well known. Even in a film such as *Partie d'écarte* (*Friendly Party in the Garden of Lumière,* 1896) where the three cardplayers constitute an unusually static scene, excessive movement is displaced onto the waiter, whose near-hysterical reactions to the card game are left unexplained. That contortions of the body and especially its involuntary and violent movements were perceived as particularly cinematic is evidenced by one of the earliest films, Edison's Kinetoscope film *Fred Ott's Sneeze* (1894), whose title encompasses its action. Similarly, the simplest of movements or gestures could be transformed into an event by being extended or prolonged (as well as performed by well-known theatrical actors). *The Irwin Rice Kiss* (Edison, 1896), which has become one of the most emblematic and recognizable of early films, receives the following description in the Edison catalogue: "They get ready to kiss, begin to kiss, and kiss in a way that brings down the house."[10] The fascination with movement specific to the cinema and which differentiates it decisively from photography and painting is explicitly articulated in a group of films that represent the transformation of a still image (usually a painting) into a "live," moving human being: *The Artist's Dream* (Edison, 1900), *Animated Painting* (Edison, 1904), and *The Artist's Dilemma* (Edison, 1900).

The actualities that reproduce ordinary, recognizable movements and actions of the order of the everyday participate in a tendency that Jacques Aumont attributes to the Impressionist painters.[11] It is the attempt to seize the moment that flees and simultaneously to grasp it as a fugitive moment.[12] All the Lumières can do is multiply the number of such moments, seemingly indefinitely, and produce a series of catalogues containing 1,424 films, dividing the films ("vues") into such categories as "vues militaires," "vues comiques," "vues diverses." Theoretically, the topics are inexhaustible, but the Lumières' cinematic career was in fact quite brief. This approach to cinematic movement and time was historically short-lived, semiotically insufficient. The one-shot film, that slice of the apparently continuous indivisible unity of time and movement that displayed the capabilities of the cinema, was soon extinct.[13]

Up to now I have deliberately left vague the relation between movement and time. At the philosophical level, they are frequently addressed as inseparable issues, indeed as the same ontological problem. If Zeno can disprove the possibility of movement, he can demonstrate that there is no change, hence, effectively, no passage of time. When Bergson argues for the indivisibility of movement as a continuous whole, he is arguing the same for duration. Movement is often represented as the embodiment of time, and it is difficult to conceive of an access to time which is not mediated by movement or change (which itself seems ineluctably wedded to movement). The early cinema seems to corroborate these assumptions by foregrounding movement as the guarantee of its ability to capture or store time. Time becomes visible as the movement of bodies through space. Nevertheless, theoretically, time and movement are distinguishable as concepts. Deleuze, in what he claims is "the style of ancient philosophers," refers to time as the "number of movement";[14] it is sometimes dependent upon what it measures (that is, movement) and sometimes an entirely independent instance. The classical cinema, according to Deleuze, maintains the subordination of time to movement, but the modernist cinema (primarily of the 1960s and 1970s) demonstrates that the cinema is capable of producing an image of pure time, liberated from movement.[15] Whereas even classical cinema disengages movement from bodies through processes of montage and camera movement, the "primitive" cinema, in Deleuze's analysis, does not extract movement "for itself," but leaves it attached to "elements, characters and things which serve as its moving body or vehicle."[16] Hence the primitive cinema could not realize the full potential of the cinematic representation of time.

Regardless of how one assesses Deleuze's history of cinema, he is not alone in noting that movement, time, and bodies are welded together in the continuity of the single-shot actuality. Given assumptions about the "real time" of the shot, this welding also implies a certain adherence of the film to reality. As André Gaudreault claims, "The filmic monstrator [the implied subject-producer of the display or exhibition in the actuality] . . . is 'captured' by the shackles of reality, of *his* reality: the apparatus of cinematography. That reality is one of twenty-four frames per second. The work of the camera-monstrator is necessarily of the order of the continuous," and "all monstrators have their 'noses' glued to the here and now of the 'representation.'"[17]

The single-shot actuality may not acknowledge the discontinuity upon which it is based, but it does embody a certain understanding of time and even a philosophy concerning its representation, that implicit in the development of the apparatus itself. For the true technological ancestor of the cinema, as Deleuze has pointed out, was not simply photography, but *instantaneous* photography, which allowed the registration of evenly spaced and sequenced moments. Cinematography made possible the synthesis through projection of such moments, but nevertheless depended upon their spacing and separate articulation. The apparatus here requires a certain leveling; time is a series of equivalent and equidistant instants (twenty-four frames per second) subjected to no hierarchy whatsoever. Cinema deals with the "any-instant-whatever."[18] Although Bergson asserts the "impossibility of real instants" in his own philosophy, he acknowledges that there have been historically two different ways of erring in the attempt to define or specify the instant. The ancients believed in "privileged" instants, characteristic and essential poses. These were the embodiments or actualizations of a transcendent form, eternal and immobile. The transitional moments between privileged ones were of no interest. Time was punctuated by a hierarchy in which certain moments were privileged as the actualization of an ideal or essential form. The moderns err, on the other hand, by refusing to hierarchize instants (as well as by proclaiming their very existence), by assigning them all to the same banal ontology. Instantaneous photography, for Bergson the quintessential apparatus of modernity, isolates "any moment" and "puts them all in the same rank."[19] In the thought of the ancients, significance was transcendental and preceded embodiment; in that of the moderns, significance emerges from an immanence with no hierarchical guarantees. An instant may *become* remarkable or privileged, but at its origin it is as ordinary and banal as any other. Deleuze allies this thinking with that of modern science, which understands time as a "mechanical succession of instants," rather than in the ancient fashion as "the dialectical order of poses." Bergson rejects both attitudes as a misrecognition of the true (that is, nonspatial) character of time, but Deleuze claims that the philosophy of any-instant-whatever, built into the technology of the cinema, is in line with Bergson's theory of time insofar as it allows for thinking the production of the new, which can be connected to *any* moment. Meaning is predetermined not in ideal forms, but in a process of emergence and surprise. According to Deleuze this is a "complete conversion of philosophy" and goes by the name of modernity.[20]

Early actualities seem to confirm this thinking about time: "any-instant-whatever" becomes cinema's proper topic. Although the placement of the camera may be precisely calculated and the recorded activities foreseen or tightly regulated, these films depend on the fascination associated with the camera's ability to "catch" moments, to itself be surprised by meaning. Dai Vaughan's homage to the Lumières rests on an affirmation of precisely this kind of unprecedented alliance between representation and unpredictability. Deleuze aligns the cinematic apprehension of temporality with movements in the other arts (ballet, mime) toward the end of the nineteenth century that exploit accidents of the environment. Significance is not predetermined in an ideal form, but emerges out of the accident; it is variable and unpredictable. An early actuality, *What Happened on Twenty-third Street* (Edison, 1901), explicitly plays out this scenario, tracing the emergence of meaning.[21] The single-shot film begins as an almost unreadable frame encompassing the varied activities on a city street and the sidewalk next to it (Figure 6.1). People and carriages pass by in no particular order, some of them glancing at or acknowledging the presence of the camera, and the film at this point resembles the "purest" of actualities, in which the camera is simply aimed at a street scene and allowed to record whatever happens. But gradually a man and woman, walking together, emerge from the mass of details and walk toward the camera (Figures 6.2 and 6.3). As they cross a grating, a gust of air blows up through it and lifts the woman's skirt (Figure 6.4). She is momentarily embarrassed, but recovers and laughs (Figure 6.5). It is perhaps not accidental that the meaning which emerges from the chaos of detail in the street scene is an eroticized one, calling for a voyeuristic gaze; I will return to this question later. What I would like to emphasize now is that the film effectively demonstrates that contingency presupposes a certain originary evacuation of meaning. Moreover, the early cinema gives the spectator the opportunity of witnessing the ceaseless production of meaning *out of* contingency.

Hence the early cinema is very much about instants and their accountability with respect to meaning. Aumont also invokes a binary opposition in conceptualizing the instant and links it to a history of painting, photography, and cinema. Gotthold Ephraim Lessing's notion of the "pregnant instant" in painting—the best instant, the most significant, typical instant—is opposed to the any-instant-whatever that Aumont associates with Impressionism and photography. The pregnant instant is linked to processes of symbolization and the production of meaning, while a focus on any-instant-whatever is evidence of the lure of realism and of "revelation." But the term *pregnant instant* is, according to Aumont, an oxymoron. One cannot effectively conjoin instantaneity (or the authenticity of the event, the real) with an immediacy and fullness of meaning, for "meaning has no place in the real."[22] Yet Aumont claims that the term is particularly useful, for it perfectly describes a transitional moment in the history of painting—the movement from a form of representation that maximizes "pregnancy" to one that maximizes the instantaneous and the accidental. The credo of the "pregnant mo-

6.1 *What Happened on Twenty-third Street* (1901). Edison.

6.2 *What Happened on Twenty-third Street.*

6.3 *What Happened on Twenty-third Street.*

6.4 *What Happened on Twenty-third Street.*

6.5 *What Happened on Twenty-third Street.*

ment" is antithetical to tendencies within Impressionism, which cultivates the values of the ephemeral, the circumstantial, and sensation as opposed to meaning. Early photography may strive to transform any-instant-whatever into a pregnant instant (a process that has more to do with "revelation" than with symbolization), but the tendencies that dominate modernity circulate around impossible desires—how to represent the unrepresentable (as in Turner) or the impalpable (light for the Impressionists), and how to fix the ephemeral. The persistent conflict between meaning and contingency which haunts the efforts of photography and painting in relation to the representation of time seems to be neutralized by the camera, which replaces choice and intentionality with an automatic inscription of duration.

Whereas painting has to struggle to produce the sign of time, temporality is one of the signifying materials of the cinema, a part of its experience for the spectator. However, there is a sense in which the very concept of the instant is inappropriate for defining the cinema, which always deals with an extensive duration. Even the shortest shot traces a process in time, and a freeze frame dictates the duration of its own reception. The instant, properly speaking, belongs to photography and to the individual film frame, which is never seen as such by the spectator. A single shot inevitably produces the effect of temporal continuity and, hence, of "real time." In theories of the early cinema, this adherence to continuity is almost always perceived as a limitation that must be overcome before the cinema as a significant form of representation can truly emerge. Gaudreault refers to the continuity of the apparatus as a form of "shackles." Deleuze believes that the essence of the cinematic is not visible until time can be disengaged from the movement of bodies within the diegesis and *articulated* through montage. Ultimately it is editing, the possibility of a *cut* in the temporal and spatial continuity of the shot, that is fetishized as the semiotic imperative of the cinema. For general cultural theorists such as Walter Benjamin and Siegfried Kracauer, the cut was *the* incarnation of temporality in film, and it constituted the formal response to the restructuring of time in modernity.

Hence a hole or breach is perceived (at the levels both of filmmaking and of its theorization) as crucial to cinematic signification. This hole is not located, as it might be, in what is lost at the edges of the frame, or in the lack of a third dimension or color, but as the possibility of an interruption in the linear forward movement of the film strip, of its *rearticulation* in editing. According to Gaudreault, the filmic monstrator, subjected to the tyranny of temporal continuity in the single-shot actuality, does not have the option of "opening a temporal breach," an action that would permit the inscription of a reflection on the narrated world, a "filtering" through the eyes of a narrator.[23] For Gaudreault, it is editing which allows the inscription within film of "temporal '*différance*'"; the present tense of the spectator's reception is conjoined with the past tense of a filmic narration. The spectator sees *now* what the narrator *has seen* before and rearranged, rearticulated for the benefit of the spectator.

Despite the antiteleological thrust of current film historiography, its desire to grant to early cinema its own autonomy in relation to later "developments" in classical narrative cinema, the temporal continuity of the single-shot actuality continues to be conceptualized as a limitation, as a primitive moment. Hence the literature stresses the necessity of the cinematic discovery of (at least) two temporalities, two types of movement. For Deleuze, camera movement and montage provide an alternative, specifically cinematic temporality, which liberates film from the shackles of a temporality enslaved to the movement of bodies and things within the frame. Gaudreault also outlines the historical necessity of a "double mobility." He claims that, in the single-shot film, "The double mobility which characterizes film narrative—mobility of objects depicted and motility of time-space segmentation—*had yet to materialize completely.* All that was known was the mobility of objects depicted in the frame, a mobility made possible by the new invention which could seize, fix and reproduce movements of beings and things."[24] This seems to suggest that the alignment of film with a pure storage/recording of time was at the same time desired and spurned. Theories of double mobility or double temporality in the cinema respond to the necessity of accounting for both film's indexicality and its possibility of articulation (of syntax). On the one hand, the cinematic image appears as the imprint of time, its automatic rendering and recording. But the implicit history in the official histories dictates the intolerability of this state of affairs; plenitude poses a threat. A gap or interval is required and is found in the form of editing. On the other hand, the solution to the threat of the overpresence of the image—editing—generates its own anxieties about discontinuity and absence. As a reinscription of the gap between film frames, editing potentially constitutes a persistent reminder of the abyss of darkness that subtends cinema.[25] Aumont claims that the fear of overpresence outweighs the fear of a hole or gap because it is "easier, mentally *and* visually, to fill a hole than to assimilate [*résorber*] a too-full [*trop-plein*]."[26] But I think it would be more accurate to say that it is in the tension between the fear of surfeit and the fear of absence that the specificity of the cinema's inscription of time lies.

Nevertheless, it remains clear that editing—as the possibility of departure from temporal and spatial continuity—is consistently perceived as the sine qua non of cinematic signification. Aumont maintains that the "interval" (usually conceived as the "visual distance maintained between two shots") is what permits the cinema to make of time a formal material.[27] Kracauer finds the spatial continuity of photography abhorrent and fully in collusion with the temporal continuity embraced by historicism. What both disallow are the gaps conducive to the production of significance and authentic memory. However, the blanketing of the world by photographs evacuated of meaning is countered, in a utopian discursive moment toward the end of Kracauer's essay, by an appeal to film's "capacity to stir up the elements of nature" by combining "parts and segments to create strange constructs." The fact that editing in itself does not provide an authentic or true arrangement, but instead, in the manner of dreams, reveals that "the valid organization of things remains unknown," indicates that for Kracauer it is the process of editing itself which can counter the semiotic-historical deficiencies of photographic continuity.[28]

Given the critical emphasis on the interval, the gap and the production of temporalities freed from the movement of objects and bodies in the frame, it is easy to see why film historians dwell on the vicissitudes of editing in the earliest years of the cinema. For the struggles to produce legibility and logic in sequencing shots reveal the complexities of creating an articulated time that does not undermine the authenticity/authority of recorded time—the "real time" of the shot. The joining together of two shots takes place very early in film history, but the implications of that act have varying levels of significance. In early actualities, such as *Electrocuting an Elephant* (Edison, 1903) and *The Burning of Durland's Riding Academy* (Edison, 1902), cuts (or camera stoppages) represent a simple ellipsis, eliding "uneventful" time, or they enable the presentation of multiple views of the same "event" (as in *Burning*). The cut (or camera stoppage) in some execution films (*The Execution of Mary Queen of Scots* [Edison, 1895], *Execution by Hanging* [Mutoscope/Biograph, 1905]) is designed precisely *not to be seen,* so that the substitution of a dummy for the real person in the execution will be invisible to a duped spectator. Here, the contents of the image are changed, but not its framing. This is a tactic used extensively in the trick film and especially in Méliès's work, where what is at stake is the fascination associated with sudden appearances and disappearances of bodies and things. Also, it is frequently noted that editing in the early cinema assumes the role of a simple addition or accumulation of shots constituted as tableaux, shots that could easily stand on their own as independent films. The instability of such editing is demonstrated by the fact that exhibitors were given the option of renting single shots.

Yet there is also a pronounced tendency to utilize editing in such a way that cuts will be technically visible but not disruptive, and their location stable and necessary in the effort to build a recognizable filmic world. What I am interested in isolating and examining here are three logics of early film editing that involve the deliberate construction of a diegesis, the concerted effort to formulate a coherent relation to filmic space and time. These logics are not exhaustive of such efforts, but historians nevertheless return to them again and again as exemplary moments in the development and stabilization of a cinematic syntax. I am interested in analyzing these moments specifically in relation to their assumptions about temporality, about the potential form of a cinematic time. The three editing practices involve: the logic of repetition (in which a change in the position of the camera instigates a repetition of a narrative event—*The Life of an American Fireman* (Edison, 1903) is the most frequently cited example); the logic of the chase (the insistent linearization of time); and the logic of parallel editing and suspense (the dramatization of time). Ultimately I will examine the relation of these logics to the difficulties posed by Zeno's paradoxes in their reemergence at the turn of the century.

In retrospect, the logic of repetition strikes us as closer to an antilogic, or the violation of a coherent set of rules for the construction of filmic space and time. These rules—those of classical continuity editing—did not emerge until much later than the films considered here, and therefore it is not the question of "violation" which is at stake.[29] The most famous example is Edwin S. Porter's *The Life of an American Fireman*. The overall organization of the film is that of linear narrative, but the crucial scene—in which the mother and daughter are rescued by the firemen—is repeated in toto, represented from two different points of view. In the first scene, the camera is located "inside" the house and records the mother waking, running to the window, and collapsing on the bed. A fireman enters the bedroom, breaks the window, and carries the mother out the window and down a ladder. A few seconds later he returns up the ladder to get the child. This scene is repeated from the "outside" of the house, the fireman descending the ladder with the mother, the mother pleading with the fireman to save her child, and the fireman returning to get the child. In each case, any elapsed time is situated in the "other," unseen space. Although this is the most elaborate example of temporal repetition in early cinema, there are other examples clustered around the same year, 1903. *Next!* (Mutoscope/Biograph, 1903) is a short, two-shot skit that takes place in a barbershop. Two clownish-looking patrons (Alphonse and Gaston) graciously defer to each other, bowing repetitively as the barber calls for the next customer. Impatient and frustrated, the barbers and the other customers finally throw the two clowns out the window, one after the other. The next and final shot repeats the same action (the two being thrown through the window) from another camera position, outside the barbershop. In another Porter film, *The Strenuous Life, or Anti-Race Suicide* (Edison, 1904), a cut-in to a closer shot of the father holding and weighing his new baby initiates a replay of a previous action. In each of these examples, temporal repetition seems to compensate for spatial dislocation. The spectator's "anchor" would be the familiarity/recognizability of a filmic time already "lived."

Around 1903–04, concerns about the stability of point of view seem to outweigh the disadvantages of temporal repetition in films that are in other respects quite linear. Noël Burch astutely links this temporal repetition to the specificity of the spectator's relation to the screen in the early cinema. Referring to *The Life of an American Fireman,* he claims that

> the fact that once these two shots were filmed, it was decided to connect them in a manner implying an obvious non-linearity rather than disturb the unity of the spatial viewpoint, seems to me to say a good deal about the *alterity* of the relationship these early films entertained with the spectators who watched them. Does it not suggest that the feeling of being seated in a theatre in front of a screen had, for spectators then, a sort of priority over the feeling of being carried away by an imaginary time-flow, modelled on the semblance of linearity which *ordinary time* has for us?[30]

The logic of temporal repetition implies a resolute literalism in the cinematic depiction of time. In a medium so strongly applauded for its ability to store or record time, it becomes difficult to think time as figurable, manipulable. The linearity and irreversibility of film would seem to make it most resistant to the depiction of simultaneity when different spaces are involved. In the first shot of *The Life of an American Fireman,* a fireman dozes at his desk. A balloon insert appears in the upper right corner of the frame, and within it the mother puts her child to bed. This has been interpreted in various ways as the fireman's dream about his own family or as the representation of simultaneous events in different spaces. Since the mother and child are never connected in any other way to this particular fireman, the argument that the superimposition depicts simultaneity strikes me as more plausible. Other films of the period, such as *The Story the Biograph Told* (Biograph, 1903), also resort to superimposition for the depiction of simultaneity. In this instance, the resolute literalism of the representation of time is apparent. What happens simultaneously in the narrative happens simultaneously in the image. Filmic time and diegetic time coincide. There is a certain spatial violence enacted here, and the coherence and contiguity of space are sacrificed to a literalism of time. Parallel editing is the historical "solution" to the problem of representing simultaneity, but in order for it to be viable, succession must be accepted as the signifier of its opposite, simultaneity. The cinematic troping of time begins.

For the most part, visible time in the cinema is equal to "real time," and any manipulation or troping of time takes place in the invisible realms of off-screen space or the interstices between shots. (Fast motion, slow motion, the freeze frame, and other distortions of time become, precisely, *special* effects, relegated to the marginal status of heavily coded—and rare—moments.) In *The Life of an American Fireman*, time is in fact condensed whenever events take place off-screen. In the "inside" view, the time that elapses between the moment when the fireman disappears down the ladder with the mother and the moment when he reappears to save the child is hardly sufficient to take the mother to safety and receive her pleas for the rescue of her child (events that are depicted in the "outside" portion). As Charles Musser has pointed out, "In keeping with theatrical conventions, whenever actions take place off screen, time is elided."[31] Time is manipulable when it is invisible. But *The Life of an American Fireman,* by repeating the scene, reveals what was "off" and formerly condensed, and "reexpands" it. From the point of view of later developments in continuity editing, this could only be perceived as a "mistake" or a "violation."

Although temporal repetition in *The Life of an American Fireman* and other films of the period certainly reveals spatial anxieties and apprehensions about the mobility of the camera, and hence the imaginary mobility of the spectator, it also very crucially indicates the forcefulness of the representational struggles over cinematic temporality. The manifest project of modernity—and of the cinema in the wake of Marey and Muybridge—is to make time visible, representable, to store and, hence, to defeat time as relentless passage. But visible time in the cinema is yoked to the body, movement, space, and the potential excesses of "real time." The primary viable articulation of time takes place off-screen, between frames, in darkness. It is in the intervals, invisible aspects, blind spots, the gaps, that time becomes accessible to manipulation, narrativization, and ultimately commodification. The cinematic production of temporality, for the most part, goes unseen, is naturalized through a logic of "real time." The representational struggles over temporality are fought on the terrain of the visible versus the invisible.

In *The Life of an American Fireman* and *Next!* what is "lost" to invisibility, and then "filled in" by the temporal repetition, is the depth of the image, its missing dimension. The window on the back wall of each set suggests the existence of an unseen narrative realm, but even more insistently, the fact that characters *cross* that semiotic barrier, transgress the spatial/temporal limits of the frame in an action central to the narrative, makes the invisibility of the "beyond" of the frame intolerable. It is made visible at the cost of a temporal jolt, a redundancy. Such a logic cannot survive, because it violates the perceived alliance of the medium with temporal irreversibility (see Chapter 4). The chase film, on the other hand, yokes invisibility to a logic of succession, to a horizontal imperative of linearity. Here, however, the desire to make and keep everything visible is also strongly evident, this time in the convention whereby all characters are allowed to leave the frame before the cut to the next location. An empty frame fills with pursued and pursuers, is evacuated, and the cycle continues. The cut is made when there is no longer anything to be seen. As numerous critics have pointed out, editing in the early cinema is often a matter of the simple juxtaposition of autonomous tableaux, as in *The Passion Play of Oberammergau* (Eden-Musee, 1898). Given what Noël Burch refers to as the "autarchy" and unicity of the frame, the space and time of the first shot do not interpenetrate the space and time of the second; any connections between the two are external. The logic is that of the sheer addition or accumulation of views. The chase film introduces a tension and a direction to filmic temporality and vectorizes space. Time is structured through anticipation and delay. *Personal* (Biograph, 1904), in which a dandy advertises for a wife and, overwhelmed with applicants for the position, is pursued down a city street, through fields, down a country road, across a fence, and so on, until he is finally "caught" by one of the women (who pulls a gun on him), is in many ways paradigmatic of the genre (extremely popular, it was remade at least three times).[32] Each shot is set in a different location but encompasses the same action—pursuers chasing the pursued. The spaces are not connected geographically or filmically in any way other than through their similar functions as the field or background traversed by the characters. The same general logic informs films such as *The Lost Child* (Biograph, 1904), in which a large crowd (including an old man in a wheelchair and a woman with a stroller) chases a man mistakenly thought to have abducted a child, and *Getting Evidence* (Edison, 1906), in which a photographer attempts unsuccessfully to photograph an "illicit" couple in a variety of comic situations and, once he obtains the desired photograph, is subject to an extended chase.

In all these films the movement of characters is either toward or away from the camera, extending the amount of time they are visible within a single frame. And although the chase film is often described as the insistent linearization of filmic temporality, there is something curiously static about these films. Aside from the beginning and ending shots, the order of shots is entirely arbitrary. It does not matter whether the dandy in *Personal* is chased across a fence before or after he is chased down a road. The middle of the film is basically constituted by repetition masquerading as difference. The chase stretches, elongates, fills the time of filmic representation, often to the point of monotony. Burch claims: "And this was the role of the chase: to extend the film experience, to initiate a certain 'imaginary' production of duration and succession exploiting an off-screen space which although it was still amorphous would eventually make possible the diegetic production characteristic of the institution."[33] Since repetition, duration, and succession were the laws of this logic, it was not in fact fully confined to the chase film, and characterized films such as *Rescued by Rover* (Hepworth, 1905), *Rube and Mandy at Coney Island* (Edison, 1907), and *Laughing Gas* (Edison, 1907), although these films lack the tension of heavy pursuit. In *Laughing Gas* (Edison, 1907), a black woman named Mandy is given laughing gas by a dentist when her tooth is pulled. She goes on, in a succession of different locations and situations (the subway, the street, a court, a church), to infect everyone she meets with her unstoppable laughter.

There is something excessive, almost hysterical, about the films that deploy this logic. Nearly all of them are comic, but the comedy seems only to intensify the anxiety they reveal. In *Laughing Gas,* what is clearly at stake is a fear of contagion linked to racial difference. In *Rescued by Rover* and *The Lost Child,* it is the safety and security of the bourgeois nuclear family that are threatened from without (by a gypsy or stranger), and the figure of the lost child acts as the emblem of loss in general. In *Personal,* it is femininity itself which constitutes a threat through the incessant multiplication of the figure of the demanding and quasi-hysterical potential wife. A mob of women repeatedly fill and empty the frame, and the dandy becomes a besieged and sympathetic character. There is a certain hysteria of sexual difference here, the inscription of an excessive heterosexuality gone awry. Lubin's remake of *Personal,* titled *Meet Me at the Fountain* (1904), comments upon the insistency of this heterosexual matrix by including, as one of the pursuing "women," a well-known female impersonator (Gilbert Saroni), who, though always the last to enter and exit the frame, "gets" the man in the end, a scene that is constituted by a closer shot in which the female impersonator caresses and kisses the dandy, who wipes his mouth with his handkerchief. The "joke" assumes heterosexuality as a norm and as normal. Similarly, *Getting Evidence* circulates around heterosexuality, the sought-after evidence constituted by photographic proof of the intimate relation of a man and a woman. The constitution of a cinematic syntax and the incessant inscription of heterosexuality as norm are in collusion.

The structure of the chase film partakes of the logic of the series, subsuming individual irregularity beneath the rule of aggregate regularity, and allying itself with a growing social emphasis upon statistics and probability. Each shot generates a sense of difference but reiterates the same dilemma: the pursuers chase the pursued, traversing the depth of field, until some arbitrary moment of closure, usually catastrophic, ends the series. And the series is repeated again in the next film, with the same expectations, the same use of delay to construct filmic duration. As Ian Hacking has demonstrated, during this period, correlation began to displace causality, and "A story of the erosion of determinism is also an account of the invention of normalcy."[34] The isolation of causal factors gives way before the observation of statistical regularities and processes of normalization. The films use the combination of individual irregularity with aggregate regularity in order to buttress the norms of family, heterosexuality, and whiteness, all of which are perceived as threatened at the turn of the century. Filmic duration is organized to suggest that each shot entertains differences, implies a progression, when the procedure involved is instead one of static addition, accumulation. As Hacking points out, the ideology of normalization deploys simultaneously two different understandings of the "normal"—"what is," the usual, the average, the typical (which may be subject to deviation, deflection), and, second, what ought to be, what we should strive for, the ethical standard of the "norm." Such a double temporality implies a dual understanding of progress as both the restoration of an ideal average (for example, "lost health" as restoration of the "norm") and the movement toward a future goal (normalization). Both are curiously static teleologies. The insistent linearization usually attributed to the chase film, which conceals an equally insistent redundancy and repetitiveness in the service of normalization, invests in this ideology of progress.

While the first two logics of film editing have been perceived as stages, as evidence of a certain stylistic "primitiveness," the use of parallel editing is frequently treated as the telos of early cinema, the attainment of a fully and specifically cinematic discourse. Parallel editing successfully eroticizes time, injects it with desire, expectation, anticipation, and displaces the spectatorial time of viewing by contributing to the construction of a "lived," imaginary temporality. Parallel editing is generally defined as cutting alternately between two scenes that are assumed to have some form of relation with each other and are usually understood as taking place simultaneously or nearly simultaneously. Simultaneity is signified by succession rather than by the spatial disruption of the image through balloon inserts or superimposition. Filmic time no longer matches, in a one-to-one correspondence (as in the single-shot actuality so long dominant), diegetic time. Spectatorial time— the time of sitting in the theater—is emptied and replaced by the cinematic articulation of a temporality whose strategies are concealed by an appeal to the grounding referentiality/indexicality of its base.

In parallel editing, the relations between the two shots are no longer the benign ones of addition or accumulation, but are intensified by the interpenetration of anxiety, desire, or horror. This is most evident in the parallel editing that links shots of an imperiled heroine or heroines, or family, with shots of the potential rescuers (*The Lonely Villa* [1909], *An Unseen Enemy*

[1912], or *The Lonedale Operator* [1911]), but is also characteristic of its discursive or metaphorical activation, as in the comparison of rich to poor in *A Corner in Wheat* (1909) and *The Usurer* (1910) (all Biograph). D. W. Griffith's significance here lies in his extensive use of parallel editing and his insistence upon making the articulation of time as crisis crucial to cinematic signification. *The Fatal Hour* (1908), the first film in which Griffith used extensive parallel editing,[35] ends with a scene in which shots of a female detective immobilized in front of a gun timed to shoot her when the clock strikes twelve are intercut with shots of the police coming to the rescue. They, of course, reach her in "the nick of time."

The yoking together of noncontiguous spaces through parallel editing forced a certain denaturalization of the filmic discourse. It required the spectator to accept enormous leaps in space and to allow the disfiguration of continuous time, its expansion or contraction. As Gunning has argued, the temporal simultaneity signified by parallel editing demands an abstraction that was countered by the incorporation of recent technology—the telephone, the telegraph, the railroad—into plots, in order to "naturalize film's power to move through space and time."[36] Editing borrowed the authority of the telephone to rationalize the instantaneous movement from site to site effected by the cut. Telephones are indeed ubiquitous in the films of this period. In *An Unseen Enemy,* two orphaned sisters are trapped in a room by their "slatternly" maid and her accomplice, who attempt to steal the contents of the father's safe. It is only when one of the sisters manages to reach the telephone that she is able to summon her brother to help them. In *The Lonely Villa,* Gunning's primary example, a bourgeois home is threatened by three itinerants, and the wife, hiding in an interior room with her three daughters, is able to alert her husband to the danger when he phones her. In both of these examples, a telephone call initiates a sequence of parallel editing chronicling a rescue. In *The Medicine Bottle* (1909), the telephone itself constitutes the solution to the problem (a woman has mistakenly instructed her daughter to administer poison instead of medicine to her sick grandmother), and the only possible hindrance or delay is in the telephone system itself (the switchboard operators gossip instead of attending to their duties). In *Death's Marathon* (1913), when a friend is too late to prevent her husband from killing himself, the wife "witnesses" the suicide over the telephone after a prolonged sequence of parallel editing. *The Lonedale Operator* combines railroad and telegraph in its narrative of separation, threat, and rescue.

As Gunning astutely points out, the motivation for this type of parallel editing is most frequently the desire to overcome a distance or physical separation, to "join . . . loved ones."[37] Suspense is predicated on absence or separation and driven by an external threat to the home, the family, the woman. The gap between shots mimics the gap constitutive of desire. Suspense in the cinema, as Pascal Bonitzer has extensively demonstrated, is on the side of invisibility, and depends upon the activation of off-screen space, or the "blind spot."[38] In parallel editing, when shot B is on the screen its legibility is saturated by the absent presence of shot A, and vice versa. Duration is energized by invisibility, by the inability to see all. It is not accidental that the "invention" of parallel editing and an increased exploitation of the frame as the threshold of an unseen yet semiotically dense space should coincide. In many of Griffith's last-minute-rescue films, the women are encased in a room in a house or in a series of adjoining rooms, an architecture that allows for an intense awareness of encroaching danger "just beyond" a frame which coincides with and rearticulates the walls of the room. In *The Lonely Villa,* when the three vagabonds break through the door of the first room in which the women are hiding, they move to a second, adjacent room, and the process is repeated. In *An Unseen Enemy,* the contiguity of the room in which the orphaned sisters hide and that in which the maid and her accomplice attempt to break into the safe is vividly incarnated in a small hole connecting them through which a hand with a gun appears to threaten the sisters. Jacques Aumont's reading of this spatial arrangement is provocative:

> It has been remarked, in the context of *Intolerance:* in Griffith's cinema, "partir c'est toujours mourir un peu" ("to leave is always to die a little") and leaving the scene signifies at least potentially the death of the character. What closes the scene, via the frame, is in a sense this threat of death, always implicitly and metaphorically proffered from beyond the frame. The revolver of *An Unseen Enemy* can, God knows, be read in more ways than one, but . . . can we not still see in it the literal agent of this threat, openly articulated in this way?[39]

Time, death, and invisibility are welded together at the edge of the frame and between shots, in the unseen space that makes it possible for the cinema to say anything at all. Perhaps this is why suspense (and its deployment in parallel editing) was so crucial to the forging of a cinematic syntax in modernity. Fatality is the perpetually deferred that drives the linear movement, and, as Bonitzer has shown, it is the "image of the worst" that governs the progression of shots in suspense, as a system.[40]

This fatality most frequently takes the clichéd form of the woman in distress, the imperiled heroine. *The Fatal Hour* is only the most explicit instance of the early cinema's tendency to yoke together the figure of the threatened woman and a discursive insistence upon temporality. Time itself seems to menace the woman, and it is in "the nick of time" that she is saved. In *The Fatal Hour,* it is the Law that comes to the rescue, but more frequently it is a lover or a husband (as in *The Lonedale Operator* or *The Lonely Villa*), so that, in effect, it is the mechanism of heterosexuality which ensures her salvation. Closure is effected by the embrace or the kiss, over and over again, as the resolution to the problem of an ending in a cinema that affirms time as continuity. In *The Lonedale Operator,* as Raymond Bellour has demonstrated, the logic of the parallel editing is basically the logic of an alternation between "he" and "she." The film begins with a scene in which the operator playfully parries the attentions of the engineer. It is only after their separation and the ensuing threat to her well-being that they are successfully reunited and embrace at the end of the film. The "thrilling of intelligibility" that Barthes associates with suspense is in the service of the confirmation and reconfirmation of heterosexuality, which in turn lends its "intelligibility" to the cinematic desire to overcome distance, separation, the inevitability of absence.[41]

The compulsive replaying of the scenario of heterosexual union exploits its mishaps and potential misses, energizing time and injecting it with a direction. Anxieties about the rationalization of time in modernity, about the confrontation with racial otherness, about emerging instabilities of gender identity, can be allayed by the insistent repetition of an imperative, normative, and fully realizable heterosexuality that overcomes division itself (a difference and a division that the cinematic medium itself has a stake in overcoming in the production of movement). Perhaps this is why the kiss has constituted such a crucial semiotic event in the cinema, from Edison's 1896 *Irwin Rice Kiss* to *The Lonedale Operator,* and throughout the period of the classical Hollywood narrative. In this respect, the 1903 *What Happened in the Tunnel* (Edison) is quite telling.[42] The film begins with a shot of a middle-class woman and her black maid sitting together in a train compartment

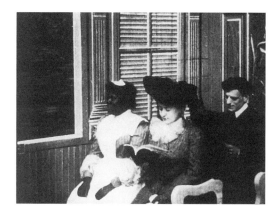

6.6 *What Happened in the Tunnel* (1903). Edison.

6.7 *What Happened in the Tunnel.*

(as a matte shot of a changing landscape on the window produces the illusion of the train's movement) (Figure 6.6).[43] A man sitting behind them is energetically flirting with the white woman (Figure 6.7). The train enters a tunnel (signified by a cut to black), and when it emerges (in a return to the first shot), the man finds that the women have changed places and he is kissing the black maid (Figure 6.8). Both women laugh heartily as the embarrassed would-be lover hides behind his newspaper (Figure 6.9).

Fashioning itself in the "what happened" mode of *What Happened on Twenty-third Street* (Edison, 1901), the film's pretense is that of having "captured" a particularly comic moment hinging on sexual difference. But in *What Happened on Twenty-third Street* contingency is conquered in a single shot—the revealing of the female body as spectacle binds the apparent anar-

6.8 *What Happened in the Tunnel.*

6.9 *What Happened in the Tunnel.*

chy of details in a focused look. *What Happened in the Tunnel,* on the other hand, utilizes editing, at a very basic level, in order to activate blindness, invisibility, as a structuring component of the cinema's articulation. On the one hand, the cut to blackness that bisects the film acts as the reinscription of the gap between frames and of the darkness built into cinematic duration through the operation of the shutter. On the other hand, that gap is recuperated for meaning through its narrativization, its diegetic incarnation as the passage through a tunnel. Nevertheless, the gap continues to embody a deeply felt threat, that of miscegenation, an "improper" sexual relation, which the film fends off through its transformation into comedy (although the laughter provoked is, no doubt, an anxious one). The kiss has been misplaced; it has gone awry.

The silent cinema did not fully master the darkness subtending the medium until the cranking of camera and projector was fully regularized through electrical power and the three-blade shutter introduced.[44] It is only then that the phenomenon called "flicker" could disappear. In the 1960s, the avant-garde film movement known as structural or materialist film refocused attention on the phenomenon of flicker in its investigation of the ontological implications of the material base of the medium—hence the short-lived genre of the "flicker film." Thom Andersen's remarkable documentary, *Eadweard Muybridge, Zoopraxographer* (1974), is very much in the spirit of this celebration of filmic materiality. Here Muybridge emerges as the heroic figure in the passage from photography to cinema, from static immobility to the successful reproduction of time and movement. Obsessed with movement, the camera is rarely still in Andersen's film, even when it confronts the enormous range of Muybridge's work in still photography, where the camera insistently moves into or out from the photographs, isolating details or placing them in context. Andersen also incessantly transforms Muybridge's sequential photography into cinema, presenting it in a way that, given advances in cinematic technology, as Andersen points out, Muybridge himself could never have seen it. In *Eadweard Muybridge, Zoopraxographer,* athletes jump over fences repeatedly, women sweep floors and walk up stairs over and over again in a vertiginous display of, and incantation to, movement.

In a very striking sequence toward the end of the film, Andersen returns to the thematics of Zeno's paradox and proposes the cinema anticipated by Muybridge as the solution. The sequence begins with a statement in a male voice-over, "But in Muybridge's work, photography in its passage to cinema overcame a philosophical obstacle," which precedes a cut to black. The shot that accompanies the discussion of this philosophical obstacle is a restaging of one of Muybridge's scenarios (shown earlier in Andersen's film) in which two women walk toward each other and kiss. The scene is clearly a "rewriting" of Muybridge—the two women are naked, they "perform" against a background constituted as a grid of white lines over black, and their gestures mimic precisely those of the women in Muybridge's sequence. The flicker effect of this scene is at first pronounced, so that the spectator is intensely aware of the intervals of blackness between illuminations of the image (Figure 6.10). But as the scene progresses, the camera moves forward toward the women, and the flicker gradually decreases (Figures 6.11 and 6.12), until, at

6.10 *Eadweard Muybridge, Zoopraxographer* (1974).
Thom Andersen.

6.11 *Eadweard Muybridge,*
Zoopraxographer.

6.12 *Eadweard Muybridge,*
Zoopraxographer.

6.13 *Eadweard Muybridge,*
Zoopraxographer.

the moment of the kiss, it disappears and the sequence becomes cinema (Figure 6.13). The overcoming of the darkness and the lost time it signals are coincident with the kiss. It is worth quoting the voice-over at length:

> The modern motion picture camera bisects time into equal moments of light and darkness,[45] their duration regulated by the constant rotation of the shutter. Between each frame, when the shutter closes over the lens as the strip of film is repositioned, there is a moment of darkness, a fragment of time which is not recorded. Time, like any continuous quantity, is infinitely divisible. It cannot be reconstituted in its unity by a mechanical instrument which bisects it finitely. [At this point, the women touch hands.] So we might question the possibility of cinema, asking how can we recapture motion in a finite number of still pictures just as Zeno asked, how can we cross space in a finite number of movements, since it is infinitely divisible? The solution to this paradox lies in the persistence of vision, metaphorically described in the fifteenth century by Leonardo da Vinci, "Every body that moves rapidly seems to color its path with the impression of its hue. Thus when lightning moves among dark clouds, the speed of its sinuous flight makes its whole course resemble a luminous snake. This is because the organ of perception acts more rapidly than the judgment." [During a moment of silence, the kiss is fully transformed into a cinematic kiss; the flicker disappears and continuity is dominant.] Through the persistence of vision, human perception is able to bridge the darkness, which always alternates, coequally with the light, on every motion picture screen.

At this point the shot fades out and is replaced by a shot of Muybridge walking across the screen repeatedly (reconstituted from his own sequential photographs) as the camera pulls back (Figures 6.14 and 6.15). The film ends with the observation in voice-over that "Muybridge transformed photography from the Zenonian reverie on movement it had been into the modern instrument that recovers the unity of human motion, the motion by which Zeno's paradoxes are refuted in a single step."

It matters little, I think, that persistence of vision is no longer considered to be an adequate explanation for the perception of movement in the cinema.[46] What matters for Andersen is that in the cinema darkness has been

6.14 *Eadweard Muybridge,
Zoopraxographer.*

6.15 *Eadweard Muybridge,
Zoopraxographer.*

banished and immobility has been successfully translated into mobility. Zeno has been refuted by cinematic technology. But what is most significant is Andersen's insistence on articulating this through the image of the human contact of a kiss. At the moment that the kiss becomes fully visible and continuous, the cinema begins. Yet this kiss is between two women; it is not the heterosexual kiss of Griffith, Porter, or the mainstream Hollywood cinema. Unlike Linda Williams, who sees Muybridge's work as the reinscription of scenarios that regulate the terms of a very conventional understanding of sexual difference,[47] Andersen emphasizes Muybridge's violation of Victorian norms and understandings of sexuality. Victorian society was, in Henry James's account cited by the film, a society whose "greatest triumph" was the "suppression of sex." Many of Muybridge's female models were prostitutes (as was common for artists of the period working with nudes). They have close-cropped hair and smoke cigarettes languorously, and Muybridge exploits the conventional association of prostitutes with lesbianism in scenarios in which two women walk together, arms around each other, or dance, or kiss. But the scandal or radical subversiveness of Muybridge's work, for Andersen, is not, ultimately, lesbianism, but nakedness. According to the film's voice-over, Muybridge's work was "necessarily subversive of the taboo against realistic representation of nudity." For his society, materiality was equivalent to "evil," and nudity was therefore acceptable only if it was *dematerialized* through "lyricism, idealization, and good taste." There is a certain slippage here between nakedness, materiality, and, ultimately, radical materialism (the film begins with a quotation from Mao Zedong to the effect that "Man's knowledge of matter is knowledge of its forms of motion"). For Andersen, Muybridge's insistence upon nakedness is of the same order as the filmmaker's concern with the materiality of his or her own medium, which, in its turn, is compatible with the radical subversiveness associated with a Marxist materialism. Lesbianism would in this context be something of an afterthought, a further confirmation of Muybridge's assault on orthodoxy.

Nevertheless, in remaining faithful to Muybridge, in scrupulously miming his pseudoscientific grid, the gestures of the performers, and the fact that it is two women who kiss, Andersen's film makes visible an enabling mechanism of mainstream cinema's attempt to "bridge the darkness"—its insistent normalization of heterosexuality, a fact that strikes the film theorist with the force of an obviousness that makes it appear to resist analysis, to require no further dissection of its logic. Yet cinematic heterosexuality, at a very early stage, becomes fully imbricated in an attempt to grapple with the paradoxes of movement and temporality in the medium. Andersen's film calls attention to the absence of a lesbian kiss in most of the cinema following Muybridge, indeed, its contradiction or suppression through the constant reiteration of the heterosexual kiss as closure. In the classical cinema, it is the heterosexual kiss that "bridges the darkness."

A paradox is a statement that is contrary to received opinion or common sense but may actually be true. The etymology of the word traces it to the Greek *para* (beyond) and *doxon* (opinion). For Zeno, the kiss never really takes place; its suggestion of union is only illusory, because movement can never be born from a series of immobilities. Infinitely halving the distance between them, the women never reach each other. In the classical cinema, the kiss is consistently returned to as the quite particular disproof of the paradox of Zeno's philosophy, as the guarantee of the cinema's ability to "bridge the darkness." The kiss here is the reassertion of the reigning doxa of family, race, nation, buttressed by a formal drive toward continuity.

Modernity has been delineated as the establishment of a social order based on mobility, flux, exchange. Perhaps this is why Walter Benjamin read Baudelaire's sonnet "A une passante" as exemplary of both the thematics of the crowd and the ephemeral temporality of the modern city. In it, a solitary woman emerges from the crowd, captures the gaze of the urban poet, and then disappears ("A lightning flash . . . then night"). The sonnet ends with the line "O you I would have loved (o you who knew it too!) [*O toi que j'eusse aimée, ô toi qui le savais!*]." Benjamin refers to this as "love—not at first sight, but at last sight."[48] Both the fascinations and the anxieties of modernity are figured as the failure of heterosexual contact, and all of this takes place in an instant. Benjamin derives his by now very familiar theory of shock in the course of his investigation of Baudelaire's poetry. And in this same essay he makes the following remark about photography: "The camera imparts to the instant an as it were posthumous shock."[49] As Samuel Weber has pointed out, the word translated as "instant" here is *Augenblick,* which is, literally, "eye-look," and has been translated as "in the blink of an eye."[50] In the crowded and "deafening" street, the urban poet loses his potential love "in the blink of an eye." Instantaneous photography, the basis of cinema, gives the instant a posthumous shock—it *takes* a picture, inscribes a moment (in the case of the cinema, eighteen to twenty-four per second). And the mechanism of the shutter in the camera (itself understood as a prosthetic extension of vision, as a figuring of the human eye) has been envisaged as "the blink of an eye." But the blink of an eye encompasses both light and darkness, vision and invisibility. The cinematic representation and celebration of mobility are founded on a basic stillness or immobility subtended by darkness. Its narrative denial of this is buttressed by the articulation of a series of imbricated obviousnesses—movement, instantaneity, heterosexuality, and visibility. The "flicker film" of the 1960s attempted to shatter this illusion and its allied comfort by assaulting the spectator at the level of perception. But many flicker films were contentless and failed to engage with the thematic matrix historically interpenetrating the illusion. Both modernity and the cinema have a stake in refuting Zeno, in affirming the reality, indeed the allure, of a mobility that is, in film, quite simply not there.

7

The Instant and the Archive

Rather than pass the time, one must invite it in. To pass the time (to kill time, expel it): the gambler. Time spills from his every pore.—To store time as a battery stores energy: the flâneur. Finally, the third type: he who waits. He takes in the time and renders it up in altered form—that of expectation.

WALTER BENJAMIN, *The Arcades Project*

The archive: if we want to know what that will have meant, we will only know in times to come. Perhaps. Not tomorrow but in times to come, later on or perhaps never. A spectral messianicity is at work in the concept of the archive and ties it, like religion, like history, like science itself, to a very singular experience of the promise.

JACQUES DERRIDA, *Archive Fever*

A 1901 actuality titled *A Mighty Tumble* (Mutoscope/Biograph) chronicles in two brief shots, barely seventeen seconds long, the razing of a four-story brick building. In the first shot the building leans slowly, then topples over as a cloud of white dust rises to obscure everything except a few silhouettes of men with top hats moving parallel to and toward the camera. The second shot is simply that of a crowd of adults and children watching the spectacle, their backs to the camera. There is an insistence upon the witness here, both in the form of the random trajectories of the top-hatted men, deindividualized by a lighting that renders them as silhouettes, and in the guise of anonymous members of a crowd. In each case the gaze at the event is assumed but not shown. It is as if the camera operator felt compelled to demonstrate that the event was worth watching or, perhaps, that watching was in itself an event worth recording. The seemingly unpredictable movements of the shadowy figures appear to incarnate the intimacy of the filmic and the aleatory, the contingent.

On May 23, 1995, the remains of the bombed-out Alfred P. Murrah Building in Oklahoma City were also subjected to demolition, and the implosion was recorded, this time as television. CNN carried local KWTV's coverage "live," explaining that the television station had placed a camera within the demolition zone, in effect sacrificing the camera to produce a closer and more intense experience of the violence of the implosion. The shot echoes *A Mighty Tumble,* recording the process by which the building begins to lean and finally collapses. A large cloud of dust and debris hurtles toward the camera/spectator, and the screen turns gray, yellow, red, and finally black as the camera is destroyed. Here, there is a form of intimacy between witness and event, so much so that the two merge in a mutual annihilation. The gaze itself implodes. Such an excessive technique registers the extraordinary desire of "liveness"—to be there at the instant of the catastrophic event, to witness death as ultimate referent or as the collision with the real in all its intractability. The liveness and presence of the camera at the instant of the implosion act as forms of compensation for the absence of a camera at the original bombing/explosion on April 19, 1995. The mourning of this loss— that of an image of the Ur-event—accompanies and fortifies the mourning for the loss of lives in the explosion.[1]

The record of the Alfred P. Murrah Building bombing is also available in digital form. The "Archives" of KWTV's website contain a digitized video clip of the May 23 implosion (which can be played forward and backward as the user desires), as well as the "first" broadcast images after the bombing on April 19, taken from a KWTV helicopter.[2] Also contained in the digital archive are a video clip of the crowd reacting to Timothy McVeigh leaving the courthouse on the day of his arrest, the complete text of the indictments, a chronology of events related to the bombing, and photographs of the 168 victims. At the click of a mouse, the computer user can move among textual, video, and photographic documents—a storehouse of details reconstructing the event. As the website produces its archive, the bombing is forced to participate in the much-touted "information explosion"—a metaphor whose semantic value is derived from its association with the notions of instantaneity, dispersal, fragmentation, and violence. In this case, the gaze is dispersed.[3]

There clearly are vast differences between the filmic, video, and digital accounts of explosiveness outlined here, but they hold in common a core and formative indexicality and a strong investment in the lure of instantaneity.

The 1901 actuality, with its photographically based guarantee of indexicality, exploits the fascination with recorded movement and change—the marks of time itself. An explosion—with its abrupt and violent juxtaposition of presence and absence, stability and change—provides the perfect target for such a fascination. Although the televisual and digital representations of explosions are not photographically based, their indexicality is a function of the strength of their exhortation to "Look here!," "See this," acting as the pointing finger of Peirce's empty indexical sign. The "liveness" of the televisual image ensures its adhesion to the referent just as the index adheres to its object, and the website makes that "liveness" relivable at the touch of a finger. The "Look here!" of the televisual and digital representations is prefigured by the insistence upon the witness in *A Mighty Tumble*.

Indexicality is inevitably linked with the singular, the unique, with the imprint of time and all its differentiating force. What the three historically successive forms of representation outlined above have in common is the obsession with instantaneity and contingency. In the face of the increasing rationalization and systematization of time, the lure of the singular instant is that of the free and undetermined moment, which holds out the promise of newness itself. Part of its attraction is its very resistance to meaning (as exemplified by the choice of an explosion and even more so by the annihilation of the camera in the news clip). The power of chance, for Charles Sanders Peirce, lies in the absolute discontinuity of the instant, which enables the emergence of the new. Yet this prized singularity of the instant is also always pitted against its legibility as generalized information, against the reassurance of a meaningful temporal continuity. The project of the cinema in modernity is that of endowing the singular with significance without relinquishing singularity. That project is not necessarily abandoned with the emergence of even newer technologies of representation.

The achievement of modernity's temporality, as exemplified by the development of the cinema, has been to fuse rationality and contingency, determination and chance. In line with the logic of statistics, the cinema has worked to confirm the legibility of the contingent. Cinema's decisive difference from photography was its ability to inscribe duration, temporal process. Yet it was a duration based upon division, upon the sequential serialization of still photographs which, projected, produced the illusion of motion and the capturing of time. The emphasis upon the afterimage and the persistence of vision as the first explanations for the illusion of motion in cinema and early "philosophical toys" (the Zoopraxinoscope, Thaumatrope, and so on) provides a context for the turn-of-the-century debate on the nature of time: whether it is a series of discrete instants or, as Bergson and others claimed, a continuous, nondivisible process.

The cinema is indebted to the nineteenth-century drive to fragment and analyze time and motion exemplified most fully, perhaps, by the work of Etienne-Jules Marey. The work of the chronophotographers was in turn dependent upon the development of an instantaneous photography that was capable of fixing, without loss of sharpness or legibility, an instant of an extremely fast movement. Hence there is a sense in which the logic of photography inevitably inhabits that of cinema.[4] The photographic instant becomes the basis for the representability of time as duration. The description and understanding of this "instant" have taken various forms, but remain epistemologically central to the endeavor. Marey and others have defined the image made possible by instantaneous photography as that which is beyond the limits of human vision, as that which no one has ever seen before. Tom Gunning claims that these frozen moments reveal ungraceful or awkward positions and hence contribute to a de-idealization of the body.[5] Thierry de Duve goes further and maintains that, in effect, instantaneous photography "captures" a moment that does not really exist (since "reality is not made out of singular events; it is made out of the continuous happening of things"). It immobilizes the runner forever in the midst of a stride, the jumper in midair, the discus thrower at a moment in the process of winding up. For de Duve, the instantaneous photograph does not represent movement but "only produces a petrified analogue of it" and reveals "an unperformed movement that refers to an impossible posture." This ambiguous status creates a complex temporality. Since the photograph is in the past tense the viewer will always come to it "too late"; the action will have already taken place. On the other hand, since the instantaneous photograph arrests an action before its completion, the viewer will always be "there" too soon. The trauma that structures instantaneous photography, for de Duve, lies in this "sudden vanishing of the present tense, splitting into the contradiction of being simultaneously too late and too early."[6] Similarly, for Benjamin, instantaneous photography gives the moment a "posthumous shock."[7]

It could be said, then, that the trauma, strangeness, or uncanniness of this impossible instant is rectified by the cinema, which restores to things their "continuous happening." Nevertheless, fragmentation of motion and time was historically the condition of the possibility of cinematic time, and the instantaneous photograph is still its crucial substrate. This is why Marey's work and that of the other chronophotographers remains central to film studies, despite the current injunction to see it independently, in its own terms, rather than to dissolve its specificity in the generalized category of "pre-Cinema." Michel Frizot, who has an investment in analyzing Marey's scientific contributions in their own right, nevertheless delineates the way in which Marey's approach to chronophotography and the analysis of movement defined the crucial conditions for reversibility (that is, the synthesis of movement that takes place in the cinema). Despite the fact that Marey was not interested in the cinema, according to Frizot his work entailed the isolation of five "physical operators" that established the "theoretical reversibility of the device."[8] Marey's primary interest was in the analysis of motion by breaking it down into the smallest possible units of time. He strove to dissect movement and produce a scientific understanding of its minutest implications. The phrase "theoretical reversibility of the device," for Frizot, signals the fact that Marey's "device," that is, his chronophotographic apparatus, was theoretically reversible; it could be used to resynthesize these minute units of movement into continuous movement even though Marey had no interest whatsoever in doing so. Despite himself, Marey, with his five "operators," actually isolated the five necessary conditions for cinema.

Frizot defines a physical operator as an artifact, machine, or method that makes it possible to carry out operations, for instance, to measure something. The first operator for Marey is the zero base or point zero, which is required to establish a measurement. Marey's scientific quantification of movement necessitated a zero point, and the instrument itself had to record its starting point. The chronophotographic method addressed two problems that were associated with the graphic method. First, the transmission time of the signal (for instance, air pressure in the tubes of his early devices) was too long and always entailed an intolerable delay between the movement and its record. Photography was an ideal solution in this respect, since the transmission time of light was effectively zero. The second problem involved the width of the signal (air pressure being, again, an example of a defective transmitter). The early devices using air pressure relied on force provided by the object being measured (the horse's hoof or man's foot hitting the ground). Furthermore, the air pressure encountered the inertia of the objects constituting the recording apparatus (the stylus, for instance). With light transmission in the photographic method there is no inertia, and hence the signal is not thickened.[9] What this first operator guarantees for Marey is quantifiability—through the representation of time/movement as a series of points, each point potentially actualizable as a zero point. This mandates a conceptualization of the instantaneous image as a *point* (a crucial issue, to which I will return).

The second operator in Marey's system was the reaction time of the registering system and entailed achieving extremely fast exposure times. A signal takes time to leave a trace, and this time must be reduced as much as possible. Marey gradually refined his cameras and moved from an exposure time of 1/500 second in 1882 to one of 1/25,000 second in 1891. The goal here is to obtain an image that gives the impression that the object has not moved during the observation time. In other words, the aim is that of the instantaneous snapshot—to immobilize the object *in medias res*, in a potentially awkward, ungainly, or ungraceful position that nevertheless possesses a sharpness which ensures legibility. But of course there is no truly instantaneous photograph, only the asymptotic movement toward an ideal, and, as de Duve has shown, the boundary between the snapshot and the time exposure is entirely arbitrary. Yet, again, the aspiration to instantaneity and the yearning to delineate the category of the instant are fully in evidence.

The third operator in Frizot's analysis of Marey is iteration, the apprehension of continuity through discontinuity. The periodic intermittence of the shutter replaces the continuous curve of the graphic method with a series of points. This also entails a loss of time, as described in Chapter 6, and the corresponding necessity for extrapolation. When a series of points is used as the basis for the representation of continuous time, that representation always rests on something of a void. The fourth operator is synthesis as a control. The accuracy of the analytic method could be demonstrated by reversing the process and ascertaining whether the phenomenon (the analyzed movement) could be reproduced. According to Frizot, this synthesis was not a goal for Marey; instead, it was nothing more than a control procedure. The fifth and final operator entailed the total and complete separation of images and hence the move from a fixed plate to a mobile film strip. Marey's desire here was legibility, to separate images that were superimposed. But this did require a conceptual sacrifice that Marey was never comfortable with: giving up the overall image of a phenomenon that had been attained in the past with a static plate as recording surface. In one sense, however, this fifth operator returns to a principle of the graphic method—the shifting or mobility of the recording surface.

Frizot's analysis of Marey's five operators does succeed in demonstrating that Marey's approach generated the theoretical reversibility of the apparatus and hence laid the groundwork for the emergence of cinema.[10] Marey's aim, as Frizot points out, was not cinema, but the cinema could certainly be seen as a by-product of his chronophotographic method. Frizot sees the various devices of the nineteenth century for recording and analyzing movement as basically disconnected or autonomous, as mechanical solutions that were ultimately heterogeneous. Nevertheless, he also concedes that occasionally there were shifts from one figure to another, and that one of these crucial shifts was from Marey to Lumière. It is also possible to see these interconnections as demonstrating the permeability of Claude Lévi-Strauss's categories of the engineer and the bricoleur.[11] The engineer is what we tend to think of as the true scientist. She or he uses tools designed for quite specific purposes in order to achieve precise goals. The bricoleur, on the other hand, uses what "comes to hand." Tools designed for one purpose may be used for an entirely unanticipated task; there is a certain contingency or chance always at work in the accomplishments of bricolage. Marey certainly conceived of himself as a scientist, but his tools were not there, already designed for the specific purpose he had in mind—the analysis of movement in time. Like a bricoleur (and like Muybridge, Anschütz, Edison, and Lumière), he adopted and adapted the photographic tools that existed, and the cinema emerged as the unexpected product of such bricolage. Nevertheless, all these figures were united by a fascination with the representation of movement and time, by the insistence upon breaking down or fragmentation as the first step in the reconstitution of a continuity of time, and by the embrace of the photographic instant as time's minimal unit. And this subterranean unity is not accidental, but the symptom of a historical shift in thinking about the representability of time.

There are at least three aspects of Frizot's analysis that invite further elaboration. The first is the idea that reversibility, or synthesis, was an inevitable outcome of Marey's approach but nevertheless functioned merely as a form of control for him. The fragmentation and analysis of movement was his explicit goal, critical to his project. Synthesis was necessary only as a control procedure to prove that his analytic method was valid, that in the process of fragmentation nothing critical to the phenomenon was lost. If the movement could be reproduced through synthesis as smooth and legible, the analytic method was justified. However, this reading poses problems with respect to Marey's understanding of what constitutes the properly "scientific." Marey elsewhere designates the cinema as antiscientific insofar as it "adds nothing to the power of our sight, nor does it remove its illusions." Science by its nature must exceed the limitations of our senses, and chronophotography should "renounce the representation of phenomena as they are seen by the eye."[12] Given Marey's distrust of the eye, it is difficult to see how the synthesis of movements he had previously subjected to analytic fragmentation (a functional equivalent of cinema) could act as a *scientific* control or "prove" anything. Since the eye is constantly vulnerable to illusion or delusion, its confirmation that a movement looked normal or accurate would be meaningless. In this sense, Marey's method is haunted by contradiction.

What Marey's dilemma makes apparent is how the normalization of cinematic vision conceals an intense epistemological work of fragmentation. The reconstitution of a "naturalized" movement is a laborious process subject to certain standards for the reconstruction of time. The ease and obviousness of cinematic movement are deceptive. Much recent avant-garde work in film and, now, digital media no longer takes this reconstitution for granted but instead works to defamiliarize this motion and time, in short, to bare the device. Bill Brand's *Demolition of a Wall* (1973), in the manner of the structural/materialist films of the 1970s, activates the frame as a minimal unit. Brand takes six frames from Lumière's *Démolition d'un mur* (*Demolition of a Wall*, 1896) and organizes them successively in each of the 720 permutations possible in their ordering. The result is a series of jerky and disorienting movements. Raymond Bellour has analyzed a CD-ROM by Jean-Louis Boissier, *Moments de Jean-Jacques Rousseau,* which allows links between the text of *The Confessions* and short scenes, made up of single shots characterized by pans. The CD program cuts out one frame of every ten, and the resulting movement is strange, artificial, somewhat uncanny. As Bellour points out, the CD-ROM "draws its strangeness and its strength from its deviation from the standards for the reproduction of movement."[13] These works acknowledge the temporal lapse, the lost time inherent in the cinematic representation of movement. They also force a rupture between bodily movement and temporality—a work against the turn of the century's suturing of these two (in the chronophotography of Muybridge, Marey, and Anschütz, as well as in the early cinema of Edison and Lumière).

The second aspect of Frizot's analysis that invites further attention is the demand for quantifiability and measurability in Marey's chronophotographic work. Evidence of this can be observed in the presence of a small clock or "chronometric dial" in the corner of many of Marey's chronophotographs. The chronometric dial was a black velvet disk with uniform markings. A bright needle spinning on the disk at a constant speed would be frozen in its path by the operation of the camera's shutter. This allowed Marey to measure accurately the intervals of time between successive exposures, in effect, to quantify the lost time inherent in this intermittent method. It would also allow him to measure the time of a gesture or movement on the basis of the clock's registration of the action's point of origin. Given his scientific aspirations, this ability to quantify time was crucial. The clock in chronophotography, as a part of the apparatus itself, was a constant reminder of referential time. The cinema, on the other hand, had to eliminate the scientific clock, the clock as a record of referential time. Instead the cinema, as the production of a generalized experience of time, of duration, had to ensure that its temporality was nonspecific, nonidentifiable, indeterminable. The cinematic image, unlike the chronophotographic image, does not speak its own relation to time. Hence the pans at the beginning of *Execution of Czolgosz,* despite their carefully choreographed relation to the time of the real execution, inevitably become unanchored, detached from any specifiable referential time, and subject only to internal markers of cinematic time. The effectiveness of the cinematic representation of time rests precisely on its unquantifiability. It was necessary to eliminate the temporal specificity of the image in order to produce the experience of time.

The third, and perhaps most significant, aspect of Frizot's analysis that bears striking implications for the analysis of cinematic time is the repeated emphasis upon Marey's conceptualization of the image as point. The central importance of a transmission time that was virtually instantaneous, the reduction of the shutter speed to 1/25,000 second, the iterative mechanism of the shutter producing time's record as a series of points, and geometric chronophotography's camouflaging of the body as an array of points—all testify to the crucial role of the concept of the point in Marey's project. Anschütz's German terms for chronophotography—*Momentphotographie, Augensblickphotographie*—also highlight the centrality of the temporal instant as point. Thinking the photographic frame as point enables separability and hence, eventually, the clarity of the reconstituted illusion of movement.

What is at stake in instantaneous photography is the sharpness and precision associated with the point. With respect to the controversy over the acceptability of blurring in the photography of moving objects, de Duve claims: "Photography may not become totally abstract, because that would constitute a denial of its referential ties. One point of sharpness suffices to assert its own space, for the essence of the point is precision." The word *point* is also a verb; it is the gesture Peirce associates with indexicality, another property of the photographic image and the promise of its intimacy with the referent. According to de Duve, the focal point is a concept that conflates the connotations of both noun and verb:

> In a sense, the very activity of finding a "focal point"—that is, selecting one particular plane out of the entire array of the world spread in depth before us—is itself a kind of pointing, a selection of this cut through the world at this point, here, as the one with which to fill the indexical sign. Finding the point of focus is in this sense a procedural analogue for the kind of trace or index that we are aware of when we hold the printed snapshot in our hands. Both poles of this phenomenon—the means to the image and the result—have in common a contraction of space itself into a point: *here* as a kind of absolute.

This condensation of the image as point leads to a difficulty in reading or interpretation: "Now a *point* is not subject to any description, nor is it able to generate narration. Language fails to operate in front of the pin-pointed space of the photograph, and the onlooker is left momentarily aphasic."[14] For de Duve, this speechlessness is a symptom of the traumatic effect of the photograph, its breakdown of the symbolic function.

It is striking that Roland Barthes, as well, builds his theory of photography around the Latin term for point—*punctum*. The *punctum* is that detail of the photograph which "pricks" or "wounds" the viewer—it is a mark, a form of punctuation, an accident. It is that aspect of the photograph, entirely unanticipated by the photographer, that fascinates the viewer, makes him or her pensive. An effect of the indexicality of the image, it is, for Barthes, a kind of absolute particularity and is opposed to the culturally generated meaning of the photograph (which Barthes labels the *studium*).[15] In this analysis, it is not the image which is condensed or contracted into a point but the point which inhabits the image.[16]

The confusions or contradictions surrounding the concept of the point are, in the case of cinema, productive. On the one hand, the point is a mathematical abstraction, existing nowhere but incarnating an ideal significance. On the other hand, the point is allied with particularity and contingency as well as the evacuation of meaning. In 1902 Henri Poincaré evoked the mathematical concept of the point when he asked the question "What is a point of space? Everybody thinks he knows, but that is an illusion." He went on to disengage the geometric concept of the point from experience through an analysis of the senses of touch and sight and the relation of the body to space. Poincaré concluded that "geometry is not true, it is advantageous."[17] "True," for Poincaré, seems to mean "grounded in experience." But the concept of the point, despite its resistance to experiential definition, *enables* things to be done, it enables certain mathematical operations: it is, in short, advantageous. The dictionary provides a multiplicity of definitions for *point,* including "an individual detail," "a distinguishing detail," "the most important essential in a discussion or matter." The mathematical definitions given by the dictionary are "a geometric element of which it is postulated that at least two exist and that two suffice to determine a line" and "a geometric element determined by an ordered set of coordinates." The temporal definitions of *point* are "an exact moment" and "a time interval immediately before something indicated: verge."[18] The point, as Poincaré is careful to argue, is not an object; it cannot be felt or seen. Rather, it is an abstraction, a geometrical construction that is ultimately bodiless, spaceless, and timeless. As in Frizot's discussion of Marey, the point functions as an origin that allows quantification, specification. David Berlinski has an elegant description of the process of evacuation that accompanies the positing of a point as origin:

the origin is a mathematical point, something that has sucked from the concept of place its essential property, that of being *here* rather than there, the infinitely extended line itself balanced perfectly on that slim solitary and singular spike. But a point, it must be remembered, is *not* a number; holding place without size and arising whimsically whenever two straight lines are crossed, it is a geometrical object, a kind of fathomless atom out of which the line is ultimately created.[19]

Although contracting the image to a point was, for Marey, the means of quantifying time/motion, it was also the condition of possibility for the reversibility of the analytic method, for synthesis—in short, for cinema. If the line emerges from a series of points, the cinema emerges from that irreversible line of images which is the filmstrip. The film is a series of sequential singularities.

The conceptualization of the instantaneous photograph as point opens up a number of possibilities. It allows for thinking the image as a critical specification of time—the exact moment. It entails a halting of time; the image is perpetually "on the verge of" completion. Perceiving the image as allied with the point, with the *punctum,* foregrounds its alignment with singularity and contingency and, therefore, its resistance to meaning, its promotion of aphasia, and the breakdown of the symbolic function. The point is an absolute particularity.

Of course, in the cinema, the image as point is precisely what the spectator does not see, what is not accessible. Just as the line conceals its ontological dependence upon the point, the projected illusion of continuity in cinema hides the independent existence of the photogram. The frozen performance of the instantaneous photograph is not left uncompleted, and it is only at the point of a cut or the end of the film that one can claim there is a suspension of time or an incomplete performance of an action. But despite its alliance with "real time," with flow, with continuity, cinema still strives for the reduction of time and space consistent with its understanding of the image in relation to the category of the point. And in this regard the cut is the most exemplary cinematic operation. For the cut is the haunting echo of the frameline—its reiteration at a different level. The cut reasserts the instantaneity of the individual photogram. Time is subject to a miniaturization, a contraction. It becomes something that can be held or possessed in a metaphorical sense. This is why the cut as ellipsis is a crucial figure. Time becomes delimitable, commodifiable, objectlike. In relation to an instantaneous photograph of a dancer by Man Ray, André Breton invokes the term *fixed-explosive,* with its suggestion of an impossible conflation of stability and movement.[20] The idea of fixed-explosiveness is also redolent with implications for the three records of building demolitions described at the beginning of the chapter. The buildings are subject to a violent change, but this change is permanently fixed through the operations of the different media. Technologies of representation here work to capture the vitality of change and movement without sacrificing a lust for fixity and stability.

For Marey, the mathematical representability of motion/time was dependent upon the concept of the point. For Charles Sanders Peirce, the present instant became philosophically representable, within his grasp, only when it became figurable as "point" and as "discontinuity." The present instant differed dramatically from any other instant, past or future; for time, in Peirce's view, is a true continuum except at the moment of the punctual present, the now. This understanding of the present's absolute difference and uniqueness allowed Peirce to sustain the dream of modernity, to embrace the possibility of the emergence of the truly new. Thinking the instant/image as point makes the temporal present a point of origin. Hence, the concept of the point has a double valence: it is the support of rationalization (for Marey) and simultaneously the embodiment of the contingency that acts as a resistance to rationalization (for Peirce). It is both the ultimate abstraction and the ultimate indicator of the concrete, the particular, the present instant in its absolute singularity.

Marey was not the first to challenge the notion of time/motion as continuum by fragmenting it. From Joseph Plateau's Phenakistoscope to the Thaumatrope, Zoetrope, and work of the other chronophotographers, the breakdown of movement into punctual units was required as a first moment in the operation of its illusory reconstruction. But there was a historical alternative. Early magic-lantern presentations in the nineteenth century also produced simulated movement, but they did so in a way that often affirmed continuity rather than fragmentation. Cut-out figures moved across a background, in an arc or vertically, by means of slippers and levers operated mechanically by the projectionist. In this process, movements, though jerky, are nevertheless continuous, without the gaps between positions characterizing, for instance, the Zoetrope or chronophotography.[21]

Yet in its later developments the magic lantern embraced fragmentation through its recourse to photographic records of poses assumed by real actors. In the life-model studios constructed in the 1870s and 1880s, photographs were taken of human models assuming the action poses required for a particular narrative.[22] Projecting these slides in sequence roughly simulated the trajectory of the narrative. In competition with the cinema, the number of slides used to represent an action increased from twelve to twenty-four to thirty-six. When the life model replaced trick movement in the magic-lantern presentation, continuity in the simulation of movement was sacrificed for a photographic indexicality that mandated fragmentation. Movement in itself was not the goal, but an indexically based movement. Similarly, although Marey felt a continuing nostalgia for the continuity of the graphic method, that method was rejected in favor of the indexically grounded one of chronophotography. The decisive difference of cinema was the transformation of movement into an indexical sign.[23] Making represented movement (the signifier of time) indexical weds time to contingency. In this gesture, time is allied strongly with the absolute particularity of the indexical, with the pressure of the real.

In positing the necessity of the absolute discontinuity of the present instant, Peirce contradicted his own very strong investment in the logic of the afterimage, in the idea of the inevitable infusion of the present with the past. For Peirce, time was the perfect continuum, and this, in turn, was the very foundation for the possibility of logical thought. But describing the present instant as unique in its disjunctiveness allowed him simultaneously to acknowledge the power of chance, of contingency. It is no accident that Peirce, who held this complex and contradictory view of the present instant, should also be the one who developed in his semiotics the concept of the index, which was to become the operative term in understanding the signifying work of the photographic image. Yet the index also harbors within itself a temporal tension. On the one hand, the indexical trace—the footprint, the fossil, the photograph—carries a historicity, makes the past present. At the other extreme, the deictic index—the signifiers "here," "now," "this," "that"—are inextricable from the idea of presence. While the index hovers on the cusp of presence and pastness, it always seems to be haunted by an aspiration to presence, as exemplified by the asymptotic movement toward the instant of instantaneous photography. This is also an aspiration of the archaeologist and the historian, who strive to imaginatively recreate the past as a present lived moment. The obsession with indexicality in the nineteenth century is a desire for revivification, for endowing the "dead" past with life.[24]

Freud's fascination with Jensen's *Gradiva* (1903), the story of an archaeologist whose desire is sparked by a bas-relief of a young woman in the act of walking, and who returns to Pompeii in search of her footprint, is a fascination with the limits of indexicality.[25] Nobert Hanold, the story's protagonist, wants to go beyond the threshold of the sign and bring Gradiva back to life. As Jacques Derrida points out, Hanold dreams

> of reliving the other. Of reliving the singular pressure of impression which Gradiva's step [*pas*], the step itself, the step of Gradiva herself, that very day, at that time, on that date, in what was inimitable about it, must have left in the ashes. He dreams this irreplaceable place, the very ash, where the singular imprint, like a signature, barely distinguishes itself from the impression. And this is the condition of singularity, the idiom, the secret, testimony. It is the condition for the uniqueness of the printer-printed, of the impression and the imprint, of the pressure and its trace in the unique *instant* where they are not yet distinguished the one from the other, forming in an *instant* a single body of Gradiva's step, of her gait, of her pace *(Gangart)*, and of the ground which carries them. The trace no longer distinguishes itself from its substrate.[26]

It is significant that Hanold's desire fastens upon Gradiva's footstep and that its origin is a representation that fixes a moment in the act of walking. It is the movement of Gradiva that activates Hanold's obsession and fuels his dream of presence. Chronophotography is the scientific sublimation of this fascination and the cinema the reactivation of its desire. Film represents an indelible past that produces a highly cathected experience of presence. The inflated rhetoric of movement, life, and death that accompanied the emergence of cinema confirms the cinematic debt to a dream of revivification and "presencing."

According to Derrida, Hanold suffers from "archive fever," a condition determined by the death drive, by finitude and destruction as limits. Archival desire strives to halt that destruction, to deny finitude. Yet, as Derrida points out, the archive's work is not simply conservative or preservative; "the technical structure of the *archiving* archive also determines the structure of the *archivable* content even in its very coming into existence and in its relationship to the future."[27] For Derrida, Hanold's impossible archival desire to revivify, to discover the originary moment of singularity, when impression and imprint are not yet separated, when representation is not riven by difference, is a consequence of a transhistorical metaphysics. Yet this analysis neglects the extent to which processes of archivization are accelerated and intensified in the nineteenth century, producing historical changes in the very terms of the archive and archivability. Photography, film, and mechanical reproduction in general are products of and help to produce a transformation in ideas about memory, recording, storage, and knowledge. What is at stake for these technologies of representation is the recording of the singular, the instantaneous, the contingent—that which is most accessible to indexical signification.

In the nineteenth century, according to Philip Rosen, "Documents, remains, survivals, ruins and edifices, fossils—in short, indexical traces that attest to a past by emerging into the present from it—achieved a kind of epistemological prestige in an era of intensifying time consciousness."[28] It is not only the past which seems "lost" and in dire need of reconstitution, but the present as well, a present that is the victim of rationalization and estrangement. The intensification of interest in dissecting and reunifying time in the nineteenth century, in manipulating it in order to produce both the possibility of its record/representation and the opportunity to construct alternative temporalities, is not some reflection of a perennial psychical order, but a reflection of a quite precise historical trauma. The subject is no longer immersed in time, no longer experiences it as an enveloping medium. Through its rationalization and abstraction, its externalization and reification in the form of pocket watches, standardized schedules, the organization of the work day, and industrialization in general, time becomes other, alienated. The desire to package or commodify time, to represent and distribute its experience in a highly controlled medium that nevertheless seems to be structured by a free, unsystematic alliance with contingency, is simultaneously a revolt against rationalization *and* its extension. What film archives, then, is first and foremost a "lost" experience of time as presence, time as immersion.

Yet because film is capable of registering and recording singularities, contingencies—theoretically without limit—it inevitably raises the specter of an archive of noise, linked to issues of legibility, cataloguing, and limitless storage. Typically, an archive is thought to preserve objects or artifacts imbued with value and meaning (whether the value and meaning preexist the archival process is another question). However, film as an archival medium is constrained not only by its affinity with the contingent and always potentially meaningless detail, but also by its problematic relation with the notion of the origin and the original delineated so well by Benjamin in "The Work of Art in the Age of Mechanical Reproduction."[29] For the archival object is preeminently unique, an original rather than a copy. Film as a form of mechanical reproduction realizes the multiplication and dissemination of copies without an original, for a print is never an original. In this sense it is, in Benjamin's terms, fundamentally anti-auratic, while the archive preserves and perpetuates the aura of the original. The archival object is singular; it must exist at only one place at any one time.[30] Hence, archival desire is an attempt to halt the vertiginous movement of mechanical and electronic reproduction.

While by virtue of its indexical and recording properties the medium of film can be understood as an archival process, films themselves are also the artifacts of archivization, despite their undermining of the logic of the original. And this is indeed the direction of much of the new film historiography—the accumulative, additive, safeguarding collection of artifacts (as well as facts). A print of a film may not be an original, but it can be "definitive," that is, not subject to the various distortions of editing, cropping, shortening, and so on, which postdate its release. The aim of this historiographic/archival impulse is to retrieve everything possible, driven by a temporal imperative (before it is "too late") and the anticipation of a future interpretation (in this sense, the archival process is a wager that stacks the deck: this object, because it is preserved, *will* be interpreted). The fear is that of the destruction of an original object, its irretrievable loss; hence the grasping for a totalizing fullness, a refusal of the finite. This is the sense in which the anarchival—destructiveness, the death drive—for Derrida, always haunts and shapes archival desire. This process is legible in the "meta-archival" processes of documenting destruction discussed at the beginning of this chapter. The explosions reduce the corrupting, dismantling work of time to an instant that can be seized and circulated.

Yet, to return to a question posed briefly in Chapter 1, what exactly is being archived in the preservation of an early film, for example, Lumière's well-known *Sortie d'usine* (*Workers Leaving the Factory*, 1895)? Is it the details of the workers' costume in 1895? The gestures of the workers as they walk toward the sides of the frame? The dog playfully leaping at a bicyclist? The patterns of light and shade across the entranceway to the factory? Or is the preservation aimed at the film itself as meaningful artifact, as one of the earliest films screened in a public setting? While it might seem obvious that it is the last possibility which fuels archival desire in this instance, in fact the two salvaging or preservative processes—that of the film as historical artifact and that of the moment as historical event, as lost presence—are inextricably welded together. The archive is a protection against time and its inevitable entropy and corruption, but with the introduction of film as an archival process, the task becomes that of preserving time, of preserving an experience of temporality, one that was never necessarily "lived" but emerges as the counterdream of rationalization, its agonistic underside—full presence. In its indexical dimension, film functions as the empty deictic signifier, the "this" or "that" which can theoretically be filled with any content whatever. But once it is allied with that content, it is the imprint not only of the content but of the temporal moment of the imprinting, of a "now" which has become a "then," but which, in its screening, becomes a resurrected, revivified "now." In addition, the archive is always a wager about the future: a future screening, a future interpretation. The artifact's significance is a function of what it "will have meant." As Derrida points out, "archival technique has commanded that which in the past even instituted and constituted whatever there was as anticipation of the future."[31]

Film's potential as an archive of noise hinges upon its intimate alliance with contingency, its perceived ability to represent *by chance* or even to represent chance. For Peirce, who embraced many of the theories of indeterminism of the period, chance was "absolute."[32] Benjamin's obsession with the figure of the gambler is an acknowledgment of modernity's investment in the concept of contingency. The "coup" of the gambler is comparable to the various and disconnected "shocks" of modern life; it is autonomous, dependent upon no previous conditions or history. Each game begins anew, positing a fresh origin: "A game passes the time more quickly as chance comes to light more absolutely in it."[33] To safeguard the epistemological purity of chance, the gambler revels in making bets at the last possible moment, ensuring that chance is not subject to interpretation, to the assignment of a meaning. The epistemological and representational privileging of chance gained force through both the accelerating secularization of the modern and new forms of conceptualization in the sciences. Discourses of indeterminism were strengthened by a host of epistemological developments in fields as diverse as evolutionary theory, history, and physics. The Second Law of Thermodynamics in physics—that concerning entropy and temporal irreversibility—necessitated a new mechanism of determination other than the cause-effect logic of classical dynamics. Statistics emerged as a way of acknowledging the force of contingency, of individuality, of singularity, while nevertheless posing as its regulation.

The concept of entropy proclaims the ultimate reign of contingency. Time is characterized by irreversibility, increasing randomness, the dissipation associated with the contingent. Film finds a place here only through the relentless forward movement of the apparatus and in its unedited form, when it presents itself as "real time," devoid of cuts.[34] For the long take is a gaze at an autonomous, unfolding scene whose duration is a function of the duration and potential waywardness of events themselves. Its length situates it as an invitation to chance and unpredictability, an invitation that is abruptly canceled by the cut. The cut is the mechanism whereby temporality becomes a product of the apparatus, repudiating the role of cinema as a record of a time outside itself. The cinema becomes a Freudian time machine rather than the pure promise of an indexical link to the referent. Nevertheless, although the indexical link may be compromised, it is not lost.

The intense debates about continuity and discontinuity, archivability, contingency and determinism, temporal irreversibility, and the conception of the photographic image as point or instant form the context for the emergence of cinematic time. In the nineteenth century, time becomes unfamiliar, uncanny, something with which we must suddenly reckon. The discovery of "deep time"—that the age of the Earth is not the thousands of years of biblical time but the millions or thousands of millions of years indicated by the fossil record—signals an alarming extension that had previously been quite manageable under the condensed rule of biblical narrative.[35] The theological destabilization was accompanied by a blow to humanism. As Rosen points out, "There is something epistemologically disordering about modern temporality." The advent of Darwinian theories of evolution indicated that "human reason itself would have to be temporalized."[36] Jonathan Crary has demonstrated the relentless linking of temporality and the body in the nineteenth century, and claims that Schopenhauer exemplifies cultural modernity in his "identification of temporality itself as a source of subjective anguish."[37]

The reconceptualization of time as a source of anxiety is accompanied by the rationalization, standardization, and tight regularization of temporality effected by industrialization and the forces of modernity. Rationalization transforms time into a form of constant pressure and constraint. The lure of contingency in such a context lies precisely in its resistance to systematicity, in its promise of unpredictability and idiosyncrasy. This lure and promise have been, precisely, *historical.* Chance and contingency have been assigned an important ideological role, supporting the fascination with the apparently alternative temporalities offered by the cinema.

Such a lure and such a promise have also been the basis of the historical phenomenon of cinephilia. In the face of newer technologies such as television and digital imaging that seem to threaten the cinema with obsolescence, film theorists have manifested a renewed interest in cinephilia and cinematic contingency. This work seems to respond to Niklas Luhmann's question "Is there a *theory* that can make use of the *concept* of contingency?"[38] For Paul Willemen and Miriam Hansen, this project takes the form of a return to and rethinking of the historical role of indexicality in the cinema. Indexicality would appear to ensure the availability of the particular, the singular, the unpredictable—in short, the antisystematic—within the cinematic domain. In the work of both theorists, the indexical trace as filmic inscription of contingency is indissociable from affect. In the case of Willemen, that affect takes the precise form of cinephilia. Cinephilia is usually considered a somewhat marginalized, furtive, even illicit relation to the cinema rather than a theoretical stance. It is the property of the film buff rather than the film theorist. Willemen conceives of it as a fully historical concept, noting that it flourished from the early 1950s to the late 1960s in relation to the emergence of a different kind of "mediatic society." It has affinities with earlier attitudes toward cinema such as that embodied in Jean Epstein's concept of *photogénie* and in the Surrealists' celebration of chance. Willemen claims that cinephilia is a kind of zero degree of spectatorship—it "doesn't do anything other than designate something which resists, which escapes existing networks of critical discourse and theoretical frameworks."[39] The word indicates the domain of the inarticulable in the film viewing experience.

What is cinephilia? And how does it come to embody the hope in a different epistemological grounding of cinematic pleasure? Cinephilia, at its most basic, is love of the cinema, but it is a love that is attached to the detail, the moment, the trace, the gesture. Willemen, in attempting to specify it, refers to the Surrealists' discussion of photography as the "capturing of fleeting, evanescent moments," to Catholic discourses of revelation, to the intensity of a spark, and to the concept of excess.[40] It seems to be most readily localizable in relation to acting or its perceived lack—to a gesture, a body position, a facial expression, or an uncontrolled utterance that somehow escapes scripting. For instance, Epstein isolated as an instance of *photogénie* the moment when Sessue Hayakawa comes into the room in *The Cheat*. Willemen describes that moment: "his [Hayakawa's] body at a certain angle, in a particular position, opening the door, entering with a particular body language."[41] Epstein was exuberant in the face of the power of the cinema to convey the telltale signs of the body itself: "I can see love. It half lowers its eyelids, raises the arc of the eyebrows laterally, inscribes itself on the taut forehead, swells the massiters, hardens the tuft of the chin, flickers on the mouth and at the edge of the nostrils."[42]

Rarely does cinephilia fasten onto a cinematic technique such as a pan or a dissolve; it is to be distinguished from the technophilia Christian Metz glosses as fetishism.[43] And because cinephilia has to do with an excess in relation to systematicity, it is most appropriate for a cinema that is perceived as highly coded and commercialized. It triggers in the viewer the sense "that what is being seen is in excess of what is being shown . . . What matters is that something should be perceived as in excess of the film's register of performance, as potentially undesigned, unprogrammed." What Willemen gestures toward here is the uncontrollable aspect of cinematic representation, its material predilection for the accidental, the contingent. These moments "show you where the cinematic institution itself vacillates, where it might tip over or allow you a glimpse of the edge of its representation." Or, in other words, you are allowed to glimpse "something you are not meant to see."[44] It is not surprising that Willemen invokes the Surrealist discourse on photography, for what is visible but not shown must be a function of the indexicality of the medium, of its photographic base. What cinephilia names is the moment when the contingent takes on meaning—a necessarily private, idiosyncratic meaning nevertheless characterized by the compulsion to share what is unsharable, inarticulable (Willemen refers to the desire to write about the experience as crucial to cinephilia). Whether the moment chosen by the cinephiliac was really unprogrammed, unscripted, or outside codification is fundamentally undecidable. It is also inconsequential, since cinephilia hinges not on indexicality but on the knowledge of indexicality's potential, a knowledge that paradoxically erases itself. The cinephile maintains a certain belief, an investment in the graspability of the asystematic, the contingent, for which the cinema is the privileged vehicle.

The apparent indexical guarantee of an access to contingency also grounds much of Miriam Hansen's reading of Kracauer's *Theory of Film*. Although she does not invoke the term *cinephilia,* the significance of the cinema in modernity is linked to "the love it inspired along with new forms of knowledge and experience." For Hansen (as for Willemen), cinema is "the aesthetic matrix of a particular historical experience"—the historical experience of modernity, of accelerating technological expansion, of the phenomenological and representational dominance of urban space, and of the potential for mass destruction. History here is not a discourse foreign to theory, not an evocation of a gradual but certain accumulation of knowledge. But the access to contingency, to the imprint of temporality, is made possible by a cinema heavily imbued with historicity. An emphasis upon chance reveals Kracauer's affinity with the Surrealists and with slapstick, and it is chance alone "which offers a tiny window, at once hope and obligation, of survival, of continuing life after the grand metaphysical stakes have been lost." According to Hansen, it is not the camera's iconicity which ensures its realism for Kracauer, but its indexicality which undergirds the "medium's purchase on material contingency."[45]

What is at stake here, as in Willemen's description of cinephilia, is a *relation* between spectator and image, but it is the photographic base which acts as the condition of possibility for such a relation. As in cinephilia, the cinema has the "ability to subject the viewer to encounters with contingency, lack of control and otherness."[46] These encounters are always individual, idiosyncratic, with the flavor of Barthes's *punctum* in photography. The content of cinephilia is never generalizable—it must be unique to the viewer—but the form of the relation can be specified. The terms of Hansen's discussion of the relation between viewer and film are remarkably similar to those of Willemen's description of cinephilia. She claims: "What is at stake is the possibility of a split-second meaninglessness, as the placeholder of an otherness that resists unequivocal understanding and total subsumption. What is also at stake is the ability of the particular, the detail, the incident, to take on a life of its own, to precipitate processes in the viewer that may not be entirely controlled by the film."[47] For both Hansen and Willemen, the cinematic inscription of contingency constitutes a process whereby history leaves its mark on the film. The content gleaned is not that of history (the historical "fact" is only a subset of all contingencies), but this relation to the film is deeply historical, emblematic of a modernity dominated by a highly technologically mediated rationalization. In this context, the lure of contingency is that it seems to offer a way out, an anchoring point for the condensation of utopian desires. It proffers itself as an escape from systematicity—both that of a tightly regulated classical system and that of its vaguely oppressive abstract analysis.

It is no accident that cinephilia and the consequent return to ontology should now emerge as the bearer of such high theoretical stakes. A certain nostalgia for cinema precedes its "death." One doesn't—and can't—love the televisual or the digital in quite the same way. It is as though the aim of theory were to delineate more precisely the contours of an object at the moment of its historical demise. Willemen claims that cinephilia is specific only to the historical form of cinema: "The cinephile shares the notion of an ontology of cinema and the less the image has a Bazinian ontological relation to the real (the death-mask notion of the real), the more the image gets electronified, with each pixil becoming programmable in its own terms, the less appropriate cinephilia becomes."[48] It is arguable that cinephilia could not be revived at this conjuncture were the cinema *not* threatened by the accelerating development of new electronic and digital forms of media. Hansen already refers to cinema in the past tense (along with a striking variety of other tenses) in claiming that Kracauer's book "elucidates the tremendous significance of cinema, the love it inspired . . . As we embrace, endure or resist the effects of the digital, the cinematic still remains the sensorial dominant of this century, of a modernity defined by mass production, mass consumption, and mass destruction. At the very least, *Theory of Film* may help us understand the experience that cinema once was and could have been, whatever may become of it."[49] It is the intense and privileged relation to contingency, assured by photographic indexicality in the abstract, which can be loved again, this time as lost.

Is this theorizing of contingency limited to the status of death knell of the cinema? Does the theory adequate to its object emerge only at the moment of its loss? There is a confusion here of the two senses of object—perhaps a deliberate confusion. If the object is characterized by mortality—it *can* die—it is then the object external to theory, more properly, perhaps, the historical object. On the other hand, it is not the cinema as such which is the object of analysis, but cinephilia (named in Willemen, suggested in Hansen by the description of a free-floating attention to detail and contingency)—a historical and historicized stance, the historical moment of a relation to cinema. That relation is one which may be definable only negatively, as that which resists systematicity, rationalization, programming, and standardization. It is the leakage of the system, potentially mobilizable as its ruin. Cinema spectatorship, from this perspective, involves cognition, but it is not the cognition of cognitive studies, which stakes its account on universal processes of reasoning and perception in film viewing.[50] Rather, it is a knowing through cinema which hinges upon the effectivity of contingency.

But is the cinema's relation to contingency really that of the utopian moment other to or in excess of all structure or systematization? Because the theorized object is located by Willemen and Hansen as profoundly historical, I think it would be wise to look again at the historical status of contingency—and indexicality as well—in modernity. It has been the aim of this book to demonstrate that an indexically ensured contingency played a major role in thinking about the cinema as the archival representation of time. Photography presented itself as the indexical tracing of space; the cinema went further to claim that it was the indexical tracing of both space and an unfolding time. In the late nineteenth and early twentieth centuries, the moment of the emergence of cinema, processes of rationalization were countered by an intense epistemological investment in contingency and chance. Physicists and biologists acknowledged the limitations of strict laws of cause and effect and explored the dynamic activity of chance, particularly at the microscopic level. Evolutionary theory made chance determinant in the appearance, disappearance, and transformation of species. Statistical epistemologies in general assumed the idiosyncratic particularity of the individual, its autonomy and resistance to typification. The contingent was crucial but unknowable. Nevertheless, it was conquered at another level, through the demonstration of the regularities of large numbers. Statistics acknowledged indeterminacy, excess, and diversity, but simultaneously worked to make the contingent legible.

Cinema has also historically worked to make the contingent legible. The actualities of early cinema presented themselves as the potential catalogues of everything—from scenes of daily life to natural catastrophes, executions, parades, and spectacles. They promoted the sense that contingency, and hence the filmable, have no limit. And despite the development of stricter limitations and codes regulating the cinematically representable, the mainstream classical narrative continued to exploit the idea of the filmability of the contingent without limit, of the lush overabundance of things, of details, diversity, and multiplicity characterizing the diegesis, of its access to a time uncontaminated by rationalization and necessity, and as the antithesis of systematicity and the site of newness and difference itself. In the face of the abstraction and rationalization of time, chance and the contingent are given the crucial ideological role of representing an outside, of suggesting that time is still allied with the free and indeterminable. Contingency and ephemerality are produced as graspable and representable, but nevertheless antisystematic. The isolation of contingency as embodying the pure form of an aspiration, a utopian desire, ignores the extent to which the structuring of contingency, as precisely asystematic, became the paradoxical basis of social stability in modernity.

A cinephilia that hinges upon the envisaged death of cinema stipulates the death as that of the photographic base. This is because we tend to see photography as the exemplary instance of indexicality and, hence, the privileged bearer of contingency. But for Peirce, who defined the indexical sign, photography was by no means the central example. In Peirce's description, the index is evacuated of content; it is a hollowed-out sign. It designates something without describing it; its function is limited to the assurance of an existence. The demonstrative pronouns "this" and "that" are "nearly pure indices."[51] Hence, indexicality together with its seemingly privileged relation to the referent—to singularity and contingency—is available to a range of media. The insistency and compulsion Peirce associates with the indexical sign are certainly attributes of television and digital media as well; witness the televisual obsession with the "live" coverage of catastrophe, the ultimate representation of contingency, chance, the instantaneous, as well as the logistics of an Internet which promises to put diversity, singularity, and instantaneity more fully within our grasp. From this perspective, the desire fueling cinephilia will not die with the cinema as we know it. Cinephilia is only a slightly illicit subset of a larger and ongoing structuring of the access to contingency.

It might seem that I am simply constructing a metasystem with no outside, characterized by the sheer impossibility of envisaging an exit. But this is not my intention. For the metasystem itself is fully historical and hence could have been different. Willemen and Hansen are attracted to the notion of a love for the cinema which fastens on the contingent because they see it as an homage to the cinema's historical dimension. The indexically inscribed contingency is not the embodiment of history as the mark of the real or referent, but history as the mark of what could have been otherwise. Hence the lack of importance accorded to the precise (cinematic) moment chosen by the cinephile. In the manner of all utopian discourses, it is an homage to possibility.

In a chapter titled "Contingency as Modern Society's Defining Attribute," Niklas Luhmann provides an Aristotelian definition of contingency: "Anything is contingent that is neither necessary nor impossible. The concept is therefore defined by the negation of necessity and impossibility."[52] There is an apparent contradiction internal to the definition itself which allows it a productive ambiguity. For it is difficult to think the compatibility of necessity and impossibility, except perhaps through their simultaneous negation. What is necessary is difficult to think of as impossible, and what is impossible is hard to imagine as necessary. However, as the negation of necessity, cinematic contingency participates in the resistance to systematicity discussed earlier and hence, ironically, becomes susceptible to a form of systematicity. In resisting, it *partakes* of systematicity, locked within the terms of its antagonist. But as the negation of impossibility, contingency has the potential to become a reflexive concept, to force a meditation on the history of its own impossible fate within modernity. As the negation of impossibility, contingency is a witness against technology as inexorability, a witness that it could have been otherwise. Through the tensions internal to its own definition, contingency might take up a double function—allowing us to derive what is positive, even utopian, from the cinema while not losing sight of what links it to future technologies and the continuing structuring/systematization of chance.

NOTES

BIBLIOGRAPHY

INDEX

Notes

1. The Representability of Time

Epigraph: Siegfried Kracauer, "Photography," in *The Mass Ornament: Weimar Essays,* trans. and ed. Thomas Y. Levin (Cambridge, Mass.: Harvard University Press, 1995), p. 49.

1. Brander Matthews, "The Kinetoscope of Time," *Scribner's Magazine* 18.6 (1895): 733–744, reproduced in George C. Pratt, *Spellbound in Darkness: A History of the Silent Film* (Greenwich, Conn.: New York Graphic Society, 1973), pp. 8–14.

2. The confusion of fiction and nonfiction here indicates a strong sense of an inherently historiographic tendency in the apparatus itself.

3. Count Alessandro di Cagliostro (1743–1795) was a celebrated Italian charlatan who posed as an alchemist, dispenser of aphrodisiacs and elixirs of youth, medium, and soothsayer. Fashionable society of pre-Revolutionary Paris was enamored with him, and many believed him to be several hundred years old. Cagliostro was eventually denounced by his own wife for heresy and imprisoned in the fortress of San Leo in the Apennines, where he died.

4. André Bazin, *What Is Cinema?* trans. and ed. Hugh Gray, vol. 1 (Berkeley: University of California Press, 1967), p. 14.

5. Phonography is clearly a crucial representational technology in this respect as well. I have limited my investigation, however, primarily to questions of *imaging* time in the cinema, addressing photography only insofar as its analysis sheds light on the photographic base of the cinema. Sound in the early cinema is multifaceted and erratic—often involving the "live" sound of a lecturer or piano accompaniment—until technologies of synchronous sound are consolidated and institutionalized in the late 1920s. For an excellent analysis of sound and issues of the technology of representation, see James Lastra, *Sound Technology and the American Cinema: Perception, Representation, Modernity* (New York: Columbia University Press, 2000).

6. Andreas Huyssen, *Twilight Memories: Marking Time in a Culture of Amnesia* (New York: Routledge, 1995), p. 4.

7. Walter Benjamin, "On Some Motifs in Baudelaire," in *Illuminations,* trans. Harry Zohn, ed. Hannah Arendt (New York: Schocken, 1969), p. 184 (hereafter "Motifs").

8. Stephen Kern, *The Culture of Time and Space, 1880–1918* (Cambridge, Mass.: Harvard University Press, 1983), p. 110.

9. Georg Simmel, "The Metropolis and Mental Life," in *The Sociology of Georg Simmel,* trans. and ed. Kurt H. Wolff (London: Collier-Macmillan, 1950), pp. 412, 410, 413.

10. Wolfgang Schivelbusch, *The Railway Journey: The Industrialization of Time and Space in the 19th Century* (Berkeley: University of California Press, 1986), pp. 42–44.

11. Kern, *Culture of Time and Space,* p. 14.

12. Ibid., p. 15.

13. See Siegfried Giedion, *Mechanization Takes Command: A Contribution to an Anonymous History* (New York: W. W. Norton, 1975), pp. 96–102.

14. Ibid., pp. 102–106.

15. Quoted in Giedion, *Mechanization Takes Command,* p. 102.

16. Walter Benjamin, "Theses on the Philosophy of History," in Arendt, *Illuminations,* p. 261; Karl Marx, *Capital,* trans. Ben Fowkes, vol. 1 (New York: Random House, 1977), pp. 129, 168; Simmel, "The Metropolis and Mental Life," p. 412.

17. E. P. Thompson, "Time, Work-Discipline, and Industrial Capitalism," *Past and Present* 38 (1967): 69, 60, 61.

18. Benjamin, "Theses on the Philosophy of History," p. 261; Charles Sanders Peirce, *Collected Papers of Charles Sanders Peirce,* ed. Charles Hartshorne and Paul Weiss, vol. 6: *Scientific Metaphysics* (Cambridge, Mass.: Harvard University Press, 1935), p. 65; Benjamin, "Motifs," p. 163. See Schivelbusch, *The Railway Journey,* p. 36.

19. See Paul Souriau, *The Aesthetics of Movement,* trans. and ed. Manon Souriau (Amherst: University of Massachusetts Press, 1983), p. 116.

20. Gilles Deleuze, *Cinema 1: The Movement-Image,* trans. Hugh Tomlinson and Barbara Habberjam (Minneapolis: University of Minnesota Press, 1986), p. 7.

21. Jacques Aumont, *L'Oeil interminable: Cinéma et peinture* (Paris: Librairie Séguier, 1989), p. 43.

22. Peter Galassi, *Before Photography: Painting and the Invention of Photography* (New York: Museum of Modern Art, 1981), p. 25.

23. In his discussion of the increasing rationalization of public time in *The Culture of Time and Space,* Stephen Kern formulates what he believes was a reigning opposition of the era—that between public time and private time. This opposition perpetuates other, fairly intransigent oppositions: technology versus aesthetics, industrial capitalism versus the individual, the social versus the psychological. Public time conforms to the dictates of the rationale of industrial capitalism; it is homogeneous, uniform, irreversible, and standardized, permitting a regularization of la-

bor, production, distribution, and consumption. There is only *one* public time that must be acknowledged by all in order to be efficient and effective. However, Kern believes that in the period 1880–1920 this public time was felt to be unreal and constricting and encouraged a counternotion of private time as multiple and heterogeneous. He locates this conceptualization of private time in the realms of literature, art, philosophy, and psychology. Its emblematic figure might be that of the anarchist in Joseph Conrad's *The Secret Agent,* whose assigned task is to blow up the Greenwich Observatory—in effect, to destroy the prime meridian. Private time is enacted, in Kern's account, in Proust's representation of the reversibility of time as sensuous experience and in Joyce's constant interruptions and expansions of time in *Ulysses.* It is further elaborated in Bergson's theorization of time as fluid duration and in his critique of the division of time into distinctive units as effectively a means of spatializing it—rejecting its essential features and reducing it to space. At the end of his investigation of a variety of texts, Kern concludes, in the tradition of *Zeitgeist* studies: "The thrust of the age was to affirm the reality of private time against that of a single public time and to define its nature as heterogeneous, fluid, and reversible" (p. 34). Such a conceptualization of private time is perceived as a reaction against the dominant homogeneous public time and its intrusions upon individual privacy, upon the very notion of the unique. Kern's opposition between public and private time has the unfortunate effect of corroborating and leaving completely intact solid ideas about bourgeois individualism and about an inner psychical life impervious to the sociohistorical. The opposition pits technology against aesthetics and, ultimately, high art and high thought against a notion of the popular. Kern argues, "The popular idea that time is made up of discrete parts as sharply separated as the boxed days on a calendar continued to dominate popular thinking about public time, whereas the most innovative speculation was that private time was the real time and that its texture was fluid" (p. 34). Kern acknowledges the influence of the cinema upon writers such as Joyce and Bergson, but, ironically, his recognition of this process transforms the cinema into a manifestation of high art—a way out of an overly technologized and rationalized public sphere. In Kern's analysis, subjectivity is unassimilable to the social realm, and hence to industrial and consumer capitalism. In fact, it constitutes something of a haven from such regimentation.

24. Charles Baudelaire, *The Painter of Modern Life and Other Essays,* trans. and ed. Jonathan Mayne (New York: Da Capo, 1964), p. 16.

25. Georg Lukács, "Narrate or Describe?" in *Writer & Critic and Other Essays,* trans. and ed. Arthur D. Kahn (New York: Grosset and Dunlap, 1971), pp. 112, 130.

26. Kracauer, "Photography," pp. 52, 61. There has been a great deal of excellent work in film theory devoted to Kracauer's approach. See, for instance, Gertrud Koch, *Siegfried Kracauer: An Introduction,* trans. Jeremy Gaines (Princeton: Princeton University Press, 2000); Patrice Petro, "Kracauer's Epistemological

Shift," *New German Critique* 54 (Fall 1991): 127–139; Heide Schlüpmann, "The Subject of Survival: On Kracauer's Theory of Film," ibid., pp. 111–127; and Miriam Hansen, "America, Paris, the Alps: Kracauer (and Benjamin) on Cinema and Modernity," in *Cinema and the Invention of Modern Life,* ed. Leo Charney and Vanessa R. Schwartz (Berkeley: University of California Press, 1995), pp. 362–402.

27. Benjamin, "Motifs," p. 175.

28. Sigmund Freud, *Beyond the Pleasure Principle,* in *The Standard Edition of the Complete Psychological Works of Sigmund Freud,* trans. and ed. James Strachey (hereafter *Standard Edition*), vol. 18 (London: Hogarth Press, 1955), p. 25; Benjamin, "Motifs," p. 161.

29. Benjamin, "Motifs," p. 163.

30. Ibid., pp. 174–175.

31. Peirce, *Collected Papers,* 6: 425.

32. See Ian Hacking, "Was There a Probabilistic Revolution 1800–1930?" in *The Probabilistic Revolution,* ed. Lorenz Krüger, Lorraine J. Daston, and Michael Heidelberger, vol. 1: *Ideas in History* (Cambridge, Mass.: MIT Press, 1987), pp. 52–53.

33. Theodore M. Porter, *The Rise of Statistical Thinking, 1820–1900* (Princeton: Princeton University Press, 1986), p. 11.

34. Ibid., p. 5.

35. See, for instance, Schivelbusch, *The Railway Journey,* pp. 159–170; and Benjamin, "Motifs," pp. 160–162, on the concept of shock and Freud's stimulus shield. Freud's concepts are not simply *like* those of physics or physiology. Often they are the same conceptual frameworks simply transported to another intellectual domain. The most striking of these is the notion of the conservation of energy (the First Law of Thermodynamics). Freud's economic point of view dictates that psychical energy circulates and is subjected to displacement and equivalence, but all within a system in which its quantity is finite. The pressure of the instinct is defined as "the measure of the demand for work which it represents" (Freud, "Instincts and Their Vicissitudes," in *Standard Edition,* vol. 14, p. 122). As Jean Laplanche and Jean-Bertrand Pontalis point out, "This requirement of Freudian thought [the economic point of view] derives on the one hand from a scientific spirit and a conceptual framework which are shot through with notions of energy, and, on the other hand, from a clinical experience that had immediately provided Freud with a certain number of data which, it seemed to him, could only be accounted for in economic terms"; *The Language of Psychoanalysis,* trans. Donald Nicholson-Smith (New York: W. W. Norton, 1973), p. 127. It is the very vagueness, indeterminacy, and malleability of the concept of energy that allow its migration between different disciplines and its centrality to the epistemological framework of the nineteenth century. This does not involve the reduction of psychoanalysis to either physics or physiology but links them all to certain developments and emphases within capitalist modernity (distribution, circulation, energy, displacement, quantification).

36. Michel Foucault, "History of Systems of Thought," in *Language, Counter-Memory, Practice,* trans. Donald F. Bouchard and Sherry Simon, ed. Donald F. Bouchard (Ithaca: Cornell University Press, 1977), p. 200.

37. Michel Foucault, *Power/Knowledge: Selected Interviews and Other Writings, 1972–1977,* trans. Colin Gordon, Leo Marshall, John Mepham, and Kate Soper, ed. Colin Gordon (New York: Random House, 1980), pp. 139–142.

38. A second caveat with respect to Foucault's work has to do with the viability of the category of the subject. Because he emphasizes the surface effectivity of discourse, the illegitimacy of the act of interpretation, and the consequent refusal of the concept of the unconscious, a delineation of the subject as subject of desire is inaccessible to a Foucauldian methodology. The subject becomes the site of enunciation of a confession in *The History of Sexuality,* trans. Robert Hurley, 3 vols. (New York: Pantheon, 1978), or the nodal point of a system of psychological, penal and ethical discourses in *Discipline and Punish,* trans. Alan Sheridan (New York: Pantheon, 1977). A subject explicable as the subject of desire, pleasure, anxiety, and lure would have no place in the Foucauldian domain.

39. See Noël Burch, *Life to Those Shadows* (Berkeley: University of California Press, 1990), p. 21.

40. Kracauer, "Photography," p. 56.

41. Tom Gunning, "An Aesthetic of Astonishment: Early Film and the (In)Credulous Spectator," in *Viewing Positions: Ways of Seeing Film,* ed. Linda Williams (New Brunswick, N.J.: Rutgers University Press, 1995), p. 118.

42. See Tom Gunning, "The Cinema of Attractions: Early Film, Its Spectator and the Avant-Garde," in *Early Cinema: Space, Frame, Narrative,* ed. Thomas Elsaesser (London: British Film Institute, 1990), pp. 56–62.

43. Quoted in Porter, *The Rise of Statistical Thinking,* p. 105.

44. Pratt, *Spellbound in Darkness,* p. 18.

2. Temporality, Storage, Legibility

1. Siegfried Kracauer, "Photography," in *The Mass Ornament: Weimar Essays,* trans. and ed. Thomas Y. Levin (Cambridge, Mass.: Harvard University Press, 1995), p. 58.

2. Allan Sekula, "The Body and the Archive," *October* 39 (1986): 3–64.

3. Friedrich A. Kittler, "Gramophone, Film, Typewriter," trans. Dorothea von Mücke with Philippe L. Similon, *October* 41 (1987): 104.

4. Jacques Derrida, "Freud and the Scene of Writing," in *Writing and Difference,* trans. Alan Bass (Chicago: University of Chicago Press, 1978), p. 201; Michel Serres, *Hermes: Literature, Science, Philosophy,* ed. Josué V. Harari and David F. Bell (Baltimore: Johns Hopkins University Press, 1982), pp. 72, 71.

5. Sigmund Freud, "The Unconscious," in *The Standard Edition of the Complete Psychological Works of Sigmund Freud,* trans. and ed. James Strachey (hereaf-

ter *Standard Edition*), vol. 14 (London: Hogarth Press, 1957), p. 187; idem, *Beyond the Pleasure Principle*, ibid., vol. 18 (London: Hogarth Press, 1955), pp. 1–64.

6. Sigmund Freud, *The Interpretation of Dreams*, ibid., vol. 5 (London: Hogarth Press, 1953), pp. 577–578.

7. Sigmund Freud, "A Note upon the 'Mystic Writing-Pad,'" ibid., vol. 19 (London: Hogarth Press, 1961), p. 231.

8. Freud, *Beyond the Pleasure Principle*, p. 28.

9. Freud, "Note upon the 'Mystic Writing-Pad,'" p. 228.

10. Sigmund Freud, "Project for a Scientific Psychology," ibid., vol. 1 (London: Hogarth Press, 1966), pp. 281–397, quotation p. 300.

11. Derrida, "Freud and the Scene of Writing," pp. 329, 226.

12. Freud, *Beyond the Pleasure Principle*, p. 26.

13. Although Derrida's conceptualization of writing situates it beyond and against the narrow understanding of phonetic writing, locating it in the more general context of the logic of the trace and deferred action, his concept is inescapably propped upon and dependent upon that of phonetic writing.

14. Freud, "The Unconscious," pp. 174, 175.

15. Freud, *The Interpretation of Dreams*, p. 536.

16. Jean Laplanche, *Seduction, Translation, Drives*, trans. Martin Stanton, ed. John Fletcher and Martin Stanton (London: Institute of Contemporary Arts, 1992), p. 174.

17. Freud, *Beyond the Pleasure Principle*, p. 27.

18. Freud, "Project for a Scientific Psychology," p. 304; idem, *Beyond the Pleasure Principle*, p. 27.

19. Walter Benjamin, *Charles Baudelaire: A Lyric Poet in the Era of High Capitalism*, trans. Harry Zohn (London: Verso, 1973), pp. 113–117.

20. Freud, "Note upon the 'Mystic Writing-Pad,'" p. 230.

21. The German is "mit dem Aufleuchten und Vergehen des Bewusstseins." See Sigmund Freud, "Notiz über den 'Wunderblock,'" in *Gesammelte Werke*, ed. Anna Freud et al., vol. 14 (London: Imago, 1948), p. 7.

22. Freud, "Note upon the 'Mystic Writing-Pad,'" p. 231.

23. Freud, *Beyond the Pleasure Principle*, p. 25.

24. Sigmund Freud, "Constructions in Analysis," in *Standard Edition*, vol. 13 (London: Hogarth Press, 1964), pp. 255–269; idem, "Remembering Repeating and Working-Through (Further Recommendations on the Technique of Psycho-Analysis II)," ibid., vol. 12 (London: Hogarth Press, 1958), pp. 145–156.

25. This does not mean that the conscious and unconscious are never in relation but that this relationship is a complex and mediated one, never direct. If conscious memory is produced at the moment that the layers are in contact in the Mystic Writing-Pad analogy, then it can hardly be called memory, since this moment is, by definition, transitory; for Freud, storage and receptivity are incompatible.

26. Freud, *Beyond the Pleasure Principle*, p. 25.

27. See Henri Bergson, *Creative Evolution* (New York: Henry Holt, 1926), pp. 336–343; idem, *Matter and Memory,* trans. Nancy Margaret Paul and W. Scott Palmer (New York: Zone, 1988); idem, *Time and Free Will,* trans. R. L. Pogson (New York: Macmillan, 1913).

28. Walter Benjamin, "A Short History of Photography," in *Classic Essays on Photography,* ed. Alan Trachtenberg (New Haven: Leete's Island, 1980), pp. 202–203.

29. Lisa Cartwright, *Screening the Body: Tracing Medicine's Visual Culture* (Minneapolis: University of Minnesota Press, 1995), p. viii. See also Fatimah Tobing Rony, *The Third Eye: Race, Cinema, and Ethnographic Spectacle* (Durham, N.C.: Duke University Press, 1996), pp. 45–76, for an analysis of the chronophotographic work of Félix-Louis Regnault and its relation to race.

30. E. J. Marey, *Animal Mechanism: A Treatise on Terrestrial and Aërial Locomotion* (New York: D. Appleton, 1874), p. 27.

31. Marey, *Animal Mechanism,* pp. 43, 44.

32. Anson Rabinbach, *The Human Motor: Energy, Fatigue, and the Origins of Modernity* (Berkeley: University of California Press, 1990), p. 93.

33. E. J. Marey, *Movement,* trans. Eric Pritchard (New York: D. Appleton, 1895), p. 3.

34. François Dagognet, *Etienne-Jules Marey: A Passion for the Trace,* trans. Robert Galeta with Jeanine Herman (New York: Zone, 1992), pp.30, 63.

35. Marey, *Movement,* p. 2.

36. Marta Braun, *Picturing Time: The Work of Etienne-Jules Marey (1830–1904)* (Chicago: University of Chicago Press, 1992), p. 66.

37. Marey, *Movement,* pp. 58, 62, 33.

38. Ibid., p. 134.

39. Ibid., p. 57.

40. Quoted in Braun, *Picturing Time,* p. 83.

41. See, for example, ibid., pp. 150–198, 255–262.

42. Marey, *Movement,* pp. 282 n., 287, 145.

43. Rabinbach, *The Human Motor,* p. 97.

44. The work of Marcel Duchamp (especially *Nude Descending a Staircase No. 2,* 1912), Anton Giulio Bragaglia, and Giacomo Balla is frequently cited as indicative of the range of Marey's influence in art and photography. See Braun, *Picturing Time,* chap. 7; and Rabinbach, *The Human Motor,* p. 115.

45. In Freud's discussion it is clear that the unconscious is responsible for the receptivity of consciousness by cathecting it. When the cathexis is withdrawn, neither receptivity nor inscription is possible. Hence the discontinuous functioning, actually initiated by the unconscious, characterizes both reception and inscription.

46. For an account of the debates over G. W. Pabst's *Secrets of the Soul* (1926), for which Karl Abraham and Hanns Sachs acted as consultants, see Ernest Jones,

The Life and Work of Sigmund Freud, vol. 3 (New York: Basic Books, 1957), pp. 114–115. Jones claims that Freud's "main objection was his disbelief in the possibility of his abstract theories being presented in the plastic manner of a film" (p. 114). Anne Friedberg also discusses the conflict between Abraham and Freud over *Secrets of the Soul,* referring to "Freud's vehement distrust of the cinema," in "An *Unheimlich* Maneuver between Psychoanalysis and the Cinema: *Secrets of a Soul* (1926)," in *The Films of G. W. Pabst: An Extraterritorial Cinema,* ed. Eric Rentschler (New Brunswick, N.J.: Rutgers University Press, 1990), p. 42.

Freud's objections to the cinema focused on its particularity, concreteness, and affinity with contingency and hence its incompatibility with the processes of abstraction crucial to psychoanalytic theory. These objections, however, do not preclude the possibility of Freud's enjoyment of the cinema as a diversion or distraction; and indeed, the fact that Freud was entertained and enchanted by the cinema is demonstrated by a letter sent to his family during a visit to Italy in 1907. Here Freud claims that he was "spellbound" by the "short cinematographic performances" screened in the Piazza Colonna in Rome. See *The Letters of Sigmund Freud,* ed. Ernst L. Freud (New York: Basic Books, 1960), pp. 261–263. Ernest Jones also reproduces this letter in *The Life and Work of Sigmund Freud,* vol. 2 (New York: Basic Books, 1955), pp. 36–37. See also Jonathan Crary, *Suspensions of Perception: Attention, Spectacle, and Modern Culture* (Cambridge, Mass.: MIT Press, 1999), pp. 362–370, for an analysis of this letter in relation to issues of spectatorship, attention, and absorption. As Crary points out, Freud "does not even indicate the content of the cinematographic performances" (p. 366) in his letter, remaining content to simply describe the atmosphere of the crowd and its relation to spectacle. Crary compares the phenomenon of spectatorship with Freud's espousal of a freefloating attention to the patient's discourse in psychoanalytic practice.

47. Quoted in Braun, *Picturing Time,* p. 255. See Braun, especially pp. 155–156, for a discussion of Marey's attempts to develop a motion picture camera.

48. Quoted in Noël Burch, *Life to Those Shadows,* trans. and ed. Ben Brewster (Berkeley: University of California Press, 1990), pp. 20–21.

49. Quoted in Dagognet, *Etienne-Jules Marey,* p. 162.

50. This would be an attribute of phonography as well—another technology for inscribing time. Although I do not have the space or time to pursue this question here, phonography raises many of the same issues with respect to the representation of time as cinematography. I have chosen to limit my investigation here to photographically based modes of representation (sequential photography, cinema).

51. Friedrich A. Kittler, *Discourse Networks, 1800/1900,* trans. Michael Metteer with Chris Cullens (Stanford: Stanford University Press, 1990), p. 211.

52. Ibid., pp. 282, 283.

53. Ibid., pp. 338, 206.

54. *Webster's New Collegiate Dictionary* (Springfield: G. and C. Merriam, 1973), s.v.

55. Dai Vaughan, "Let There Be Lumière," in *Early Cinema: Space, Frame, Narrative*, ed. Thomas Elsaesser (London: British Film Institute, 1990), pp. 65, 66–67.

56. However, Bergson certainly knew Marey, since both worked at the Collège de France during the years 1900–1904 and both were members of a group organized to study psychic phenomena (including telepathy and levitation). See Braun, *Picturing Time*, p. 279.

57. Bergson, *Creative Evolution*, pp. 306, 332.

58. Rainer Maria Rilke, *The Notebooks of Malte Laurids Brigge*, trans. M. D. Herter Norton (New York: W. W. Norton, 1964), quoted in Kittler, *Discourse Networks*, p. 326.

3. The Afterimage, the Index, and the Present

1. Charles Sanders Peirce, *The Essential Peirce: Selected Philosophical Writings*, ed. Nathan Houser and Christian Kloesel, vol. 1 (Bloomington: Indiana University Press, 1992), p. 226.

2. See Hermann von Helmholtz, *Treatise on Physiological Optics*, trans. and ed. James P. C. Southall, vol. 1 (Menasha, Wis.: Optical Society of America, 1924), p. 91.

3. Film theorists or historians who appeal to persistence of vision (sometimes in combination or confusion with the phi phenomenon) as an explanation for the illusion of motion in cinema include, among others, Sergei M. Eisenstein, "Synchronization of Senses," in *The Film Sense*, trans. and ed. Jay Leyda (New York: Harcourt, Brace and World, 1942); Raymond Spottiswoode, *Film and Its Techniques* (Berkeley: University of California Press, 1963), p. 47; L. F. Johnson, *Film, Space, Time* (New York: Holt, Rinehart and Winston, 1973), p. 3; Louis Gianetti, *Understanding Movies*, 2d ed. (Englewood Cliffs, N.J.: Prentice-Hall, 1976), pp. 123–124; Thomas W. Bohn and Richard L. Stromgren, *Light and Shadow: A History of Motion Pictures*, 2d ed. (Sherman Oaks, Calif.: Alfred, 1978), pp. 5–6; James Monaco, *How to Read a Film: The Art, Technology, Language, History, and Theory of Film and Media*, rev. ed. (New York: Oxford University Press, 1981), p. 73; Richard L. Stromgren and Martin F. Norden, *Movies: A Language in Light* (Englewood Cliffs, N.J.: Prentice-Hall, 1984), pp. 14–15; David A. Cook, *A History of Narrative Film*, 2d ed. (New York: W. W. Norton, 1990), pp. 1–2; Gerald Mast and Bruce Kawin, *The Movies: A Short History*, rev. ed. (Boston: Allyn and Bacon, 1996), pp. 9–10; Chris Webster, "Film and Technology," and Paul Wells, "Animation: Forms and Meaning," in *An Introduction to Film Studies*, ed. Jill Nelmes, 2d ed. (London and New York: Routledge, 1999), pp. 62 and 239, respectively.

4. C. W. Ceram, *Archaeology of the Cinema* (New York: Harcourt, Brace and

World, 1965), p.24; Joseph A. F. Plateau, quoted in Georges Sadoul, *Histoire général du cinéma*, vol. 1 (Paris: Denoel, 1948), p. 25.

5. See, for instance, Joseph and Barbara Anderson, "Motion Perception in Motion Pictures," and Bill Nichols and Susan J. Lederman, "Flicker and Motion in Film," in *The Cinematic Apparatus*, ed. Teresa de Lauretis and Stephen Heath (London: Macmillan, 1980), pp. 76–95 and pp. 96–105, respectively. Research into the perception of motion in cinema is ongoing and in flux. For an explanation of critical flicker fusion and apparent motion, see David Bordwell and Kristen Thompson, *Film Art: An Introduction*, 5th ed. (New York: McGraw-Hill, 1997), pp. 4 and 33.

6. Michael Chanan, *The Dream That Kicks: The Prehistory and Early Years of Cinema in Britain* (London: Routledge and Kegan Paul, 1980), p. 59.

7. Hugo Münsterberg, *The Film: A Psychological Study* (New York: Dover, 1970), p. 29.

8. Frederick A. Talbot, *Moving Pictures: How They Are Made and Worked* (Philadelphia: J. B. Lippincott, 1912), p. 5; Chanan, *The Dream That Kicks*, p. 56; Silvanus Phillips Thompson, "Optical Illusions of Motion," in *Visual Perception: The Nineteenth Century*, ed. William N. Dember (New York: John Wiley and Sons, 1964), p. 84.

9. Johann Wolfgang von Goethe, *Theory of Colours*, trans. Charles Lock Eastlake (Cambridge, Mass.: MIT Press, 1970), pp. 22, 7, 17.

10. Sir David Brewster, "Accidental Colours," in *Edinburgh Encyclopaedia*, 1: 88–93, quoted in *Brewster and Wheatstone on Vision*, ed. Nicholas J. Wade (London: Academic, 1983), p. 235.

11. See Sir Charles Wheatstone, "Contributions to the Physiology of Vision. No. I," *Journal of the Royal Institution* 1 (1830): 101–117, reprinted in Wade, *Brewster and Wheatstone on Vision*, pp. 248–262.

12. Ibid., p. 251.

13. A. R. Luria, *The Working Brain*, trans. Basil Haigh (New York: Basic, 1973), p. 229, quoted in Chanan, *The Dream That Kicks*, p. 57; Helmholtz, *Treatise on Physiological Optics*, 1: 91.

14. Brewster, "Accidental Colours," p. 243.

15. Henri Bergson, *Matter and Memory*, trans. N. M. Paul and W. S. Palmer (New York: Zone, 1988), pp. 218–219, 66, 69.

16. Gilles Deleuze, *Bergsonism*, trans. Hugh Tomlinson and Barbara Habberjam (New York: Zone, 1988), p. 60.

17. See Anson Rabinbach, *The Human Motor: Energy, Fatigue, and the Origins of Modernity* (Berkeley: University of California Press, 1990).

18. Goethe, *Theory of Colours*, p. 17; Brewster, "Accidental Colours," p. 238; Hermann von Helmholtz, "The Recent Progress of the Theory of Vision," in *Science and Culture: Popular and Philosophical Essays*, ed. David Cahan (Chicago: University of Chicago Press, 1995), pp. 164–165.

19. Jonathan Crary, *Techniques of the Observer: On Vision and Modernity in the Nineteenth Century* (Cambridge, Mass.: MIT Press, 1990), p. 98.

20. Ibid., p. 96.

21. Ernst Mach, *Contributions to the Analysis of the Sensations,* trans. C. M. Williams (Chicago: Open Court, 1897), p. 9n.

22. Johannes Müller, "Of the Senses," in Dember, *Visual Perception,* pp. 42, 50.

23. For a fuller discussion of this process of feminization and its attendant anxiety, see Mary Ann Doane, "Technology's Body: Cinematic Vision in Modernity," *differences* 5.2 (1993): 1–23.

24. Helmholtz also elaborates an extensive theory of experience and verification in order to "save" human access to the external world; "Recent Progress," p. 202.

25. Ibid., pp. 173, 203.

26. Müller, "Of the Senses," p. 52.

27. Rabinbach, *The Human Motor,* argues that fatigue was resistant to modernity but also enabled it.

28. Jacques Derrida, *Archive Fever: A Freudian Impression,* trans. Eric Prenowitz (Chicago: University of Chicago Press, 1996), p. 19.

29. Paul Souriau, *The Aesthetics of Movement,* trans. and ed. Manon Souriau (Amherst: University of Massachusetts Press, 1983), pp. 114–115, 116, 118.

30. Ibid., pp. 119, 120–121.

31. Anton Giulio Bragaglia, "Futurist Photodynamism 1911," in *Futurist Manifestos,* ed. Umbro Apollonio (New York: Viking, 1973), p. 43.

32. Umberto Boccioni et al., "Futurist Painting: Technical Manifesto 1910," in Apollonia, *Futurist Manifestos,* p. 30; Bragaglia, "Futurist Photodynamism 1911," p. 43.

33. Umberto Boccioni, "Futurist Painting and Sculpture (extracts) 1914," in Apollonia, *Futurist Manifestos,* p. 178.

34. Boccioni et al., "Futurist Painting," p. 28.

35. Bragaglia, "Futurist Photodynamism 1911," pp. 45, 40, 44.

36. Marta Braun, *Picturing Time: The Work of Etienne-Jules Marey* (Chicago: University of Chicago Press, 1992), p. 310. There was a limited amount of work in film in Futurism. See especially F. T. Marinetti et al., "The Futurist Cinema 1916," in Apollonia, *Futurist Manifestos,* pp. 207–219.

37. F. T. Marinetti, "The Founding and Manifesto of Futurism 1909," in Apollonia, *Futurist Manifestos,* p. 22. Marinetti goes on to reject "moralism, feminism, every opportunistic or utilitarian cowardice." The connection between museums and feminism is not immediately obvious.

38. Although the Futurists seemed to embrace the cinema (and made a number of films), they often reduced it to the same problematic as painting: "The cinema, being essentially visual, must above all fulfill the evolution of painting, detach itself from reality, from photography, from the graceful and the solemn. It must become antigraceful, deforming, impressionistic, synthetic, dynamic, free-wording"

(Marinetti et al., "The Futurist Cinema 1916," p. 208). The sixth tenet of the manifesto on cinema calls for "Daily exercise in freeing ourselves from mere photographed logic" (p. 218).

39. Even Benjamin was immensely more suspicious of the snapshot (instantaneous photography) than of the long exposures required for the early daguerreotype (which had, for him, a certain charm). See Walter Benjamin, "A Small History of Photography," in *One Way Street and Other Writings,* trans. Edmund Jephcott and Kingsley Shorter (London: Verso, 1985), pp. 240–257.

40. Charles Sanders Peirce, *Collected Papers of Charles Sanders Peirce,* ed. Charles Hartshorne and Paul Weiss, vol. 2: *Elements of Logic* (Cambridge, Mass.: Harvard University Press, 1932), p. 267.

41. Charles Sanders Peirce, *Writings of Charles S. Peirce: A Chronological Edition,* ed. Christian J. W. Kloesel, vol. 3 (Bloomington: Indiana University Press, 1986), p. 69.

42. Ibid., pp. 70, 71.

43. Charles Sanders Peirce, *Peirce on Signs: Writings on Semiotic by Charles Sanders Peirce,* ed. James Hoopes (Chapel Hill: University of North Carolina Press, 1991), p. 49.

44. Ibid., p. 24.

45. For a complex and provocative reading of Peirce's theory of signs in relation to experience, purpose, and habit, see Teresa de Lauretis, *Alice Doesn't: Feminism, Semiotics, Cinema* (Bloomington: Indiana University Press, 1984), pp. 172–182; idem, *Technologies of Gender* (Bloomington: Indiana University Press, 1987), pp. 39–42.

46. Peirce, *Peirce on Signs,* pp. 239, 183, 142.

47. Peirce, *The Essential Peirce,* 1: 226.

48. Peirce, *Collected Papers,* 2: 161.

49. Peirce, *The Essential Peirce,* 1: 226.

50. Oswald Ducrot and Tzvetan Todorov, *Encyclopedic Dictionary of the Sciences of Language,* trans. Catherine Porter (Baltimore: Johns Hopkins University Press, 1979), p. 86.

51. Roman Jakobson, "Shifters, Verbal Categories, and the Russian Verb," in *Selected Writings,* vol. 2: *Word and Language* (The Hague: Mouton, 1971), pp. 131–133.

52. Peirce, *Collected Papers,* 2: 163 n.

53. Peter Wollen, *Signs and Meaning in the Cinema* (Bloomington: Indiana University Press, 1972), pp. 116–154.

54. Peirce, *Collected Papers,* 2: 159.

55. Ibid., p. 143.

56. Peirce, *Peirce on Signs,* pp. 251, 25, 239–240.

57. It is true that animal footprints and smoke from a fire are, in a sense, representations linked to chance, accident, and the lack of human control. But the ad-

vent of photography marks the first time that a representation mimicking a three-dimensional space and registering a time could be produced without human agency.

58. Charles Sanders Peirce, *Collected Papers of Charles Sanders Peirce,* ed. Charles Hartshorne and Paul Weiss, vol. 6: *Scientific Metaphysics* (Cambridge, Mass.: Harvard University Press, 1935), pp. 409, 425.

59. Ibid., pp. 28, 37, 41.

60. Peirce, *The Essential Peirce,* 1: 221.

61. Peirce, *Collected Papers,* 6: 197, 54.

62. Ibid., p. 32.

63. Peirce, *The Essential Peirce,* 1: 149.

64. Ian Hacking, *The Taming of Chance* (Cambridge: Cambridge University Press, 1990), p. 1.

65. Peirce, *Collected Papers,* 6: 43; idem, *Essential Papers,* 1: 222.

66. Peirce, *Collected Papers,* 6: 139, 85, 426, 69.

67. Ibid., p. 66.

68. Ibid.

69. Ibid., p. 234.

70. Peirce, *Essential Papers,* 1: 226; idem, *Collected Papers,* 2: 161.

71. Bragaglia, "Futurist Photodynamism 1911," p. 40.

72. Paul de Man, "Literary History and Literary Modernity," in *Blindness and Insight: Essays in the Rhetoric of Contemporary Criticism* (New York: Oxford University Press, 1971), p. 148.

73. Siegfried Kracauer, "Photography," in *The Mass Ornament: Weimar Essays,* trans. and ed. Thomas Y. Levin (Cambridge, Mass.: Harvard University Press, 1995), pp. 54, 62, and 59.

74. Roland Barthes, *Camera Lucida: Reflections on Photography,* trans. Richard Howard (New York: Hill and Wang, 1981), p. 77.

75. Roland Barthes, "Rhetoric of the Image," in *Image-Music-Text,* trans. Stephen Heath (New York: Noonday, 1988), p. 45.

76. Christian Metz, "On the Impression of Reality in the Cinema," in *Film Language: A Semiotics of the Cinema* (New York: Oxford University Press, 1974), p. 8.

77. Chanan, *The Dream that Kicks,* pp. 15–16; Derrida, *Archive Fever,* p. 18.

78. Pier Paolo Pasolini, "Observations on the Long Take," *October* 13 (1980): 3.

79. This form of "presence," however, can be only a theoretical ideal. The datedness of the film stock together with the spectator's historical knowledge inevitably makes the event "historical."

80. Pasolini, "Observations on the Long Take," pp. 5, 6.

81. See Mary Ann Doane, "Information, Crisis, Catastrophe," in *Logics of Television,* ed. Patricia Mellencamp (Bloomington: Indiana University Press, 1990), pp. 222–239.

82. Walter Benjamin makes a similar claim about death in storytelling in "The

Storyteller," in *Illuminations,* trans. Harry Zohn, ed. Hannah Arendt (New York: Schocken, 1969), pp. 83–110.

4. Temporal Irreversibility and the Logic of Statistics

1. Tom Gunning, "The Cinema of Attractions: Early Film, Its Spectator and the Avant-Garde," in *Early Cinema: Space, Frame, Narrative,* ed. Thomas Elsaesser (London: British Film Institute, 1990), p. 58.

2. In a similar way, in the auditory realm, music subjects its listener to the time of its own forward movement (as do theater and other forms of performance). This movement can vary, however, from performer to performer, and it is only mechanical or electronic reproduction that adds the element of invariability. Film is inconceivable without mechanical reproduction; music can be "exhibited" as a performance in the present or delivered through mechanical reproduction. This is not to suggest that the sound recording process does not "add" something or inform the perception of the recorded sound, or that phonography does not constitute a signifying procedure in its own right. Phonography itself does share many of the aspects of temporal irreversibility described here in relation to the cinema (for example, in "aberrant" experiments in playing recorded sounds in reverse). But film was the first *visual* form of mechanical reproduction to engage temporal irreversibility.

3. *Post-Express,* 20 February 1897, p. 14, quoted in George C. Pratt, *Spellbound in Darkness: A History of the Silent Film* (Greenwich, Conn.: New York Graphic Society, 1973), p. 18.

4. *The Artist's Dilemma* was one of a group of films from 1900 acquired by the Edison Company and copyrighted in Edison's name. See Charles Musser, *Before the Nickelodeon: Edwin S. Porter and the Edison Manufacturing Company* (Berkeley: University of California Press, 1991), p. 192. The film can be viewed on the Library of Congress's online American Memory collection at http://memory.loc. gov/cgibin/query/D?papr:26:./temp/~ammem_fE1I::

5. Georges Méliès had also used extensively the transformation of representations (statues, dummies, skeletons, figures in paintings, posters, photographs, playing cards, etc.) into living beings. Paul Hammond traces this strategy back to the magic theater, to Robert Houdin's mechanical figures, which came to life and which Méliès imitated during the 1880s. Hammond also points to John Nevil Maskelyne's attempt to bring a painting to life in an illusion invented by David Devant in 1893, titled *The Artist's Dream.* See Hammond, *Marvelous Méliès* (London: Gordon Fraser, 1974), p. 90.

6. Although clocks were frequently part of a painted set in this period and could not "move" to indicate the passage of time, the fact that the artist is asleep at both the beginning and end of the film and the similarity between this film and

the Maskelyne illusion, *The Artist's Dream,* strongly suggest that the diegesis is a dream and that time does not advance within it.

7. Jacques Aumont, "The Variable Eye, or the Mobilization of the Gaze," in *The Image in Dispute: Art and Cinema in the Age of Photography,* ed. Dudley Andrew (Austin: University of Texas Press, 1997), p. 245.

8. Richard Morris, *Time's Arrows: Scientific Attitudes toward Time* (New York: Simon and Schuster, 1985), pp. 110–111.

9. Michel Serres, *Hermes: Literature, Science, Philosophy,* ed. Josué V. Harari and David F. Bell (Baltimore: Johns Hopkins University Press, 1982), pp. 71–72.

10. Anson Rabinbach, *The Human Motor: Energy, Fatigue, and the Origins of Modernity* (Berkeley: University of California Press, 1990), p. 63.

11. Although the Second Law of Thermodynamics is associated more strongly with decline or dissipation, the idea of a directionality in time is crucial to thermodynamics, so that degeneration in effect gives birth to the possibility of thinking its opposite—progress.

12. See, for instance, James Clerk Maxwell's definition—"Work is done when resistance is overcome, and the quantity of work done is measured by the product of the resisting force and the distance through which that force is overcome"—and his subsequent discussion of work and energy in relation to entropy, in *Theory of Heat* (New York: D. Appleton, 1872), pp. 87 and 185–188.

13. P. M. Harman, *Energy, Force and Matter: The Conceptual Development of Nineteenth-Century Physics* (Cambridge: Cambridge University Press, 1982), p. 58.

14. Quoted in Rabinbach, *The Human Motor,* p. 151.

15. Morris, *Time's Arrows,* p. 117.

16. François Jacob, *The Logic of Life: A History of Heredity,* trans. Betty E. Spillmann (Princeton: Princeton University Press, 1973), p. 198.

17. Claude E. Shannon and Warren Weaver, *The Mathematical Theory of Communication* (Urbana: University of Illinois Press, 1963), p. 12.

18. A film shown in reverse may also be indexical. However, in the examples from physics textbooks, film must be indexical (as opposed to iconic, that is, animated) to act as authentic evidence of the irreversibility of time.

19. Ilya Prigogine and Isabelle Stengers, *Order out of Chaos: Man's New Dialogue with Nature* (New York: Bantam, 1984), p. 61. Prigogine and Stengers are comparing the time of classical physics to a practice of film projection that is far from the norm. My argument here is that mainstream film, in its classical forms, reaffirms the irreversibility of time. Jean Epstein extolled the possibilities of reversible time and motion in cinema and cited their effects in "older" films (a usage of reversible time that had already become marginalized by the time he wrote the following):

Experience since time immemorial has created the dogma of life's irreversibility. The course of evolution in both the atom and the galaxy, in inorganic matter as in both animal and human forms, derives its irrevocably unique meaning from the loss of energy. The constant increase in entropy is the catch which stops the gears of the terrestrial and celestial machine from ever moving in reverse. Time cannot return to its origin; no effect can precede its cause. And a world which would claim to break with or modify this vectorial order seems both physically impossible and logically unimaginable.

Focus attention, however, on a scene in an old avant garde film or a slap-stick comedy that has been filmed in reverse motion. Suddenly, with an un-deniable precision, the cinema describes a world which moves from its end to its beginning, an anti-universe which until now man had hardly managed to picture for himself. Dead leaves take off from the ground to hang once again upon tree branches; rain drops spurt upwards from the earth to the clouds; a locomotive swallows its smoke and cinders, inhales its own steam; a machine uses the cold to produce heat and work. Bursting from a husk, a flower with-ers into a bud which retreats into the stem. As the stem ages, it withdraws into a seed. Life appears only through resurrection, crossing old age's decrep-itude into the bloom of maturity, rolling through the course of youth, then of infancy, and finally dissolving in a prenatal limbo. Universal repulsion, the energy loss of entropy, the continual increase of energy constitute truth val-ues contrary to Newton's law and the principles of Carnot and Clausius. Ef-fect has become cause; cause, effect.

Could the structure of the universe be ambivalent? Might it permit both forward and backward movements? Does it admit of a double logic, two determinisms, two antithetical ends?

Jean Epstein, "Magnification and Other Writings," trans. Stuart Liebman, *October* 3 (1977): 20–21. Epstein celebrates the significance of a filmic capability that had been seriously minimized in the mainstream cinema. His writing often conveys a utopian dream of what the cinema might have been.

20. Prigogine and Stengers argue that this is still the case today. See *Order out of Chaos*.

21. Ibid., p. 60.

22. Quoted in Ilya Prigogine, *From Being to Becoming: Time and Complexity in the Physical Sciences* (New York: W. H. Freeman, 1980), p. 2.

23. Michel Serres, *Zola* (Paris: Editions Grasset et Fasquelle, 1975), p. 73; my translation.

24. Prigogine and Stengers, *Order out of Chaos*, pp. 22, 111.

25. Ibid., p. 116.

26. François Jacob, on the other hand, claims that the contradiction is only ap-parent: "Every human being remains in a sense permanently plugged into the gen-eral current which carries the universe towards disorder. It is a sort of local and

transitory eddy which maintains organization and allows it to reproduce"; *Logic of Life*, p. 253.

27. Ibid., p. 176.

28. Ibid., p. 198.

29. Prigogine and Stengers, *Order out of Chaos*, p. 232.

30. See Prigogine, *From Being to Becoming*, p. 12.

31. Maxwell himself objected to the term, calling the figure "no more a demon but a valve" and asserting that there were no supernatural resonances to the argument; Harman, *Energy, Force, and Matter*, p. 140.

32. Jacob, *Logic of Life*, p. 196.

33. Maxwell, *Theory of Heat*, pp. 308–309. See also N. Katherine Hayles, *Chaos Bound: Orderly Disorder in Contemporary Literature and Science* (Ithaca: Cornell University Press, 1990), pp. 42–44, for an insightful discussion of Maxwell's demon in the context of Victorian culture.

34. See Harman, *Energy, Force, and Matter*, pp. 139–140; and Prigogine and Stengers, *Order out of Chaos*, pp. 122–123.

35. See Prigogine and Stengers, *Order out of Chaos*, pp. 123, 241; and Ian Hacking, *The Taming of Chance* (Cambridge: Cambridge University Press, 1990), p. 107.

36. Prigogine and Stengers, *Order out of Chaos*, p. 241.

37. Jacob, *Logic of Life*, pp. 197, 200.

38. Ibid., p. 173.

39. Hacking, *The Taming of Chance*, pp. 109, 108.

40. See Kathleen Woodward, "Statistical Panic," *differences* 11 (Summer 1999): 177–203.

41. Francis Galton, *Inquiries into Human Faculty and Its Development* (New York: Macmillan, 1883), pp. 4, 5, 10, 17.

42. For an extended discussion of the concept of degeneration in art and aesthetics, see Max Nordau, *Degeneration* (1892) (Lincoln: University of Nebraska Press, 1993).

43. Galton, *Inquiries into Human Faculty*, p. 25.

44. Ibid., p. 14.

45. Allan Sekula, "The Body and the Archive," *October* 39 (1986): 48.

46. Walter Benjamin, "The Work of Art in the Age of Mechanical Reproduction," in *Illuminations*, trans. Harry Zohn, ed. Hannah Arendt (New York: Schocken, 1969), pp. 222, 223.

47. Benjamin's position on this shifts, even within a single article. Elsewhere in "The Work of Art in the Age of Mechanical Reproduction," he writes of the "optical unconscious," the special effects (slow motion, microscopic cinematography, etc.) that make visible what is ordinarily beyond the reach of human vision and hence a mechanism by means of which cinema displays an affinity with the unique, the individual, the contingent rather than the generalizable. This is also

the case in his discussion of the daguerreotype and of Eugene Atget's work in "A Small History of Photography," in *One Way Street and Other Writings,* trans. Edmund Jephcott and Kingsley Shorter (London: Verso, 1985), pp. 240–257.

48. Peter Coveney and Roger Highfield, *The Arrow of Time* (New York: Ballantine, 1990), p. 147.

49. *Memento* (Christopher Nolan, 2001) is a particularly good example. Although the film begins with a striking sequence of reversed motion, in which blood returns to a body, a bullet flies back to a gun, the gun is reinserted in a belt, etc., this reversal is not sustained throughout the film and, indeed, acts as a trope for the backward movement of the film's narrative as a whole, which unfolds, in the tradition of the detective story, to reveal the critical event allowing an understanding of the character's destiny. For the most part, the fragmentation and reordering of time in this film is supported by a basic irreversibility of movement.

50. Charles Musser, "Rethinking Early Cinema: Cinema of Attractions and Narrativity," *Yale Journal of Criticism* 7.2 (Fall 1994): 216–217.

51. Charles Musser, *History of the American Cinema,* vol. 1: *The Emergence of Cinema: The American Screen to 1907* (Berkeley: University of California Press, 1990), pp. 117, 189.

52. Roy Rosenzweig, *Eight Hours for What We Will* (Cambridge: Cambridge University Press, 1983), p. 199.

53. Eileen Bowser, *History of the American Cinema,* vol. 2: *The Transformation of Cinema: 1907–1915* (Berkeley: University of California Press, 1990), p. 125. In "The Cult of Distraction," Siegfried Kracauer analyzes the architecture and form of presentation of the Berlin picture palaces, describing the juxtaposition of films and production numbers as a striving for *"the total artwork [Gesamtkunstwerk] of effects."* He argues that although film has the potential to foreground "a kind of distraction that exposes disintegration instead of masking it," it does not, in practice, accomplish this. Instead, he describes the programs of the large movie theaters in the following fashion: "For even as they summon to distraction, they immediately rob distraction of its meaning by amalgamating the wide range of effects—which by their nature demand to be isolated from one another—into an "artistic" unity. These shows strive to coerce the motley sequence of externalities into an organic whole"; *The Mass Ornament,* pp. 324 and 327–328.

54. Whereas the earlier nickelodeon encouraged patrons to enter in the middle of a "show" (usually a succession of short news programs, documentaries, comedies, and dramas lasting about an hour), this practice was progressively undermined with the advent of the picture palace in the late 1910s and early 1920s, where a corps of trained ushers managed and directed an audience of around four thousand in the auditorium while another four thousand waited for the next show. Ushers "maintained a quiet decorum in the theatre that went along with, and even underlined, the upper-class atmosphere so sought after by suburbanite patrons"; Douglas Gomery, *Shared Pleasures: A History of Movie Presentation in*

the United States (Madison: University of Wisconsin Press, 1992), p. 49. Despite the practice of continuous showings, which might seem to allow for temporal reversibility in the cinema, the regulation of ushers, the rise of the double feature in the 1930s, and the accelerating tendency to view a feature film as a self-contained unit all buttressed the association between film and temporal irreversibility.

55. Prigogine and Stengers argue that new developments in the analysis of far-from-equilibrium situations qualify this assertion and suggest that irreversibility may be at work at the microscopic level as well; *Order out of Chaos*, pp. 12–18.

56. Laura Mulvey, "Visual Pleasure and Narrative Cinema," in *Narrative, Apparatus, Ideology*, ed. Philip Rosen (New York: Columbia University Press, 1986), p. 203.

57. See the debate between Charles Musser and Tom Gunning on the issue of narrativity in Méliès' films, in Musser, "Rethinking Early Cinema," especially pp. 207–209; and Gunning, "The Cinema of Attractions," pp. 56–62.

58. As Tom Gunning argues, there is strong evidence that so-called stop-motion filming always involved an actual splice and therefore constituted a form of editing. See "'Primitive' Cinema: A Frame Up? Or, The Trick's on Us," in Elsaesser, *Early Cinema*, pp. 97–99.

59. Hammond, *Marvellous Méliès*, p. 89.

60. Lucy Fischer, "The Lady Vanishes: Women, Magic and the Movies," *Film Quarterly* 33.1 (1979): 35; Linda Williams, "Film Body: An Implantation of Perversions," in Rosen, *Narrative, Apparatus, Ideology*, pp. 527–528.

61. For a discussion of the relations between masculinity and error and masculinity and entropy in modernity, see Mary Ann Doane, "Technology and Sexual Difference: Apocalyptic Scenarios at Two 'Fins-de-Siècle,'" *differences* 9.2 (1998): 1–24; idem, "Technology's Body: Cinematic Vision in Modernity," *differences* 5.2 (1993): 1–23.

62. Tom Gunning also denies the legitimacy of a polarization of Lumière and Méliès, claiming that the films of both can be more accurately understood as belonging to the tradition of visual illusions, including the transforming tricks and magic lanterns of vaudeville. See "'Primitive' Cinema," p. 96.

63. Georges Méliès, "Cinematographic Views," trans. Stuart Liebman, in Richard Abel, ed., *French Film Theory and Criticism: A History/Anthology*, vol. 1: *1907–1929* (Princeton: Princeton University Press, 1988), p. 44. Originally published as "Les Vues cinématographiques," in *Annuaire général et international de la photographie* (Paris: Plon, 1907), pp. 362–392.

64. See, for example, Katherine Singer Kovács, "Georges Méliès and the *Féerie*," in *Film before Griffith*, ed. John L. Fell (Berkeley: University of California Press, 1983), p. 254 n.; and David A. Cook, *A History of Narrative Film*, 2d ed. (New York: W. W. Norton, 1990), p. 15. Although Cook points out in a footnote that the story may be apocryphal, he repeats it without qualification, as a historical incident, in the text. See also Lewis Jacobs, *The Rise of the American Film* (1939; re-

print, New York: Teachers College Press, 1968), p. 23; and Kenneth MacGowan, *Behind the Screen: The History and Technique of the Motion Picture* (New York: Dell, 1965), p. 100.

65. Michel Foucault, "Of Other Spaces," trans. Jay Miskowiec, *Diacritics* 16 (1986): 24.

5. Dead Time, or the Concept of the Event

1. Jean-François Lyotard, *The Inhuman: Reflections on Time*, trans. Geoffrey Bennington and Rachel Bowlby (Stanford: Stanford University Press, 1991), p. 68.

2. Peter Galassi, *Before Photography: Painting and the Invention of Photography* (New York: Museum of Modern Art, 1981), pp. 25, 29.

3. Walter Benjamin, "A Small History of Photography," in *One Way Street and Other Writings*, trans. Edmund Jephcott and Kingsley Shorter (London: Verso, 1985), p. 243; Siegfried Kracauer, "Photography," in *The Mass Ornament: Weimar Essays*, trans. and ed. Thomas Y. Levin (Cambridge, Mass.: Harvard University Press, 1995), p. 54. For a provocative discussion of this essay and its relation to Kracauer's later theory of film, see Gertrud Koch, *Siegfried Kracauer: An Introduction*, trans. Jeremy Gaines (Princeton: Princeton University Press, 2000), pp. 95–113.

4. Roland Barthes, *Camera Lucida: Relections on Photography* (New York: Hill and Wang, 1981), pp. 40–43.

5. Roland Barthes, *Image-Music-Text*, trans. Stephen Heath (New York: Noonday, 1977), p. 45.

6. André Gaudreault, "The Cinematograph: A Historiographical Machine," in *Meanings in Texts and Actions: Questioning Paul Ricoeur*, ed. David E. Klemm and William Schweiker (Charlottesville: University Press of Virginia, 1993), p. 95.

7. Thomas Elsaesser, "Early Cinema: From Linear History to Mass Media Archaeology," in *Early Cinema: Space, Frame, Narrative*, ed. Elsaesser (London: British Film Institute, 1990), p. 17.

8. *Execution by Hanging* and *Reading the Death Sentence* are clearly segments of the same film. In line with the practices at this time, the exhibitor was given the option of buying the parts as separate entities.

9. See Charles Musser, *Before the Nickelodeon: Edwin S. Porter and the Edison Manufacturing Company* (Berkeley: University of California Press, 1991), p. 187.

10. The threat of this seemingly absolute contingency is only underlined by the desperate attempts of religion to confer a meaning upon death, to domesticate it by bringing it back within the realm of the knowable. Religion responds to the fear of meaninglessness contaminating death. With the increasing secularization of modernity, the effectivity of religion's solace is diminished.

11. Quoted in *Before Hollywood: Turn-of-the-Century Film from American Archives* (New York: American Federation of the Arts, 1986), p. 109.

12. For a discussion of this film in relation to discourses of physiology and as "evidence of a widespread popular interest in the power of technology to regulate and discipline bodies," see Lisa Cartwright, *Screening the Body: Tracing Medicine's Visual Culture* (Minneapolis: University of Minnesota Press, 1995), pp. 17–18.

13. See Musser, *Before the Nickelodeon*, pp. 162–167.

14. Ibid., p. 187.

15. David E. Nye, *Electrifying America: Social Meanings of a New Technology, 1880–1940* (Cambridge, Mass.: MIT Press, 1990), p. 1; David Levy, "Re-constituted Newsreels, Re-enactments, and the American Narrative Film," in *Cinema 1900/ 1906: An Analytical Study*, ed. Roger Holman (Brussels: Fédération Internationale des Archives du Film, 1982), p. 251.

16. Mark Seltzer, *Bodies and Machines* (New York: Routledge, 1992), p. 11.

17. Walter Benjamin, "On Some Motifs in Baudelaire," in *Illuminations*, trans. Harry Zohn, ed. Hannah Arendt (New York: Schocken, 1969), pp. 174–175.

18. The media insisted upon identifying Czolgosz as an immigrant despite the fact that he had been born in the United States. The assassination provoked a public hysteria about immigration, foreignness, and anarchy.

19. Benjamin, "A Small History of Photography," p. 256.

20. In its own fashion, electrocution also involves a taming and structuring of the accidental: the idea of electrocution allegedly emerged from the witnessing of accidental electrical death (a man being killed instantly by a live wire). See Tim Armstrong, "The Electrification of the Body at the Turn of the Century," *Textual Practice* 5.3 (1991): 315.

21. The exhibitor was given the option of buying the narrative section with or without the opening panoramas; Musser, *Before the Nickelodeon*, p. 188.

22. See Dolf Sternberger, *Panorama of the Nineteenth Century*, trans. Joachim Neugroschel (New York: Urizen, 1977), p. 185. For a discussion of the differences between the European stationary panorama and the American moving panorama, see Jacques Aumont, "The Variable Eye," in *The Image in Dispute: Art and Cinema in the Age of Photography*, ed. Dudley Andrew (Austin: University of Texas Press, 1997), pp. 236–240. For an excellent analysis of the history of the panorama and its spectacular effects in relation to the cinema, see Angela Miller, "The Panorama, the Cinema, and the Emergence of the Spectacular," *Wide Angle* 18.2 (April 1996): 35–69. See also Vanessa R. Schwartz, *Spectacular Realities: Early Mass Culture in Fin-de-Siècle Paris* (Berkeley: University of California Press, 1998), pp. 149–176.

23. Sternberger, *Panorama of the Nineteenth Century*, pp. 8, 9, 11.

24. See Levy, "Re-constituted Newsreels," p. 248.

25. Ibid., pp. 248–249.

26. See Raymond Fielding, *The American Newsreel, 1911–1967* (Norman: University of Oklahoma Press, 1972), p. 38.

27. Levy, "Re-constituted Newsreels," p. 247.

28. Fielding, *The American Newsreel, 1911–1967*, p. 42.

29. Miriam Hansen, *Babel and Babylon: Spectatorship in American Silent Film* (Cambridge, Mass.: Harvard University Press, 1991), p. 31.

30. Quoted in Fielding, *The American Newsreel, 1911–1967,* p. 43.

31. Musser, *Before the Nickelodeon,* p. 193.

32. André Gaudreault, "The Infringement of Copyright Laws and Its Effects (1900–1906)," in Elsaesser, *Early Cinema,* pp. 115–117.

33. See Gaudreault, "Infringement," p. 120.

34. Quoted in Levy, "Re-constituted Newsreels," p. 214.

35. Gaudreault, "Infringement," p. 119.

36. Levy, "Re-constituted Newsreels," pp. 243–258.

37. Ibid., p. 254.

38. André Gaudreault, "Temporality and Narrativity in Early Cinema, 1895–1908," in *Film before Griffith,* ed. John L. Fell (Berkeley: University of California Press, 1983), p. 326.

39. Michael Chanan, *The Dream That Kicks: The Prehistory and Early Years of Cinema in Britain* (London: Routledge and Kegan Paul, 1980), p. 41.

40. Siegfried Kracauer, "Boredom," in Levin, *The Mass Ornament,* pp. 332, 334.

41. For a discussion of theories of boredom, modernity, and postmodernity, including Kracauer's work as well as that of Walter Benjamin and Frederic Jameson, see Patrice Petro, "After/Shock: Between Boredom and History," in *Fugitive Images: From Photography to Video,* ed. Patrice Petro (Bloomington: Indiana University Press, 1995), pp. 265–284. Petro argues for the recognition of boredom as a historical category and for its close affiliation with issues of gender and sexual difference.

42. Sigmund Freud, "Thoughts for the Times on War and Death," in *The Standard Edition of the Complete Psychological Works of Sigmund Freud,* trans. and ed. James Strachey (hereafter *Standard Edition*), vol. 14 (London: Hogarth Press, 1955), p. 289.

43. The striking exception to this statement is the snuff film, which aspires to the direct, nonfictional representation of death and the arousal of the voyeuristic urges associated with it. However, it is crucial that the snuff film is not simply marginal, but illicit. The obscenity of filming death extends beyond the necessity for murder which is entailed and is linked to a notion of "proper" and "improper" objects of the gaze.

44. Jacques Derrida, "Structure, Sign, and Play in the Discourse of the Human Sciences," in *Writing and Difference,* trans. Alan Bass (Chicago: University of Chicago Press, 1978), p. 278.

45. Claude Lévi-Strauss, "The Science of the Concrete," in *The Savage Mind* (Chicago: University of Chicago Press, 1966), pp. 21, 22.

46. Ibid., pp. 25, 29.

47. Derrida, "Structure, Sign, and Play," p. 291.

48. For a related and extremely provocative reading of Freud's concept of the

screen memory, see Naomi Schor, *Reading in Detail: Aesthetics and the Feminine* (New York: Methuen, 1987), pp. 71–78.

49. Sigmund Freud, "Screen Memories," in *Standard Edition,* vol. 3 (London: Hogarth Press and Institute of Psycho-Analysis, 1962), pp. 305, 309.

50. Sigmund Freud, *The Psychopathology of Everyday Life,* in *Standard Edition,* vol. 6 (London: Hogarth Press, 1960), p. 257.

51. Jean Laplanche and Jean-Bertrand Pontalis, "Fantasy and the Origins of Sexuality," in *Formations of Fantasy,* ed. Victor Burgin, James Donald, and Cora Kaplan (London: Methuen, 1986), p. 18.

52. Charles Baudelaire, *The Painter of Modern Life and Other Essays,* trans. and ed. Jonathan Mayne (New York: Da Capo, 1964), pp. 13, 12, 13, 30.

53. Ibid., pp. 16.

54. Laura Mulvey, "Visual Pleasure and Narrative Cinema," in *Narrative, Apparatus, Ideology,* ed. Philip Rosen (New York: Columbia University Press, 1986), pp. 198–209.

55. See Hansen, *Babel and Babylon.*

56. Ian Hacking, *The Taming of Chance* (Cambridge: Cambridge University Press, 1990).

6. Zeno's Paradox

1. Jean Epstein, "Magnification and Other Writings," trans. Stuart Liebman, *October* 3 (1977): 23; Henri Bergson, *Creative Evolution,* trans. Arthur Mitchell (New York: Henry Holt, 1926), p. 308.

2. Epstein, "Magnification," pp. 24, 21.

3. Bergson, *Creative Evolution,* pp. 305–306, 308.

4. Gilles Deleuze, *Cinema 1: The Movement-Image,* trans. Hugh Tomlinson and Barbara Habberjam (Minneapolis: University of Minnesota Press, 1986), p. 25; idem, *Cinema 2: The Time-Image,* trans. Hugh Tomlinson and Robert Galeta (Minneapolis: University of Minnesota Press, 1989), p. 82.

5. Deleuze, *Cinema 1,* pp. 1, 2.

6. See Tom Gunning, "An Aesthetic of Astonishment: Early Film and the (In)Credulous Spectator," in *Viewing Positions: Ways of Seing Film,* ed. Linda Williams (New Brunswick, N.J.: Rutgers University Press, 1995), pp. 118–119.

7. Epstein, "Magnification," p. 23; Christian Metz, *Film Language: A Semiotics of the Cinema* (New York: Oxford University Press, 1974), p. 9.

8. Marshall Deutelbaum has argued that, contrary to traditional opinion, Lumière films were in fact highly structured and that films like *Sortie d'usine* manifest a sequential logic, with a clearly marked beginning, middle, and end, suggesting a narrative organization. I agree with this in some instances. However, my point here is that, as tightly structured and planned as the films might be, time is sutured to movement, and the films reveal a fascination with movement itself.

See Marshall Deutelbaum, "Structural Patterning in the Lumière Films," in *Film before Griffith,* ed. John L. Fell (Berkeley: University of California Press, 1983), pp. 299–310. See also Roy Armes, *French Cinema* (New York: Oxford University Press, 1985), p. 10; and Alan Williams, *Republic of Images: A History of French Filmmaking* (Cambridge, Mass.: Harvard University Press, 1992), pp. 27–31. Both Armes and Williams also point out that the subject matter of the films reflects the lifestyle and ideology of the turn-of-the-century bourgeoisie.

9. The dates for these Lumière films are taken from *La Production cinématographique des Frères Lumières,* ed. Michelle Aubert and Jean-Claude Sequin (Lyon: Centre National de la Cinématographie, l'Université Lumière–Lyon 2, et Bibliothèque du Film, 1996). The difficulty in determining the dates of production of these earliest films is linked to the fact that some surviving prints were remakes of earlier versions. For instance, for a discussion of the relation of the 1897 version of *Barque sortant du port* to a possible version of the same film made in 1896, see *La Production,* pp. 212–213.

10. Quoted in Tom Gunning, "'Now You See It, Now You Don't': The Temporality of the Cinema of Attractions," *Velvet Light Trap* 32 (1993): 6.

11. This is why Aumont corroborates Godard's claim and labels Lumière the last Impressionist. See Jacques Aumont, *L'Oeil interminable: Cinéma et peinture* (Paris: Librairie Séguier, 1989), p. 16.

12. Ibid., p. 43.

13. As André Gaudreault and Jean-Marc Lamotte have shown in their ongoing research on fragmentation of the film strip in the work of Lumière and Edison, early actualities often made use of hiatuses that were sometimes produced by camera stoppages and at other times produced by splicing the film. They warn, however, against anachronistically using the term *editing* to characterize this fragmentation, which responds to various needs (most frequently ellipsis of unwanted or "dead" time, as in *Electrocution of an Elephant,* discussed in Chapter 5). Gaudreault and Lamotte claim that by 1898 18 percent of Lumière films and by 1900 36 percent of Edison films contained some sort of visual hiatus. However, it is nevertheless true that the bulk of actualities produced during this period were composed of a single shot that preserved "real time." See Gaudreault and Lamotte, "Fragmentation des prises de vues Lumière," paper presented at the conference "Stop Motion and Fragmentation of Time: Cinematography, Kinetography, Chronophotography," Montreal, October 4–7, 2000. See also Gaudreault, "Les Traces du montage dans la production Lumière," in *L'Aventure du Cinématographe: Actes du Congrès mondial Lumière* (Lyon: Aléas Editeur, 1999), pp. 299–306.

14. Deleuze, *Cinema 2,* p. 35.

15. Despite a wealth of recent work reevaluating the so-called primitive cinema and questioning its alleged status as simply a more naive precursor of the later, more highly developed cinema, Deleuze espouses a fairly predictable and teleolog-

ical history in which the early, "primitive" cinema is really not-yet cinema, the classical cinema refines and standardizes narrative, and the modernist cinema of the 1960s and 1970s comes to fulfill the true potential of cinema to manipulate and defamiliarize time. For a more sympathetic analysis of Deleuze's approach to cinema, see D. N. Rodowick, *Gilles Deleuze's Time Machine* (Durham, N.C.: Duke University Press, 1997).

16. Deleuze, *Cinema 1,* p. 24.

17. André Gaudreault, *Du littéraire au filmique: Système du récit* (France: Presses de l'Université Laval Méridiens Klincksieck, 1988), pp. 112, 110; my translation. For a different view about continuity and discontinuity in early film, see Tom Gunning, "Non-Continuity, Continuity, Discontinuity: A Theory of Genres in Early Films," in *Early Cinema: Space, Frame, Narrative,* ed. Thomas Elsaesser (London: British Film Institute, 1990), pp. 86–94; and idem, "The Non-Continuous Style of Early Film, 1900–1906," in *Cinema 1900/1906: An Analytical Study,* ed. Roger Holman (Brussels: Fédération Internationale des Archives du Film, 1982), pp. 219–230.

18. Deleuze, *Cinema 1,* pp. 4–5.

19. Bergson, *Creative Evolution,* p. 332.

20. Deleuze, *Cinema 1,* pp.4, 7.

21. For an insightful analysis of this film in relation to the "staged" and the "unstaged" and the dialectical absorption of the actuality into narrative, see James Lastra, "From the Captured Moment to the Cinematic Image: A Transformation in Pictorial Order," in *The Image in Dispute: Art and Cinema in the Age of Photography,* ed. Dudley Andrew (Austin: University of Texas Press, 1997), pp. 263–291. Judith Mayne discusses *What Happened on Twenty-third Street* in terms of the early cinema's narrativization of the female body in *The Woman at the Keyhole: Feminism and Women's Cinema* (Bloomington: Indiana University Press, 1990), pp. 161–164. See also Constance Balides, "Scenarios of Exposure in the Practice of Everyday Life: Women in the Cinema of Attractions," *Screen* 34 (Spring 1993): 19–37, for an analysis of voyeurism and the exposure of the female body in early cinema.

22. Aumont, *L'Oeil interminable,* p. 76.

23. Gaudreault, *Du littéraire au filmique,* p. 110.

24. André Gaudreault, "Temporality and Narrativity in Early Cinema, 1895–1908," in Fell, *Film before Griffith,* p. 314; emphasis added.

25. For a discussion of the consequences of this relation betweeen continuity and discontinuity, see Jean-Louis Baudry, "Ideological Effects of the Basic Cinematographic Apparatus," in *Narrative, Apparatus, Ideology,* ed. Philip Rosen (New York: Columbia University Press, 1986), pp. 286–298.

26. Aumont, *L'Oeil interminable,* p. 100.

27. Ibid., pp. 98–99.

28. Siegfried Kracauer, "Photography," in *The Mass Ornament: Weimar Essays,*

trans. and ed. Thomas Y. Levin (Cambridge, Mass.: Harvard University Press, 1995), pp. 62–63.

29. The power of classical continuity editing reveals itself, however, in the fact that the widely used Museum of Modern Art print of *The Life of an American Fireman* was reedited at some point, using parallel editing to intercut inside and outside scenes and avoid the repetition of time. Only quite recently has the Library of Congress paper print version been accepted as the authentic version. See Charles Musser, *Before the Nickelodeon: Edwin S. Porter and the Edison Manufacturing Company* (Berkeley: University of California Press, 1991), pp. 230–234.

30. Noël Burch, "Porter, or Ambivalence," *Screen* 19.4 (Winter 1978–79): 104.

31. Musser, *Before the Nickelodeon*, p. 225.

32. Remakes include, but are not limited to, *How a French Nobleman Got a Wife through the New York Herald "Personal" Columns* (Edison, 1904), *Meet Me at the Fountain* (Lubin, 1904), and *Dix Femmes pour un mari* (*Ten Women for One Husband*) (Pathé, 1905).

33. Noël Burch, *Life to those Shadows,* trans. and ed. Ben Brewster (Berkeley: University of California Press, 1990), p. 150.

34. Ian Hacking, *The Taming of Chance* (Cambridge: Cambridge University Press, 1990), p. 161.

35. Tom Gunning, *D. W. Griffith and the Origins of American Narrative Film: The Early Years at Biograph* (Urbana: University of Illinois Press, 1991), p. 99. Gunning argues that the strategy of parallel editing allowed the developing cinema both to reaffirm and to contest the rationalization and oppression of industrial time: "Making the passage of time more palpable, parallel editing offers both a celebration and an overcoming of the new rhythms of modern production in an art form which—like the major attractions of the new amusement parks—was itself the product of industrial production. Griffith's parallel editing, like much of contemporaneous popular culture, clothes a new experience of time and labor in the forms of fantasy and desire" (p. 106).

36. Tom Gunning, "Heard over the Phone: *The Lonely Villa* and the deLorde Tradition of the Terrors of Technology," *Screen* 32.2 (Summer 1991): 187.

37. Tom Gunning, "Weaving a Narrative: Style and Economic Background in Griffith's Biograph Films," in Elsaesser, *Early Cinema*, p. 343.

38. Pascal Bonitzer, "Partial Vision: Film and the Labyrinth," trans. Fabrice Ziolkowski, *Wide Angle* 4, no. 4 (1981): 57–58.

39. Jacques Aumont, "Griffith—The Frame, the Figure," in Elsaesser, *Early Cinema*, p. 354.

40. Pascal Bonitzer, "Here: The Notion of the Shot and the Subject of the Cinema," *Film Reader*, no. 4 (1979): 113.

41. Raymond Bellour, "To Alternate/To Narrate," in *Early Cinema: Space, Frame, Narrative*, ed. Thomas Elsaesser (London: BFI, 1990), pp. 360–374; Roland

Barthes, "Introduction to the Structural Analysis of Narratives," in *Image-Music-Text,* trans. Stephen Heath (New York: Hill and Wang, 1977), p. 119.

42. See Mayne, *The Woman at the Keyhole,* pp. 173–174, for a provocative analysis of this film in terms of both racial and sexual difference. Her analysis, however, deals with the narrative and elides the formal issue of the cut and the use of black leader to signify a tunnel.

43. See Musser, *Before the Nickelodeon,* pp. 262–263, for a discussion of the various predecessors of this film and of its place in the railway subgenre.

44. As Charles Musser points out, "By early 1897 scores of different projectors were available to American showmen. Although little noted by historians, these machines had diverse capabilities and construction. Some depended on electricity for power, but most were hand-cranked and the operator could use limelight as an illuminant"; *History of the American Cinema,* vol. 1: *The Emergence of Cinema: The American Screen to 1907* (Berkeley: University of California Press, 1990), p. 167. See also p. 442 for a discussion of the hardships of hand cranking early film projectors.

45. As pointed out at the beginning of this chapter, this statement is not accurate. Because the shutter breaks the projection beam twice, once while the frame is moved into position and once while it is held in place, the frame is illuminated three times for every two periods of darkness. The frame is dark for about 40 percent of the time, light for about 60 percent of the time. For a fuller discussion of this phenomenon, see David Bordwell and Kristin Thompson, *Film Art: An Introduction,* 5th ed. (New York: McGraw-Hill, 1997), p. 33.

46. See, for instance, Joseph Anderson and Barbara Anderson, "Motion Perception in Motion Pictures," and Bill Nichols and Susan J. Lederman, "Flicker and Motion in Film," in *The Cinematic Apparatus,* ed. Teresa de Lauretis and Stephen Heath (London: Macmillan, 1980), pp. 76–95 and 96–105. Research into the perception of motion in cinema is ongoing and in flux. For an explanation of critical flicker fusion and apparent motion, see Bordwell and Thompson, *Film Art,* pp. 4 and 33.

47. See Linda Williams, "Film Body: An Implantation of Perversions," in Rosen, *Narrative, Apparatus, Ideology,* pp. 507–534.

48. Walter Benjamin, "On Some Motifs in Baudelaire," in *Illuminations,* trans. Harry Zohn, ed. Hannah Arendt (New York: Schocken, 1969), p. 169.

49. See Samuel Weber, *Mass Mediauras: Form, Technics, Media,* ed. Alan Cholodenko (Stanford: Stanford University Press, 1996), p. 98. This is Weber's translation. The translation in the *Illuminations* essay is: "The camera gave the moment a posthumous shock, as it were" ("On Some Motifs in Baudelaire," p. 175).

50. Weber, *Mass Mediauras,* p. 98. As Weber points out, this is an inaccurate but "suggestive" translation. See also Jacques Derrida's use of the term *Augenblick* in

his deconstruction of presence through an analysis of Husserl: "As soon as we admit this continuity of the now and the not-now, perception and nonperception, in the zone of primordiality common to primordial impression and primordial retention, we admit the other into the self-identity of the *Augenblick;* nonpresence and nonevidence are admitted into the *blink of the instant.* There is a duration to the blink and it closes the eye. This alterity is in fact the condition for presence, presentation, and thus for *Vorstellung* in general"; *Speech and Phenomena and Other Essays on Husserl's Theory of Signs,* trans. David B. Allison (Evanston, Ill.: Northwestern University Press, 1973), p. 65.

7. The Instant and the Archive

Epigraphs: Walter Benjamin, *The Arcades Project,* trans. Howard Eiland and Kevin McLaughlin (Cambridge, Mass.: Harvard University Press, 1999), p. 107; Jacques Derrida, *Archive Fever: A Freudian Impression,* trans. Eric Prenowitz (Chicago: University of Chicago Press, 1996), p. 36.

1. This chapter was written before the events of September 11, 2001, which provided an extreme example of the cultural reverberations of the collapse of a building (in this case, two—the twin towers of the World Trade Center in New York). This time, no compensation was necessary for the absence of cameras at the Ur-event. Nevertheless, the inevitable sense that one lacks the perfect image of such an event, an image that would be adequate to its enormity, is evident not only in the incessant replaying of the moments of collapse but in the myriad of books, magazines, and exhibitions that strove to capture the event photographically, to reduce it to an instant.

2. The KWTV website is http://www.kwtv.com/news/bombing.

3. Unlike film, both digital and video representations are eminently reversible and, in this sense, mark a break with the properties of the cinematic apparatus as discussed in Chapter 4.

4. See Garrett Stewart, *Between Film and Screen: Modernism's Photo Synthesis* (Chicago: University of Chicago Press, 1999).

5. Tom Gunning, "Bodies in Motion: The *Pas de Deux* of the Ideal and the Material at the Turn of the Century," paper delivered at the conference "Stop Motion and Fragmentation of Time: Cinematography, Kinetography, Chronophotography," Montreal, October 4–7, 2000.

6. Thierry de Duve, "Time Exposure and Snapshot: The Photograph as Paradox," *October* 5 (1978): 115, 114, 121. For de Duve, the news photograph (the instantaneous photograph) and the photographic portrait (the time exposure) are two poles that structure the reception of every photograph as an oscillation between trauma and consolation. The time exposure, with its greater degree of blurring, builds duration into our sense of the lost object and hence always entails a process of mourning.

7. Walter Benjamin, "On Some Motifs in Baudelaire," in *Illuminations,* trans. Harry Zohn, ed. Hannah Arendt (New York: Schocken, 1969), pp. 174–175.

8. Michel Frizot, "Les Opérateurs physiques de Marey et la réversibilité cinématographique," paper delivered at the conference "Stop Motion and Fragmentation of Time: Cinematography, Kinetography, Chronophotography," Montreal, October 4–7, 2000. Frizot expands upon the significance of these operators in his recent book, *Etienne-Jules Marey: Chronophotographie* (Paris: Nathan, 2001). I became aware of this book only as the final proofs were being prepared for my book and therefore could not take into account its more detailed arguments about Marey.

9. As Marey himself pointed out, "In the study of movement, photography has the advantage of not being obliged to borrow any motive power from the object observed"; *Movement,* trans. Eric Pritchard (New York: D. Appleton, 1895), p. 50. Marta Braun claims that the graphic method "could not grasp movements too weak to move a stylus or the movements of subjects that obviously could not be physically harnessed to any measuring apparatus"; *Picturing Time: The Work of Etienne-Jules Marey (1830–1904)* (Chicago: University of Chicago Press, 1992), p. 41.

10. Frizot also points out, quite crucially, the necessity for a single camera and, hence, a single viewpoint in order to produce the synthesis of images. Muybridge's multicamera setup did not allow for this.

11. Claude Lévi-Strauss, "The Science of the Concrete," in *The Savage Mind* (Chicago: University of Chicago Press, 1966), pp. 16–22.

12. Quoted in Marta Braun, *Picturing Time,* p. 255.

13. Raymond Bellour, "Rousseau avec Marey: Repensés par l'orinateur," paper delivered at the conference "Stop Motion and Fragmentation of Time: Cinematography, Kinetography, Chronophotography," Montreal, October 4–7, 2000.

14. de Duve, "Time Exposure and Snapshot," p. 119.

15. Roland Barthes, *Camera Lucida: Reflections on Photography,* trans. Richard Howard (New York: Hill and Wang, 1981), pp. 26–27.

16. The relation of the image to the point depends upon the phenomenon being represented or measured. If that phenomenon is movement (its illusion in the cinema), the image itself is a point. If the image stands alone, as it does for Barthes in his discussion of photography, the image *contains* a multiplicity of points (each a potential *punctum*).

17. Henri Poincaré, *Science and Hypothesis,* trans. George Bruce Halsted (New York: Science Press, 1905), pp. 63, 65.

18. *Webster's New Collegiate Dictionary* (Springfield, Mass.: G. & C. Merriam, 1973), p. 887.

19. David Berlinski, *A Tour of the Calculus* (New York: Vintage, 1995), p. 17.

20. The term *fixed-explosive* is a way of defining compulsive beauty for Bréton. The entire quotation is in *Mad Love,* trans. Mary Ann Caws (Lincoln: University of

Nebraska Press, 1987), p. 19. I am grateful to Tom Gunning for pointing out this use of the term.

21. Some magic-lantern presentations did make use of fragmentation. See Charles Musser, *History of the American Cinema*, vol. 1: *The Emergence of Cinema: The American Screen to 1907* (Berkeley: University of California Press, 1990), pp. 42–45.

22. David Francis, "Simulated Movement in Nineteenth Century Magic Lantern Presentations," paper delivered at the conference "Stop Motion and Fragmentation of Time: Cinematography, Kinetography, Chronophotography," Montreal, October 4–7, 2000. See also Deac Rossell, *Living Pictures: The Origins of the Movies* (Albany: State University of New York Press, 1998), pp. 24–25.

23. Emile Reynaud's Théâtre Optique projected drawings of sequenced movement using intermittent motion in 1892, but film histories have consistently downplayed his contribution in favor of the photographically based apparatuses of Edison and Lumière. See Rossell, *Living Pictures*, pp. 21 and 158.

24. See Philip Rosen, *Change Mummified: Cinema, Historicity, Theory* (Minneapolis: University of Minnesota Press, 2001), especially chap. 3.

25. Sigmund Freud, "Delusions and Dreams in Jensen's *Gradiva*," in *The Standard Edition of the Complete Psychological Works of Sigmund Freud*, trans. and ed. James Strachey, vol. 9 (London: Hogarth Press, 1959), pp. 1–95.

26. Derrida, *Archive Fever*, pp. 98–99.

27. Ibid., p. 17. Derrida focuses on print technologies of archivization, preeminently e-mail and letters, but says nothing about indexicality (photographic or filmic imaging) in relation to the archive.

28. Rosen, *Change Mummified*, p. 115. Thomas Richards claims that this fascination with collecting and stockpiling knowledge and artifacts was associated strongly with imperialism: "This operational field of projected total knowledge was the archive. The archive was not a building, nor even a collection of texts, but the collectively imagined junction of all that was known or knowable, a fantastic representation of an epistemological master pattern, a virtual focal point for the heterogeneous local knowledge of metropolis and empire"; *The Imperial Archive: Knowledge and the Fantasy of Empire* (London: Verso, 1993), p. 9.

29. Benjamin, "The Work of Art in the Age of Mechanical Reproduction," in *Illuminations*, pp. 217–251.

30. This is, of course, complicated by any mode of mechanical reproduction—comic books, records, films, printed books; none of these are singular or have "originals." However, it is crucial to note the importance of handwritten manuscripts for determining the definitive edition of a text. And any copy of a product of mechanical reproduction (a first edition comic book, for instance) can and often does *stand in* for the nonexistent original. It becomes archivable as soon as it becomes scarce or inaccessible.

31. Derrida, *Archive Fever*, p. 18.

32. Charles Sanders Peirce, *Collected Papers of Charles Sanders Peirce,* ed. Charles Hartshorne and Paul Weiss, vol. 6: *Scientific Metaphysics* (Cambridge, Mass.: Harvard University Press, 1935), p. 425.

33. Benjamin, *The Arcades Project,* p. 512.

34. A film, of course, always has an ending, no matter how arbitrary. This fact necessarily limits its alliance with entropy. An infinitely long film would theoretically fully embody entropy and ultimately chronicle the death of the universe. There is a sense, then, in which every film ending mimics or simulates the "end of the world."

35. See Stephen Jay Gould's contribution to *Conversations about the End of Time,* trans. Ian Maclean and Roger Pearson, ed. Catherine David, Frédéric Lenoir, and Jean-Philippe de Tonnac (New York: Fromm International, 2000), pp. 19–23.

36. Rosen, *Change Mummified,* p. 104.

37. Jonathan Crary, *Suspensions of Perception: Attention, Spectacle, and Modern Culture* (Cambridge, Mass.: MIT Press, 1999), p. 55.

38. Niklas Luhmann, *Observations on Modernity,* trans. William Whobrey (Stanford: Stanford University Press, 1998), p. 46.

39. Paul Willemen, *Looks and Frictions: Essays in Cultural Studies and Film Theory* (Bloomington: Indiana University Press, 1994), pp. 228, 231.

40. Ibid., p. 232. For an intriguing discussion of the Surrealists' relation to photography, see Rosalind Krauss, "The Photographic Conditions of Surrealism," in *The Originality of the Avant-Garde and Other Modernist Myths* (Cambridge, Mass.: MIT Press, 1985), pp. 87–118.

41. Willemen, *Looks and Frictions,* p. 233.

42. Jean Epstein, "Magnification and Other Writings on Film," trans. Stuart Liebman, *October* 3 (1977): 13. See also idem, "*Bonjour cinéma* and other writings by Jean Epstein," trans. Tom Milne, *Afterimage* 10 (1981): 8–38.

43. Although Epstein fastens on the technique of the close-up, he is more interested in it as a conveyor of the signs of the body, especially the face, than in its inherent characteristics as a technique. He is not interested in close-ups of objects or of aspects of landscape. The close-up simply magnifies the legibility of the body.

44. Willemen, *Looks and Frictions,* pp. 237, 238–239, 240, 241.

45. Miriam Hansen, "Introduction," in *Theory of Film,* ed. Siegfried Kracauer (Princeton: Princeton University Press, 1997), pp. xxxv, x, xxii, and xxxii.

46. Ibid., p. xxi.

47. Ibid., p. xxxi.

48. Willemen, *Looks and Frictions,* p. 243.

49. Hansen, "Introduction," p. xxxv.

50. See David Bordwell and Noël Carroll, "Introduction," in *Post-Theory: Reconstructing Film Studies,* ed. David Bordwell and Noël Carroll (Madison: University of Wisconsin Press, 1996), p. xvi. See also Bordwell's discussion of "contingent universals" in his essay in the same volume, "Convention, Construction, and Vi-

sion," especially pp. 91–93; and Joseph Anderson and Barbara Anderson, "The Case for an Ecological Metatheory," in Bordwell and Carroll, *Post-Theory,* pp. 347–367.

51. Charles Sanders Peirce, *The Essential Peirce,* ed. Nathan Houser and Christian Kloesel, vol. 1 (Bloomington: Indiana University Press, 1992), p. 226. Since "this" and "that" are also symbolic signs, Peirce would no doubt have been more accurate in isolating the pointing finger as the "purest" form of the index. In this respect, it is interesting to note the significance of the mouse and the pointing arrow or finger in computer technology.

52. Luhmann, *Observations on Modernity,* p. 45.

Bibliography

Abel, Richard, ed. *French Film Theory and Criticism: A History/Anthology.* Vol. 1: *1907–1929.* Princeton: Princeton University Press, 1988.

Ager, Derek. *The New Catastrophism: The Importance of the Rare Event in Geological History.* Cambridge: Cambridge University Press, 1993.

American Federation of the Arts. *Before Hollywood: Turn-of-the-Century Film from American Archives.* New York, 1986.

Anderson, Joseph, and Barbara Anderson. "The Case for an Ecological Meta-theory." In *Post-Theory: Reconstructing Film Studies.* Edited by David Bordwell and Noël Carroll. Madison: University of Wisconsin Press, 1996, 347–367.

————— "Motion Perception in Motion Pictures." In *The Cinematic Apparatus.* Edited by Teresa de Lauretis and Stephen Heath. London: Macmillan, 1980, 76–95.

Apollonia, Umbro, ed. *Futurist Manifestos.* New York: Viking, 1973.

Armes, Roy. *French Cinema.* New York: Oxford University Press, 1985.

Armstrong, Nancy. *Fiction in the Age of Photography: The Legacy of British Realism.* Cambridge, Mass.: Harvard University Press, 1999.

Armstrong, Tim. "The Electrification of the Body at the Turn of the Century." *Textual Practice* 5.3 (1991): 303–325.

Aubert, Michelle, and Jean-Claude Sequin, eds. *La Production cinématographique des frères Lumières.* Lyon: Centre National de la Cinématographie, L'Université Lumière-Lyon 2, and Bibliothèque du Film, 1996.

Aumont, Jacques. *L'Oeil interminable: Cinéma et peinture.* Paris: Librairie Séguier, 1989.

————— "The Variable Eye, or the Mobilization of the Gaze." In *The Image in Dispute: Art and Cinema in the Age of Photography.* Edited by Dudley Andrew. Austin: University of Texas Press, 1997, 236–240.

Balides, Constance. "Scenarios of Exposure in the Practice of Everyday Life: Women in the Cinema of Attractions." *Screen* 34.1 (Spring 1993): 19–37.

Barthes, Roland. *Camera Lucida: Reflections on Photography.* Translated by Richard Howard. New York: Hill and Wang, 1981.

———— *Image-Music-Text.* Translated by Stephen Heath. New York: Noonday, 1988.

Batchen, Geoffrey. *Burning with Desire: The Conception of Photography.* Cambridge, Mass.: MIT Press, 1999.

Baudelaire, Charles. *The Painter of Modern Life and Other Essays.* Translated and edited by Jonathan Mayne. New York: Da Capo, 1964.

Baudry, Jean-Louis. "Ideological Effects of the Basic Cinematographic Apparatus." In *Narrative, Apparatus, Ideology.* Edited by Philip Rosen. New York: Columbia University Press, 1986, 286–298.

Bazin, André. *What Is Cinema?* Translated and edited by Hugh Gray. Vol. 1. Berkeley: University of California Press, 1967.

Bellour, Raymond. *L'Analyse du film.* Paris: Editions Albatros, 1979.

———— "Rousseau avec Marey: Repensés par l'originateur." Paper delivered at conference "Stop Motion and Fragmentation of Time: Cinematography, Kinetography, Chronophotography," Montreal, October 4–7, 2000.

Benjamin, Walter. *The Arcades Project.* Translated by Howard Eiland and Kevin McLaughlin. Cambridge, Mass.: Harvard University Press, 1999.

———— *Charles Baudelaire: A Lyric Poet in the Era of High Capitalism.* Translated by Harry Zohn. London: Verso, 1973.

———— *Illuminations.* Translated by Harry Zohn. Edited by Hannah Arendt. New York: Schocken, 1969.

———— *One Way Street and Other Writings.* Translated by Edmund Jephcott and Kingsley Shorter. London: Verso, 1985.

Bergson, Henri. *Creative Evolution.* Translated by Arthur Mitchell. New York: Henry Holt, 1926.

———— *Matter and Memory.* Translated by N. M. Paul and W. S. Palmer. New York: Zone, 1988.

———— *Time and Free Will.* Translated by R. L. Pogson. New York: Macmillan, 1913.

Berlinski, David. *A Tour of the Calculus.* New York: Vintage, 1995.

Bohn, Thomas W., and Richard L. Stromgren. *Light and Shadow: A History of Motion Pictures.* 2d ed. Sherman Oaks, Calif.: Alfred, 1978.

Bordwell, David. "Convention, Construction, and Vision." In *Post-Theory: Reconstructing Film Studies.* Edited by David Bordwell and Noël Carroll. Madison: University of Wisconsin Press, 1996, 87–107.

Bordwell, David, and Noël Carroll. "Introduction." In *Post-Theory: Reconstructing Film Studies.* Edited by David Bordwell and Noël Carroll. Madison: University of Wisconsin Press, 1996, xiii–xvii.

Bordwell, David, and Kristen Thompson. *Film Art: An Introduction.* 5th ed. New York: McGraw-Hill, 1997.

Bowser, Eileen. *History of the American Cinema.* Vol. 2: *The Transformation of Cinema: 1907–1915.* Berkeley: University of California Press, 1990.

Braun, Marta. *Picturing Time: The Work of Etienne-Jules Marey (1830–1904)*. Chicago: University of Chicago Press, 1992.

Breton, André. *Mad Love*. Translated by Mary Ann Caws. Lincoln: University of Nebraska Press, 1987.

Brewster, Sir David. *The Stereoscope*. London: John Murray, 1856.

Burch, Noël. *Life to Those Shadows*. Translated and edited by Ben Brewster. Berkeley: University of California Press, 1990.

———. "Porter, or Ambivalence." *Screen* 19.4 (Winter 1978–79): 91–105.

Capek, Milic. *The Philosophical Impact of Contemporary Physics*. Princeton: D. Van Nostrand, 1961.

Cartwright, Lisa. *Screening the Body: Tracing Medicine's Visual Culture*. Minneapolis: University of Minnesota Press, 1995.

Ceram, C. W. *Archaeology of the Cinema*. New York: Harcourt, Brace and World, 1965.

Chanan, Michael. *The Dream That Kicks: The Prehistory and Early Years of Cinema in Britain*. London: Routledge and Kegan Paul, 1980.

Charney, Leo. *Empty Moments: Cinema, Modernity, and Drift*. Durham, N.C.: Duke University Press, 1998.

Chevalier, Jacques. *Henri Bergson*. Translated by Lilian A. Clare. New York: Macmillan, 1928.

Comolli, Jean-Louis. "Depth of Field: The Double Scene." In *Narrative, Appartus, Ideology*. Edited by Philip Rosen. New York: Columbia University Press, 1986, 422–430.

Cook, David A. *A History of Narrative Film*. 2d ed. New York: W. W. Norton, 1990.

Coveney, Peter, and Roger Highfield. *The Arrow of Time*. New York: Ballantine, 1990.

Crary, Jonathan. *Suspensions of Perception: Attention, Spectacle, and Modern Culture*. Cambridge, Mass.: MIT Press, 1999.

——— *Techniques of the Observer: On Vision and Modernity in the Nineteenth Century*. Cambridge, Mass.: MIT Press, 1990.

Dagognet, François. *Etienne-Jules Marey: A Passion for the Trace*. Translated by Robert Galeta with Jeanine Herman. New York: Zone, 1992.

de Duve, Thierry. "Time Exposure and Snapshot: The Photograph as Paradox." *October* 5 (1978): 113–125.

de Lauretis, Teresa. *Alice Doesn't: Feminism, Semiotics, Cinema*. Bloomington: Indiana University Press, 1984.

——— *Technologies of Gender*. Bloomington: Indiana University Press, 1987.

Deleuze, Gilles. *Bergsonism*. Translated by Hugh Tomlinson and Barbara Habberjam. New York: Zone, 1988.

——— *Cinema 1: The Movement-Image*. Translated by Hugh Tomlinson and Barbara Habberjam. Minneapolis: University of Minnesota Press, 1986.

—— *Cinema 2: The Time-Image.* Translated by Hugh Tomlinson and Robert Galeta. Minneapolis: University of Minnesota Press, 1989.

de Man, Paul. *Blindness and Insight: Essays in the Rhetoric of Contemporary Criticism.* New York: Oxford University Press, 1971.

Derrida, Jacques. *Archive Fever: A Freudian Impression.* Translated by Eric Prenowitz. Chicago: University of Chicago Press, 1996.

—— *Speech and Phenomena and Other Essays on Husserl's Theory of Signs.* Translated by David B. Allison. Evanston, Ill.: Northwestern University Press, 1973.

—— *Writing and Difference.* Translated by Alan Bass. Chicago: University of Chicago Press, 1978.

Doane, Mary Ann. "Information, Crisis, Catastrophe." In *Logics of Television.* Edited by Patricia Mellencamp. Bloomington: Indiana University Press, 1990, 222–239.

—— "Technology and Sexual Difference: Apocalyptic Scenarios at Two 'Fins-de-Siècle.'" *differences* 9.2 (1997): 1–24.

—— "Technology's Body: Cinematic Vision in Modernity." *differences* 5.2 (1993): 1–23.

Ducrot, Oswald, and Tzvetan Todorov. *Encyclopedic Dictionary of the Sciences of Language.* Translated by Catherine Porter. Baltimore: Johns Hopkins University Press, 1979.

Eco, Umberto, Stephen Jay Gould, Jean-Claude Carrière, and Jean Delumeau. *Conversations about the End of Time.* Translated by Ian Maclean and Roger Pearson. New York: Fromm International, 2000.

Eisenstein, Sergei M. *The Film Sense.* Translated and edited by Jay Leyda. New York: Harcourt, Brace and World, 1942.

Elsaesser, Thomas, ed. *Early Cinema: Space, Frame, Narrative.* London: British Film Institute, 1990.

Epstein, Jean. "*Bonjour cinéma* and Other Writings by Jean Epstein." Translated by Tom Milne. *Afterimage* 10 (1981): 8–38.

—— "Magnification and Other Writings on Film." Translated by Stuart Liebman. *October* 3 (1977): 9–25.

Fell, John L., ed. *Film before Griffith.* Berkeley: University of California Press, 1983.

Fielding, Raymond. *The American Newsreel, 1911–1967.* Norman: University of Oklahoma Press, 1972.

Fischer, Lucy. "The Lady Vanishes: Women, Magic, and the Movies." *Film Quarterly* 33.1 (1979): 30–40.

Foucault, Michel. *Discipline and Punish.* Translated by Alan Sheridan. New York: Pantheon, 1977.

—— *The History of Sexuality.* Translated by Robert Hurley. 3 vols. New York: Pantheon, 1978.

———— "History of Systems of Thought." In *Language, Counter-Memory, Practice.* Translated by Donald F. Bouchard and Sherry Simon. Edited by Donald F. Bouchard. Ithaca: Cornell University Press, 1977, 199–204.

———— "Of Other Spaces." Translated by Jay Miskowiec. *Diacritics* 16.1 (1986): 22–27.

———— *Power/Knowledge: Selected Interviews and Other Writings, 1972–1977.* Translated by Colin Gordon, Leo Marshall, John Mepham, and Kate Soper. Edited by Colin Gordon. New York: Random House, 1980.

Francis, David. "Simulated Movement in Nineteenth-Century Magic Lantern Presentations." Paper delivered at conference "Stop Motion and Fragmentation of Time: Cinematography, Kinetography, Chronophotography," Montreal, October 4–7, 2000.

Freud, Ernst L., ed. *The Letters of Sigmund Freud.* New York: Basic, 1960.

Freud, Sigmund. *Beyond the Pleasure Principle.* In *The Standard Edition of the Complete Psychological Works of Sigmund Freud.* Translated and edited by James Strachey. Vol. 18. London: Hogarth Press, 1955, 1–64.

———— "Constructions in Analysis." In ibid. Vol. 13. London: Hogarth Press, 1964, 255–269.

———— "Delusions and Dreams in Jensen's *Gradiva.*" In ibid. Vol. 9. London: Hogarth Press, 1959, 1–95.

———— *Gesammelte Werke.* Edited by Anna Freud et al. Vol. 14. London: Imago, 1948.

———— *The Interpretation of Dreams.* In *Standard Edition.* Vols. 4–5. London: Hogarth Press, 1953, 1–627.

———— "A Note upon the 'Mystic Writing-Pad.'" In ibid. Vol 19. London: Hogarth Press, 1961, 225–232.

———— "Project for a Scientific Psychology." In ibid. Vol. 1. London: Hogarth Press, 1966, 281–397.

———— *The Psychopathology of Everyday Life.* In ibid. Vol 6. London: Hogarth Press, 1960.

———— "Remembering, Repeating, and Working-Through (Further Recommendations on the Technique of Psycho-Analysis)." In ibid. Vol. 12. London: Hogarth Press, 1958, 145–156.

———— "Screen Memories." In ibid. Vol. 3. London: Hogarth Press and the Institute of Psycho-Analysis, 1962, 299–322.

———— "Thoughts for the Times on War and Death." In ibid. Vol. 14. London: Hogarth Press, 1955, 273–302.

———— "The Unconscious." In ibid., 159–215.

Friedberg, Anne. "An *Unheimlich* Maneuver between Psychoanalysis and the Cinema: *Secrets of a Soul* (1926)." In *The Films of G. W. Pabst: An Extraterritorial Cinema.* Edited by Eric Rentschler. New Brunswick, N.J.: Rutgers University Press, 1990, 41–51.

———— *Window Shopping: Cinema and the Postmodern.* Berkeley: University of California Press, 1993.

Frizot, Michel. "Les Opérateurs physiques de Marey at la réversibilité cinématographique." Paper delivered at conference "Stop Motion and Fragmentation of Time: Cinematography, Kinetography, Chronophotography," Montreal, October 4–7, 2000.

Galassi, Peter. *Before Photography: Painting and the Invention of Photography.* New York: Museum of Modern Art, 1981.

Galton, Francis. *Inquiries into Human Faculty and Its Development.* New York: Macmillan, 1883.

Gaudreault, André. "The Cinematograph: A Historiographical Machine." In *Meanings in Texts and Actions: Questioning Paul Ricoeur.* Edited by David E. Klemm and William Schweiker. Charlottesville: University Press of Virginia, 1993, 90–97.

———— *Du littéraire au filmique: Système du récit.* Paris: Presses de l'Université Laval Méridiens Klincksieck, 1988.

Gianetti, Louis. *Understanding Movies.* 2d ed. Englewood Cliffs, N.J.: Prentice-Hall, 1976.

Giedion, Siegfried. *Mechanization Takes Command: A Contribution to an Anonymous History.* New York: W. W. Norton, 1975.

———— *Space, Time, and Architecture: The Growth of a New Tradition.* 3d ed. Cambridge, Mass.: Harvard University Press, 1954.

Goethe, Johann Wolfgang von. *Theory of Colours.* Translated by Charles Lock Eastlake. Cambridge, Mass.: MIT Press, 1970.

Gomery, Douglas. *Shared Pleasures: A History of Movie Presentation in the United States.* Madison: University of Wisconsin Press, 1992.

Gould, Stephen Jay. *Time's Arrow, Time's Cycle: Myth and Metaphor in the Discovery of Geological Time.* Cambridge, Mass.: Harvard University Press, 1987.

Gunning, Tom. "An Aesthetic of Astonishment: Early Film and the (In)Credulous Spectator." In *Viewing Positions: Ways of Seeing Film.* Edited by Linda Williams. New Brunswick, N.J.: Rutgers University Press, 1995, 114–133.

———— "Bodies in Motion: The *Pas de Deux* of the Ideal and the Material at the Turn of the Century." Paper delivered at conference "Stop Motion and Fragmentation of Time: Cinematography, Kinetography, Chronophotography," Montreal, October 4–7, 2000.

———— *D. W. Griffith and the Origins of American Narrative Film: The Early Years at Biograph.* Urbana: University of Illinois Press, 1991.

———— "Heard over the Phone: *The Lonely Villa* and the deLorde Tradition of the Terrors of Technology." *Screen* 32.2 (Summer 1991): 184–196.

———— "The Non-Continuous Style of Early Film 1900–1906." In *Cinema 1900/ 1906: An Analytical Study.* Edited by Roger Holman. Brussels: Fédération Internationale des Archives du Film, 1982, 219–230.

—— "'Now You See It, Now You Don't': The Temporality of the Cinema of Attractions." *Velvet Light Trap* 32 (1993): 3–12.

Hacking, Ian. *The Taming of Chance.* Cambridge: Cambridge University Press, 1990.

—— "Was There a Probabilistic Revolution 1800–1930?" In *The Probabilistic Revolution.* Edited by Lorenz Krüger, Lorraine J. Daston, and Michael Heidelberger. Vol. 1: *Ideas in History.* Cambridge, Mass.: MIT Press, 1987, 45–55.

Hammond, Paul. *Marvellous Méliès.* London: Gordon Fraser, 1974.

Hansen, Miriam. "America, Paris, the Alps: Kracauer (and Benjamin) on Cinema and Modernity." In *Cinema and the Invention of Modern Life.* Edited by Leo Charney and Vanessa R. Schwartz. Berkeley: University of California Press, 1995, 362–402.

—— *Babel and Babylon: Spectatorship in American Silent Film.* Cambridge, Mass.: Harvard University Press, 1991.

—— "Introduction." In *Theory of Film.* Edited by Siegfried Kracauer. Princeton: Princeton University Press, 1997, vii–xiv.

Harman, P. M. *Energy, Force, and Matter: The Conceptual Development of Nineteenth-Century Physics.* Cambridge: Cambridge University Press, 1982.

Hayles, N. Katherine. *Chaos Bound: Orderly Disorder in Contemporary Literature and Science.* Ithaca: Cornell University Press, 1990.

Helmholtz, Hermann von. *Helmholtz's Treatise on Physiological Optics.* Translated and edited by James P. C. Southall. Vol. 1. Menasha, Wis.: Optical Society of America, 1924.

—— "The Recent Progress of the Theory of Vision." In *Science and Culture: Popular and Philosophical Essays.* Edited by David Cahan. Chicago: University of Chicago Press, 1995, 127–203.

Hockberg, Julian E. *Perception.* Englewood Cliffs, N.J.: Prentice-Hall, 1964.

Hopkins, Albert A., ed. *Magic: Stage Illusions and Scientific Diversions Including Trick Photography.* New York: Munn, 1897.

Huyssen, Andreas. *Twilight Memories: Marking Time in a Culture of Amnesia.* New York: Routledge, 1995.

Jacob, François. *The Logic of Life: A History of Heredity.* Translated by Betty E. Spillmann. Princeton: Princeton University Press, 1973.

Jacobs, Lewis. *The Rise of the American Film.* 1939; reprint, New York: Teachers College Press, 1968.

Jakobson, Roman. "Shifters, Verbal Categories, and the Russian Verb." In *Selected Writings.* Vol. 2: *Word and Language.* The Hague: Mouton, 1971, 130–147.

Johnson, L. F. *Film, Space, Time.* New York: Holt, Rinehart and Winston, 1973.

Jones, Ernest. *The Life and Work of Sigmund Freud.* Vols. 2 and 3. New York: Basic, 1955, 1957.

Kemple, Thomas M. *Reading Marx Writing: Melodrama, the Market, and the "Grundrisse."* Stanford: Stanford University Press, 1995.

Kern, Stephen. *The Culture of Time and Space, 1880–1918.* Cambridge, Mass.: Harvard University Press, 1983.

Kittler, Friedrich A. *Discourse Networks, 1800/1900.* Translated by Michael Metteer with Chris Cullens. Stanford: Stanford University Press, 1990.

———— "Gramophone, Film, Typewriter." Translated by Dorothea von Mücke with Philippe L. Similon. *October* 41 (1987): 101–118.

Koch, Gertrud. *Siegfried Kracauer: An Introduction.* Translated by Jeremy Gaines. Princeton: Princeton University Press, 2000.

Kracauer, Siegfried. *The Mass Ornament: Weimar Essays.* Translated and edited by Thomas Y. Levin. Cambridge, Mass.: Harvard University Press, 1995.

Krauss, Rosalind. *The Originality of the Avant-Garde and Other Modernist Myths.* Cambridge, Mass.: MIT Press, 1985.

Laplanche, Jean. *Seduction, Translation, Drives.* Translated by Martin Stanton. Edited by John Fletcher and Martin Stanton. London: Institute of Contemporary Arts, 1992.

Laplanche, Jean, and Jean-Bertrand Pontalis. "Fantasy and the Origins of Sexuality." In *Formations of Fantasy.* Edited by Victor Burgin, James Donald, and Cora Kaplan. London: Methuen, 1986, 5–34.

———— *The Language of Psychoanalysis.* Translated by Donald Nicholson-Smith. New York: W. W. Norton, 1973.

Lastra, James. "From the Captured Moment to the Cinematic Image: A Transformation in Pictorial Order." In *The Image in Dispute: Art and Cinema in the Age of Photography.* Edited by Dudley Andrew. Austin: University of Texas Press, 1997, 263–291.

———— *Sound Technology and the American Cinema: Perception, Representation, Modernity.* New York: Columbia University Press, 2000.

Lévi-Strauss, Claude. *The Savage Mind.* Chicago: University of Chicago Press, 1966.

Levy, David. "Re-constituted Newsreels, Re-enactments and the American Narrative Film." In *Cinema 1900/1906: An Analytical Study.* Edited by Roger Holman. Brussels: Fédération Internationale des Archives du Film, 1982, 243–260.

Luhmann, Niklas. *Observations on Modernity.* Translated by William Whobrey. Stanford: Stanford University Press, 1998.

Lukács, Georg. "Narrate or Describe?" In *Writer & Critic and Other Essays.* Translated and edited by Arthur D. Kahn. New York: Grosset and Dunlap, 1971, 110–148.

Lyotard, Jean-François. *The Inhuman: Reflections on Time.* Translated by Geoffrey Bennington and Rachel Bowlby. Stanford: Stanford University Press, 1991.

MacGowan, Kenneth. *Behind the Screen: The History and Technique of the Motion Picture.* New York: Dell, 1965.

Mach, Ernst. *Contributions to the Analysis of the Sensations.* Translated by C. M. Williams. Chicago: Open Court, 1897.

Mannoni, Laurent, Donata Pesenti Campagnoni, and David Robinson. *Light and Movement: Incunabula of the Motion Picture, 1420–1896.* Gemona, Italy: Giornate del Cinema Muto, 1995.

Marey, Etienne-Jules. *Animal Mechanism: A Treatise on Terrestrial and Aërial Locomotion.* New York: D. Appleton, 1874.

———— *Movement.* Translated by Eric Pritchard. New York: D. Appleton, 1895.

Marx, Karl. *Capital.* Translated by Ben Fowkes. Vol. 1. New York: Random House, 1977.

Mast, Gerald, and Bruce Kawin. *The Movies: A Short History.* Rev. ed. Boston: Allyn and Bacon, 1996.

Maxwell, James Clerk. *Theory of Heat.* New York: D. Appleton, 1872.

Mayne, Judith. *The Woman at the Keyhole: Feminism and Women's Cinema.* Bloomington: Indiana University Press, 1990.

Metz, Christian. *Film Language: A Semiotics of the Cinema.* Translated by Michael Taylor. New York: Oxford University Press, 1974.

Miller, Angela. "The Panorama, the Cinema, and the Emergence of the Spectacular." *Wide Angle* 18.2 (April 1996): 35–69.

Monaco, James. *How to Read a Film: The Art, Technology, Language, History, and Theory of Film and Media.* Rev. ed. New York: Oxford University Press, 1981.

Morris, Richard. *Time's Arrows: Scientific Attitudes toward Time.* New York: Simon and Schuster, 1985.

Müller, J. *Elements of Physiology.* Translated by William Baly. Vol. 2. London: Taylor and Walton, 1842.

———— "Of the Senses." In *Visual Perception: The Nineteenth Century.* Edited by William N. Dember. New York: John Wiley and Sons, 1964, 35–69.

Mulvey, Laura. "Visual Pleasure and Narrative Cinema." In *Narrative, Apparatus, Ideology.* Edited by Philip Rosen. New York: Columbia University Press, 1986, 198–209.

Münsterberg, Hugo. *The Film: A Psychological Study.* New York: Dover, 1970.

Musser, Charles. *Before the Nickelodeon: Edwin S. Porter and the Edison Manufacturing Company.* Berkeley: University of California Press, 1991.

———— *History of the American Cinema.* Vol. 1: *The Emergence of Cinema: The American Screen to 1907.* Berkeley: University of California Press, 1990.

———— "Rethinking Early Cinema." *Yale Journal of Criticism* 7.2 (Fall 1994): 203–232.

Nichols, Bill, and Susan J. Lederman. "Flicker and Motion in Film." In *The Cinematic Apparatus.* Edited by Teresa de Lauretis and Stephen Heath. London: Macmillan, 1980, 96–105.

Nordau, Max. *Degeneration.* Lincoln: University of Nebraska Press, 1993.

Nye, David E. *Electrifying America: Social Meanings of a New Technology, 1880–1940.* Cambridge, Mass.: MIT Press, 1990.

Pasolini, Pier Paolo. "Observations on the Long Take." *October* 13 (1980): 3–6.

Peirce, Charles Sanders. *Chance, Love, and Logic.* Edited by Morris R. Cohen. New York: Harcourt, Brace, 1923.

——— *Collected Papers of Charles Sanders Peirce.* Edited by Charles Hartshorne and Paul Weiss. Vol. 2: *Elements of Logic.* Cambridge, Mass.: Harvard University Press, 1932.

——— Vol. 6: *Scientific Metaphysics.* Cambridge, Mass.: Harvard University Press, 1935.

——— *The Essential Peirce: Selected Philosophical Writings.* Edited by Nathan Houser and Christian Kloesel. Vol. 1. Bloomington: Indiana University Press, 1992.

——— *Peirce on Signs: Writings on Semiotic by Charles Sanders Peirce.* Edited by James Hoopes. Chapel Hill: University of North Carolina Press, 1991.

——— *Writings of Charles Sanders Peirce: A Chronological Edition.* Edited by Christian Kloesel. Vol. 3. Bloomington: Indiana University Press, 1986.

Petro, Patrice. "After/Shock: Between Boredom and History." In *Fugitive Images: From Photography to Video.* Edited by Patrice Petro. Bloomington: Indiana University Press, 1995, 265–284.

——— "Kracauer's Epistemological Shift." *New German Critique* 54 (Fall 1991): 127–139.

Poincaré, Henri. *Science and Hypothesis.* Translated by George Bruce Halsted. New York: Science Press, 1905.

Poovey, Mary. *A History of the Modern Fact: Problems of Knowledge in the Sciences of Wealth and Society.* Chicago: University of Chicago Press, 1998.

Porter, Theodore M. *The Rise of Statistical Thinking, 1820–1900.* Princeton: Princeton University Press, 1986.

Pratt, George C. *Spellbound in Darkness: A History of the Silent Film.* Greenwich, Conn.: New York Graphic Society, 1973.

Prigogine, Ilya. *From Being to Becoming: Time and Complexity in the Physical Sciences.* New York: W. H. Freeman, 1980.

Prigogine, Ilya, and Isabelle Stengers. *Order out of Chaos: Man's New Dialogue with Nature.* New York: Bantam, 1984.

Rabinbach, Anson. *The Human Motor: Energy, Fatigue, and the Origins of Modernity.* Berkeley: University of California Press, 1990.

Richards, Thomas. *The Imperial Archive: Knowledge and the Fantasy of Empire.* London: Verso, 1993.

Rodowick, D. N. *Gilles Deleuze's Time Machine.* Durham, N.C.: Duke University Press, 1997.

Rony, Fatimah Tobing. *The Third Eye: Race, Cinema, and Ethnographic Spectacle.* Durham, N.C.: Duke University Press, 1996.

Rosen, Philip. *Change Mummified: Cinema, Historicity, Theory.* Minneapolis: University of Minnesota Press, 2001.

Rosenzweig, Roy. *Eight Hours for What We Will.* Cambridge: Cambridge University Press, 1983.

Rossell, Deac. *Living Pictures: The Origins of the Movies.* Albany: State University of New York Press, 1998.

Russell, Bertrand. *A History of Western Philosophy.* New York: Simon and Schuster, 1945.

Sadoul, Georges. *Histoire général du cinéma.* Vol. 1. Paris: Denoel, 1948.

Schivelbusch, Wolfgang. *The Railway Journey: The Industrialization of Time and Space in the 19th Century.* Berkeley: University of California Press, 1986.

Schlüpmann, Heide. "The Subject of Survival: On Kracauer's Theory of Film." *New German Critique* 54 (Fall 1991): 111–127.

Schor, Naomi. *Reading in Detail: Aesthetics and the Feminine.* New York: Methuen, 1987.

Schwartz, Vanessa R. *Spectacular Realities: Early Mass Culture in Fin-de-Siècle Paris.* Berkeley: University of California Press, 1998.

Sekula, Allan. "The Body and the Archive." *October* 39 (1986): 3–64.

Seltzer, Mark. *Bodies and Machines.* New York: Routledge, 1992.

Serres, Michel. *Genesis.* Translated by Geneviève James and James Nielson. Ann Arbor: University of Michigan Press, 1995.

———— *Hermes: Literature, Science, Philosophy.* Edited by Josué V. Harari and David F. Bell. Baltimore: Johns Hopkins University Press, 1982.

———— *Zola.* Paris: Editions Grasset et Fasquelle, 1975.

Shannon, Claude E., and Warren Weaver. *The Mathematical Theory of Communication.* Urbana: University of Illinois Press, 1963.

Simmel, Georg. "The Metropolis and Mental Life." In *The Sociology of Georg Simmel.* Translated and edited by Kurt H. Wolff. London: Collier-Macmillan, 1950, 409–424.

Souriau, Paul. *The Aesthetics of Movement.* Translated and edited by Manon Souriau. Amherst: University of Massachusetts Press, 1983.

Spottiswoode, Raymond. *Film and Its Techniques.* Berkeley: University of California Press, 1963.

Sternberger, Dolf. *Panorama of the Nineteenth Century.* Translated by Joachim Neugroschel. New York: Urizen, 1977.

Stewart, Garrett. *Between Film and Screen: Modernism's Photo Synthesis.* Chicago: University of Chicago Press, 1999.

Stromgren, Rochard L., and Martin F. Norden. *Movies: A Language in Light.* Englewood Cliffs, N.J.: Prentice-Hall, 1984.

Talbot, Frederick A. *Moving Pictures: How They Are Made and Worked.* Philadelphia: J. B. Lippincott, 1912.

Thompson, E. P. "Time, Work-Discipline, and Industrial Capitalism." *Past and Present* 38 (1967): 56–97.

Thompson, Silvanus Phillips. "Optical Illusions of Motion." In *Visual Perception: The Nineteenth Century.* Edited by William N. Dember. New York: John Wiley and Sons, 1964, 84–93.

Trachtenberg, Alan, ed. *Classic Essays on Photography.* New Haven: Leete's Island, 1980.

Turbayne, Colin Murray. *The Myth of Metaphor.* New Haven: Yale University Press, 1962.

von Baeyer, Hans Christian. *Maxwell's Demon: Why Warmth Disperses and Time Passes.* New York: Random House, 1998.

Wade, Nicholas J., ed. *Brewster and Wheatstone on Vision.* London: Academic, 1983.

Weber, Samuel. *Mass Mediauras: Form, Technics, Media.* Edited by Alan Cholodenko. Stanford: Stanford University Press, 1996.

Webster, Chris. "Film and Technology." In *An Introduction to Film Studies.* Edited by Jill Nelmes. 2d ed. London: Routledge, 1999, 59–88.

Wells, Paul. "Animation: Forms and Meaning." In ibid., 237–264.

Willemen, Paul. *Looks and Frictions: Essays in Cultural Studies and Film Theory.* Bloomington: Indiana University Press, 1994.

Williams, Alan. *Republic of Images: A History of French Filmmaking.* Cambridge, Mass.: Harvard University Press, 1992.

Williams, Linda. "Film Body: An Implantation of Perversions." In *Narrative, Apparatus, Ideology.* Edited by Philip Rosen. New York: Columbia University Press, 1986, 507–534.

Wollen, Peter. *Signs and Meaning in the Cinema.* Bloomington: Indiana University Press, 1972.

Woodward, Kathleen. "Statistical Panic." *differences* 11.2 (Summer 1999): 177–203.

Index

Actualities, 22–25, 28, 63, 65–67, 68, 109, 137, 141–142, 143–146, 147, 150–153, 156–157, 158, 159–161, 163–164, 169–170, 177–178, 179, 180–181, 184–185, 186, 193, 206, 207–208, 230

Aesthetics, 10, 25, 165; and the afterimage, 27, 82–88; modernism in, 79

Afterimages, 219; and cinema, 9–10, 21, 69, 78; role in aesthetics, 27, 82–88; role in vision, 9–10, 21, 26, 69–74, 76–82, 83, 88–89, 101, 208–209; Brewster on, 69, 73–74, 76, 77–78, 88; and Plateau, 69, 71, 74, 78, 88, 218; Purkinje on, 74; and fatigue, 77–78. *See also* Traces

Andersen, Thom, 29, 199, 202–204

Animated Painting, 178

Anschütz, Ottomar, 212, 215

Archaeology, 112, 220

Archivability of time, 27, 29, 30–31, 33–34, 61–62, 81–82, 185; in cinema, 2, 3, 4, 22–25, 63, 82, 88, 102, 103–105, 107, 119, 221–224; in photography, 4, 33, 66–67, 82, 88, 99, 102–103, 105; Derrida on the archive, 82, 104, 206, 222–223

Aristotle, 231

Arnheim, Rudolf, 25

Arrivée d'un train en gare de La Ciotat (Arrival of a Train at the Station of La Ciotat), 177

Arrivée en gondole (Gondola Party), 177

Art, 165, 168, 176. *See also* Painting

The Artist's Dilemma, 109, 111–112, 133–134, 141, 170, 178

The Artist's Dream, 178

Atget, Eugène, 152

Aumont, Jacques, 113, 178, 195; on photography, 181; on the pregnant instant, 181, 183; on film editing, 185

Baignade de négrillons (Negroes Bathing), 177

Balla, Giacomo, 84, 85

Barker, Robert, 153

Barque sortant du port (Boat Leaving Harbour), 65, 137, 177

Barthes, Roland, 196; on photography, 103, 143, 215–216, 228; *Camera Lucida,* 143; on the point, 215–216, 228

The Battle of Sedan, 153–154

Baudelaire, Charles: Benjamin on, 4, 14, 43, 205; and trauma of modernity, 4, 11–12, 14, 15, 43, 166, 168; event and structure in, 28, 168–169, 170; celebration of present by, 102, 105; "The Painter of Modern Life," 102, 168; and contingency, 167–169, 170, 205; and female beauty, 168, 170; vs. Freud, 168; on photography, 168–169; "A une passante," 205

Bazin, André, 228; on archivability of time, 3; on photography, 3; on indexicality of cinema, 25

Beheading the Chinese Prisoner, 145

Bell curves, 17, 97, 124, 126–127, 128–129, 136

Bellour, Raymond, 196, 213–214

Benjamin, Walter, 156; on Baudelaire, 4, 14, 43, 205; on historical progress, 7, 8; on shock, 8–9, 13–15, 33, 160, 163, 205, 209; on the auratic, 13–14, 129–130, 222; on Freud, 13, 14, 15; on Proust, 13, 14, 15, 43; on cinema, 14–15, 133, 151–152, 184; on photography, 14–15, 129–130, 142–143, 151, 152, 205, 209; and contingency, 15, 142–143; on gambling, 15, 206, 222–224; on montage, 15; on dissecting time, 46; on statistics, 129–130; on optical unconscious, 133; *The Arcades Project,* 206; "The Work of Art in the Age of Mechanical Reproduction," 222

Bergson, Henri, 120; on temporal continuity, 9, 21, 43, 45, 174–176, 177, 178, 209; on Zeno's paradoxes, 29, 35, 174–176, 177, 178; vs. Freud, 45; on spatialization of time, 45, 66, 174–176, 178, 180; on photography, 66–67, 180; *Matter and Memory,* 76–77, 175; on memory, 76–77, 78, 90, 101; vs. Souriau, 83; vs. Peirce, 90, 101; on cinema, 174–176; *Creative Evolution,* 175

Berlinski, David, 216–217

Bertillon, Alphonse, 129

Biograph films, 31, 145, 155, 157–158, 186, 188, 189, 190–191, 193–194, 206

Biology, 10, 22, 112, 114, 116, 118, 120, 121–122, 127. *See also* Evolutionary theory

Bioscope, 108

Boccioni, Umberto, 84

Bogart, Humphrey, 104

Boissier, Jean-Louis, 213

Boltzmann, Ludwig, 18, 121, 124

Bonitzer, Pascal, 195, 196

Boredom, 162

Bragaglia, Anton Giulio, 84, 86–88

Brand, Bill, 213

Braun, Marta, 49, 88

Breton, André, 218

Brewster, Sir David, 69, 73–74, 76, 77–78, 88

Bricolage, 165, 212

Buckle, Henry Thomas, 17, 97

Burch, Noël, 62, 188, 190–191

The Burning of Durland's Riding Academy, 153, 156, 186

Cagliostro, Count Alessandro di, 2

Capitalism: structuring of time and contingency in, 3–4, 7–8, 11, 21–22; assembly lines in, 5–6, 15; Industrial Revolution, 7–8, 115; labor time in, 7–8, 21–22; money in, 7, 8; leisure time in, 8, 11, 106; and the subject, 11; and photography, 12; commodification in, 20, 21–22, 79, 80, 106, 162, 190, 221

Carnot, Sadi, 114, 121

Carrà, Carlo, 84

Cartwright, Lisa, 46

Cemeteries, 138–139

Ceram, C. W., *Archaeology of the Cinema,* 70

Chanan, Michael, 72, 104, 105, 162

Chance, 4, 10–12, 230, 231, 232; Peirce on, 15–16, 27, 95–101, 106–107, 112, 208, 219, 223; and singularity, 16, 95, 100–101, 208; and statistics, 18, 27–28, 31–32, 126–127; relationship to cinema, 113, 136–138, 170, 225; and Surrealism, 226, 227. *See also* Contingency

The Cheat, 226

Chemistry, 116

Christening and Launching Kaiser Wilhelm's Yacht "Meteor," 156–157

Chronocyclographs, 6

Chronophotography: vs. graphic inscription, 9, 29, 49, 54–56, 57, 59–61, 210–212; relationship to cinema, 26, 35, 46, 49, 57, 61–62, 63, 66–67, 68, 133, 190, 209, 210–215, 217; and legibility, 54, 56–57, 60; vs. photodynamism, 87. *See also* Marey, Etienne-Jules

Cinephilia, 26, 30, 225–227, 228–229, 231

Class, socioeconomic, 19

Clausius, Rudolf, 97, 114

Colonialism, 82, 152

Commodification, 20, 21–22, 79, 80, 106, 162, 190, 221

The Conjurer (Le Magicien), 134

Conrad, Tony, 131

Contingency: in modernity, 3–4, 10–19, 28, 168–169, 176, 208, 223–224, 229–230, 231–232; structuring of, 3–4, 10–11, 29–30, 31–32, 138, 140, 141, 144, 161–162, 163, 230, 231–232; and cinema, 10, 22–25, 27–28, 29, 30, 31–32, 65–67, 68, 82, 106–107, 113, 130–131, 135–138, 140–145, 152, 163, 169, 170–171, 180–181, 208, 219, 221–222, 223, 225–228, 229–232; the ephemeral, 10–13, 14–15, 22, 30, 102–104, 168–169, 176, 181, 183, 205, 230; and photography, 10, 12, 14–15, 102–103, 129–130, 142–143, 152, 168–169, 181, 183, 221, 230–231; relationship to rationalization, 10–11; as meaninglessness, 11–12, 33, 66–67, 103, 105, 106, 107, 140, 141, 144, 145, 163, 164, 166–167, 169, 181, 183; as resistance to systematicity, 11, 28, 106, 225, 227, 228, 229–230, 231–232; and shock, 13–14, 163, 164; and statistics, 16–19, 22, 27–28, 31, 124, 127, 135–136, 138, 170, 224; and death, 28, 68, 106–107, 145, 163–164; and indexicality, 94, 227, 230–231; and the present, 105; and television, 106; in the event, 140, 144, 164–165, 171; of the spectator, 157–158; and spectacle, 170; and the point, 216–217, 218; and unpredictability,

225; definition of, 231–232; relationship to impossibility, 231–232; relationship to necessity, 231–232

Continuity and discontinuity, 8–10, 21; time as continuous, 8–9, 20, 25, 26, 29, 35–36, 45–46, 61, 67–68, 77, 89–91, 99–100, 106, 177, 196, 202, 209, 211, 218, 219; time as discontinuous, 9, 25, 26, 28–29, 35–36, 45–46, 61, 67–68, 89–91, 99–101, 106, 208, 209, 218, 219; in Freud, 26, 35, 61, 67–68; in Marey, 26, 35, 61, 67–68, 211–212; in cinema, 28–29, 36, 57, 173–174, 176, 179–180, 184–196, 211–212, 217–218

Cooke, George A., 135

A Corner in Wheat, 194

Course en sacs (*Sack Race*), 177

Crary, Jonathan, 225; on the afterimage, 70, 78–79; on modernity, 79, 80, 105; on subjectivization of vision, 79, 80, 81

Criminality, 127, 152

Critical flicker fusion, 71

Cut, the, 29, 147, 190, 194, 197, 198; importance in development of cinema, 31, 66, 137, 224; Pasolini on, 105, 106–107; as ellipsis, 131, 152, 159–160, 169, 186, 217–218; Benjamin on, 184; Kracauer on, 184

"Cyclograph of an Expert Surgeon Tying a Knot," 6

Dagognet, François, 48

Darwin, Charles: on natural selection, 16, 96–97, 98, 122; vs. Carnot, 121. *See also* Evolutionary theory

Da Vinci, Leonardo, 202

Dead time, 159–160, 162, 169, 186

Death: and cinema, 2, 3, 22, 28, 62, 68, 105, 106–107, 145–147, 150–155, 159–160, 161, 163–164, 169, 186, 195–196; and contingency, 28, 68, 106–107, 145, 163–164; execution films, 28, 145–147, 150–155, 156, 159–160, 161, 163–164, 169; death drive, 36, 82, 221, 222; Freud on, 36, 68, 163; Peirce on, 96, 97, 106–107; and cinematic cut, 105, 106–107; electricity as conveyor of, 147, 150–152

Death's Marathon, 194

De Duve, Thierry, 209, 211, 215

Deleuze, Gilles: on Bergson, 77, 175–176, 180; on cinema, 175–176, 179, 180–181, 184, 185; on montage, 184, 185

De Man, Paul, 102

Demeny, Georges, 62

Démolition d'un mur (*Demolition of a Wall*) (Lumière), 213

Demolition of a Wall (Brand), 213

Derrida, Jacques: on Freud, 36, 39–40, 76; on memory, 36, 76; on facilitation, 39–40; on the archive, 82, 104, 206, 220–223; on Lévi-Strauss, 164–166; "Structure, Sign, and Play in the Discourse of the Human Sciences," 164–166; on Jensen's *Gradiva*, 220–221

Descartes, René, 114

Description, Lukács on, 12

Determinism, 122, 139, 192, 224; vs. chance, 16, 95–96, 97–98, 124; vs. statistics, 112, 124, 135–136, 138, 192; Freud on, 167. *See also* Necessity

Diegesis, 24, 28, 30, 184, 188–189, 193, 198

Digital media, 20, 26, 29, 207–208, 213–214, 225, 228–229, 231

Discursive practice, 21

Ducrot, Oswald, 93

Dynamism of a Dog on a Leash, 85

Eadward Muybridge, Zoopraxographer, 29, 199, 202–204

Ebbinghaus, Hermann, 63–64

Eddington, Sir Arthur Stanley, 118

Edison, Thomas: kinetoscopes of, 1–3, 177–178; films of, 28, 109, 111–112, 133–134, 141, 145, 146–147, 150–159, 160, 161, 164, 169, 170, 177–178, 178, 181, 186, 188, 191–192, 196–198, 212, 214

Editing, film, 25, 184–196; montage, 15, 105, 179, 184, 185; continuity, 29, 187, 189; the cut, 29, 31, 66, 105, 106–107, 131, 137, 147, 152, 159–160, 169, 184, 186, 190, 194, 197, 198, 217–218, 224; flashbacks, 30, 131; ellipses in, 131, 152, 159–160, 169, 186, 189, 217–218; flashforwards, 131; logic of chase in, 187, 190–193; logic of parallel editing and suspense in, 187, 189, 193–196; logic of repetition in, 187–190; and simultaneity, 188–189, 193

Einstein, Albert, 122

Electricity, 147, 150–152, 160, 162, 164

Electrocuting an Elephant, 28, 145–146, 147, 150–152, 159–160, 163–164, 169–170, 186

Elsaesser, Thomas, 144

Entropy, law of. *See* Thermodynamics: Second law of

Ephemeral, the, 10–13, 183, 205; as seized by photography, 10, 14–15, 102–103, 168–169; and cinema, 22, 25, 30, 176, 230. *See also* Contingency

Epstein, Jean, 172–174, 176; on Zeno's paradoxes, 29; on *photogénie,* 226

Ethnicity, 19

Eugenics, 19, 128, 129

Events: and Structuralism, 28, 164–166, 169; structure in, 28, 140–141, 144, 160, 164–167, 169–171; contingency in, 140, 144, 164–165, 171; and dead time, 160

Evolutionary theory, 25, 224, 225, 230; natural selection, 16, 96–97, 98, 122; irreversibility of time in, 112, 118, 120, 121–122; vs. thermodynamics, 120, 121–122, 124–125

An Execution by Hanging, 145, 155, 159, 186

Execution of a Spy, 145

Execution of Czolgosz, with Panorama of Auburn Prison, 28, 145, 146–147, 150–155, 159, 160, 161, 164, 169, 214

The Execution of Mary Queen of Scots, 145, 186

Extraordinary Illusions, 135

Fairgrounds, 138–139

Faraday, Michael, 70–71

The Fatal Hour, 194, 196

Fechner, Gustav, 74, 78

Fielding, Raymond, 155

Firemen Fighting the Flames at Paterson, 156

Fischer, Lucy, 135

Flashbacks, 30, 131

Flashforwards, 131

The Flicker, 131

Flicker films, 199, 205

Foucault, Michel, 80; on cinema, 3; on heterotopia/heterochrony, 3, 138–139; on episteme, 20–21; on power, 21

Frame, film, 9, 21, 29, 31, 57, 70, 87, 154, 172, 177, 179–180, 185, 195–196, 202, 217

Fred Ott's Sneeze, 177–178

Freud, Sigmund, 34–46; on consciousness and time, 9, 13, 26, 34–35, 37–38, 43–46, 61, 67, 76; on memory and the unconscious, 9, 13, 26, 36–42, 43–45, 61, 67, 76; *Beyond the Pleasure Principle,* 13, 37, 38, 40, 42–43, 44, 45; on stimulus shield of consciousness, 13, 26, 34–35, 38–39, 42–43, 45, 61, 67, 68; and industrialization, 19; and thermodynamics (conservation of energy), 19, 36; and legibility of time, 20, 63, 76; and recording of

time, 20; and physiology, 21, 35, 39–40, 63–64; and cinema, 26, 61–62, 63, 67, 68, 167; continuity and discontinuity in, 26, 35, 61, 67–68; event and structure in, 28, 167, 168, 169; on shock/trauma, 34, 36, 43, 140; vs. Marey, 35–36, 61, 63, 67–68; and Mystic Writing-Pad, 35, 37–38, 39, 40, 43–44, 61, 76; *Project for a Scientific Psychology,* 35, 37, 39–40, 42–43; on resistance, 35, 39–41; on death, 36, 68, 163; on deferred action *(Nachträglichkeit),* 36; and inscriptions/traces, 36, 39–42, 44–46, 61, 68; on sexuality, 36; "The Unconscious," 36–37, 41; *The Interpretation of Dreams,* 37, 166; on facilitation *(Bahnung),* 39–41; on memory as inscription/trace, 39–42, 44–46, 61, 68; on permeable/impermeable neurones, 39–41; "Constructions in Analysis," 44; "Remembering, Repeating and Working-Through," 44; vs. Bergson, 45; on slips of the tongue, 64, 167; Wolf-Man case, 64; "Thoughts for the Times on War and Death," 163; and contingency, 166–167; *The Psychopathology of Everyday Life,* 166, 167; on screen memories, 166–167; on chance, 167; on paranoia, 167; on phylogenesis, 167; on superstition, 167; vs. Baudelaire, 168; and Jensen's *Gradiva,* 220

Frizot, Michel, 210–215, 216

Future, the, 3, 30, 131, 218, 223

Futurism, 27, 60, 78, 84–88, 102, 105

Galassi, Peter, 10, 142

Galton, Francis, 19, 128–129, 130

Gambling, 15, 206, 223–224

Gaudreault, André, 24, 143, 157–158, 161, 179, 184

Gaussian curves, 17, 97, 124, 126–127, 128–129

Gender, 19, 127, 196

Getting Evidence, 167, 192

Gibbs, Josiah, 122

Giedion, Siegfried, *Mechanization Takes Command,* 6

Gilbreth, Frank B., 6

"Girl Folding a Handkerchief," 6

Goethe, Johann Wolfgang von: on the afterimage, 69, 72–73, 77, 88; *Theory of Colours,* 72–73

Gradiva, 220

Graphic inscription, 46, 47–49; vs.

chronophotography, 9, 29, 49, 54–56, 57, 59–61, 210–212. *See also* Marey, Etienne-Jules

Griffith, D. W., 194, 195, 203

Gunning, Tom, 24, 141–142, 194, 195, 209

Guys, Constantin, 102

Hacking, Ian, 16, 126–127, 192–193

Hammond, Paul, 134–135

The Hand of the Violinist, 85

Hansen, Miriam, 155–156, 225, 227, 228–229, 231

Harman, P. M., 116

Hayakawa, Sessue, 226

Helmholtz, Hermann von, 21, 47, 82; on the afterimage, 69, 78; on vision, 69, 76, 81, 89, 105; on thermodynamics, 114

Hepworth films, 191

Herschel, Sir William, 97

Heterosexuality, 29, 192, 193, 196–198, 203, 204–205

Heterotopia/heterochrony, 3, 138–139

Historicism, 12, 33, 186

History, 15, 17, 20–21, 104–105, 220, 224; historical progress, 7, 8, 115; and irreversibility of time, 20, 112, 120; historical decline, 115; and thermodynamics, 115, 120

Homosexuality, 127

How a French Nobleman Got a Wife through the New York Herald "Personal" Columns, 157

Huyssen, Andreas, 4

Iconicity, 93, 227

Imperialism, 2–3, 19, 127

Impressionism, 10, 178, 181, 183

Imprints/impressions. *See* Traces

Indexicality, 4; of cinema, 10, 15, 22–23, 24–25, 26, 31–32, 64–65, 68, 69, 93, 103, 107, 119, 140–141, 146, 154, 162–163, 172, 185, 193, 207–208, 219, 221, 222, 223, 224, 225, 227, 229; of photography, 10, 16, 21, 69, 83–84, 89, 92, 93–95, 103, 129, 143, 215–216, 219, 221, 227, 229, 230–231; Peirce on, 16, 26–27, 69, 70, 88–89, 91–95, 101, 140, 208, 215, 219–220, 230–231; and Marey, 47–49; and the afterimage, 88–89; and singularity, 92–93, 94, 100–101, 208, 219, 221, 225; and contingency, 94, 227, 230–231; and the event, 140; of television, 207–208

Individual, the, 124–127, 129–130, 138, 192–193, 224, 230. *See also* Particularity; Singularity

Industrial Revolution, 7–8, 115

Information theory, 114, 118; noise in, 64–65

Instantaneity: modern fascination with, 4, 13, 20, 27, 29–30, 70, 78, 82, 105–106, 107, 151, 207–208, 218; instants of time, 9–10, 29, 30, 45–46, 60, 77, 78, 82, 88, 89–91, 99–106, 109, 174, 179–180, 181, 183–184, 205, 208, 209, 211, 212, 218–219, 223; of digital media, 29, 231; and Marey, 29, 48–49, 214–215; of television, 29, 106, 206–207, 231; of photography, 66, 83–84, 86–87, 89, 101, 103, 104, 179–180, 181, 183, 184, 205, 209–210, 211, 214–215, 217–218; vision's lack of, 69, 74, 76–77, 78, 81; and photodynamism, 88; and electricity, 151. *See also* Present, the

Internet, 231

Intolerance, 195

irreversibility, temporal, 27, 108–109, 111–113, 117–120, 131–133, 136, 139, 141, 188, 190

The Irwin Rice Kiss, 178, 196

Jacob, François, 118, 119, 121, 122, 124, 125

Jakobson, Roman, 93

James, Henry, 203

Janssen, Jules, 55

Jensen, Wilhelm, 220

Joule, James Prescott, 114

Kelvin, Lord, 114, 123

Kepler, Johannes, 113

Kern, Stephen, 5

Kinetoscopes, 177–178; "The Kinetoscope of Time," 1–3, 8, 22. *See also* Edison, Thomas

Kittler, Friedrich: on storing time, 34; on cinema, 64; on Freud, 64; on noise, 64–65; on psychophysics, 63–64

Klee, Paul, 6

Koyré, Alexandre, 120

Kracauer, Siegfried: on photography, 1, 12, 23, 33, 68, 102–103, 143, 185–186; and contingency, 15, 143; on the present, 105, 143; on mass culture, 162; on cinema, 184, 186, 227; *Theory of Film,* 227, 229

Kraepelin, Emil, 116

Lamprecht, Karl, 4

Language, 91–93; demonstratives in, 25, 69, 70, 93, 101, 231; written texts, 34, 63; vs. the unconscious, 42; Marey on, 48

Laplace, Pierre-Simon, marquis de, 114
Laplanche, Jean, 42, 167
Laughing Gas, 191–192
Legibility: Freud and legibility of time, 20, 63, 76; Marey and legibility of time, 20, 48–49, 54, 56–57, 60, 61, 63, 67, 84, 102, 211–212; vs. storage, 20, 21, 26; of time, 20, 25, 26, 45–46, 48–49, 54, 56–57, 60, 61, 63, 67–68, 76, 82, 83–88, 102, 153, 162–163, 208, 211–212, 222; cinema and legibility of time, 26, 63, 67–68, 162–163, 222; and chronophotography, 54, 56–57, 60; of contingency, 230
Leibniz, Gottfried Wilhelm, 114
Lesbianism, 199, 202–204
Lessing, Gotthold Ephraim, 181
Lévi-Strauss, Claude, 164–166, 168, 212; "The Science of the Concrete," 165
Levy, David, 150, 155, 157, 158
The Life of an American Fireman, 187–190
Literature, 114, 143, 157, 176
Logic, 25
The Lonedale Operator, 194, 196
The Lonely Villa, 193, 194, 195, 196
The Lost Child, 191–192
Lubin, Siegmund, 153, 156–157, 192
Luhmann, Niklas, 225, 231
Lukács, Georg: on narration vs. description, 12; and contingency, 15
Lumière, Auguste and Louis: films of, 1, 22, 23–24, 25, 62, 63, 65, 113, 137, 144, 177, 178, 180, 212, 213, 214, 223; vs. Méliès, 28, 113, 136–138; Cinématographe of, 108–109, 132
Luria, A. R., 74, 76
Lyotard, Jean-François, 140

Mach, Ernst, *The Analysis of Sensations*, 80
Magic films, 109, 111–112, 133–136, 141, 186
Magic lanterns, 218–219
Mao Zedong, 204
Marey, Etienne-Jules, 59–68, 116; and chronophotography, 9, 29, 35, 46, 47, 49, 54–57, 59–61, 85, 87, 209–215, 218–219; and graphic inscription, 9, 29, 35, 46, 47–49, 54–56, 57, 59–60, 210–212, 219; and legibility of time, 20, 48–49, 54, 56–57, 60, 61, 63, 67, 84, 102, 211–212; and recording of time, 20; and cinema, 26, 35, 46, 49, 57, 61–62, 63, 66–67, 68, 133, 190, 209, 210–215, 217; continuity and discontinuity in, 26, 35, 61,

67–68, 211–212; on time, 26; on the image as point, 29–30, 211, 214–215, 216, 217, 218; and instantaneity, 29, 48–49, 214–215; vs. Freud, 35–36, 61, 63, 67–68; and storage of time, 35; and time as continuum, 35; on movement, 46–47, 56–57; and air currents, 47; and fluid dynamics, 47; on Helmholtz, 47; and indexicality, 47–49; and lost time, 47; and myograph, 47; and sphymograph, 47; on language, 48; *Movement*, 49, 54; vs. Muybridge, 49, 60–61, 66, 78, 82, 102, 105, 190, 212; Frizot on, 210–215, 216, 217; as bricoleur, 212
Marinetti, F. T., 88
Marx, Karl, on labor time, 7
Maskelyne, John Nevil, 135
Masking, 71
Mass culture, 229; and statistics, 19; and the individual, 112, 129–130, 138; and boredom, 162; relationship to time, 162
Maxwell, James Clerk, 18, 97, 123–124, 133
Mayer, Robert, 114
McKinley, William, 146–147, 150–151
The Medicine Bottle, 194
Meet Me at the Fountain, 192
Méliès, Georges: films of, 28, 113, 134–138, 155, 177, 186; vs. Lumières, 28, 113, 136–138
Memory: Freud on memory and the unconscious, 9, 13, 26, 36–42, 43–45, 61, 67, 76; Freud on memory as inscription/trace, 39–42, 44–46, 61, 68; Ebbinghaus on, 63–64; Bergson on, 76–77, 78, 90, 101
Metz, Christian, 93, 103, 176–177, 226
A Mighty Tumble, 206, 207–208
Miró, Joan, 6
Modernity: technological change in, 2, 4, 5, 6, 10, 11, 13, 20, 29, 33, 68, 82, 102, 106, 112, 114, 115, 147, 150–151, 194, 208, 225, 227, 228–229; contingency in, 3–4, 10–19, 28, 168–169, 176, 208, 223–224, 229–230, 231–232; fascination with instantaneity/the present in, 4, 13, 20, 27, 29–30, 70, 78, 82, 105–106, 107, 151, 207–208, 218; obsession with temporal exactitude in, 4–5; rationalization of time in, 4–5, 5–11, 14, 20, 31–32, 108, 162, 184, 190, 196, 208, 221, 225, 228, 229–230; time management in, 5–6, 10, 162; shock factor in, 8–9, 13–15, 33–34, 43, 77, 163, 164, 166, 205, 223–224; mass culture in, 19, 112, 129–130, 138, 162, 229; newness

in, 20, 46, 100–101, 102, 180, 218; the present in, 27, 78, 151, 218; mobility and flux in, 33, 79, 88, 105, 205; as antireferential, 79; vs. postmodernity, 105–106; role of art in, 165, 168–169; archivization in, 221
Moments de Jean-Jacques Rousseau, 213–214
Money, 7, 8
Montage, 15, 105, 179, 184, 185. *See also* Editing, film
Morris, Richard, 117, 118–119; *Time's Arrows,* 118
Movement: in cinema, 9–10, 21, 29, 69, 70, 71–72, 78, 109, 111–112, 131, 133–134, 172–179, 199, 202–204, 205, 208–209, 213–214, 217; relationship to time, 46–47, 56–57, 178–179; divisibility of, 174. *See also* Zeno's paradoxes
Müller, Johannes, 80, 81
Mulvey, Laura, 170
Münsterberg, Hugo, 71
Museums, 82, 88, 138–139
Musical scores, 34
Musser, Charles, 132, 141–142, 153, 156, 189
Muybridge, Eadward, 49, 60–61, 66, 78, 82, 102, 105, 190, 212; Andersen's *Eadward Muybridge, Zoopraxographer,* 29, 199, 202–204
Myograph, 47
Mystic Writing-Pad, 35, 37–38, 39, 40, 43–44, 61, 76

Narration, Lukács on, 12
Narrative, 67, 68, 106–107, 109, 131, 134, 136, 138, 141–142, 156, 157, 158–159, 160, 161, 162, 164, 169, 170, 184–185, 188–189, 190, 196, 198, 230
Nationalism, 127, 205
Natural law, 95–96, 122–123, 126–127
Natural selection, 16, 96–97, 98, 122. *See also* Evolutionary theory
Necessity, 95–96, 97–98, 124, 138, 165, 166, 231–232. *See also* Determinism
Newness, 20, 100–101, 102, 180, 218
Newton, Isaac, 71; Newtonian physics, 18, 27, 113, 120, 122–123
Next!, 188, 190
Nietzsche, Friedrich, 102
Niver, Kemp, 155
Noise in information theory, 64–65
Nye, David E., 150

Optical toys, 21, 71–72, 80–81, 132, 209, 218–219
Orientalism, 2–3

Painting, 6, 82, 83–88, 89; Impressionism, 10, 178, 181, 183; Futurism, 27, 60, 78, 84–88, 102, 105
The Palace of the Arabian Nights, 134
Pan, 147, 153–156, 158, 160, 161–162, 169, 214, 226
Panoramas, 153–155, 162
Paris, J. A., 71
Particularity, 162–163, 168, 219, 225; and statistics, 27–28, 230; and the point, 30, 216–217, 218. *See also* Individual, the; Singularity
Partie d'écarte (Friendly Party in the Garden Lumière), 177
Pasolini, Pier Paolo, 104–105, 106
The Passion Play of Oberammergau, 190
Past, the: relationship to photography, 1, 23, 103, 105, 143, 209; relationship to cinema, 3, 23, 30, 184, 220; relationship to the present, 9–10, 12, 70, 76–77, 78, 83, 101, 103–106, 184, 218, 219–220, 223
Peirce, Charles Sanders, 89–101; on time as continuous, 8, 9, 29, 35, 89–91, 99–100, 106, 218, 219; on time as discontinuous, 9, 29, 35, 89–91, 99–101, 102, 106, 208, 218, 219; on chance, 15–16, 27, 95–101, 106–107, 112, 208, 219, 223; on the index, 16, 26–27, 69, 70, 88–89, 91–95, 101, 140, 208, 215, 219–220, 230–231; on statistics, 16, 27, 97; on demonstrative pronouns, 69, 70, 93, 231; on icons, 69, 92; on symbols, 69, 92, 93; on logical thought, 89–90, 91, 97, 101, 219; on photography, 89, 93–95, 101, 230; on the present, 89–91, 99–101, 102, 106, 218, 219; vs. Bergson, 90, 101; on intuition, 91; "On the Nature of Signs," 91–92; on the singular, 92–93, 94, 100–101, 208; on death, 96, 97, 106–107; on natural selection, 96–97, 99; on Second Law of Thermodynamics, 96; "Design and Chance," 98; "The Doctrine of Necessity," 98; on habit, 98, 100; on mind, 98–99; "Notes on Metaphysics," 100–101; vs. Pasolini, 106–107
"Perfect Movement," 6
Persistence of vision, 70, 71–72, 78, 202
Personal, 157, 190–191
Phenakistiscope, 71, 72, 80, 218

Philosophy, 15, 101–102; relationship to cinema, 19–20, 170, 174–176; and inaccessibility of the present, 76–77, 218. *See also* Bergson, Henri; Peirce, Charles Sanders; Zeno's paradoxes

Phi phenomenon, 71

Phonography, 4; as storing time, 34, 62, 82

Photodynamism, 86–88

Photography: relationship to past, 1, 23, 103, 105, 143, 209; representation of time in, 1, 3, 4, 22, 23, 48–49, 89, 95, 102–103, 105, 143, 209; archivability of time in, 4, 33, 66–67, 82, 88, 99, 102–103, 105; cyclographs, 6; and contingency, 10, 12, 14–15, 102–103, 129–130, 142–143, 152, 168–169, 181, 183, 221, 230–231; the ephemeral seized by, 10, 14–15, 102–103, 168–169; indexicality of, 10, 16, 21, 69, 83–84, 89, 92, 93–95, 103, 129, 143, 215–216, 219, 221, 227, 229, 230–231; and capitalism, 12; relationship to shock, 14–15, 205; vs. cinema, 24, 29, 62–63, 87, 103, 104, 105–106, 131, 143, 151–152, 156, 157, 178, 179–180, 184, 199, 208–210, 219, 229; and the point, 29–30, 211, 214–216, 217, 218, 224, 228; instantaneity of, 66, 83–84, 86–87, 89, 101, 103, 104, 179–180, 181, 183, 184, 205, 209–210, 211, 214–215, 217–218; as compensation for flawed vision, 80–81; and Futurism, 86–87; iconicity of, 89, 93–94; relationship to the present, 95, 102–103, 105, 143; relationship to statistics, 127–130; composite portraiture, 128–129, 130. *See also* Chronophotography

Physics, 10, 15, 98; thermodynamics, 4–5, 17–18, 27; and statistics, 17–18, 27–28; Newtonian physics, 18, 27, 113, 120, 122, 133, 224; relationship to cinema, 19–20, 70–72; reconceptualization of time in, 20, 25, 112; concept of life as movement in, 46; symmetry of time in, 113. *See also* Thermodynamics

Physiology, 15, 22, 45–46, 101–102; the afterimage in, 9–10, 26, 69–74, 75–76, 77–79, 85, 101; relationship to cinema, 19–20; and Freud, 21, 35, 39–40, 63–64; reconceptualization of time in, 25, 112; lost time in, 47; irreversibility of time in, 112. *See also* Helmholtz, Hermann von; Marey, Etienne-Jules

Plateau, Joseph, 69, 71, 74, 78, 88, 218

Pocket watches, 4, 6, 7, 221

Poincaré, Henri, 216

Point, the: and photography, 29–30, 211, 214–216, 217, 218, 224, 228; and singularity, 29–30, 216–217, 218; and particularity, 30, 216–217, 218; the present as point, 100; and cinema, 216–217, 218; and contingency, 216–217, 218

Pontalis, Jean-Bertrand, 167

Porter, Edwin S., 157, 187, 188, 203

Porter, Theodore, on statistics, 16–17, 18

Praxinoscope, 132

Present, the: modern fascination with, 4, 13, 20, 27, 29–30, 70, 78, 82, 105–106, 107, 151, 207–208, 218; relationship to past, 9–10, 12, 70, 76–77, 78, 83, 101, 103–106, 184, 218, 219–220, 223; relationship to cinema, 23, 27, 30, 102, 103–105, 106, 107, 143, 151–152, 184, 220; accessibility of, 25, 70, 76–77, 78, 82, 88, 89, 90, 99–100, 101–102, 104–106, 107, 218; relationship to photography, 95, 102–103, 105, 143; as point, 100; and contingency, 105; relationship to the future, 218. *See also* Instantaneity

Prigogine, Ilya, 119–121, 122

Probability, 17, 97–98, 106, 107, 124–127, 131, 135–136, 170, 192; and irreversibility of time, 112, 121–122. *See also* Statistics

Progress, 7, 8, 116, 193

Prostitution, 127

Proust, Marcel, 13, 14, 43, 78

Psychoanalysis, 15, 22, 114; relationship to cinema, 19–20, 39, 43, 64–65, 68; reconceptualization of time in, 25, 112; Kittler on, 64; irreversibility of time in, 112. *See also* Freud, Sigmund

Psychophysics, 63–64

Purkinje, Jan, 74

Quetelet, Adolphe, 18, 21, 31; and Gaussian curves, 17, 97, 124, 126–127, 136; "average man" invented by, 124, 126–127, 128

Rabinbach, Anson, 47, 115, 116

Race, 2–3, 19, 127, 152, 192, 193, 196–198, 205

Railroads, 5, 6, 194

Ray, Man, 218

Ray Gun Virus, 131

Reading the Death Sentence, 145

Real time, 25, 31, 66–67, 136–137, 159, 161–163, 172, 174, 186, 189–190, 217, 224

Repas de bébé (Feeding the Baby), 109, 177

Rescued by Rover, 191–192
Rhythm of the Violinist, 85
Robert-Houdin, Jean-Eugène, 135
Roget, Peter Mark, 70–71
Rosen, Philip, 221, 225
Rosenzweig, Roy, 132–133
Rube and Mandy at Coney Island, 191
Russolo, Luigi, 84

Saroni, Gilbert, 192
Sauts au cheval en longueur (Leaping over a Horse), 177
Sauts d'obstacles (German Hussars Jumping Fences), 177
Scenes of the Wreckage from the Waterfront, 153
Schopenhauer, Arthur, 225
Sekula, Allan, 33, 129
Seltzer, Mark, 151
Serres, Michel: on history, 20; on thermodynamics, 113–114, 120
Severini, Gino, 84
Sharits, Paul, 131
Shock: Benjamin on, 8–9, 13–15, 163, 205, 209; in modernity, 8–9, 13–15, 33–34, 43, 77, 163, 164, 166, 205, 223–224; and contingency, 13–14, 163, 164; relationship to cinema, 14, 15, 24, 151–152; relationship to photography, 14–15, 205; Freud on, 34, 36, 43, 140
Simmel, Georg, 4, 7, 33
Singularity, 142, 220, 231; and chance, 16, 95, 100–101, 208; and statistics, 27–28, 124–127, 224, 230; and the point, 29–30, 216–217, 218; and cinema, 64–65, 67; and indexicality, 92–93, 94, 100–101, 208, 221, 225. *See also* Individual, the; Particularity
Social sciences, 10, 17
Sortie d'usine (Workers Leaving the Factory), 23–24, 177, 223
Souriau, Paul, 27, 82–84, 89, 105; *Aesthetics of Movement,* 83; vs. Bergson, 83; on photography, 83–84; on the sketch, 84, 102; vs. Futurism, 85–86, 87, 88
Space, 41–42, 54, 56–57
Special effects, 109, 111–112, 133–136, 189
Spectators of cinema, 1–3, 11, 132–133, 139, 157–158, 160–161, 188
Sphymograph, 47
Spinoza, Baruch, 114
Stampfer, Simon, 71

Statistics: in social sciences, 10, 17; Hacking on, 16, 126–127, 192–193; and contingency, 16–19, 22, 27–28, 31, 124, 127, 135–136, 138, 170, 224; and Gaussian curves, 17, 97, 124, 126–127, 128–129; and physics, 17–18, 27–28; and mass culture, 19; relationship to cinema, 19–20, 25, 31, 106–107, 127–128, 130–131, 135–136, 138, 170, 192–193, 208; reconceptualization of time in, 25; and particularity, 27–28, 230; and singularity, 27–28, 124–127, 224, 230; and irreversibility of time, 112, 121–122; and thermodynamics, 121–124, 131; and the individual, 124–127, 138, 224, 230; relationship to photography, 127–130; and normality, 192–193
Stengers, Isabelle, 119–121, 122
Stereopticon, 132
Sternberger, Dorf, 153–154
The Story the Biograph Told, 189
The Strenuous Life, or Anti-Race Suicide, 188
Stroboscopic disc, 71
Structuralism, 28, 164–166, 169
Stuttgart: 26ᵉ Dragons, 177
Surrealism, 226, 227

Talbot, Frederick A., 72
Taylor, Frederick W., 5–6, 10, 81
Telegraphy, 5, 6, 29
Telephones, 194
Television, 4, 26, 105, 225, 228; instantaneity of, 29, 106, 206–207, 231
Thaumatrope, 71, 72, 132, 209, 218
Theaters, motion picture, 132–133, 139
Thermodynamics: Second Law of, 4–5, 17–18, 27, 96, 112, 114–125, 133–134, 136, 224; vs. Newtonian physics, 18, 27, 113, 120, 122–123, 133; First Law of, 19, 36, 114–117, 124; relationship to cinema, 19–20, 23, 117–120, 131, 133–134, 136–137; influence of Quetelet on, 21; reconceptualization of time in, 25; and Helmholtz, 47; irreversibility of time in, 112, 113–122, 131, 133–134; and steam engines, 114, 115, 120, 123; and decline, 115, 128; energy in, 115–117, 128; and history, 115, 120; and work, 115–117; and progress, 116; and disorder, 117–120, 136–137; vs. evolutionary theory, 120, 121–122, 124–125; and statistics, 121–124, 131; Maxwell's demon, 123–124, 133
"Thisness," 10, 25, 64–65, 69, 70, 93, 101, 223, 231. *See also* Indexicality

Thompson, E. P., 7–8

Thompson, Silvanus Phillips, 72

Thomson, Sir William, 114, 123

Time: cinema as representation of, 1–4, 22–25, 27, 30–32, 35–36, 39, 61–62, 67–68, 102, 103–105, 106, 107, 131, 136, 141, 143, 151–152, 161, 163, 172–176, 183–184, 185–196, 213–214, 220; photography as representation of, 1, 3, 4, 22, 23, 48–49, 89, 95, 102–103, 105, 143, 209; recording/storage of, 1, 2, 3, 4, 20, 22, 22–25, 26, 30–31, 33–34, 61–62, 67, 68, 81–82, 104–105, 107, 119, 143–144, 151, 153–156, 158, 160–161, 162–163, 164, 169, 178–179, 185, 190, 222–223, 224; archivability of, 2, 3, 4, 22–25, 27, 29, 30–31, 33–34, 61–62, 66–67, 81–82, 88, 102–104, 105, 107, 119, 185, 221–224; rationalization of, 3–11, 14, 22, 31–32, 35, 106, 108–109, 162, 196, 221, 225, 228, 229–230; structuring of, 3–4, 11, 21–22, 25, 31–32, 67, 139, 140, 160, 161–162, 184, 230, 231–232; and pocket watches, 4, 6, 7; efficient management of, 5–6, 10, 32, 81–82, 116, 162; standardization of, 5, 6, 8, 106, 221, 225; and Taylorism, 5–6, 10, 162; abstraction of, 6, 7–8, 10–11, 22, 29–30, 32, 221; divisibility of, 6, 7–8, 14, 45–46, 60, 67, 202, 210, 211–212; irreversibility of, 6, 20, 23, 25, 27, 30, 36, 108–109, 111–125, 131–133, 136, 139, 141, 188, 190, 224; as uniform/homogeneous, 6–7, 67–68, 81, 180–181, 183; historical progress and rationalization of, 7, 8; industrialized time vs. task-oriented sense of, 7–8; labor, 7–8, 21–22; as money, 7, 8; as continuous, 8–9, 20, 25, 26, 29, 35–36, 45–46, 61, 67–68, 77, 89–91, 99–100, 106, 177, 196, 202, 209, 211, 218, 219; leisure, 8, 11, 106; as discontinuous, 9, 25, 26, 28–29, 35–36, 45–46, 61, 67–68, 89–91, 99–101, 106, 208, 209, 218, 219; instants of, 9–10, 20, 29, 30, 45–46, 60, 77, 78, 82, 88, 89–91, 99–106, 109, 174, 179–180, 181, 183–184, 205, 208, 209, 211, 212, 218–219, 223; relationship to consciousness, 9, 13, 26, 34–35, 37–38, 43–46, 61, 67, 76; legibility of, 20, 25, 26, 45–46, 48–49, 54, 56–57, 60, 61, 63, 67–68, 76, 82, 83–88, 102, 153, 162–163, 208, 211–212, 222; relationship to movement, 46–47, 56–57, 178–179; relationship to space, 54, 56–57; relationship to mass culture, 162. *See also* Future, the; Past, the; Present, the

Todorov, Tzvetan, 93

Traces, 26, 69–70, 81–82, 83, 88–89, 92, 101, 119, 220, 226; and Freud, 36, 39–42, 44–46, 61, 68; and Marey, 47–48. *See also* Afterimages; Indexicality

Trauma. *See* Shock

The Treasures of Satan, 135

A Trip to the Moon, 134, 135

Turner, J. M. W., 183

Typewriter, 82

Uncle Tom's Cabin, 1, 3, 152

An Unseen Enemy, 193, 194, 195

The Usurer, 194

Vaughan, Dai, 65–66, 68, 180

Vision: role of afterimages in, 9–10, 21, 26, 69–74, 76–82, 83, 88–89, 208–209; theory of persistence of, 9–10, 21, 70–72, 78, 85, 101, 202, 208–209; as lacking instantaneity, 69, 74, 76–77, 78, 81; referentiality of, 70, 78–81; subjectivization of, 70, 79–81; role of failure/fatigue in, 72, 77–78, 80–82; camera obscura model of, 76, 79

Vitagraph, 109

Vitascope, 108, 132

Weaver, Warren, 118, 119

Weber, Samuel, 205

Werner, Anton von, 153–154, 155

Wertheimer, Max, 71

What Happened in the Tunnel, 196–198

What Happened on Twenty-third Street, 181, 197–198

Wheatstone, Sir Charles, on the afterimage, 69, 74

Willemen, Paul, 225–227, 228, 229, 231

Williams, Linda, 135, 203

Wollen, Peter, 93

Zapruder, Abraham, 104–105

Zeno's paradoxes, 35; and discontinuity of time, 9, 28–29; relationship to cinema, 9, 28–29, 172–176, 187, 199, 202–203, 204–205; Epstein on, 172–174; Achilles and the tortoise, 173; arrow paradox, 173; stadium paradox, 173

Zoetrope, 72, 80, 132, 218–219

Zoopraxinoscope, 209